SOULT

SOULT

Napoleon's Maligned Marshal

PETER HAYMAN

ARMS AND
ARMOUR

First published in Great Britain in 1990
by Arms and Armour Press, Villiers House, 41-47 Strand, London
WC2N 5JE.

Distributed in Australia by Capricorn Link (Australia) Pty. Ltd,
P.O. Box 665, Lane Cove, New South Wales 2066, Australia.

British Library Cataloguing in Publication Data
Hayman, Peter
Soult: Napoleon's maligned marshal.
1. France. Armée. Soult, Nicolas-Jean de Dieu, 1769–1851
I, Title
355.3'31'0924
ISBN 0-85368-931-8

Jacket illustrations: front, Soult as a young general in the Revolutionary
Army, from a contemporary print; back, 'Soult in Old Age', from the
portrait in Apsley House, reproduced by kind permission of the Victoria
and Albert Museum and His Grace the Duke of Wellington.

Designed and edited by DAG Publications Ltd. Designed by David
Gibbons; edited by John Gilbert; typeset by Ronset Typesetters Ltd,
Darwen, Lancashire; camerawork by M & E Reproductions, North
Fambridge, Essex; printed and bound in Great Britain by Butler &
Tanner Ltd, Frome.

CONTENTS

To Rosemary

ACKNOWLEDGEMENTS

MY FIRST THANKS go to the late Comte Hervé de Guitaut, Marshal Soult's great great grandson, to his wife and to their two sons, Guillaume and Antoine. The wisdom and generous hospitality of Hervé and his family have been beyond praise and he has kindly examined the family papers at Epoisses on my behalf. I am grateful too to the Comtesse de Guitaut who warmly welcomed my wife and myself to the château of Epoisses and made available to me copies of the portraits of Soult's children. Most grateful thanks are also due to the late Marquis Michel de Saint-Pierre who gave me much good advice and, with his charming wife, entertained me at his home. Additional thanks must go to the Comtesse de Croix, the sister of the late Duc de Dalmatie.

I also owe a special debt of gratitude to the long suffering *locataire* of the château of Soultberg, Madame Bruel-Pachod, whom I confronted unannounced some years ago and who at once showed me all round the house.

I should never have begun my book at all but for the hospitality and ceaseless energy of my half-sister, Sara Berthaud, who is fortunate enough to live near the Black Mountains in the department of Tarn only a few miles from the commune of St-Amans-Soult where the Marshal was born and where he died. Through her I have met many people who live in this lovely but little known region of France. I must mention in particular the mayor of the commune, Monsieur Gilbert Jougla, his predecessor, the late Louis Blanc, and various other local officials. Others who have greatly helped me have been Didier Pacaud, the author of the 1986 *Life of Jean de Dieu Soult*; my friend, François Pons of Mazamet, who generously gave me his copy of Anarchasis Combes's *Histoire Anecdotique* of Soult; J-C Averous of St-Amans-Soult who provided me with information about the Marshal's mother's family, the de Greniers, who were among the remarkable *gentilhommes verriers* of the Black Mountains. (This was backed up by information on the English branch of the family kindly supplied by Eric Hemming of Bushey, Hertfordshire); Major Geoffrey Baxter who with his wife, Sylvie, entertained me at the officer's mess in Castres where the dining room is adorned with a fine portrait of the Marshal and Bertrand de Viviés of Viviers les Montagnes whose Royalist forbear, the Vicomte de Lescures, harried the unfortunate Soult when he was in flight back home after the Battle of Waterloo.

Others whom I have met either directly or indirectly through my half-sister have been Pierre-André Wimet, the Président de la Commission Départmentale d'Histoire et d'Archéologie du Pas de Calais who is a mine of information about anything relating to the camp of Boulogne; Guy and Diana Viala whose home is very near the place from which Napoleon and Soult looked longingly across the channel before the 'invasion of England that never took place' and Jean-Paul Escalettes, a real expert on the battle of Toulouse, who guided me on a tour of the battlefield and on a visit to Soultberg. I am also grateful to my niece, Anne Destenay, and to Georges Ferrato for advice and help.

Among historians and 'Napoleonists' I must mention especially Professor Jean Tulard who gave me some wise advice in the middle of his busy time-table at the Sorbonne; Alan Palmer, the author of many books on the Napoleonic period who has been a real source of inspiration; Professor David Chandler, the Head of the Department of War Studies at Sandhurst whose great books *The Campaigns of Napoleon* and *Napoleon's Marshals* have been my guides; Doctor Paddy Griffiths, also of the Department of War Studies, and Charles Esdaile of Southampton University where the Wellington Dispatches are housed, who has been engaged in much new research on the Peninsular War. On Soult's invasion of Portugal I have been helped by Peter Gay, HM Consul in Oporto, John Delaforce CBE of Oporto, Nancy Hewitt of Reading, formerly of Oporto, and Jennifer Coates, my skilled Portuguese translator. A most delightful and robust 'Napoleonist' is Philip Haythornthwaite of Nelson, Lancashire, who has provided me with all the battle plans and much additional information.

I acknowledge my great indebtedness to the Bodleian Library: the Ministry of Defence (Whitehall) Library (Mrs Judith Blacklaw); the Archives de la Guerre at Vincennes; the Biblioteca Publico Municipal de Porto in Oporto; the Archives Départmentales de Morbihan in Vannes for information about Quiberon; the Stadtarchiv in Solingen for information about Soult and his German wife in the Rhineland; News International and the Public Library Department of the City of Birmingham for coverage by *The Times* and local newspapers in the north of England of Soult's visit in 1838; the Victoria and Albert Museum (Alysia Robinson) for help over the fine picture of Soult in old age which is at Apsley House; and the Royal Green Jackets (Colonel Elliot and Colonel Baker) for more information about Soult's London visit. Finally, Major Charles Blackmore who led the memorable 'Corunna Walk' of 1983-4 on the 175th anniversary of Sir John Moore's retreat, hotly pursued by Soult, has provided me with both interesting information and photographs.

Warm thanks are due to Ashley Tilley and to the Delegate Company in Henley-on-Thames for deciphering my terrible writing and typing the book.

Above all I am most grateful to my wife, a kinswoman of the famous Napier brothers, who has for so long borne with my total immersion in Soult and who has regularly corrected my inaccuracies in wording and expression.

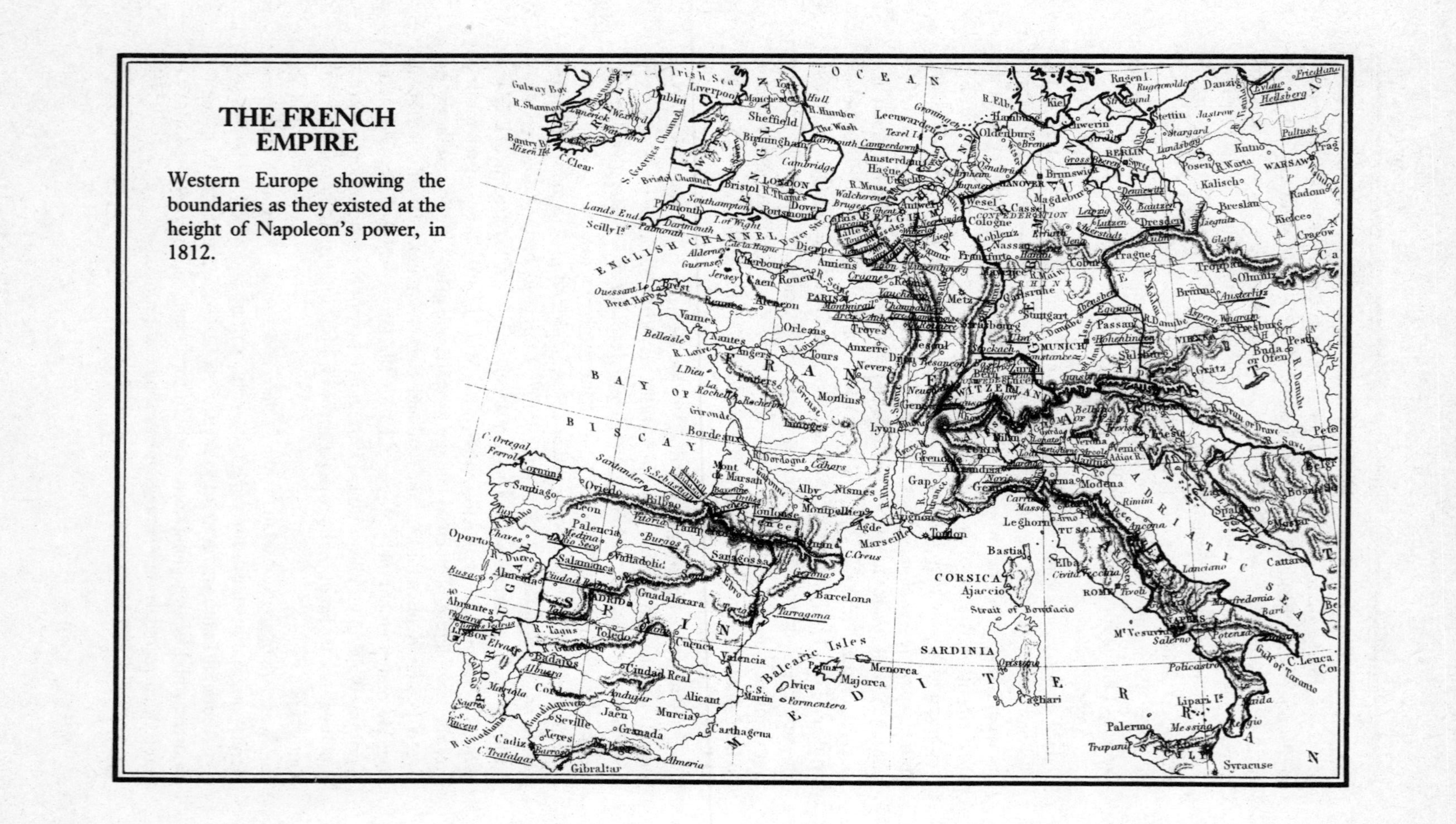

THE FRENCH EMPIRE

Western Europe showing the boundaries as they existed at the height of Napoleon's power, in 1812.

INTRODUCTION

"SILENCE is certainly history's murderer." This was a remark made to me by Michel de Saint-Pierre, Marshal Soult's great great grandson, who was himself a distinguished writer, poet and wartime Resistance leader. He was repeating a comment of his parents, Louis and Antoinette de Saint-Pierre, in one of their books which, a hundred years after Soult's death, reflected the career of one of the greatest of Napoleon's marshals.

In the 138 years since Soult died he has been, as Louis de Saint-Pierre has written, "either ignored or abused by historians". One of his bitterest critics was General Thiébault who, according to Louis Madelin, "criticized him atrociously in many pages of invective". Thiébault served several times under Soult. He was one of that "salade des maréchaux ... une détestable mélange" who, so the self-opinionated Thiébault believed, had blocked his promotion. Soult also detested and was scorned by Thiers when they were both ministers under King Louis Philippe; Thiers took his revenge in some of his comments on Soult in his monumental *History of the Consulate and the Empire*. There was, too, the *canard* about 'Roi Nicolas', initiated as Professor Tulard, the historian, suggests by his arch-enemy, Ney, when Soult had tried desperately to find a solution for France's Portuguese problem. The derisory name 'Nicolas' has stuck to him quite undeservedly ever since. His switches of loyalty from Napoleon to the Bourbons, joining as it were the *Collège des Girouettes* – 'the weathercock school' – have been criticized also, although most of his comrades in arms followed the same course of being loyal simply to France herself.

Naturally Soult appears in most of the histories and biographies of the Napoleonic period. However, since the *Histoire Anecdotique* of Anarcharsis Combes, published in 1870, until the *Life* written in 1986 by Didier Pacaud, Président de la Societé des Sciences et Belles Lettres du Tarn, no full-length biography of Soult has ever been written. His own *Memoirs* simply cover the Revolutionary Wars and the beginning of the Consulate. They are severely factual, written without malice about one of the most furiously competitive periods of French history, and predominantly military with some general comments on political affairs. They are no worse and no better than the avalanche of memoirs which were written by most of Napoleon's marshals and generals after their retirement. Soult contended, not without justification, that, as a minister under King Louis Philippe, he was too busy to write any more. His son, then an ambassador, comments with a professional diplomatist's cynicism on his father being "compelled to concern himself with the excessive and boring labours of parliamentary life". In fact, he had plenty of time to write during his foreign exile after Waterloo and on his return to France in 1819. Doubtless the real reason why he wrote no more was that he was a man of action rather than a man of letters.

Was Soult, in fact, the crafty, avaricious plunderer that he has sometimes been called ... the man who inspired loyalty among his junior officers and troops, but jealousy and hatred among some of his generals ... the man with treasonable intentions in Portugal ... the man who, after his dashing exploits in the Revolutionary Wars and his severe leg wound outside Genoa, preferred to 'lead from behind', as his bitter critic, Thiébault, and even his aide-de-camp, Saint-Chamans, suggest? Was he really little more than a talented drill sergeant with certain military capabilities? The books published by the Saint-Pierres provide a more realistic picture. They are based on the collection of family papers in the great château of Epoisses in Burgundy. They comprise an edited version of Soult's papers on the Peninsular War, a selection of his correspondence with King Louis Philippe and his talented son, the Duke of Orléans, and the reminiscences of Soult's faithful assistant, Brun de Villeret.

What are the facts about Soult? He was born in 1769, the same year as Napoleon and Wellington. He served in the ranks of Louis XVI's army. He became a marshal under Napoleon, a minister under both the senior and junior lines of the House of Bourbon, President of the Council and at least nominal head of the government for as long a period as anyone in French history and, with Turenne, Villars and Saxe, one of only four 'marshal generals' of France ever to be created. During his long career it could be argued that in the camp of Boulogne he was, under Napoleon, the chief architect of the Grande Armée – the finest military machine that the world had thus far seen, – and he might well have led the advance guard in the invasion of England. At Austerlitz he contributed more than any of his comrades to Napoleon's greatest victory. He was one of the few who kept his head during the Emperor's first serious reverse at Eylau. During his five and a half years in the Peninsula he created, as 'viceroy' in Andalusia, the real French power base in Spain. As Louis Philippe's Minister of War, he probably did more to reform the army than any other individual in nineteenth-century France. As a business entrepreneur he contributed much to the economy of his native Languedoc; and in a memorable speech in Birmingham in 1838 he foreshadowed the Entente Cordiale.

Throughout his life he displayed a real and rare political flair for getting along with foreigners. Thanks to a German wife he became, as a young general of brigade, the *Wundermann* of the Rhinelanders and, after Tilsit, a tactful military governor of Berlin so that he was warmly welcomed in Germany when he was exiled after Waterloo. He dealt in a firm but friendly way with the Swiss patriots in 1799, with the villainous Barbets in Piedmont and with the Neapolitans a year later. He might have found a political solution for Portugal in 1809 had he not been bundled out of Oporto by Wellington. Like Suchet in Valencia, he remained on good terms with most Andalusians for the years that he ruled over them as 'viceroy', his popularity being little diminished even by his plundering of their art treasures.

Above all, Soult is of special interest to Britain. To his contemporaries on this side of the Channel he was better known than any of the marshals. One of the few warships in the Royal Navy to be named after a foreigner was called *Marshal Soult.* Sir William Napier, the Peninsular War historian, described him as "the best loved Frenchman the British ever fought". He saved the life of one of the three fighting Napier brothers and they all became his warm admirers. Indeed some of Napier's *History* is based on the official papers that Soult lent him. Sir Charles Oman, that other great Peninsular War historian, considers that Napier cannot be trusted where Soult is concerned. Indeed, it is usual nowadays to point out Napier's factual inaccuracies and to claim that he was too much involved in the fighting to be reliable. But there is surely something to be said for one of the few men apart from Julius Caesar who played a full part in a major war and then wrote a detailed history of it! Many of the other British officers who fought in the War, such as Captain William Bragge, Ensign John Aitchison and Edward Charles Cocks echoed Napier's views in their writings, while the British private soldier, often a good commentator, gave Soult the grudging compliment of a nickname; the 'Duke of Dalmatia' being corrupted to the 'Duke of Damnation'. More important still, his great adversary, Wellington, while emphasizing some of Soult's tactical failings, regarded him, according to his 'conversations' with Lord Stanhope much later, as one of the greatest of the marshals.

What was Soult really like? Two hundred years after the French Revolution no final conclusion has been reached about its significance nor about the many remarkable Frenchmen such as Jean de Dieu Soult who emerged from it. Of course he was a rough diamond like many of the comrades; with his upbringing and his lack of education he was bound to be. Beneath his cold manner he was a real buccaneer, as were most of the soldiers who learned their craft in the 'Army of the Sambre et Meuse'. He was intensely ambitious; without ambition he could never have succeeded in the vicious 'game of snakes and ladders' which was the promotion scramble in the armies of Revolutionary France. He was sometimes over-deferential to his superiors while being harsh to his immediate subordinates, but he was much admired by the soldiers who served under him. He was moulded by Napoleon but, when he thought Napoleon was wrong, he became his own man, and in 1814 he defended France for several days after the Emperor had abdicated. He was avaricious, yet he turned his business abilities not only to his own profit but to the benefit of his fellow countrymen. Like most of those who fought in the Napoleonic Wars, he plundered works of art, but this turned out to be for the ultimate benefit of numerous picture galleries in Europe and North America! All in all, he was a fine fighting soldier, probably the best and hardest working administrator in Napoleon's armies, a supreme pragmatist who used to say – "inspiration is nothing but rapid calculation", a talented civil administrator and a minister with at least plenty of 'gravitas'. In his later years he was the 'illustre épée' of King Louis Philippe, the grand old soldier who, in the mid-nineteenth century, reflected the glories of the First Empire, both in Paris and at Queen Victoria's coronation in London. Louis de Saint-Pierre, married to one of his descendants and his memorialist, records that in 1814 the returning Bourbons regarded him with Davout and Masséna as one of 'the three greats' of Napoleon's marshals. This is surely a reasonable assessment.

1

THE MAKING OF A MARSHAL: THE REVOLUTIONARY WARS IN GERMANY

JEAN DE DIEU SOULT was born in 1769 – the same year as Napoleon and Wellington. His family came from a long line of small merchants and local officials in Languedoc. The family, originally 'Soulz', was at first Protestant but changed its name to 'Soult' when it prudently became Catholic at the time of the Revocation of the Edict of Nantes. Jean Soult, the third in succession with that Christian name and the Marshal's grandfather, was for a time collector of taxes in the small village of St-Amans-Labastide. He had, as one of thirteen children, a son, also Jean, who married a young woman, Marie-Brigitte de Grenier de la Pierre, a member of a celebrated family of 'gentlemen glass-makers of the Tarn'. These were a group of French Protestants from the remote region of the Black Mountains who earned their living making glass by using charcoal from the huge forests that covered the whole area. Ennobled by Saint Louis in the thirteenth century, they fought on the king's behalf against other religious dissentients such as the Cathars. At the time of the Revocation of the Edict of Nantes many of them became Catholic. Others who remained Protestant emigrated to England but maintained close ties with their French family. By now there were more sophisticated ways of glass-making and the glass-makers had become poor – if still noble. Jean Soult was not especially anxious for his son, Jean, who had become the local village notary, to marry Marie-Brigitte, who was much younger than himself, while the noble de Greniers themselves did not consider it much of a match. However, the obstacles were overcome and in 1765 the middle-aged notary married the youthful Brigitte de Grenier. Four years later their eldest son was born, followed by three brothers and two sisters.[1]

Perhaps due to his mother's piety or to the influence of his uncle, an itinerant curé named Abbé Soult, the eldest son, the future Marshal, was given the unusual name of 'Jean de Dieu'. The original Jean de Dieu, the founder of a small Catholic religious order, was born in Portugal and first served as a soldier in Andalusia in the armies of the Emperor Charles V in the sixteenth century. Considering the Marshal's own long service in both Portugal and Spain, this name was strangely prophetic. Many of his descendants have been given the baptismal name of Jean de Dieu. The name 'Nicholas', which became attached to him over the years, appears nowhere in his baptismal, marriage or death certificates, nor in his patents of appointment as a marshal of the Empire or as a peer of France. In fact it was a slang name used on various occasions and especially in derisory terms by the soldiers of his rival Ney's army who called him 'Roi Nicolas' after that mysterious incident when, as conqueror of Oporto in 1809, he was supposed to have aspired to be a king. The name clung to him. It has been used by some historians and also in reference books. Incidentally, Napoleon himself was derisively called 'Nicolas' too – perhaps the English equivalent is 'Old Nick' – when he was being abused by the country folk of the Midi on his way to exile in Elba. So Soult was in fair company.

The Soult family lived in a small stone house in the 'Grande Rue' of St-Amans-Labastide.[2] It was only one of five houses in the tiny village with an upper floor and Jean, as the local notary, shared leadership of the community with the curé. The village was dominated by the Black Mountains and in the eighteenth century it was very poor and very remote. (The area became a centre of the Resistance during the Second World War, as a monument on one of the peaks south of Labrugière testifies, but even now it is a part of France little known to tourists.) The story that Mazamet, the sizeable town near by, became famous for providing cloth for the French army when Soult was Minister of War under King Louis Philippe is something of a myth. But Soult and his immediate descendants, several of whom represented the department of the Tarn in the Chamber of Deputies for 100 years after Soult's death, did much to develop the whole area. A far more important role in the cloth industry was played by Pierre-Elie Houlès and his descendants. Many of the delightful families who live in this part of France are still involved in the higher levels of the textile industry.[3]

In the eighteenth century life in the little communities in and around the Black Mountains was very hard. Since there were only tracks and no roads, families had to be completely self-supporting. The Soults had a small back garden full of cabbages and other vegetables: bread was their staple diet and Jean de Dieu and his brothers had to collect logs from the forest and even dung from the horses that used the narrow track from Mazamet to St-Pons to keep the dank little house in the Grande Rue reasonably warm in the winter.[4] Jean de Dieu was a tough, thickset youngster well used to hard work. When, many years later, a flatterer asked him whether he found his braided minister's uniform too heavy for him, he replied sardonically that it was not nearly as heavy as the burdens he habitually carried when he was a boy.

Jean de Dieu's father died when he was only ten. His mother, still a youngish woman of great spirit, wanted to carry on the notary business until Jean de Dieu could take it over, but there were problems. Except for some elementary learning that he received from his uncle, the abbé, he had had little formal education – a fact which he bitterly regretted in later life. As a boy he also spoke with a strong Languedoc accent, using on occasions the Black Mountains patois which is akin to Catalan and is still used by old people in some of the mountain villages. Indeed some say that ethnographically this area was once a kind of Catalan 'finger' pointing northwards into France. It was another link between Soult and Spain although he was never to soldier in Catalonia. He corrected his speech over the years and it was never a problem for him in the army, but his rather heavily accented voice often made him hard to understand in later years when he was speaking as a minister in the Chamber.

Another problem for the boy at this time was one of discipline. Young Jean de Dieu was already the leader of the more rumbustious village boys and, partly to check his high spirits and partly to train him to take over his father's business, he was successively apprenticed to notaries in two other villages. Neither move was a success; in the first village there was an even rowdier element than in St-Amans, while in the second his employer was such a tyrant that young Jean de Dieu hated him. One cold February day in 1785 the boy, now nearly sixteen, escaped through the window of the little garret room in which he was more or less imprisoned and returned home to find that his poor mother had the bailiffs in the house. He took an instant decision. The prospect of being a village notary had always bored him. He had secret longings to be a soldier so he went straight off to the nearby château of La Rembergue and joined up as a military volunteer. For this he received ten crowns which he immediately sent to his mother to pay her debts.

Soult undoubtedly inherited from his mother much of his drive and toughness, and from his father his strong love of order. Like many strong-willed men, he often deferred to the three most important women of his family – his mother, his elder sister, Sophie, and his wife, Louise. He had a particularly deep affection for his mother. She lived on into her 90s and, whenever he got the chance – which was rare – he used to pay flying visits to her at St-Amans. When he and Louise later gave grand dinner parties, he always insisted that his mother should occupy the place of honour on his right.

During his two years serving in the Royal Regiment of Infantry in the army of Louis XVI stationed at St-Jean d'Angély, he felt baffled and restless. He was made a corporal but had no hope of becoming an officer since at that time all promotions to commissioned rank were reserved for young men of noble birth. His general impatience and ruffianly behaviour seem to have brought him very near to being court-martialled.[5] In the end sheer boredom and frustration led him to try to resign from the army altogether and to set himself up in a bakery business in St-Amans. He returned to the depot in the château of La Rembergue but failed to secure his release. From now on he was to be even more actively embroiled in the dramatic military events that were shaping world history. Characteristically, despite the failure of his present mission, he maintained friendly ties with the La Rembergue family, most of whom joined the *émigré* army abroad, although one branch supported the Revolution. He also kept in touch with some of his other comrades: one of them, Laporte, remained a private soldier throughout his army career but ended up as a gardener in Soult's house in Paris.

Soult's resumed military career began in 1792 when the Austrians and Prussians invaded Revolutionary France. It has been suggested by critics delving into his republican past when he was a tough Minister of War under King Louis Philippe that at this early stage he was a prominent member of a Revolutionary political club, making violent speeches in his neighbourhood attacking those who "opposed the glorious system of social equality that has now been established." In fact they seem to have been little more than the outpourings of a hotheaded young man at a time when his country was being invaded. There is no evidence that he engaged in serious political activity like many of his future comrades in the new Revolutionary armies. Indeed he was now far too busy as a soldier to become involved in Revolutionary politics. The National Assembly, in desperate need of larger armies, had ordered the raising of volunteer battalions from the newly created departments. Officers in these units would be elected by the rank and file except for an 'adjutant major' from the regular army. Serving officers could hold these posts in the new *fédérés* battalions without forfeiting their regular army ranks. By now many former officers had resigned their commissions either to retire or to join the *émigré* army across the Rhine. Some 2,000 vacancies could only be filled from the commissioned ranks, giving Soult and others their chance. Soult, who was stationed at Schelestadt in Alsace, was already a *caporal fourrier* – a 'corporal quartermaster' – in the Royal Infantry which was now named the 23rd Infantry. In July he was appointed sergeant and, early in 1792, he was chosen to be instructor to the First National Guard battalion of the Haut Rhin with the rank of *sous-lieutenant* of the grenadier company, a post reserved for exceptional young men promoted from the ranks.[6] His task was the training of raw recruits for embodiment in the regular army. The commanding officers of these volunteer battalions were often inexperienced old men: within a few months Soult was virtually commanding the battalion himself as acting adjutant major, elected with acclamation by the whole unit. For the first time he began to make full use of his remarkable training and organizational abilities – qualities that he was to display in full measure ten years later when he was creating the Grande Armée in the camp at Boulogne. Napoleon Bonaparte gained his own promotion in the same way and at the same time, becoming adjutant major of the Ajaccio Volunteers in Corsica. Both he and Soult were then 22.

In the strange war that now followed, swinging backwards and forwards across southern Germany, the Revolutionary armies were fighting a coalition joined by England, Spain and Portugal. For the French generals the price of failure was often the guillotine, especially if they were in trouble with the terrible 'Representatives of the People' – the political commissars of the day – who accompanied the armies. Two of Soult's generals, Custine, or 'General Moustache', as he was called, who had joined the Revolutionary cause without really understanding what it was all about, and de Beauharnais, the first husband of the future Empress Josephine, were among those guillotined. Soult was too junior to be involved in such matters. His brisk, soldierly *Memoirs* covering this period make few allusions to politics, although he does refer to the desperate anxiety of some of his leaders not to be "too passive", which sometimes led them into frightening decisions. The young adjutant major was typical of those patriotic Frenchmen who recognized that "in this time of disaster and anarchy, the honour of France took refuge in the army".[7] Nevertheless, despite his habitual prudence, Soult's name did appear in one of the dreaded Representative of the People lists for expressing himself too freely about the Revolutionary Government. It seems likely that he was saved, like many others, by the fall of Robespierre.

What really mattered to him, however, was fighting. He was in the thick of Custine's hasty withdrawal from Mainz at the beginning of the war and he emerged as an excellent regimental officer. Later at Wissembourg he commanded two battalions in his first offensive action which caused heavy Austrian losses following a successful enveloping attack. Before the end of 1792 the army was engaged in a desultory war of outposts in which Soult showed great initiative and determination. He had learned the necessity for close military cooperation especially during the Allied invasion of Alsace in 1793 and later when in each of the three years from 1795 to 1797 the French armies invaded southern Germany. Fortunately for the French, Allied cooperation was also bad but Soult sharply criticized his general-in-chief, Jourdan, for "deploying the army over too wide a front so that it was impossible for the various corps to support each other". In contrast to Bonaparte's well-knit Army of Italy, he considered it a great mistake for Jourdan to allow several disjointed offensives to go forward at the same time and to be commanded by subordinate chiefs who were often acting quite independently.[8] Indeed the army deserved a better chief than the ex-journeyman pedlar, Jourdan, who was nicknamed 'The Anvil' because the enemy so often hammered him. Soult would often tangle later with this strange, patriotic but indecisive man, especially when, as King Joseph Bonaparte's chief of staff in Spain, the latter was much involved in Soult's unending quarrels with the king.

Another quality that Soult developed was his ability to get on well with his military superiors. Some critics have said that he flattered the great while remaining remote from his juniors. Occasionally he did lay flattery on with a trowel but it was as usual then as it is now. Getting oneself noticed by senior officers was the best way of securing advancement in the armies of Revolutionary France.

Hoche was the first senior officer with whom Soult developed a close relationship. Lazare Carnot, the head of the war section of the committee of Public Safety – the 'Organizer of Victory' – had doubled the number of Frenchmen under arms. He also created the 'Bureau Typographique', an embryonic general staff. Training and a staff organization were urgently needed for Carnot's *levée en masse*. The 'Amalgame' of 1793 had created *demi-brigades* which brought together one regular battalion with two volunteer battalions, and Soult was transferred with his volunteers to Hoche's Army of the Moselle. In order to gain new experience, he applied for a staff post. Hoche immediately agreed and Soult joined the staff of General Taponier at Zweibrücken. In those days there was much less distinction between staff and command, and Soult was also given a mixed force of all arms – a feature of the old Royal army – to attack the Austrians near Niederbronn. Soult, who was specially skilful at handling these mixed forces, was victorious, taking some 300 prisoners. From then on Hoche urged him in characteristically expansive terms to be a "true sans-culotte" and gave him various independent commands.

In January 1794 he became chief of staff to General Lefebvre, the general of division commanding the advance guard of the Army of the Moselle. This link with the 'elderly' and gallant Lefebvre (he was 40) was the second military association that Soult treasured and was important to his future. In June a vigorous battle with the Austrians took place at Fleurus near Brussels. The battle had little strategic value since Vienna had already decided to evacuate the Austrian Netherlands, at least for the time being, but Lefebvre's division greatly distinguished itself. The brave Alsatian had no great tactical skill but he was beloved by his troops and Soult made him an excellent assistant. "It was fifteen hours of the most desperate fighting that ever I saw," Soult wrote in his *Memoirs.* There is the story that at a critical moment in the battle the hot headed Marceau appeared at Lefebvre's headquarters threatening to blow out his brains if he did not get some badly needed reinforcements. Soult, very much Marceau's junior, calmed him down and quietly told him to return to his men until reinforcements arrived. Marceau did not resent this advice and is supposed to have said afterwards, "You have given me a lesson in calmness that I shall not forget. It is you that have gained the victory!"[9] This is not the kind of colourful story that Soult was likely to include in his severely factual *Memoirs* but he does emphasize that he constantly urged Lefebvre to stand firm until the Austrians themselves began to retreat. "We were determined", he wrote, "only to emerge victorious from this 'volcano'."[10] He was to show the same coolness and obstinacy in adversity with Napoleon himself on the bloody field of Eylau thirteen years later. Soult and Marceau became firm friends until Marceau was killed in battle in 1796.

After Fleurus there was also some scrappy fighting near Waterloo when Soult had three horses killed under him. Writing his *Memoirs* in exile after the great battle in which he had been Napoleon's chief of staff, and doubtless anxious to make his peace with Louis XVIII, it is not surprising that Soult makes no mention of these earlier experiences on Victor Hugo's "doleful plain". However, as he had fought all over the Waterloo countryside twenty years before, it is a pity that the Emperor did not take more notice of his advice in June 1815.

Soult describes his service as Lefebvre's chief of staff as one of the happiest periods of his military life. Lefebvre was very dependent on him but he was an exacting master. Soult, however, revelled in hard work and enjoyed this mixture of command and staff duties. One French historian suggests that Soult makes too much of the period in his *Memoirs*, claiming that it was the only time until 1815 that he was ever a chief of staff, in order to justify his much criticized appointment by Napoleon at Waterloo.[11] This is unfair. Soult always showed a keen interest in military organization, sometimes perhaps more than in the battle itself. He was to be an excellent if imperious 'major general' to King Joseph in Spain but there is possibly truth in Wellington's celebrated comment that although he was very good at bringing his troops into battle he did not always know what to do with them when he got them there.

After Fleurus Jourdan's army became the 'Army of the Sambre et Meuse'. The 'Sambre et Meuse' never acquired the lustre of Bonaparte's Army of Italy, partly because of its ineffectual commander, but its soldiers contributed quite as much to Napoleon's future glories as did the victors of Arcola and Rivoli. There was a difference in style and some mutual ill will between what has been called the 'puritan' and more orthodox republican armies in Germany and the warmer, more relaxed Army of Italy. However, from the potentially hostile environment across the Rhine which produced 'dedicated republicans' such as Jourdan himself and Bernadotte, as well as traitors like Dumouriez, Pichegru and Moreau, Napoleon later obtained some of his finest generals. Within the ranks of the 'Sambre et Meuse' Soult needed all his toughness to hold his own against such turbulent warriors as Marceau, Kléber or Bernadotte.[12] Moreover, it was a period of quick promotion.[13] For the first time Soult came into contact with Michel Ney. Their careers were to be fatally entwined for years. Born within a few months of eath other, they were totally different in temperament. Soult, a shrewd soldier and excellent administrator who was to develop considerable political skills, had plenty of inner fire but appeared cold and restrained. Ney, "the bravest of the brave", indolent when not fighting and by no means the open hearted paladin as often portrayed, was a quarrelsome, tricky and difficult man who repeatedly let down his comrades, Masséna, Soult and even Napoleon himself; for some time the Swiss-born Jomini, his chief of staff, supplied him with much of his tactical skill and he has been called one of the "Grande Armée chargers" rather than an effective general.[14] For most of their lives Soult and Ney detested each other. "Do you think it is an easy matter to control a Soult or a Ney?" asked Napoleon ruefully, referring to their famous quarrel at Lugo in Galicia in 1809. But at this time the 'Sambre et Meuse' was a kind of family for them both.

The "immoral and incompetent" government of the Directory, as Soult called it, intended to make the 'Sambre et Meuse' the main spearhead of the three major French offensives through southern Germany during the years 1795 and 1797. Although Bonaparte's victories in Italy stole the limelight, the early successes of the 'Sambre et Meuse' in the Low Countries and over the Rhine extended the frontiers of France further than ever before in her history. Soult, now commanding a *demi-brigade*, took a full part in all these operations. In the 1796 offensive he was on the extreme left of the line. At the battle of Altenkirchen he was attacked by a superior force of Austrian cavalry but he resisted strongly, taking about 3,000 prisoners with only a small loss. Later his semi-independent unit was assailed at Herborn by a much stronger enemy force; again he held out until Kléber came to his aid and then, without losing a gun or a colour, he fought his way back to the main army. However, the appalling state of French finances and a dreadful commissariat system meant that the army had to live off the land when it was abroad. Soult commented that this living by plunder was both bad for discipline and enraged the countries in which the French armies were operating. With 'respectable' Royal army precedents it was a policy pursued relentlessly by Napoleon on the grounds that war must be made to pay for itself, but it caused endless difficulties both for the Emperor and his lieutenants.[15]

French relations with their conquered peoples had now become a serious problem. At the beginning, whatever might be the attitude of governments, the spread of revolutionary ideas was welcomed by some of the people in Germany, Italy and the Low Countries if not nearly as enthusiastically as the Revolutionary Armies expected. But 'living off the land' and the endless fighting had painful effects even on the easy-going Rhinelanders. As a strict disciplinarian, somewhat lacking in personal warmth, Soult might have been expected to inspire foreigners with loathing. But this was never the case. His first experience in this context came in Bonn in 1795. As a young and confident general of brigade, aged 26, he followed normal practice by insisting on a lavish provision of food and wine for his table. He also made sizeable financial demands as required by the French government. When the Rhinelanders, accustomed to the mild regime of the Electoral Archbishop of Cologne, protested, Soult threw one of the municipal officers into prison and threatened Bonn with dire penalties. His chief, Lefebvre, went much further, calling the town council "good for nothing rascals" and promising "fire and blood" all round. Soult was more restrained and finally established fairly peaceful relations with the town.[16]

An event now occurred which unquestionably influenced his attitude towards foreigners. In January 1796 his *demi-brigade* was stationed in Solingen in the duchy of Berg, famous since the Middle Ages for the manufacture of sword blades and still an important cutlery town in the Ruhr. The Duke of Berg, who was subsequently dethroned by Napoleon to make way for his brother-in-law, Murat, had marriage links with the Russian imperial family and little love for France. Having heard about French army oppressions in the Rhineland, the inhabitants of Solingen were alarmed by the forceful young general of brigade who established his headquarters in the house of a certain Frau Berg, the widow of Johann Abraham Berg, a maker of sword blades and a former mayor of Solingen. Despite his name, Johann had no connection with the ruling family of the duchy. Almost at once Soult made the usual burdensome quartering demands. He was increasingly fond of good living: he was 'on his way up' in the hurly burly of the 'Sambre et Meuse'; he entertained Lefebvre and the other generals frequently and the needs of his table were considerable. But he was careful to ensure that his *demi-brigade* were well quartered too. He had also acquired quite a sense of self-importance, going one better than his fellow generals in having a special seal designed for himself which, unusually, bore his own name above the Republican emblem.

Frau Berg had a 24-year-old daughter, Louise, who was romantically involved at this time with a French *émigré* officer named Duffieux de la Grange-Merlin, and they were planning to elope. Duffieux was occupied in recruiting Rhineland Germans to serve in the British army in accordance with the well-established eighteenth-century tradition. Soult, however, met Louise, as it was said, on the staircase in his headquarters, fell in love with her and determined to marry her. There are conflicting reports of what happened next. One tale relates how this Languedoc peasant boy (sic) who commanded an army of "bootless flotsam" demanded to marry the daughter of a prosperous Solingen craftsman and threatened harsh punishment if he did not get his way, so that the agitated townsfolk begged Frau Berg to encourage the match. But the Solingen archives show that Frau Berg disliked her daughter's involvement with the French *émigré* anyway, especially when a French Republican army was quartered in the town, so that she was quite willing to help disentangle her daughter from Soult's rival. Moreover, the duchy government, too, had become increasingly nervous about French *émigrés* with the 'Sambre et Meuse' on their doorstep. Frau Berg was a woman of spirit from a prominent Rhineland family. She used much influence in favour of Louise's betrothal to the dashing young general. Duffieux appeared no more.

From her pictures Louise was obviously no raving beauty but it was a love match: no doubt, too, the ambitious Soult wanted to marry into a stable bourgeois family. Of course he was no 'peasant boy' – indeed as a notary's son he was socially on much the same level as the Bergs. Soult's own comments on the marriage in his *Memoirs* are characteristically low-key. "My wife provided me with a happiness which only increased with the passing years."[17] Despite his numerous infidelities she made him an excellent wife, nursing him devotedly when he was seriously wounded and taken prisoner by the Austrians in one of his heroic sallies from Genoa, performing social duties when he commanded in Boulogne, and presiding as hostess in his fine town house in the Rue de l'Université in Paris and in their country property near St-Cloud. She was at his side during many of the vicissitudes of his later life. She was sensible enough to be on excellent terms with his aides de camp and she was also very forceful. Napoleon, who was often as good a judge of able women as he was of men, once commented: "Soult is very ambitious but it is his wife who manages him!" Congratulating Soult on the birth of his daughter in 1804, Napoleon expressed the hope that she would be as like her mother as possible.[18] In fact, Hortense Soult, who was to marry the Marquis de Mornay, a liberal politician, was a young woman of considerable ability.

By 1804 the Soults were becoming well established in the imperial hierarchy, thanks not a little to Louise's personality. She was made 'Dame of Honour' to Napoleon's mother, – the formidable 'Madame Mère', and, sitting on Madame Mère's right, she is one of the few marshal's wives included by the scrupulously obedient David in the painting of Napoleon's coronation – although, in fact, it is doubtful whether either of them was actually present at the ceremony! Like King Joseph Bonaparte's wife, Louise never accompanied her husband to Spain: with the continuous campaigning and the fierce guerilla activities, the Peninsula was no place for the wives of generals on either side. This did not much please the Emperor but Louise was unabashed. In fact, as will be recorded, the only battle she lost with Napoleon was at Dresden in 1813 when she tried unsuccessfully to prevent her husband being sent back to Spain for the fateful campaign which ended with the battle of Toulouse. When Soult was a minister under Louis XVIII the redoubtable Louise was not 'put down' by the snubs of Royalist *grandes dames* such as poor Aglaé Ney, who having held a minor court appointment before the Revolution, was mercilessly humiliated by the returning Bourbons. In the dangerous days after Waterloo, when Soult had to go into exile, Louise was at her best. She had always maintained excellent relations with her German family so that it was in the Solingen area and then in neighbouring Düsseldorf that Soult made his home when he had to leave France. All the time that he was abroad she worked tirelessly for his return. Then, when there was another complete change in his fortunes and he became a senior minister under Louis Philippe, it was partly through his wife's influence that swords and other items of military equipment from Solingen were provided for the French army. By this time the Soults were installed in the château of Soultberg which he had built for their later years. In the event she only outlived her husband by one year.

Critics have alleged that her meteoric rise went to her head. There is little evidence of this. Certainly local records in her native town make much of this extraordinary career – a Solingen girl becoming an important figure in Napoleonic France and a duchess of that improbable place 'Dalmatia'; then achieving even greater prominence in the France of Louis Philippe as a close friend of the German wife of the heir to the throne, the Duke of Orléans. Soult also appears in a romantic light in local documents. He was the *wundermann* of Solingen – a 'gentle master' enjoying widespread popularity when he had his headquarters there. The town received him again in the friendliest way, twenty years later, when he returned as an exile after Waterloo. Of course, like most of the Revolutionary generals – and there is little evidence that he was more grasping than most of them – he also had a sharp eye for financial profit, having dealings with various prosperous German banks in Frankfurt, which gave him another strong tie with the Rhineland. When he left Solingen for the first time after his marriage he had very amicable exchanges with the town authorities. Later he returned there from time to time to make sure that the town was spared excessive military burdens.[19]

In 1797 he served once more under his much admired Hoche. Earlier Hoche had invited him to take part in an operation against the Royalists, supported by the British navy, which ended in Hoche's victory at Quiberon. But Soult refused this offer, hating, as he carefully records in his post-Restoration *Memoirs*, to fight against fellow Frenchmen. If, as seemed possible before his premature death, Hoche and not Bonaparte had become the ruler of France, Soult might well have been faced with fewer military and political problems in his career. In his *Memoirs* he suggests that Hoche could have acted as Pompey to Bonaparte's Julius Caesar and that he might at least have prevented some of the convulsions that followed Napoleon's Brumaire *coup d'état.*[20]

In 1798 Soult had his first direct involvement with the country which was to loom so large in his life – England. This initial encounter was futile. Soult was sent to command a brigade in the so-called 'Army of England' between Bruges and Ghent. Did the Directory really contemplate an invasion at this time? If so their preparations were ludicrously inadequate. Probably the whole business was intended as a distraction for the already overweening Bonaparte. Instead Bonaparte embarked on his invasion of Egypt while the 'Army of England' became more or less a propaganda diversion. However, financial help for the expedition was needed and characteristically Soult raised a large sum from his brigade, which his men could ill afford. By now England was regarded as France's chief enemy and, when a small British force unsuccessfully attacked the fortress of Ostend, Soult was doubtless reflecting current feelings of hostility towards England in describing it venomously as "a nasty expedition of no military importance – designed to spread destruction against all the rules of war".[21] Towards the end of the year this rather ridiculous 'Army of England' was disbanded and Soult returned to Germany.

Before his departure for Egypt Bonaparte had forced Austria to make a humiliating peace at Campo Formio. But, while he was away, Vienna struck back. As a partner in the Second Coalition with England and Russia, she declared war on France at the beginning of 1799. There were four theatres of hostilities – the Low Countries, southern Germany, Switzerland and Italy. A full concentration of the Allied armies could have invaded France and destroyed the Directory, especially as there were only a few able French generals available – Moreau, Joubert and, above all, Masséna. But here was a great opportunity for young brigade commanders. Soult commanded the advance guard of Jourdan's army in southern Germany. Stockach was his first big chance to handle sizeable forces in the field. Heavily outnumbered by the Austrians, he led his brigade, sword in hand, in a violent attack on the enemy's flank. After some initial success the Austrians stood their ground and a vigorous counter-attack by the Archduke Charles, commanding the Austrian forces, compelled the French to give way. Finally Jourdan broke off the battle and retreated back to the Rhine. Stockach was a serious reverse for the French but Soult could not be blamed. His first attack had almost succeeded and, on the army's retreat, he provided the rearguard, temporarily taking over command of a division.

Moreau, who then succeeded Jourdan, was a better general but he was cautious, very jealous of Bonaparte and of doubtful loyalty. Masséna, commanding the French armies in Switzerland, was a much more effective soldier and Soult longed to serve under him. However, the young general of brigade was only one of many very ambitious soldiers now serving in the French armies in Germany. He had, it was true, shown considerable military skill and *élan* at Niederbronn, Herborn and Stockach, especially in the command of mixed forces. He had been an able and intelligent chief of staff to Lefebvre, and an excellent organizer in the 'Sambre et

Meuse', playing a major part in uniting volunteers and regulars and in transforming the French forces from a herd of undisciplined ragamuffins into a fairly well-knit professional army. He was a very hard worker; and if he was aloof with his immediate subordinates he was admired by the rank and file of his brigade. Furthermore he had much impressed some of his superiors, notably the brilliant Hoche and that brave old veteran Lefebvre – indeed his real heroes were now Hoche, Lefebvre and Masséna.[22] Finally, he showed more tact and political awareness than most of his contemporaries in his relations with foreigners, particularly with Germans. All in all there were few of his comrades with better qualifications for high command. Now what he needed most was to serve directly under a first rate commander-in-chief. He found one in the wily, avaricious André Masséna, who in Bonaparte's absence in Egypt, was to save France.

2

THE MAKING OF A MARSHAL: SWITZERLAND AND ITALY

IN APRIL 1799 Soult achieved his immediate ambition – the command of a division in Masséna's 'Army of Switzerland'. The Helvetic Republic, as Switzerland had now become, was an area of the greatest danger to France. After Stockach the Archduke Charles had decided that a direct attack could best be made through that divided little country which had been brought under what the London *Times* described as "the disorganizing system of the Directory ... forced to crouch to the galling yoke of a despotic government". The various cantons disliked the French; they hated the Austrians and most of them detested each other. Throughout his campaigning in Switzerland, the politically conscious Soult considered that one important objective was to regain Swiss friendship. If only the Directory had respected Switzerland's neutrality, she would have protected France's frontiers.

After a preliminary spell in Basle, Soult was ordered to pacify the turbulent cantons in the south of Switzerland, Schwyz, Uri and Unterwald. The situation there was serious; Frenchmen had been murdered; there was an Austrian army not far away in the Engadine; the area around the St Gothard Pass was desperately hard campaigning country and an independent cantonal government had been set up in Altdorf. From Zürich Masséna gave Soult a completely free hand – his first fully independent command – and he set out at once to re-establish the French position in this desolate mountain region. It was the kind of military/political task for which he was becoming well suited and he used that mixture of firmness and conciliation which had been so successful in the Rhineland. At a conference near the great baroque monastery of Einsiedeln, he threw a veil over recent Swiss attacks on Frenchmen, praised traditional Swiss courage, played on local fears of Austrian tyranny and obtained an agreement with the *landemann* of Schwyz whereby many Swiss enlisted with the French on condition that the hated Zürich Swiss units serving under Soult were returned, with his commander-in-chief's reluctant acquiescence, to Masséna's direct command. Soult's comments on these events were unusually forthcoming. "I shall never forget," he wrote, "the welcome that I had from these good people and I get renewed pleasure from thinking about them as I write these Memoirs!"[1] However, the neighbouring cantons of Uri and Unterwald were much more of a problem, and Soult was compelled to do battle in the terrible mountainous country through which the St Gothard tunnel now runs. He ended by defeating the patriots at Airolo and pacifying the area. Then, with his newly acquired 'public relations' sense, he paid a kind of Lake Lucerne 'pilgrimage' to the shrine of William Tell, putting himself in the hands of twelve Swiss oarsmen, most of whom must have lost family fighting against the French. At the end of his visit he and his former Swiss antagonists parted from one another as good friends.

Following these hectic two months, Soult had hastily to return to support Masséna in the Zürich area. Lecourbe, that master of mountain warfare, had been driven out of the Engadine by sheer weight of numbers and the whole French position in Switzerland was threatened by two large Austrian armies under the Archduke Charles himself and under General Hötze. Soult held the right of the defence line in front of the Zürich Beg and in the June battle called 'First Zürich' his division of some 7,000 men was engaged in fierce hand to hand fighting with twice as many Austrians. There were heavy losses on both sides. Soult used Lake Zürich boats with guns mounted on them – a military innovation which he had first employed against the Swiss insurgents. He hung on to his defensive position in the Zürich Beg desperately. Finally he led forward his last reserves in person. These consisted of 700 new recruits who were ordered not to waste their fire but to attack with the bayonet, forcing the enemy at last to retreat. In his report to the government in Paris, Masséna said that he could not praise too highly Soult's bravery and military skill. But 'First Zürich' had not succeeded in stemming the Allied advance. Masséna soon had to evacuate Zürich itself and, in Germany, the Low Countries and Italy, too, France was in desperate danger. Soult refers in contemptuous terms to the poor cooperation of the French generals on other fronts in comparison with Masséna's closely knit forces. But again, fortunately for the French, there was even worse cooperation between the Allies. In a moment of total aberration, the controlling 'Aulic Council' in Vienna, still with an eye on the future of the Austrian Netherlands, relieved some of the pressure on Masséna by transferring the Archduke Charles to Germany, leaving Switzerland to the responsibility of General Hötze and to a Russian army under the comparatively inexperienced Korsakov. At the same time the brilliant Russian General, Suvarov, had defeated and killed General Joubert at the battle of Novi. Now, in supreme command of the Allied forces, his strategic plan was for Korsakov and Hötze to attack the French frontally while he surrounded them from the rear.

'Second Zürich', fought over fifteen days in September and October, was the decisive encounter. If Masséna had lost this battle or had waited until Suvarov had come into action France would have been invaded in strength. With Bonaparte and his army away in Egypt she would have faced disaster. As usual under the Directory Masséna's army was starved of money and resources but it was tightly organized in a strong defence line running along Lake Zürich and then along the River Linth which was the direct responsibility of Soult's division. It was essential that the

Austro-Russian army should be defeated before it was strengthened by the arrival of the formidable Suvarov.

The crossing of the Linth near the eastern end of Lake Zürich was Soult's immediate task. The river was strongly defended by Hötze's Austrians and its marshy banks made it a very difficult obstacle. Soult at once subjected his men to some short, sharp 'commando' training. In his *Memoirs* he makes it plain that, despite their experiences so far in war, French soldiers in general were in comparatively poor physical shape. They ought to march harder and faster, carrying heavy packs on their backs; there was no reason why they should not be trained to be as good at mountain warfare as the Austrians or even the Swiss. The infantry should display greater technical proficiency and expertise in handling their weapons; they needed more careful training than the cavalry and for a much longer period than was presently the case in the Revolutionary armies.[2] Views such as these were far removed from the positional warfare which were a feature of the eighteenth century and Soult was not alone among officers in the new French armies to hold them. Probably he held them more strongly than most of his comrades; and a few years later, in the great camp at Boulogne, he was able, uniquely, to put them into effect on the grand scale. The semi-amphibious crossing of the Linth was just a minor rehearsal for the great training operations which were to take place on the Channel coast. On this occasion elaborate bridge building was out of the question but, as in his operations against some of the Swiss insurgents, Soult collected on the river a flotilla of twelve large boats, several small skiffs and three big launches, which were capable of carrying field guns. He also ordered that most of the men should quickly be taught to swim "like the Greeks and Romans in classical times".

Characteristically, one of his first actions was to carry out a personal reconnaissance. Disguised as a private soldier with a musket in his hand and accompanied by a corporal as if on sentry duty, he made a detailed examination of the marshy bank of the river to determine the exact place where his troops should cross. A specially trained and selected unit of 160 good swimmers, most of them armed with pikes, sabres and carrying their pistols and cartridges on their heads, was detailed to ford the river. Some twenty drummers, instruments strapped to their heads, were also included to sound the signal for the attack. The special unit was given a precise timing of two and a half hours to carry out the crossing and to seize some of the formidable defences on the other bank if possible without firing a shot. However, if there was serious resistance, the drums were to beat with some Swiss crying "save yourselves" in German to stampede the Austrians, and the whole division would then attack across the river. A bridge of boats would be built by the engineers as soon as possible afterwards to transport the heavy equipment.

In the event almost complete surprise was achieved and before the Austrians could recover themselves they had lost total control of the river bank. General Hötze, the Austrian commander, was killed; some of the Russian regiments supporting the Austrians were decimated and the French took at least 8,000 prisoners. Masséna recognized that the crossing of the Linth played a big part in his own great victory of Zürich, and Soult considered this operation as one of his major exploits; it is specially recorded among his other victories on the commemorative mausoleum built in his native town of St-Amans-Soult.

Under Masséna's overall direction Soult was now given command of three divisions commanded respectively by Mortier, also to become a marshal and always a close friend of Soult; Loison, Soult's *bête noir* in the Peninsula, and the zealous Gudin. Soult's main task was to prevent Suvarov, who was marching up from the Lombard plain, from linking up with Korsakov's discomfited army and indeed to drive him out of Switzerland. In one of the very few bitter comments in his otherwise strictly factual *Memoirs*, Soult complains that "later historians" have attributed to Lecourbe the successes in carrying out mountain warfare against Suvarov. In fact, manoeuvring with ever greater assurance in what had really become the role of a Corps commander, it was Soult who directed that units from his divisions should take action against Suvarov. Campaigning once more in the St Gothard region, which by now he had come to know well, Soult endeavoured to bring Suvarov to a decisive battle at Glavus but the Russian slipped away, leaving his wounded, his artillery and 3,000 prisoners in French hands. Suvarov himself, feeling that the Austrians had been totally uncooperative, resigned in disgust. Soult, who probably had a shrewder idea of Russian aggression than many of his contemporaries, recorded that Suvarov's defeat and the Russian retirement saved France from the most serious danger that it had faced in any previous war. "One day," he recorded, "all Europe may have to combine against the Russian menace."[3] Soult was immediately ordered to turn his mobile divisions northwards so as to secure the left bank of the Rhine. One division, commanded by General Gazan, later to be Soult's chief of staff in Spain, engaged in an operation around Constance in which a mixed force of Russians and French *émigrés* were soundly defeated, Frenchmen fighting against Frenchmen in the streets of the town; a Bourbon flag was captured and the enemy was driven across the Rhine.

By now heavy falls of snow had put an end to the great Swiss campaign of 1799. Soult established his winter headquarters at Rheinfelden near Lake Constance. His divisions were tired out and, inevitably, under the Directory, penniless. Soult tried to raise money from the Swiss in the familiar manner but they proved to be much more close-fisted than the Rhinelanders. Nevertheless Masséna, with Soult directing his spearhead, had achieved great things. The large Allied army, 70,000 strong, which had threatened to invade France, had been driven out of Switzerland with heavy losses. One of the Austrian commanders had been killed and the Russian, Korsakov, had been disgraced. Suvarov had resigned and, within a few months, Russia had left the Second Coalition. Switzerland was pacified and not unfriendly; and order had been restored among its warring cantons. French losses were rather more than 6,000 killed, and a high proportion of the wounded soon returned to the colours. Soult praised Masséna as one of the great military captains of history and this admiration endured for the rest of his life despite the problems that they were both to face later in Spain. Soult also paid tributes to his various divisional commanders and to the valour of his troops. His own reputation stood high. He had shown himself to be a good and brave tactical leader – by no means just a 'military slogger'. He obviously had plenty of imagination with a real flair for daring enterprises such as the commando-style crossing of the River Linth as well as the determined use of his advanced units in pursuing Suvarov. He had also developed some sound public relations sense in dealing patiently but firmly with the Swiss patriots. All this was a rare combination for a soldier in the Revolutionary armies. Writing to congratulate him, Masséna praised him especially for his hazardous river crossing and for "falling upon the enemy with such skill and energy and beating them everywhere".[4]

Napoleon Bonaparte's return from Egypt, the *coup d'état* of the 18 Brumaire and Napoleon's assumption of the title of First Consul had a great reviving effect on the French armies everywhere. Soult makes no bones about this. In his *Memoirs*, begun a year or two after Waterloo, when Napoleon was detested by the royal government and the 'Napoleonic legend' had not yet been born, this normally cautious man writes of the event as follows: "Napoleon afforded France a protective authority, giving her safeguards which calmed down evil passions and ended the wicked forces of the Revolution. He provided for our armies not only the leadership of which he had given such excellent proofs but also limitless self-confidence. As a first step the army expected and obtained some improvement in provisioning and equipment as well as some arrears of back pay."[5]

Despite the Russian abandonment of the Second Coalition, Austria had no intention of making peace or indeed of abandoning the strong position that she now held in Italy. The French situation there after military defeats and mass withdrawals was highly precarious. Now, under Masséna, they held a narrow line from the Appenines along the borders of the new Ligurian republic, covering Genoa. A much larger French army, composed of most of the forces which had been fighting in Germany for the last six years and commanded by Moreau, faced a formidable Austrian army in southern Germany. The capture of Vienna was the First Consul's main strategic objective and he began to build up a sizeable army at Dijon which could be used to support the main offensive against Vienna either through southern Germany or through Italy. This was an important moment in Soult's military career. As a veteran of the 'Sambre et Meuse' he might have been expected to rejoin Moreau's army for renewed operations in Germany. Indeed Moreau visited him at his headquarters in Rheinfelden, passing a whole day there and evidently taking some trouble with this young, up and coming divisional general. A discussion of the recent Swiss campaign quickly turned into a talk about the personality of Napoleon Bonaparte. Soult confessed ingenuously in his *Memoirs* that higher politics were at this moment an enigma to him but he had seen how the army chiefs in the 'Sambre et Meuse', like Jourdan and Bernadotte, tended to have one eye on politics in Paris. Of course he was flattered by the way Moreau spoke to him "so expansively", praising Bonaparte's military qualities but sharply criticizing his ambitions.[6] Moreau said he had only accepted a command in the Consular armies so that he could keep an eye on the new First Consul. He was obviously bidding for this successful young general's support. But he got nowhere. Soult realized that Moreau was quite as ambitious as Bonaparte himself; he could never hide his jealousy and, when it came to the crunch in battle, Soult concluded that he would be irresolute to the point of folly. More importantly, however, Soult already had in his pocket a firm request from Masséna to join him in Genoa to take command of the right wing of his army. "I have been allowed," wrote Masséna, "to bring under my command all those for whom I have a high regard and affection. I have arranged that you will receive immediately a posting to the Army of Italy."[7] Masséna was obviously a much better bet than the sour and indecisive Moreau.

As was to be the pattern over the next fifteen years, Soult enjoyed virtually no break in his active service. There were no visits to politicians in Paris. He just had time to take Louise home to St-Amans-Labastide and introduce her to his mother before he was off again to join Masséna in Italy. He was now 31.

During his own visit to Paris before taking up his command Masséna had complained of having many cadres but few troops and next to no resources. This was partly because he was starved of assistance by the incompetent Directory. But after Brumaire there were even more serious problems. Bonaparte was concentrating all his available manpower on the big Reserve Army that he was gathering at Dijon and there was little to spare elsewhere. Moreover, on his way back to Genoa the normally astute Masséna was swindled by the commissariat agents in Marseilles. "Is our army," commented Soult, "to be the plaything of this foul horde who enrich themselves at the soldiers' expense?"[8] In addition, there were great difficulties in bringing reinforcements into Genoa by sea because of the tight blockade maintained by the British fleet under Lord Keith. But this was not merely a case of a French army being starved into submission by a blockading fleet and by a large encircling army of up to 100,000 Austrians. It was the deliberate policy of the First Consul to treat the men of his beloved Army of Italy – the heroes of Arcola and Rivoli where he first made his name – as sacrificial lambs while he made up his mind about the advance upon Vienna with the Reserve Army. Should it be in conjunction with Moreau in southern Germany, which was his first option, or should he attack the Austrians in Italy – initially very much his second choice? "As a result," comments Thiers, "the brave men of the Army of Italy were left by the country they were defending to perish for want".[9]

Soult had not yet met Napoleon but in the Army of Italy he experienced for the first time his utter ruthlessness over the lives and destinies of his generals and soldiers when he had a firm military objective. Arriving in Genoa in February 1800, he was horrified by the state of the French army. Masséna could scarcely muster

30,000 men and with the need to provide garrisons for Genoa and for Savona he had a field force of no more than half that number. The soldiers were "pale, weary, famished and dejected men, looking like ghosts; it was a worse situation than I had ever experienced" wrote Soult.[10]

In the depths of winter, with the very efficient British blockade, there was already a desperate shortage of food; disease was widespread and the hospitals were in a terrible state with hundreds of sick men lying around on the ground or on filthy palliasses. Soult's predecessor, General Marbot, the father of the military historian, had had to use force to obtain drugs from chemists in the city and he finally died of disease himself. It was much to his and Soult's credit that he never seems to have resented his young successor's arrival and he served briefly as one of Soult's divisional generals. Soult was greatly upset by his death. Part of the trouble was that the inhabitants of Genoa and Savona – particularly the wealthier ones – had no love for the French; there were numerous spies posing as Italian refugees in the French army and brigands infested the mountains. So poor was the army's morale that there had been widespread desertions, whole units trying to escape from Genoa to make their way home.

Against this background Masséna had made the most of his meagre resources. With three divisions numbering no more than 18,000 men and forming the right wing of the army, Soult had established his headquarters at Acqui in the Ligurian Mountains. The left wing was commanded by Suchet who was to serve under Soult in the camp of Boulogne and was afterwards an excellent military leader in the Peninsula but a very uncooperative colleague for Soult in southern France in 1814. At this stage Melas, the Austrian commander, really had the game in his hands. Suchet's much smaller force became separated from Masséna's main army and he retreated towards Nice. If the Austrians had followed him with the bulk of their army, leaving a small force to block Genoa, they could have penetrated into southern France before Napoleon himself was ready to move from Dijon. In fact Napoleon was in a dilemma. Moreau was making such slow progress in Germany that he now decided to switch the main offensive with his Reserve Army from Dijon to northern Italy. This, of course, made the role of Masséna – and of Soult – even more important.

Soult was once again – and in every sense – Masséna's right-hand man. In his *Memoirs* he divides the operations of the next few weeks into three distinct phases. At first he had to restore the damaged morale of his troops and to delay as much as possible the slow but inexorable advance of the much larger Austrian forces. Restoring morale by discipline and training was a task which by now he performed with great skill. But operationally he had an enormous area to cover. He tried to secure a long coast line by capturing Sestri Levante to protect himself from the direction of La Spezia. But he was mainly occupied in carrying out a series of quick and devastating attacks both in the mountains and along the coast far to the west of Genoa. Here one of his divisions under Gazan held Voltri which, especially with the tightening of the British naval blockade, was an important supply base. In the ferocious fighting the French were even reduced to eating the corpses of some Hungarian grenadiers! This first phase ended with a combined attempt by Masséna marching along the coast and Soult operating in the mountains to relieve Savona and re-establish communications with Suchet. The operation failed in the face of greatly superior Austrian forces; Masséna and Soult had to retreat to Genoa, leaving Savona to fall and severing the final links with Suchet.

The second phase, lasting for a couple of weeks, was a kind of offensive/defensive protection of Genoa as Soult made regular attacks outside the city against an enemy five or six times stronger than himself, often returning with captured prisoners. These attacks were good for French morale but they merely produced more mouths to feed as the food situation in Genoa became increasingly desperate.

By the end of April the third phase of the campaign had begun. This was a purely defensive battle fought against vastly superior Austrian forces. By now Napoleon had made his remarkable crossing of the Great St Bernard Pass and, to the astonishment of the Austrians, he had arrived in Italy. The continued retention of Genoa was obviously of great importance since it tied up a sizeable proportion of the Austrian army. Masséna was ordered to hold on until at least the beginning of June. With his utter disregard for any other considerations than his own ultimate victory, Napoleon made no immediate attempt to relieve the beleaguered army. An occasional French ship ran the British blockade and a staff officer slipped through the encircling Austrian troops with an encouraging message from Napoleon, but the First Consul's only objective was to destroy the main army in the Lombard plain. Masséna and Soult were left to hold out in Genoa as best they could.

In this final phase of the city's defence the problems were as much political as military. Under the stress of siege and starvation the Ligurian government had vanished. The French were now cordially hated and increasingly close links had been established between Genoese insurgents and the besieging Austrians. As usual, Soult's instinct was for firmness combined with conciliation, but his task remained largely a military one. Masséna ran a government as best he could with a special commission, compelling some of the townsfolk to act as auxiliaries in support of the French troops. This did not work well and he soon proclaimed that any large gatherings of Genoese would be shot on sight. The besieged forces were approaching starvation and Masséna's dark hair had turned white.

Soult was not directly involved in these administrative and police problems. His main task was still to lead desperate forays against the Austrians surrounding the city. Genoa lies inside a kind of ampitheatre framed by mountains and guarded by a series of forts. The two most important forts were 'Deux Frères' and 'Diamond'. Both were vigorously attacked by the Austrians and were simultaneously bombarded by the British fleet. 'Deux Frères' was captured by the enemy and 'Diamond' was blockaded. In the most triumphant of his forays Soult led his men, sword in hand, to recapture 'Deux Frères' and to relieve the blockade of 'Diamond'. Once more he had ordered his men to attack the Austrians with their bayonets without firing their muskets. These spectacularly successful actions gave great encouragement to the defenders of Genoa. It was a heroic period of Soult's life who was fighting desperately side by side with his soldiers. As Massena said, "So long as I am here and Soult is in 'Deux Frères' we shall remain victorious."[11] Alas, this prophecy turned out to be only too true. Buoyed up by his success, Soult now planned a more ambitious attack on Mount Creto to the north so as to relieve further pressure on the city and to obtain some much needed grain supplies. Although only 2,400 men could be spared for this expedition, Soult had ordered Gazan to launch a diversionary attack from Fort Diamond. Despite the size of the Austrian force under Prince Hohenzollern, Soult had abundant self-confidence and a fair hope of success. Thiébault, Soult's constantly carping critic, says in his *Journal of the Siege of Genoa* that Masséna was unhappy about the Mount Creto operation but after the successful attack on 'Deux Frères' he seems to have had every confidence in his young lieutenant's skill and bravery.

In the event everything went wrong. A sudden mountain storm impeded Gazan's diversionary attack, Gazan himself being severely wounded. This meant that the whole of Prince Hohenzollern's army could be concentrated on Soult's small force. In a hopeless battle against appalling odds Soult fought bravely and tried to rally his men. But he was seriously wounded in the leg and ordering his remaining troops to leave him and return safely to Genoa. His younger brother, Pierre, who had been in charge of the small cavalry element in the force, and his A.D.C. Lieutenant Hulot, tried to carry him out of danger but he was too seriously wounded to be moved on the slippery mountain paths and was taken prisoner.

At this stage of the war relations between senior officers on both sides were comparatively gentlemanly. Soult was robbed of his possessions on the battlefield itself but Prince Hohenzollern lodged him in a cottage near his own headquarters and arranged for his sword to be sent back to Masséna. Soult found the Austrian doctors to be quite useless. However, with Hohenzollern's permission, he was allowed to write a letter, actually using as a desk the stooping back of one of his Austrian surgeons, requesting Masséna for the services of his favourite French doctor, Cothenet. Cothenet was given permission to pass through the Austrian lines but, before he arrived, the wounded general had taken the Austrian surgeon's scalpel from his hands and performed a preliminary operation on himself. Soult described it as "fairly easy but very painful".

After these typical examples of bravura, Soult was taken to the Bishop's Palace in Alessandria so that he could recover from his wound in somewhat greater comfort. Here, exasperated with impatience and worry about the war, he lay prostrate in bed while his brother, his aide-de-camp and the French doctor watched through field glasses on the roof the varying fortunes of the battle of Marengo. After considering plans for escape in the general confusion that followed the Austrian defeat, Soult's wound grew worse again and he was threatened with the loss of his leg from gangrene. In the circumstances he decided to give his parole to his captors, assuming like most people that the end of the war would not long be delayed. With full freedom of movement his health began steadily to improve. He was joined by his favourite cavalry commander and ex-aide-de-camp, Franceschi, who improbably had swum out of Genoa through the British blockade, carrying dispatches for Napoleon. Franceschi was a former sculptor who had originally joined the army in the 'Régiment des Arts'. He was one of Soult's greatest admirers and was to cover himself with glory until his tragic capture and death in the Peninsula. Subsequently Soult was joined by Louise, who looked after him devotedly.

Meanwhile, events in Genoa had gone from bad to worse, thus fulfilling Masséna's gloomy forecast that things would deteriorate when Soult could no longer make his dashing forays. Before Napoleon's triumph at Marengo, Masséna's gallant, sick, half-starved army was forced to surrender. But he was treated with all the honours of war. He and his men were allowed to proceed to the south of France and were free to continue the fight from there. The magnificent defence of Genoa was naturally of inestimable help in Napoleon's victory since it kept a high proportion of the Austrian army distracted by a long and difficult siege. Napoleon afterwards was mean enough to criticize Masséna for losing contact with Suchet and indeed for not himself retreating into France. He was always jealous of subordinates who had done conspicuously well. In fact, if Masséna had retired towards southern France, it would have seriously impeded the build-up of Napoleon's Reserve Army in Dijon.

This is perhaps the moment to deal with some of the vicious comments on Soult made by his most unbalanced critic, Thiébault, in his *Journal of the Siege of Genoa* and in his *Memoirs*. Louis Madelin, the Napoleonic historian, describes Thiébault as "atrociously abusing Soult, Davout and Berthier in many pages of invective". In the *Journal of the Siege* he accuses Soult of alternately flattering Masséna and later, together with Suchet, of trying to denigrate him in favour of themselves. He also suggests that Soult was responsible for spreading stories about Masséna's subsequent financial peculations. At this stage Masséna, in Thiébault's eyes, could do no wrong but in fact the general's financial skullduggery was a byword in the French army and eventually resulted in his temporary suspension from command. Thiébault suffered from a kind of persecution mania, believing quite wrongly that Soult blocked his promotion when he later became a general of brigade in Soult's IV Corps because he did not give his corps commander sufficiently high praise in his *Journal*. Thiébault also claimed, on the basis of some probably fictitious discussion, that Masséna endorsed these views and was in turn strongly critical of Soult. This is arrant nonsense. It was Masséna's strong recommendation to Napoleon on Soult's behalf that 'translated' Soult from the comparative obscurity of a command in Italy to become one of the leading marshals of the Empire. Eventually Thiébault even turned against his beloved Masséna and accused him of "senility" in Spain.[12]

Soult finally recovered from his leg wound in the mountain spa of Acqui where he was given mud-baths; but he was to walk with a slight limp for the rest of his life. He criticized the First Consul for not bringing the war to an end more quickly. The fact that he had given his word hampered his further activities. Indeed this ambitious young man was only to be released from parole in exchange for an Austrian general captured by the French when the war ended after Moreau's victory at Hohenlinden.

Meanwhile, there was a strange interlude in Soult's military career. Although he had not been formally 'exchanged' there seemed to be no objection, under the quaint rules of war then existing, to him carrying out 'semi-administrative' duties in a country which was being brought more or less completely under French rule – Piedmont. Violent upheavals had taken place in northern Italy. The invading Austrian armies had at first swept away the various republics set up by the French but Marengo had changed the situation once again and Piedmont was now regarded by the French, like Switzerland, as an important buffer territory. The feeble ruler, Charles Emmanuel IV, had departed for Sardinia and a provisional government had been set up under French protection as a prelude to total annexation. Soult's former chief in the 'Sambre et Meuse', Jourdan, was the French minister in Turin. This old Republican had been appointed largely in order to remove him from Paris in the aftermath of Brumaire. But 'The Anvil' had little taste for diplomacy and Soult, as administrator of the French forces, exercised the main authority in Piedmont until the end of 1800 under the overall command of Brune, Masséna's successor in command of the Army of Italy. Soult had to train and organize two weak army divisions. As usual there was no money, so he had to try to get enough cash from the feeble provisional government to maintain them, to garrison numerous strong points and to deal with the chaotic administration of the military hospitals. He was confronted everywhere with a complete administrative shambles. However, after his experiences in beleaguered Genoa, it was not too difficult for this firm and intelligent disciplinarian to produce order in Turin itself. Elsewhere in Piedmont there was much confusion with the so-called Italian patriots, the supporters of Charles Emmanuel and Republican sympathizers with France at each other's throats. In addition the mountains were infested with brigands known as 'Barbets.' All this called for military command as well as for skilful organization. Soult used against the Barbets the same technique that he had employed in Switzerland – fast flying columns moving through the mountains – until he had them begging for an armistice. Then, as with the Swiss cantons, he displayed a conciliatory manner before compelling some of them to police the mountains themselves. As he wrote laconically in his *Memoirs*: "I followed my usual practice of carefully respecting the manners and beliefs of the country which I was involved in administering."[13] For his work he received fulsome praise from the provisional government in Turin. There were, however, more serious insurrections in the region of Aosta which were harder to contain. After he had done his best to cope, he received a warm letter of congratulation from his superior, Brune, commending him for his conduct of operations. "The skilful handling of Piedmont's troubles was entirely due to your wise and vigorous activities," wrote Brune.[14] Once more he had won the full confidence of his soldiers, supporting them against predatory commissariat agents and against Piedmontese brigands. As a relief from all this, Soult, increasingly enticed by good living, threw a lavish ball in one of the palaces in Turin. The principal guest, apparently, was a celebrated Italian singer with whom he was supposed to be enamoured.

However, when it comes to biographies, poor Soult can rarely win. These hectic four months – during which administrative duties had been superseded by military operations – have been carefully described by his son, the future French ambassador in Berlin, in an account based on his father's papers. Yet they have been summarized by a recent historian, somewhat unkindly, as "a little enlightened counter-insurgency against the Barbets but with little to do other than the peaceable arts of recruiting, hospital administration and logistic reorganization".[15]

At the end of this period Soult was finally exchanged for the Austrian General Spork and, at the end of 1800, he was free to resume his normal military career. He was urged by his old chief, Lefebvre, and by Masséna to visit Paris to meet the First Consul. But, with the political scene still highly charged, Soult was shrewd enough to remain 'a simple soldier' and to stay with the army. Instead he was appointed lieutenant general of the 'Army of Observation of the Midi' in southern Italy under the command of Murat, with his headquarters in Taranto. This began a fighting relationship with a man who was totally different from himself. As a counter-balance to the impetuous Murat, Soult was to supply some firm and balanced military skill. They were to operate together frequently during the War of the Third Coalition and the association was of great benefit to Napoleon himself. At the moment it was also very useful to Soult that Murat had become Napoleon's brother-in-law!

Soult had three main tasks in Taranto. The first was to build up good relations with the southern Italians. The lazy and carefree Neapolitans were quite different from the tough people of Genoa or Piedmont and he was soon on good terms with them. In the outlandish Heel of Italy, which was to remain at least for another century as uncivilized as many parts of North Africa, the countryside was at the mercy of brigands. But, often with the aid of the church, Soult was able to bring them reasonably well under control. He was in no sense a religious man but, like Napoleon himself, he knew when to make full use of the influence of the Catholic establishment.

Soult's second task was to bring Taranto and other small ports in Apulia into a state of full defence against possible British naval attacks so that they could become important supply bases for the French army still in Egypt. However, this need soon disappeared when the French surrendered in Egypt only four months after Soult's arrival in Taranto. He was to have no further dealings with Egypt until, as head of the government under Louis Philippe nearly 40 years later, he wrestled with Lord Palmerston over the problems of Mehemet Ali.

His third task, which strongly appealed to him, was to turn Taranto into a base for other overseas activities – to make it, in effect, a kind of Adriatic Gibraltar. The Ionian Islands had come under French rule at the Treaty of Campo Formio but now, after the French defeats in Italy, they were ruled jointly by Russia and Turkey. As the British discovered in the Second World War, Taranto and other ports in Apulia made excellent bases for clandestine operations across the Adriatic. Soult's son records how his father immediately made contact with those people in the Ionian Islands who wanted to renew their ties with France, and also with that formidable brigand, Ali Pasha, the 'Lion of Janina', who was anxious to develop friendly links with Napoleon.[16] From his secret information Soult informed Alquier, the French ambassador in Naples, that there was much ferment in the Ionian Islands: English influence hardly existed outside Corfu, the Russian fleet had departed and there was a good opportunity for renewed French expansion. Murat praised him for his expert interception of British diplomatic correspondence and for discovering so much about popular feelings not only in the Ionian Islands but also in Epirus and other parts of the Greek mainland. As it happened, it was unfortunate from the French viewpoint that, because of events elsewhere, Soult's clandestine activities in the Adriatic bore so little fruit. Within a few years the Ionian Islands were to enjoy a period of English rule, of English cricket and even of the vice-royalty of Mr Gladstone! Incidentally it was the nearest that Soult ever came to the territory of 'Dalmatia' from which he eventually received his dukedom.

Under the influence of those two avaricious and extravagant characters, Masséna and Murat, Soult was no doubt taught about the advantages as well as the hardships of a military career. Naturally the youthful lieutenant general was influenced by the financial manoeuvrings of his chiefs. He certainly enjoyed good living but too much should not be made of this. He was only following the practice of most successful generals and invading armies at this time. On the other hand he remained a zealous professional soldier with genuine political gifts and an undoubted ability to get along well with the civilians amongst whom he was operating. Murat brought him back to Naples assuring him that he "had made many friends for France in southern Italy".[17] In fact the future King of Naples proposed him as his own successor as general-in-chief of the Army of Observation of the Midi. This army, however, was very soon disbanded, and in any case Soult was on the brink of a much more glamorous future.

3

THE INVASION THAT NEVER TOOK PLACE

IN HIS BIOGRAPHY of Napoleon, Professor Tulard quotes a passage from Ymbert's *Moeurs Administratifs* as follows: "When a man was talented, Napoleon with his Herculean arms would seize him by the hair and place him on a pedestal saying – 'behold my creature'."[1] Soult was certainly no 'creature' but there was an element of this relationship in his sudden appearance at centre stage after his relative obscurity in southern Italy. How was it that this taciturn man of 33, who was not one of Napoleon's young men of the old 'Army of Italy' and who had never even met the First Consul, was suddenly made in March 1802, colonel general of the Chasseurs of the Consular Guard? This was a post in the First Consul's military household which brought him into immediate and regular contact with Napoleon himself. It was one of the fastest career advancements of the whole Napoleonic era.

One of the reasons was undoubtedly the strong recommendation that Napoleon had received from Masséna. Napoleon's brother-in-law, Murat, had paid an equally warm tribute to Soult's abilities. More important still, Napoleon was on the look-out for young generals who had been in no way involved in the tempestuous politics of post-Brumaire Paris. The years of the Consulate were riddled with conspiracy and treason. Many ambitious soldiers thought they had quite as good a right to rule France as Napoleon himself. Furthermore, there were numerous idealistic or mere 'tactical' Republicans, as well as Royalist plotters. These disaffections and conspiracies were rife in Paris but with so many 'political' or 'Republican' generals the army was also much affected. It was very important for the First Consul to have a cadre of young generals who had already given proofs of their military skill, who had real administrative gifts, who were more than simple straightforward soldiers but who were so far quite uncommitted politically. Among Napoleon's chief lieutenants were the all-powerful Berthier as Minister of War who was the perfect chief of staff but could not command troops in action; Davout who was a very able and intensely loyal soldier; Lannes who was an intrepid fighter but no administrator, and Ney who, as already described, was one of the 'chargers' of the army rather than an intelligent general. But it was Soult who best fulfilled most of Napoleon's requirements as an able general, a tough disciplinarian, a fine administrator and with developing political intelligence. This was probably why – of all the generals who were given command in the 'Army of the Coasts of the Ocean', the army that was to invade England – Soult was made general-in-chief of the main military camp at St-Omer by order of Berthier on August 28 1803.[2] In fact, the camp at Boulogne continued to be called officially the 'camp of St-Omer'. The Ministry of War in Paris recognized St-Omer from past experience and had determined to install army headquarters there. But the pragmatic Soult soon changed things. Writing from St-Omer to Andréossy, his new chief of staff, on September 3 1803, he said: "I have found nothing here and I am going to Boulogne. We will provisionally establish a headquarters here although the long distance from the coast disgusts me." He hardly visited St-Omer again.[3]

The invasion of England was not a brand new initiative of the First Consul. It had been preceded in 1798 by the rather pathetic affair planned by the Directory. Soult had been involved in this and, while he was in Italy in 1801, there had been another mustering of invasion ships at Boulogne. These vessels had been vigorously engaged by Nelson but it was one of his few unsuccessful operations. The attacks were beaten off with some losses.

This encounter gave the First Consul some encouragement. He had long recognized that England was his chief enemy although he was never to fight against her directly until Waterloo. But now, from the moment that the short-lived Anglo-French peace of Amiens ended until the outbreak of the War of the Third Coalition, the overwhelming military strength of France was concentrated on the Channel coast. Amongst other commentators and historians, Bourrienne, the spiteful ex-schoolmate and ex-secretary of the First Consul, has suggested in his *Memoirs* that the projected invasion was no more than a political smokescreen – "so ruinous, useless and absurd an enterprise could never have been imagined".[4] But there is overwhelming evidence to show that it was indeed a perfectly serious undertaking. Marmont and other memoir writers are quite definite on the subject. Soult himself was asked later by one of his English friends, Sir George Napier, the brother of the Peninsular War historian, whether Napoleon really meant to invade England. He replied that he certainly intended to try. When questioned further as to whether he would have succeeded, he answered: "Ah, Monsieur, c'est une autre grande question."[5]

Few British historians seem greatly interested in the plans for this large-scale French invasion. The exception is Richard Glover with his detailed study *Britain at Bay*.[6] Glover emphasizes that it would certainly have been the most carefully planned operation of its kind until Hitler's formidable invasion project in 1940. Like Hitler, Napoleon had most of the mainland of Europe from which to launch his enterprise. His aim was to invade England with an army of over 150,000 men comprising eight large formations of varying strength stationed all along the coast or at training camps inland – from Augereau's corps in the Brest area to Marmont's corps in the Low Countries. But the main invasion army was to consist of three corps. Ney was on the left in and around the fortified town of Montreuil, including the small estuary at Etaples. Davout was on the right, initially in the area of Bruges since his corps was to be carried mainly by a flotilla of ships provided by the puppet Batavian government, but later, as plans developed, concentrated in the Cap Gris Nez area. The main thrust of the invasion, however, would obviously have been in the centre. Here was much the biggest corps consisting of some 46,000 men – almost as large as those of Ney and Davout combined – stationed first in the St-Omer training camp and then in and around Boulogne. This army corps would not have relied for transport on the Batavian government, but would have been carried entirely in French-built boats. It was commanded by Soult, who also commanded the Montreuil camp until Ney arrived.[7]

So Soult was 'the first among equals' in the invasion army. He soon set up his headquarters definitively in Boulogne, using the town house of a family of aristocrats who had supported the new regime soon after the Revolution, the Hôtel Chanlaire. (The house has since been demolished to make way for a school and the trains from Boulogne to Paris now run beneath it.) Soult's corps was made up of four divisions. The 1st Division, forming the 'camp droit' in Boulogne, was commanded by the intelligent Saint-Hilaire, the 2nd, forming the Boulogne 'camp gauche', by the able but loud-mouthed Vandamme, the 3rd, stationed at Ambleteuse near Boulogne, by the toweringly tall Legrand, and the 4th, at Wimereux, by Suchet, Soult's old comrade in the Genoa fighting. Oudinot, in charge of the grenadiers of the Imperial Guard, also came under Soult's command. Additionally, he had a mass of support troops including the light cavalry brigade of General Margaron. Indeed Soult's corps, like the others, gradually became a self-contained formation of all arms. (Boulogne was badly damaged during the Second World War and the area occupied by the 'camp droit' – once the fisherman's part of the old town – was almost entirely destroyed, being replaced by modern houses. The 'camp gauche' was in the still well-preserved part of this charming old town.)

Napoleon came to Boulogne six times during this period, staying in all for about fourteen weeks. His visits are called by Boulonnais historians 'Boulogne's Hundred Days'. He took as his headquarters the small château of Pont-de Briques, which had been left empty by its *émigré* owners. (It was only saved with difficulty from demolition after the Second World War when the Route Nationale swept past its gates on either side.) The years from 1803 to 1805 have been described as the hinge between the Consulate and the Empire, and it has truthfully been said that during this period "the heart of France beat within the walls of this small château". It was the first imperial headquarters of Napoleon's reign: Caillou farm on the field of Waterloo was to be the last.[8] There was only room in Pont-de-Briques for Napoleon's immediate entourage but there was accommodation nearby for some of his family. The Hôtel Desandrouin in the town, later called the Palais Imperial, housed Berthier's large staff while Soult with his staff was only a few metres away so that all those involved in the land side of the invasion were grouped closely together. Naval affairs were even more important: Admiral Bruix had his headquarters close by as 'Admiral of the National Flotilla for the Invasion of England'. There was accommodation also for Admiral Décrès, the Minister of Marine. Bruix and Décrès hated each other. It was easier for Soult, from a different service, to have good relations with both of them, but he was especially close to Bruix.

Eustache de Bruix, now in his middle 40s, was born in San Domingo, the home of the Empress Josephine, and he had served with distinction in the French fleet during the War of American Independence. He had developed close ties with Napoleon, giving him much help at the time of Brumaire. He was an able, warm-hearted, explosive extrovert, a close friend of Talleyrand (sharing in some of his dissipations) and of course more politically involved than the younger man, Soult. Given the honorary title of 'Inspector General of the Coasts of the Ocean', he ranked with Soult and with the other newly created marshals. But for his ill health he might well have replaced the unfortunate Villeneuve. Sadly for France, he died from consumption in 1805.

Quite as important as the fighting soldiers and sailors was the famous engineer, Sganzin, who was responsible for the actual construction of the harbour works which were needed at Boulogne and all along the coast. But Napoleon's correspondence shows that Soult, as one of the principal users of these harbours, was closely involved in their design and construction. It was his engineer officer, Bertrand, later Napoleon's companion at St Helena, who was initially responsible for the shipping basins at Wimereux and Ambleteuse as well as the small wooden forts which protected them. Finally, the brilliant marine engineer, Forfait, supervised the building all over north-west Europe of the hundreds of flat-bottomed boats which were to transport the invasion army.

The Emperor would arrive at Boulogne from time to time unannounced in order to keep everyone on the alert. Afterwards he would ride round the surrounding country trying to see all he could before summoning to dinner Bruix, Soult and Sganzin for a detailed appreciation of the latest developments. On occasions he paid incognito visits as far as Calais accompanied by Soult and Bruix. These discussions were "better than a volume of written reports".[9] Savary, now one of Napoleon's closest assistants, writes glowingly about all the work that was going on in Boulogne with the troops "never without a gun or a pickaxe in their hands", actually building the harbours of Boulogne, Wimereux and Ambleteuse themselves amid their unremitting training and embarkation exercises. (There was no Todt organization to help them as there was for the Germans in 1940.) "Never", wrote Savary, "had there been so vast a concept with everyone working together with so much vigour and precision."[10] The concept was Napoleon's but the man primarily responsible for carrying it out on the army side was Soult.

An advance headquarters for Napoleon and his senior staff was established on the coast between Boulogne and Wimereux. It was called the Tour d'Ordre after an old shipping beacon dating from Roman times which had collapsed in the seventeenth century. The Tour d'Ordre commanded an excellent view of the port and channel of Boulogne, the roadstead beyond and the English Channel itself. As early as 1803 Napoleon had ordered Bruix to establish his advance base there.[11] Bruix had quickly built a small *barraque* or hut on a knoll which had been part of some old English fortifications dating from the Hundred Years War. Napoleon had a larger *barraque* constructed for himself, and similar but smaller huts were built alongside for Berthier and Soult. They were in the form of Maltese Crosses reinforced with earth: Napoleon's gossipy valet Constant called them *barraques sauvages*. Even Napoleon's hut was fairly spartan, with a council room and sleeping accommodation, but some senior officers were occasionally entertained there. Through a powerful telescope the bustle of activity in Dover Castle could be seen, according to Napoleon, as easily as Mont Valérien, on the outskirts of Paris, from the Tuileries. Much has been written sentimentally by Victor Hugo and others about these *barraques*. It is not clear how frequently they were occupied but Napoleon certainly used them as bases for his numerous tours along the coast. Few of the incessant stream of letters and instructions that came from Boulogne were actually sent from the Tour d'Ordre although, rather oddly, his formal letters about Francis II relinquishing the title of Holy Roman Emperor in favour of becoming Emperor of Austria were dated from there.[12] No doubt much discussion of invasion plans took place there between Napoleon and his principal lieutenants Berthier, Bruix and Soult.

Rapid communication between Boulogne and Paris was also essential. Before the Revolution the Chappe brothers had introduced a telegraph system in France, using semaphore arms mounted on hilltops or prominent buildings. The First Consul had the system greatly developed: no time, money nor manpower were to be spared in extending a Chappe line to Boulogne. The signal station there was fixed on the belfry tower alongside the headquarters of Berthier, Soult and Bruix. Soult sent off the first message by this system on Christmas Eve 1803. However, it never arrived so Soult refused to send any similar messages until in May 1804 he received a direct order to use the telegraph – indeed to communicate with Paris by this means twice a day. It could not be employed in bad weather but it remained a regular link with Paris so long as Soult remained in Boulogne.[13]

Commanding the largest corps in the invasion army, his authority often stretching as far as Calais, Soult was responsible for carrying out Napoleon's main instructions on the land aspects of the invasion army throughout most of 1803-5. The other corps commanders naturally had responsibilities within their own corps, but, with his headquarters in Boulogne, Soult had by far the most important role. When Napoleon was actually in Boulogne his military orders were issued through Berthier but at other times many letters on invasion problems were sent directly to Soult. His many and varied responsibilities may be grouped under five main headings. First it was his task to ensure that his huge corps and the large number of ancillary troops based in Boulogne were not only ready to fight but also to cross the Channel and invade England. His responsibilities were closely linked with those of

Bruix in the use of landing-craft and with Sganzin in the building of harbours and protective forts. Secondly, as chief land commander, he would have participated fully in the discussions about the form of the projected invasion. Thirdly, all along the coast from Boulogne to Calais, he had to deal with regular British naval attacks. Fourthly, he was responsible for security measures to counter the skilled operations of English and of French Royalist agents: moreover Napoleon relied upon him to keep him fully informed ot the army's loyalty at a time when there were plots and conspiracies everywhere. Lastly, he had to perform an important 'public relations' role. Napoleon himself was a master in this field. The famous Legion of Honour ceremony that took place in August 1804 in the amphitheatre of Terlincthun behind the Tour d'Ordre and the plan to build the great commemorative column nearby, in both of which Soult was closely involved, were superb public relations exercises which made a distinct contribution to the 'Napoleonic legend'.

It was a formidable task to convert the battle-experienced but heterogeneous units of the French army which assembled first at St-Omer and elsewhere in northern France and then at bases at Boulogne and other ports along the Channel coast into an effective force capable of invading England. In his *Memoirs* describing the crossing of the River Linth during the Swiss campaign Soult had already commented on the poor physical shape, the lack of technical proficiency and the insufficient training of French infantrymen. Now he was faced with an infinitely greater challenge. Not only had the men of the invasion army to be trained in large-scale land exercises but they had to rehearse embarking and disembarking quickly in flat-bottomed boats, and learn to row as well as to fight. In addition, special arrangements had to be made to embark cavalrymen with their horses and accoutrements and for the transport of various types of artillery. One historian has summarized the problem as follows: "It was a question in the end of getting the infantry accustomed to the sea and to taking up their quarters in the boats which would be used for the invasion. It was a totally new idea for so many thousands of men to occupy these hundreds of flat-bottomed boats night and day during the winter months. The cavalry had to get used to the rough hospitality of the 'stable boats' also. The camp at Boulogne gradually formed a real 'knighthood' in which each foot soldier and cavalryman was eager to carry out the invasion."[14] There may be pardonable exaggeration here, especially over the army's 'enthusiasm', but it would be hard to think of a greater contrast between this great amphibious army being trained by Soult, Bruix and the other corps commanders and the well-drilled 'positional' soldiers of Dettingen and Fontenoy only 50 years previously.

The little ships which were gradually being built all over France and the Low Countries were collected in Boulogne and the other small Channel ports with great difficulty. As experimental innovations they were slow to build and the British blockade was stringent. There were flat-bottomed boats able to carry 100 men with mortars mounted at the bow and the stern, large sail-driven 'prams' over 30 metres long which could carry 150 men, 20-metre pinnaces carrying 55 men, much larger *chaloupes* or *bateaux cannonières* for transporting cavalrymen with their horses and light arms or units of artillery, and small cargo ships converted into brigs, able to carry a whole company of infantry. It was the joint responsibility of Soult and of Bruix to see that good relations were maintained between the army and the navy in the use of these different boats. Various methods were adopted to solve inter-service problems. Soldiers with their officers were allocated as far as possible to the same vessels with the same naval officers in charge. In the larger ships parties of soldiers took up temporary accommodation and carried out normal duties alongside the sailors. Other sailors trained with the troops exercising on the mainland, with a view to being used as a protecting force for the ships when the army landed in England. Landing on shore from flat-bottomed boats in the face of strong opposition would have been as difficult as it proved to be for the Allies in 1944. Close over all inter-service training was thus essential.[15]

Soult was also much involved with Sganzin and Bruix in the difficult tasks of building and enlarging the small harbours and basins from which the invasion force was to embark. Boulogne was to be the main base and major works were carried out there excavating the harbour itself and widening the approach channel. Work was also concentrated in the nearby small inlets of Wimereux and Ambleteuse, at Etaples and at many other estuaries along the Channel coast. Boulogne, Wimereux and Ambleteuse came within Soult's direct operational area and Napoleon made special use of his drive and enthusiasm in carrying out all his wide-ranging ideas for the invasion. Whereas Bruix sometimes had doubts about success, Soult was habitually optimistic. Ségur describes a dramatic moment in 1805 when it really seemed that the invasion was about to take place: "On reaching Boulogne on August 2, Rapp and I announced the Emperor's arrival next day and that soon afterwards the invasion was to be launched. Marshal Soult was overcome was joy. He bounded across the room in delight."[16] This was a rare manifestation of this taciturn man's real feelings. It was of course the final and decisive false alarm. The invasion was cancelled but it was the prelude to the great Austerlitz campaign that followed.

Some of the flood of letters which Napoleon showered upon Soult during the Boulogne years give a good insight into the young general-in-chief's many and varied activities. If the overall ideas were the Emperor's, it was Soult with Bruix and Sganzin who carried them out. Unwilling, however, to allow his subordinates to get on with the job, Napoleon concerned himself with every detail of the work. To take some of his letters at random, he praises Soult for his sketch plan of the proposed harbour at Wimereux. But was the land around Wimereux healthy? His plans for projects at Ambleteuse, Camp Gris Nez and Calais appeared to be sound but how many sick men had he got under command – division by division? The soldiers must all learn to row and must exercise frequently getting in and out of the landing craft. A small French sloop had been captured by the English at Dunkirk and a reprimand must be passed on to Davout for insufficient attention to security. Every letter was filled with detailed questions and instructions. They covered even such items as boathooks, parts for muskets and portable containers to hold water![17]

How did Soult cope with it all? One of his aides-de-camp, the Comte de Saint-Chamans, describes how he was made to work for hours by day and night writing orders, at Soult's indication, on every aspect of army administration, subsistence, cantonments, police, military discipline, hospitals, etc. "He forgot nothing," wrote Saint-Chamans, "and he was as much concerned with small details as with major operations."[18] Another young lieutenant, later to become not only an aide-de-camp but a devoted admirer, Brun de Villeret, tells how he accompanied his own general at the time to a briefing session with Soult who asked a thousand questions needing precise answers rather than woolly suggestions.[19] In this, as in many other ways, Soult was behaving increasingly like Napoleon himself. Saint-Chamans describes him inspecting troops outside his headquarters every day or visiting the extensive works proceeding in the camps and in the little harbours along the coast. Three times a week he held military manoeuvres for twelve hours on end. "Never was there so excellent a school as the camp of Boulogne," he comments, "since it trained more good officers and men than any other military school that has ever existed."[20]

The appointment of Saint-Chamans was itself of significance. Soult's aides-de-camp included a Choiseul and a Lecaron de Troussures, with others of less noble birth. Republicanism had flourished in the army where, as de Tocqueville has recorded, everyone so far had profited from the Revolution and thus had a strong vested interest in it. But during this time of plots and conspiracies Napoleon began to broaden the basis of his support in the army and in the nation. His appointments to the marshalate at the beginning of the Empire reflected this policy. At the same time, during the 'Boulogne schooling', as one historian has recounted, "Veteran soldiers of the Revolution were joined by former Royalist supporters from La Vendée who took their places only in the army – young men of aristocrat birth appeared as regimental officers or on the staff – all of them wanting to use their enthusiasm and skill against the enemies of France."[21] Soult's dispassionate attitude to such changes certainly assisted the process, although not too much should be made of it. The privileged recruits were not always well liked by the army rank and file: there were to be more Vendée uprisings and several army conspiracies which turned out badly for Soult himself. But the Boulogne camp clearly did bring a number of young aristocrats into Napoleon's armies.

Life in Boulogne, nevertheless, was not all drills and manoeuvres. Consistent with the French genius for making the best of things, the soldiers were encouraged by their commander-in-chief to build their own 'houses', using wood from the national forests and stones from the seashore. These houses were laid out in long neat rows with small gardens full of flowers and vegetables. This made Boulogne a far more attractive place in which to live than many garrison towns.[22] Nor was Soult always the taciturn 'workaholic' described by Saint-Chamans who was astonished that an active man of 34 should neglect his "normal pleasures" in order to bury himself in the smallest details of administration. As in the Rhineland and in Italy, the young commander-in-chief, when off duty, had continued to develop his taste for good living. In line with the First Consul's wish to create a new 'aristocracy' from among his leading generals and ministers, he had been provided with enough money, in addition to what he had acquired already, to buy a large town house in Paris – a residence in the Rue de l'Université which had formerly belonged to the Talleyrand family – and a country property at Villeneuve l'Etang near St-Cloud. His wife, Louise, remained in these two houses for much of the time bringing up the children, Hector, born in 1802, and Hortense, born in 1804. Napoleon and Josephine were the children's godparents. But Louise paid regular visits to Boulogne. Some unpublished letters from General Marchand describe a typical evening spent with the commander-in-chief and his wife and 40 other guests; there was much dancing and card-playing. On another occasion Marchand accompanied his own chief, Ney, to dinner with the Soults, indicating that these two young rivals from the 'Sambre et Meuse' were still on social terms. The dinner was followed by a magnificent ball given in honour of Louise Soult who appeared in an elegant black dress covered with diamonds. The ball cost some six million francs to which senior officers were asked to contribute. Marchand hoped that a similar ball would not be given in honour of Madame Ney since he and his comrades just would not be able to afford it![23]

Very much a mixed blessing for Soult was the appointment in April 1804 of Joseph Bonaparte, Napoleon's elder brother, to be colonel of the 4th Regiment under his command. It is usually an embarrassment to have a close relation of one's chief under orders and Joseph took himself very seriously. He regarded himself as the head of the Bonaparte family and, when the Empire was proclaimed, he was recognized as heir presumptive. He was also a senator and had led the French delegation in the prolonged negotiations before the Treaty of Lunéville. Napoleon wrote rather pompously to Soult that Senator Joseph Bonaparte had an ambition to be a soldier: it was not enough to serve the state politically, he must also serve with the sword and he must do his duty with vigour! Whatever his real feelings, Soult was fully capable of matching such high-flown sentiments. His Order of the Day proclaimed that the army was greatly honoured by this appointment of "one of the most important personages in the state". The military historian, Bigarré, a strong protagonist of Joseph and later to be his principal aide-de-camp in Spain, describes the latter's brief sojourn in Boulogne as being very successful. He took part in some of Soult's embarkation exercises, was present at an exchange of fire between French and British warships, and helped to improve relations between the soldiers and the sailors. Soult and Bruix, who had been wrestling with some of these problems for months, may have had rather different views. In the event Joseph only stayed in Boulogne for a short time before departing on a political tour without asking permission or indeed without even informing his general-in-chief. In a letter to Berthier Napoleon complained bitterly about his brother's "totally unauthorized" activities. But the Emperor's sharpest criticism came in a letter to Soult in which he referred to Joseph holding personal military reviews, trying to ingratiate himself with the troops by giving them money and spending too much time in self-indulgence without carrying out any military duties. He praised Soult for his firm attitude, assuring him that he had made known his displeasure to his brother who should have remained firmly under Soult's orders.[24]

Thus, for the first but by no means for the last time, Soult was drawn into a conflict between the two brothers. While despising Joseph's ineptitude, Napoleon was never prepared to have a real showdown with him. It was not surprising that relations between Soult and Joseph became strained almost to breaking point, especially when in Spain their roles were reversed and Soult became King Joseph's major general and then his viceroy in Andalusia. Naturally that eager busybody, Louis Constant, Napoleon's *valet de chambre*, records some spicy information about Soult and Joseph sharing the favours in Boulogne of a certain talented 'lady of the town', Madame Fagan, from Dunkirk. In one of the lighter moments in his *Memoirs*, Soult's aide-de-camp, Saint Chamans, describes his master as something of a 'womanizer' although he was always brought to heel by his formidable German wife as if he was a little boy. It has been suggested in one biography that Soult's subsequent attitude towards King Joseph was caused partly by jealousy as a result of this incident in Boulogne. There were, in fact, far more serious reasons for the bitter quarrel which proved so disastrous to France's military prospects in the Peninsula. It is probable that Constant more or less invented the story. His *Memoirs* were made up after the Restoration by a publisher who had little regard for the truth. There was no lack of female entertainment in the camp of Boulogne but recent diligent researchers have revealed no trace whatever of Madame Fagan in the Boulogne city records – or indeed in those of Dunkirk.[25] In any case Professor Tulard affirms that no historical use should be made of Constant's *Memoirs*.

The second of Soult's responsibilities related to the land strategy of the invasion itself. As in all his campaigns, it was Napoleon, of course, who decided the overall strategy, but he must have discussed invasion plans with his land and sea commanders, especially with those who were based in Boulogne. His ignorance of naval affairs was legendary and in the end French failure to gain control of the Channel, even for a short time, proved fatal.

Napoleon also seriously underestimated the difficulties that he would have faced had he landed. Until his final imprisonment in St Helena he persisted in his absurd belief in a sympathetic 'fifth column' in England; that if he were to proclaim a republic in London the people, inspired by the ideals of the French Revolution, would rise up against the government. He firmly believed also in British unpreparedness. Although in St Helena he boasted to O'Meara, his British doctor, about the amount of intelligence that he received from French and English agents, in fact the French seemed to have had very little idea of the political situation in Britain, even though Andréossy, Soult's chief of staff, had headed the French embassy in London for the brief period after the Treaty of Amiens and must have contributed something. Privateers with some of Soult's engineer officers on board reconnoitred the Kent coast to locate shore batteries, and fishermen were bribed to bring back information, much of which was false. Despite this almost total lack of hard intelligence Napoleon was absurdly overconfident or pretended to be so. A splendid medal was struck, dated as it were from London, with the Emperor's head crowned with laurel on one side and a representation of Hercules strangling a creature, half-fish, half-human, supposed to depict England, on the other side. A ship, oddly named the *Prince des Galles*, was chosen to transport Napoleon himself. And in the summer of 1805 a vaudeville theatre group arrived in Boulogne 'en route for London'. More seriously, Soult was ordered to build a special communication system for the army when it had landed. A very high Chappe semaphore tower was constructed at Cap Gris-Nez which was to send messages to a similar tower on Dover Castle. From there it was intended to make use of the British Admiralty system which employed signal panels all the way to London.

It is customary to underestimate the state of British defensive preparations. In fact, that much abused commander-in-chief, the Duke of York, had at his disposal a fair sized regular army supported by the militia and a mass of untrained volunteers. Places such as Dover, Chatham and Portsmouth were strongly defended and the famous ring of martello towers were admirable defence points. Napoleon's intention seems to have been to land at ports between Deal and Margate, to bypass Dover at first, to storm Chatham and to make straight for London. Had he been prepared to suffer the losses which were a commonplace in his subsequent wars, he might have achieved some success; but it would undoubtedly have been a much slower business than he expected. To have transported in small flat-bottomed ships a force of 150,000 men would have needed four or five tides: he would probably have required separate operations to reduce Dover, and, as he intended, Portsmouth in order to cripple the British navy. Against this background Kircheisen, the German historian, suggests that it is most unlikely that Napoleon would have appeared in England personally until his armies were well established. At the beginning of his reign as Emperor he would hardly have risked being captured during the Channel crossing nor would he have wanted to become involved in a military shambles if the landings were bitterly opposed or if major subsidiary operations were needed against, say, Dover or Portsmouth.[26] It is pure speculation but it seems likely that Soult, the general-in-chief in Boulogne with by far the largest corps in the invasion army, would have commanded the advance formations of the assault. He was still very much 'Napoleon's man', very different, for example, from Bernadotte who would hardly have been trusted on his own in England. With his ability to get on well with foreigners, Soult would have been the obvious choice. If he had led the invasion, his first opponents would probably have been the Experimental Rifle Corps at

Shorncliffe Camp now being trained by Sir John Moore as a fast-moving light force whose main task was to cover the advance or the retreat of the main army. This fine unit was to be part of the rearguard that was to cover Moore's retreat to Corunna in 1808 – hotly pursued by Soult himself! But Soult's role in an invasion of England is a matter of conjecture. In fact he had to wait for over 30 years to come to London – and then as the representative of King Louis Philippe at the coronation of Queen Victoria. Described by his great admirer, Sir William Napier, the historian of the Peninsular War, as the "best loved Frenchman the English ever fought", it is interesting to consider what kind of reception he would have received in England in 1805![27]

The third of Soult's main tasks in Boulogne was, in cooperation with Bruix, to provide for the protection of the shipping armada gradually gathering there or in the nearby small anchorages against sudden and vigorous British naval attacks. This was achieved by carefully placed land batteries supporting the small wooden forts built on promontories around Boulogne or out at sea and by cavalry units patrolling the seashore. Many of the encounters with the English took place as the convoys of flat-bottomed boats built in shipyards up and down the coasts of Europe converged on Boulogne. Despite some losses almost 1,000 flat-bottomed boats had arrived there as early as the end of 1803. Only a comparative few were captured by the English or were shipwrecked. Napoleon, however, whilst admitting that French shipping losses were much smaller than he anticipated, was soon complaining about naval losses including, for example, a gunboat captured with valuable cannon on board.[28] But the most serious French losses were sustained in an operation for which Napoleon himself was responsible. In the summer of 1804, soon after he was proclaimed Emperor, he had come to Boulogne. Despite opposition from Bruix, Napoleon demanded a sizeable naval demonstration in and around Boulogne harbour. The operation took place at night during a fierce thunderstorm, English ships were also engaged and, as Soult reported to the Ministry of War, eight French ships ran aground with some 80 casualties. Information reaching London suggested much higher losses, yet this did not prevent Napoleon advising Soult that, according to British newspapers, his main source of information about England, the whole operation had been a great French success and had caused great alarm in London![29] In Constant's untrustworthy *Memoirs* there is a highly coloured story of a violent quarrel between the Emperor and Bruix over this incident, with Napoleon threatening Bruix with a riding-whip and the admiral half-drawing his sword in response. This may well be invention but Napoleon's relations with Bruix were certainly much sharper than with Soult.

Another area of considerable responsibility for the heavily burdened young general-in-chief was that of army loyalty, with which were associated problems of security and counter-espionage. Napoleon certainly regarded Soult, still uninvolved in Parisian politics, as uniquely well suited to keep him informed about political opinion in the army, especially over the various constitutional changes – First

Consul, Consul for Life, Emperor – that were so quickly unfolding. Pursuant with his aim of gradually moving towards a monarchy, he asked Soult as early as the spring of 1803 to "find out in some detail about the views of the army on such changes".[30] Was there still a strong Republican tradition in the army? There were many Royalist conspiracies in France which intensified after the arrival from England of the group led by Georges Cadoudal, the trial of the suspected traitors, Generals Moreau and Pichegru, and the kidnapping and execution of the young Bourbon Duke of Enghein. The Emperor needed urgently to know the reaction of the invasion army to all these developments. In fact the sharp political divisions caused by the Revolution did not greatly affect this army. Fortunately for Napoleon, the programme of constant hard work and rigorous military training, the sense of common purpose that the whole army was beginning to share and the good living conditions, especially in and around Boulogne, had an excellent effect on the soldiers' morale. The inspiration that Napoleon himself offered, coupled with the training and discipline provided by Soult and his colleagues, meant that, with few exceptions, the army was becoming more strongly united in its devotion to the Emperor even if the men were increasingly bored at being unable to fight. Soult could be relied upon to voice his soldiers' feelings in suitably flamboyant terms. At the time of the trials of Moreau and Pichegru he sent a letter to the First Consul "on behalf of the military camps at St-Omer and Montreuil" in which he called for prompt justice against the "monsters who threatened France with its greatest evils".[31]

Closely linked to all this were the related problems of security and counter-espionage. Here, as in most countries then and today, there were complicated and overlapping responsibilities. On the one hand there were police agents reporting directly to Fouché in Paris. On the other there were the security units of General Savary, that increasingly powerful member of Napoleon's personal staff, who had been primarily responsible for kidnapping and bringing to Paris for execution the Duke of Enghein. Northern France was undoubtedly the area of greatest danger since it was on the Channel coast that Royalist leaders and English agents landed. Savary was active here but the main responsibility for combating local dangers fell on Soult. Boulogne was largely Republican in sympathy. But the bishop, who was a Royalist *émigré*, had many links in the town; there were numerous Royalist sympathizers and, amazingly, even some English merchants and private residents living in the neighbourhood who were excellent espionage sources. An active spy agency organized by an Abbé Leclerque had bases in both Boulogne and Calais. The energetic churchman not only employed a good number of spies in English pay but he arranged for fishermen, in return for substantial rewards, to carry both military and political information to England.

As the trials of Moreau, Pichegru and the other Royalist leaders proceeded, Napoleon not only kept Soult well informed but continued to request the army's reactions. His letters were to be passed on to Davout – and doubtless to others to whom he had no time to write. Napoleon recognized the crucial position of Boulogne as the headquarters of the invasion army and Soult was instructed to hold secret meetings with the mayor and other civilian officials in order to concert security measures all along the coast. No foreign national should be allowed any longer to stay in the town or indeed in the neighbourhood; anyone acting suspiciously should be arrested and dealt with as a spy; and fishermen suspected of carrying information across the Channel must also be arrested and brought to trial. Napoleon was convinced that a gang of assassins was being organized in Boulogne to kill him. A new gendarmerie commander was sent to assist Soult and the military gendarmes had to go around in civilian clothes in conjunction with police agents sent from Paris. As a special protection for the Pont-de-Brique headquarters, three new companies of grenadiers were billeted in village houses nearby. Soult had to supervise all this. He began a veritable witch hunt in the Boulogne and Calais area and, among the suspects that he caught while trying to deal with Abbé Leclerque's espionage circle, were fifteen Royalists who were put on trial in Rouen, six of them being shot. Perhaps the most spectacular of Soult's captures was an English spy who had concealed between his body and the lining of his shirt a leather 'skin' on which was traced a detailed map of the whole coastline![32]

The last of Soult's responsibilities was the exact opposite of this 'cloak and dagger' stuff. Despite his reserved and taciturn nature he, like Napoleon, appreciated the publicity value of great theatrical spectacles. When Napoleon made himself Emperor, Soult used the occasion for a magniloquent address to the troops. "Today," he proclaimed, "there begins a new era and the happiness of France is assured forever. Our oath of loyalty, so long engraved on our hearts, is the pledge of our love for the father of our country! Let us swear obedience to the Empire and fidelity to the Emperor!" To which the troops responded fervently, "We swear it!" It was heady stuff and some have described such declarations as sycophantic attempts by Soult to ingratiate himself with his imperial master. In fact they were the kind of rousing exhortations that the army greatly needed in these early days of the Empire. They were entirely in line with Napoleon's own exaggerated and sometimes untrue statements in the Grande Armée bulletins that were to follow.

Then there were the meticulous preparations that Soult and others made for the magnificent ceremony in which the enthroned Emperor distributed the Legion of Honour to the army in the great amphitheatre at Terlincthun. The whole project was Napoleon's but many of the administrative arrangements on the spot were made by Soult and the occasion had an enormous effect on the army's morale. Like several of the other invasion chiefs, Soult himself was invested with the Grand Eagle of the Legion of Honour. Along with sixteen others, he had already been awarded the honorary rank of chief of the 4th Cohort of the Legion, covering various departments in northern France with which he had no connection whatever. But his appointment as colonel of the Chasseurs of the Guard assured his position in the imperial hierarchy as a member of the Emperor's military household. Moreover, he and his staff were able to share the perquisites of the Imperial Guard which were so much envied by the rest of the Grande Armée.

In these circumstances it was not surprising that he was included in the first creation of marshals in 1804. The marshals' batons were handed out for a variety of reasons – often to keep dedicated 'Republicans' quiet – but Soult and others like Davout and Ney were made marshals because of their future potential. Soult travelled to Paris with his friend, the ailing Bruix, to attend the Emperor's coronation.

In Boulogne there followed another operation for which Soult had the prime responsibility – the building of the great memorial column, 'the column of the Grande Armée', which in one form or another has stood there ever since. Without Soult's enthusiasm and his financial contribution this project would never have got off the ground. He worked on all the preliminary arrangements while he was still in Boulogne and, to help finance it, he exacted a day's pay from every man in his corps – an action which naturally caused Thiébault to question whether the soldiers could afford it, adding the snide comment: "Soult would have been the greatest man in the world if he had gained as much glory as he gained money." A plaque depicting Soult offering the plans of the column to Napoleon occupies a prominent position on the base and again it has been suggested unkindly, if with an element of truth, that this was another example of Soult seeking self-glorification. The column was raised to commemorate an invasion that never took place and it was only beginning to be built when Napoleon himself abdicated. Thereafter it had a rather chequered life. When building continued in the reign of Louis XVIII it was suggested that the Bourbon hero, Henry of Navarre, should replace Napoleon on the top. Different counsels prevailed during Louis Philippe's reign when the construction was at last finished. But then, ironically, the King's Minister of War, Marshal Soult, was debarred from attending the inauguration ceremony lest this would seem to be too militarist! The column was badly damaged during the Second World War but was repaired and reinaugurated in a solemn ceremony under the government of General de Gaulle in 1962. The Emperor's statue stands on top of it and today it is more or less how Soult originally conceived the project.[33]

Whatever may be said of these various enterprises – Soult's expansive address to the troops, the great Legion of Honour ceremony and the building of the column of the Grande Armée – they must have been a great inspiration to the army at the time and they have become part of the 'Napoleonic legend' ever since.

These were some of Soult's many activities in Boulogne. He was one of the three or four men most closely involved in the invasion, training and disciplining the great army that was afterwards to bestride Europe, acting as Napoleon's faithful watchdog in that army, taking defensive measures on land against attacks by the British navy and against Royalist plots or enemy agents, and helping to create the ardent devotion which was such a unique feature of the Grande Armée. Perhaps his work in Boulogne is best summed up in the *Journal* of the National Assembly of

December 14 1851 shortly after his death. It recorded: "Besides the creation of the harbours of Boulogne, Wimereux and Ambleteuse, Marshal Soult did very many other great things. Above all he trained the troops of the Grande Armée to develop their intelligence, giving them toughness, ability and discipline for all the many things that they were to accomplish." As Soult once said to the Emperor: "Those soldiers who cannot stand the fatigue that I myself endure will stay at the depots: those who can stand it will conquer the world!"[34]

4

"THE FIRST TACTICIAN IN EUROPE"

DESPITE their elaborate three-year training for the invasion – the drills and exercises, the embarkation practices – the enthusiastic, well fed and now united army on the Channel coast preferred the idea of a land war to the rigours of a sea crossing and the desperate resistance of a landing in England. Some said they would prefer to march into the depths of Siberia rather than invade England.[1] Would they have felt like that after 1812? There was disillusion in the French armies and the soldiers warmly welcomed the outbreak of the war with Austria and Russia. By September the 'Army of the Coasts and Ocean' had become the 'Grande Armée'. This complete change of plan did not come as a total surprise to Soult or to the other corps commanders. They had been warned as early as March 1805 to make contingency plans in secrecy.

There is a theory that Napoleon dictated to Intendant General Daru at Pont-de-Briques a comprehensive plan for the movement of the whole army from the Channel coast to the Danube. This is probably an exaggeration.[2] More likely the Emperor had a general concept in mind and, within this broad outline, with a plan laid out by Berthier, the detailed moves were left to the commanders of the eight army corps stationed along the coast from Brest to the Low Countries. By far the largest formation was the massive IV Corps numbering now some 40,000 men. Its four divisions, 40 battalions in all, were still commanded by Vandamme, Saint-Hilaire, Legrand and Suchet, though Suchet was soon transferred to another corps. Soult's corps, like all the others, was effectively organized to fight on its own if necessary with infantry, twelve squadrons of light cavalry commanded by Margaron, and artillery – a system much developed from the rudimentary system of the old Royal army.[3] Soult had had plenty of experience of commanding these mixed forces during the Revolutionary Wars. The movement of such large numbers of men needed very careful handling. In his *Memoirs* General Bigarré, no friend of Soult's, describes him "as the most skilful of all the marshals at moving great masses of troops and exploiting them to the fullest advantage on the battlefield".[4]

Soult led his corps from Boulogne to Speyer in southern Germany in 29 days without losing a man. The infantry were supposed to march along the edges of the roads, led by their colonels on horseback, the cavalry occupying the centre of the road and the generals travelling in carriages. This all sounds quite orderly but in fact the men have been described as moving along in no recognized formation, indeed flooding in a mob across the roads and fields.[5] Setting out each day at about 5 am, the infantry marched some 4 kilometres in an hour with a half-hour break, the *halte de pipe*, at stated intervals. In this way they usually covered between 30 and 50 kilometres daily, halting soon after midday for rest and forage. They carried in packs on their backs some emergency rations, cloaks and a spare pair of boots but they had been geared up to fight a maritime war and their equipment in general was poor; their boots soon worn to tatters.[6]

In theory a staff officer and a 'war commissary' were sent in advance to make preparations for each night's food and lodging. Commissariat arrangements were nominally in the hands of civilian *intendants* who were universally regarded by the army as scoundrels and they were soon completely outdistanced. As a deliberate policy there were no supply trains so that the army could move faster and once more the troops simply 'lived off the land'. Again, as Napoleon described it: "La guerre devait nourrir la guerre!" There were no special problems over this in France itself and at first the people of southern Germany were friendly. Later in 'enemy' territory, when forage turned to pillage, these activities resulted in a bitterly hostile civilian population. As already noted, this system was strongly criticized by Soult in his *Memoirs* covering the Revolutionary Wars. Soult also had his own disciplinary problems at the highest level. The rough, outspoken Vandamme invited his battalion commanders to dinner in Speyer and then beat up the host in the house where he was staying, with nearly fatal results, for being slow in serving them. And Thiébault, who was one of Saint-Hilaire's brigade commanders – the man with the permanent chip on his shoulder – was already becoming disgruntled. Otherwise morale in IV Corps remained excellent. Perhaps the most important reason for this was the close rapport that existed between officers and men, thanks largely to Soult – "the great disciplinarian of Boulogne", as Napoleon called him.[7]

In under a month IV Corps was crossing the Rhine by a bridge of boats at Speyer. A large Austrian army commanded by General Mack and the Archduke Ferdinand was at Ulm: another army under the Archduke John was in the Tyrol. At first Napoleon reckoned that Mack would inevitably retire towards the Tyrol to join up with Archduke John's forces. When he did not do so the Emperor immediately employed what the military historian Professor Chandler has called a famous strategic disposition – "la manoeuvre sur la derrière". Soult, with the largest army corps, was ordered to seize a position on the Danube far below Ulm as a key element in this manoeuvre – the biggest 'strategic overdrive' that Napoleon had so far used – in order to prevent any link up between the armies of General Mack and of the Archduke John.

Meanwhile Ney and Lannes were to hold Mack in check in Ulm while Davout and Bernadotte would protect the army's flank from the large Russian force under Kutuzov that was still some distance away. Provided with the army's main bridging equipment, Soult marched at top speed through familiar territory in southern

Germany, where he had fought in the old 'Sambre et Meuse' during the Revolutionary Wars. Napoleon's original intention was for him to cross the Danube at Inglostadt[8] but, as the first unit of the Grande Armée to reach the Danube, Vandamme's division seized the broken bridge at Donauworth, taking prisoner a reconnaissance party from Mack's army which believed that Napoleon's forces were still in France. This enabled Soult to cross the Danube there and to march quickly on Augsburg with two of his divisions while Saint-Hilaire's division was left to guard Donauworth.

Napoleon joined Soult in Augsburg, still expecting Mack to retreat. The position of IV Corps, now reduced to only two divisions amounting to 30,000 men, sandwiched between the armies of Mack and the Archduke John, could have been very dangerous. In fact the Austrians remained in Ulm. There were rumours of a British landing in northern France and of serious rioting in France itself: in any event Mack regarded Ulm as the key to half Germany and the bulwark of the Tyrol. As the Austrians made no attempt to retreat they were fiercely attacked by Ney and Lannes in the country around Ulm. Meanwhile Soult was ordered to close the trap by marching through the difficult roads of the Swabian Alps to Memmingen which he forced to surrender with 5,000 men as prisoners. It was here that Napoleon paid a warm tribute to his wheeling movement which had been carried out so quickly and which contributed significantly to Mack's eventual surrender. "The whole strategic operation," he wrote, would be "ten times more famous than Marengo. If I had only wanted to beat the enemy, I would not have needed such wearisome marching but I wanted to capture them all."[9] Soult was then ordered to cut off the last remaining Austrian line of retreat at Biberach. If by then Mack had not surrendered Soult would have continued his rapid march up the River Iller to Ulm itself. His high-speed dash over atrocious roads in pouring rain comes in for some characteristically caustic comment from Thiébault who sneers at a march which had not been properly reconnoitred. How could it have been since rapidity was so essential? Soult's infantry, cavalry and artillery were said to be "in a terrible muddle. Such a want of foresight would have been a blot on the career of a corporal – let alone a marshal of France!"[10] The 6th Bulletin of the Grande Armée puts the matter in better perspective, describing Soult's vital task in shutting off Mack's line of retreat. However, in the usual 'no win' situation for any of his corps commanders, Napoleon could not resist carping at Soult for allowing a force of enemy infantry and cavalry to escape to the Tyrol.[11] Nevertheless, IV Corps had made an important contribution to this initial Austrian disaster.

Napoleon allowed the Austrians little rest. Soult's corps was reviewed in Munich on October 26th. Then, with Murat's cavalry, IV Corps and Lannes's V Corps in the lead, the Grande Armée entered Vienna and moved onwards to confront the Austrian and Russian armies in Moravia. It was a hectic and somewhat disorganized pursuit – the first of many occasions in which the sensible and meticulous Soult came under the command of the headstrong Murat, called at that time by Saint-Chamans, Soult's aide-de-camp, "the most pathetic general-in-chief I have ever known!" An attempt was made to cut off Kutuzov from the main Russian army near Hollabrunn by using Soult's and Lannes's rapidly advancing corps but this was foiled partly because of Bernadotte's slow crossing of the Danube. Then, much to Napoleon's fury, Murat agreed to a brief armistice which allowed Kutuzov to get clear away and join the main Russian and Austrian armies, with the two Emperors now present in person, at Olmütz. Napoleon established his base at Brünn. By this time the Allies had a great strategic advantage. After its long, hectic march from the Channel coast, interrupted by its victorious operations around Ulm, the French army was exhausted. The men were described as looking like scarecrows, the lines of communication were terribly stretched and although Vienna had been captured there were considerable Austrian forces threatening from the Tyrol. Prussia had not joined the Third Coalition but she remained a strong potential menace: the main Russian army with their Austrian allies, containing the magnificent Imperial Guard, was 90,000 men strong while the French forces numbered under 60,000: moreover only Soult's and Lannes's corps with Murat's cavalry and the French Imperial Guard were right forward. Davout, coming from Vienna, and Bernadotte from the Bohemian border, were hastening by forced marches to join the main army.

Desperate as his strategic situation seemed to be, Napoleon, with characteristic boldness and self confidence, decided to persuade the much larger Allied army to take the initiative and attack him. His only alternatives were to stay on in bleak, inhospitable Moravia or to retreat ignominiously to Vienna and the Danube Valley. His plan required that Soult's IV Corps, which had played only a supporting if vital role at Ulm, should take the lead in the new battle. Although Suchet's division had now left him, IV Corps was still much the largest in the Grande Armée, consisting of three divisions commanded respectively by Vandamme, Saint-Hilaire and Legrand, with supporting light cavalry and some artillery. After its long march from France the corps was weak in artillery. Soult who understood as well as his master the importance of its role, had not had time, as he had planned, to assemble some heavy Austrian artillery captured in Vienna. Thiébault commanded a brigade in Saint-Hilaire's division but had displayed his customary awkwardness by already falling out with Soult, who had preferred Morand to himself as commander of the first brigade, and of the division itself in the event of Saint-Hilaire being killed.[12]

On November 21 Soult and Lannes were ordered to occupy the heights of Pratzen and the village of Austerlitz, which was temptingly close to the Allied positions around Olmütz, and then to retire in some apparent confusion to the west side of the Goldbach stream below Pratzen hill. This manoeuvre was carried out perfectly and, at the same time, Savary was sent to Allied headquarters to ask for an armistice as if the French were in difficulties. These activities were undertaken in order to gain time for the corps of Bernadotte and Davout to join the main army.

By November 29 Napoleon's dispositions were made. Lannes's corps on the left was based on the Santon hill: next to him was Murat's cavalry reserve, Oudinot's grenadiers and the Imperial Guard which were in an area also to be occupied by Bernadotte when he arrived. Soult's IV Corps occupied the centre behind the Goldbach stream: two of his divisions, commanded by Vandamme and Saint-Hilaire, were facing the Pratzen plateau with the third division – Legrand's – holding the two villages of Zokolnitz and Telnitz on the right of the French line. Legrand was soon to be joined by the advanced divisions of Davout's III Corps but initially half the French line was held by Soult.

At Allied headquarters there were conflicting councils. The aging Austrian Emperor favoured a waiting policy: the Tsar was in two minds but as the arguments raged the hotheads around him advocated an immediate attack. The senior Russian general, Kutuzov, known as 'General Dawdler', seemed to be asleep. Although the Austrians were very much in a minority in the Allied army, it was General Weyrother, an Austrian military lecturer, who carried the day, persuading his colleagues with staff college eloquence that the Allied plan should be to attack the right of the French army in force while it was still weak, turn Napoleon's flank, cut him off from Vienna and annihilate him

At French headquarters another of those 'Austerlitz occasions' – so much magnified by legend afterwards – was supposed to have taken place. With Napoleon temporarily absent, Murat, Soult and Lannes were said to have advocated a temporary French withdrawal in the face of obvious Allied military superiority. However, as soon as the Emperor reappeared, Soult assured him that his corps was fully ready for immediate action. Lannes, who quarrelled incessantly with the other marshals – his particular *bêtes noirs* being Murat, Bessières and Soult – claimed that on this occasion Soult had treacherously changed his mind, and challenged him to a duel. He was sharply restrained by the Emperor who declared that they were all involved in much more serious matters. This tale has encouraged a recent writer on Lannes to compare his "brutal frankness" with the "fawning cunning" of Soult.[13] On such occasions, the cold, taciturn Soult never answered back in kind: he just got on with the job.

Now he certainly had a formidable task. Napoleon already knew that the Allies would launch a major attack on his right flank: Soult was to hold this attack in check as best he could with Legrand's division occupying Zokolnitz and Telnitz until Davout's rapidly advancing corps came into position. Meanwhile the divisions of Saint-Hilaire and Vandamme were to storm the Pratzen plateau, threatening the exposed flank of the Allied forces as they attacked the French right. Lannes's corps, with Bernadotte's corps and Murat's cavalry, were to resist strong holding attacks launched by General Bagration against the French left.

It was at this supreme moment with the battle impending that the 'Boulogne schooling' was to be really tested. IV Corps had been in continuous movement. Its headlong dash across Europe had been followed by the arduous flank march to cut off Ulm from the south-east and then by the hectic advance, cooperating with Lannes's corps ahead of the rest of the Grande Armée, into the depths of Moravia. But whatever may have been his relationship with some of his senior officers – the outspoken and ill disciplined Vandamme and the cantankerous Thiébault – Soult maintained a solid hold over the rank and file of his corps. They may not have loved him – that feeling was increasingly reserved for the Emperor himself – but they had a great respect for the man who had trained them so mercilessly and effectively on the Channel coast. One French historian describes him addressing each of his regiments in turn with that "sense of occasion" which he possessed so fully. When he asked his old soldiers in the 10th Light Regiment whether they remembered beating the Russians in Switzerland they replied that they were never likely to forget it. In fact until the present campaign he and Masséna (who of course was not present) were the only marshals who had actually fought against the Russians. On such occasions Soult displayed much of the evocative genius of Napoleon himself. By now he had become as close to Napoleon professionally, if not personally, as anyone could be. There were to be many violent explosions in the future under greatly altered circumstances, but at this moment he was unquestionably "the faithful Soult". He was with Napoleon at 3 am on the fateful day, December 2, for a final discussion of battle tactics. Napoleon is supposed to have said to him, "à vous la bataille", and he was ordered to attack the Pratzen at 7.30 am.

Perhaps as much has been written about the advance of Soult's corps up the Pratzen plateau than about any other action in French military history. The lower slopes of the Pratzen were still covered in thick mist and with the smoke of the French campfires. Then, with Saint-Hilaire on the right and Vandamme on the left, Soult's two divisions advanced: the mist and smoke cleared and suddenly there appeared "pure and radiant the sun of Austerlitz".[14] The scene must have been unforgettable. The French divisions went forward in columns of three in a line preceded by the *tirailleurs* moving in zig-zag formation. Contrary to the usual practice in battle, the musicians of the band had been allowed to remain in the centre of each regiment. Captain Coignet, the military historian, who took part in the battle, describes how the band in his own regiment was at full strength, with an old soldier aged about 60 at its head playing familiar rousing tunes. Meanwhile the drum major beat out a deafening charge that would have "stirred up a paralytic!"[15] Saint-Hilaire's and Vandamme's troops fell upon the weak flank of the huge Russian column which was attacking the French right and inflicted severe losses upon them just as Napoleon had predicted. Already Prince Adam Czarytowski, confidante of the Tsar and standing beside him, observing the determined way in which Soult's divisions climbed the plateau and attacked the Russian flank, had lost all confidence in the outcome of the battle. By 9.30 am Soult's men were well established on top of the Pratzen.

Meanwhile Legrand, commanding Soult's third division, was being very hard pressed. His operations indeed had at first been even more difficult than the

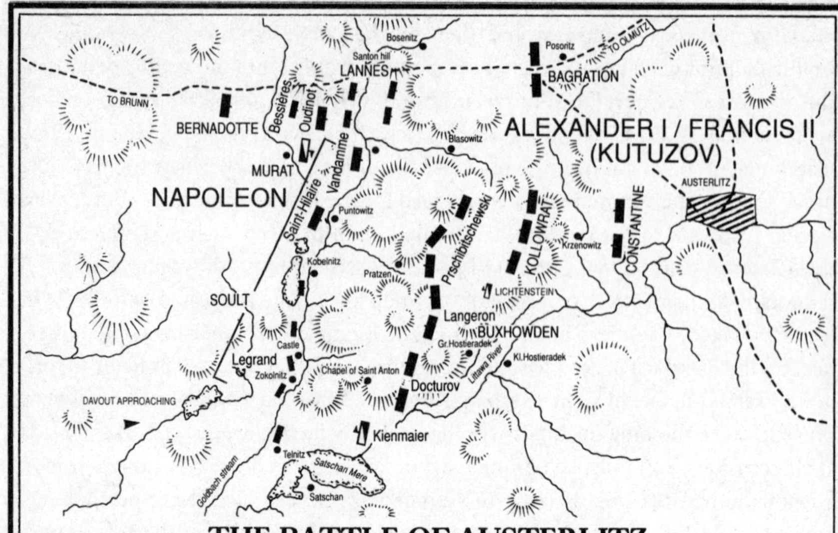

THE BATTLE OF AUSTERLITZ

The evening of December 1, before the battle. The extensive area covered by Soult's three divisions is graphically illustrated. While the divisions of Vandamme and Saint-Hilaire are poised for the famous attack on the Pratzen Plateau, Legrand's division alone has to defend Telnitz and Zokolnitz against the main thrust of the Allied offensive until Davout's III Corps arrives.

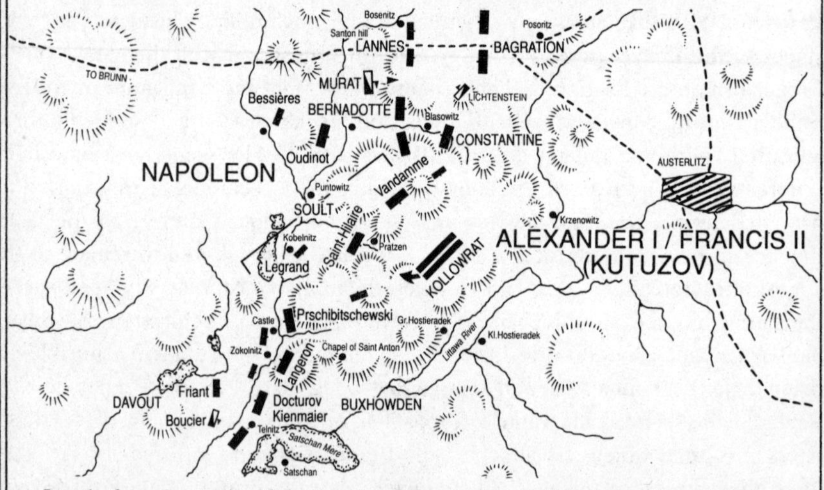

Just before the crisis of the battle on December 2. Vandamme's and Saint-Hilaire's divisions, firmly established on the Pratzen Plateau, are being counter-attacked by the Allied forces led by Kollowrat. Meanwhile the advanced divisions of Davout's Corps have come to the aid of Legrand in his defensive operation against the main Allied assault. On the French left, Lannes, Murat and Bernadotte are heavily engaged with the Russians.

spectacular attack on the plateau. His infantry included two Corsican battalions who, although not trained at Boulogne, fought bravely. There were also some foreign units – a handful of *tirailleurs de Po* from Italy. (By degrees foreign troops were to form an even larger element in the Grande Armée.) The infantry were supported by Soult's light cavalry under Margaron and a few guns but they were no match for the main Russian and Austrian attack with forces twice as large. Both Telnitz and Zokolnitz were lost and the fighting was so severe that the main streets of both villages were choked with dead and wounded making it difficult to pass through them. Davout's corps was now coming into action to help Legrand's beleaguered division. Legrand had held out stubbornly until Friant's and Boucier's divisions from III Corps took the strain. Soult's staff officers carefully guided these advancing divisions but the fog still lingered in the valley and in the general confusion regiments of the two corps fired upon each other, causing some casualties.

On the left of the French line there was a desperate battle. The role of Bagration's Russian army there was to keep the French left wing fully occupied while the main Allied onslaught developed on the French right. He made some headway against Lannes's corps partly because Murat was slow in making use of his heavy cavalry.

But it was on the Pratzen plateau that the battle was to be won or lost. Soult was now in full control but a strong Russian counter-attack developed. Kutuzov had hurriedly changed the direction of some of the Russian columns forming part of the main Allied thrust against the French right wing, reinforced by reserves striving hard to regain possession of the plateau. Soult's choice of Morand to lead the first of Saint-Hilaire's divisions was a mistake: he was a limited officer "with a notably small head"![16] Thiébault's division did its best to restore the situation but at one point Saint-Hilaire was considering partial withdrawal. The situation was restored by a fierce bayonet charge led by Saint-Hilaire himself. Soult brought up six 12-pounder guns and helped to bring them into action. Vandamme on the left was being hotly engaged but he too held his own. The fighting was fierce and Thiébault later recorded that the French had orders to take no prisoners. By midday the whole Pratzen plateau was securely in Soult's hands. The crisis of the battle had now arrived. Napoleon joined Soult at the little chapel of Saint Anton on the peak of the plateau and his headquarters were established there.

There was one last encounter on the plateau. The final Allied reserve, the Russian Imperial Guard, which included the noble born youths of the Chevalier Guard, were thrown into the attack, falling with devastating effect upon one brigade of Vandamme's division which had become separated from the rest. The 4th Regiment, which in Boulogne had been commanded by Napoleon's brother, Joseph, lost its eagle and beat a hasty retreat, still crying "Vive l'Empereur". Soult's battle weary divisions needed reinforcements and Napoleon ordered Bernadotte's corps, which had been engaged with Bagration on the French left, as well as the Guard cavalry under Bessières and Rapp, to restore the situation, causing such havoc amongst the Chevalier Guard that – another Austerlitz story – it was said there "would be many fine ladies in St Petersburg who would be heartbroken that day".

It was now decided to launch the divisions of Saint-Hilaire and Vandamme upon the flank and rear of the main Allied army which was heavily engaged with Davout's corps and the remnants of Legrand's division around the villages of Telnitz and Zokolnitz. It is said that Soult asked for orders to this effect and that Napoleon replied, "Carry on, my dear marshal, you know just as well as me what to do" – observing to his staff at the same time that it was Soult who was directing the battle. Obviously the final decisions were Napoleon's but it was Soult's corps that was principally responsible for carrying out the operations. The Emperor rarely allowed others to play the decisive role but that court propagandist, the painter David, was authorized to paint a picture of the occasion with Napoleon receiving the Russian cavalry general, Repnin, while Soult standing beside him is looking away, appearing to concentrate solely on commanding the vigorous action taking place in front of them.

The main Allied army was now in desperate straits, hemmed in by Davout's corps and elements of Legrand's division in front and by the remainder of Soult's corps, impatiently urged on by the Emperor, from the rear. The Russian and Austrian troops made strenuous attempts to cut their way through the ranks of the encircling French. Some of them perished in the freezing waters of the nearby lake – nowhere near the large number that was claimed in the Imperial Bulletin, probably much under 2,000 – but many other Allied soldiers were taken prisoner. Meanwhile there had been a hard-fought battle on the French left. Bagration and the Russians, having at least carried out their main task of keeping this part of the French army fully occupied were finally driven off the field by Lannes. But Lannes then temporarily left the Grande Armée in disgust because not enough had been said about his corps in the Imperial Bulletin. It was an odd conclusion to the pre-battle dispute between Soult and himself.

There is no reason to doubt yet another well-known Austerlitz story that at the end of the battle Napoleon described Soult enthusiastically as "the first tactician in Europe" and that he had done more than anyone else to help win the day. It was out of character for the Emperor to ascribe such glory to others: no doubt he spoke in a moment of euphoria after a great triumph but quite clearly Soult and IV Corps were main contributors to the victory.

This is perhaps the moment to dispose of other silly tales put around by Thiébault and subsequently included in his *Memoirs*. His rather confused criticisms are to the effect that Saint-Hilaire and Vandamme hardly caught a glimpse of their corps commander during the whole onslaught. Because of eye trouble he was supposed to have concealed himself under a green eye-shade; he provided no cavalry support on the plateau and he left Legrand's division with too little to do! All in all his inadequacies were supposed to have resulted in Napoleon refusing him the title of 'Duke of Austerlitz'.[17] These comments were matched by his crude criticism of Davout's part in the battle of Auerstadt – Davout's great victory. They were the outpourings of a man who was desperately disappointed over his failure to get the promotion which he thought he deserved. Poor Thiébault never became more than a lieutenant general and he and Soult were poles apart. The historians, Guénin and Nouillac, have justly called Thiébault "cet éternel mécontent!"

As regards the comment that Soult had become somewhat careful of himself in battle – a view occasionally expressed by his not always trustworthy aide-de-camp Saint-Chamans – it can only be said that, as a corps commander with his three divisions at Austerlitz operating in various parts of the battlefield, he was in quite a different situation to the dashing days when sword in hand he led his men forward during the Revolutionary Wars in Germany and Switzerland and in the mountains around Genoa. His serious wound and capture at Genoa may have affected him but to supervise the very diverse operations in which Saint-Hilaire, Vandamme and Legrand were involved required direction of a high order. He could not spare any cavalry for Pratzen because his cavalry reserve under Margaron was fully occupied with Legrand, who most certainly had more than enough to do. He intervened personally with artillery at a critical stage on the plateau and he was beside Napoleon giving orders in the chapel on the peak at the most crucial stage in the battle. As for Thiébault's gibe that he was not made Duke of Austerlitz because of his conduct during the battle, the simple fact was that the ultimate credit for Napoleon's four greatest victories – Marengo, Austerlitz, Jena and Friedland – was reserved for Napoleon himself and could not be delegated to anyone else.

Allied casualties in the battle were some 15,000 killed and wounded with about 12,000 prisoners: the French had some 7,000 casualties. One English historian of the battle has called it the most skilful and most "economical" of all Napoleon's victories.[18] The immediate result was that the Austrian Emperor begged for an armistice and Austria left the Third Coalition forthwith.

Soult's renown at Austerlitz rests firmly on several pillars – the famous 'Boulogne schooling' which benefited a substantial part of the Grande Armée; the high morale of the magnificent IV Corps despite its hectic march and its vigorous operations since leaving the Channel coast; the handling of his three divisions, one in a critical defensive role, the other two leading the great attack on the Pratzen plateau under 'the sun of Austerlitz'; and lastly his entire corps taking part in the final onslaught on the encircled Allied army. These were the elements that surely made Soult the major contributor to Napoleon's finest victory.[19]

5

FROM VIENNA TO KONIGSBERG

THE TREATY with the Austrians at Pressburg, with its heavy financial burdens, meant that large French forces had to be kept in Austria and southern Germany to ensure that the peace conditions were fulfilled. Soult and his IV Corps were mainly responsible for this task. At a review in Vienna Napoleon praised the corps warmly except for the unfortunate 4th Regiment which had lost its eagle on the Pratzen plateau. The regiment was instructed to capture at least ten enemy standards in exchange. Napoleon saw much of Soult at this time. He never became as intimate with the Emperor as, for example, Bessières or Duroc, but he remained on very close professional terms. Thus he accompanied Napoleon to a hunting party arranged by the redoubtable Archduke Charles which was really an excuse for political talks. When the Emperor left Vienna Soult established his headquarters on the Danube, first at Linz in Austria and then at Passau in Bavaria, where he lived for six months in some splendour in the country residence of the prince bishop in Freudenheim.

It was a time of rest and recovery. The Grande Armée was no longer quite the well-schooled military machine that Soult had helped to create in Boulogne nor were the men the exhausted scarecrows that they had been at the end of their long march from the Channel coast. After Austerlitz they were tough, experienced and battle hardened – the cream of the army being Davout's III Corps and Soult's IV Corps. Lannes's corps had played a less prominent role and, except for the division of Drouet d'Erlon, Bernadotte's corps had not been greatly involved. The whole army was now brought up to full strength by the arrival of less well-trained reserves from the depots on the Rhine: in general it was better clothed and it had been promised celebrations and arrears of back pay when, if ever, it returned to France. Meanwhile the soldiers could live well off the land: Napoleon's client states of the Confederation of the Rhine – Bavaria, Württemburg and Baden – were presently friendly. The marshals themselves had not yet acquired great wealth or personal advancement. At the centre of this army of occupation, keeping a firm eye on the military activities of Austria and reporting developments to the Emperor, Soult moved briskly around his bailiwick carrying out inspections and exercises and occasionally visiting the Grande Armée headquarters in Munich, where Berthier was in overall command. As usual he worked hard. Morale in his corps was high, the men respected him highly and only some of the senior officers were difficult. Soult always seemed to stand on his dignity with his divisional commanders: even the intelligent Saint-Hilaire found him aloof and unfriendly.

Life at corps headquarters has been well described by two of Soult's very contrasting aides-de-camp – Captain Brun de Villeret, the young man who had stood up to him in the briefing sessions in Boulogne, and the youthful, aristocratic Saint-Chamans. Soult had promised to take Brun de Villeret on to his staff but it took time to arrange this and Brun was too late for Austerlitz, a fact which Soult commented upon "with his customary brusquerie", when he arrived eight days later.[1] Brun came from much the same part of France as Soult but from a somewhat better social background: they soon became almost personal friends. Brun also looked after Louise when, with her family preoccupations, she paid her rare visits to her husband and he cemented a friendly alliance with her. He was quite different from some of the other aides-de-camp whom he described rather primly as "young libertines" with grand titles, a lot of money and brilliant uniforms: It took some time before his comrades shed their inhibitions towards him. But he quickly learned much about the art of war from his new master. In return he helped to compensate for the deficiencies in Soult's schooling. This cold, dour man readily admitted to his educational inadequacies when he was with someone he felt he could trust. Around the table in the evening he and Brun talked about history, science and literature, subjects of which he was quite ignorant.[2] Brun was to serve him loyally in several of the most explosive crises in his career.

It is not clear how far the other aides-de-camp – 'the libertines' – joined in these discussions but Saint-Chamans gives another picture of the marshal. His *Memoirs*, written long after the Bourbons had been restored, are entertaining but not without malice. He wrote: "It would be impossible to meet someone like the marshal who under his rough exterior could hide so much ease of manner, perspicacity and finesse in all sorts of matters and who had such firmness of character. He took decisions with great force, and, despite his cold air, he loved good cheer. On the other hand, he did not have the brilliant courage on the battlefield of a Ney or a Lannes. He did not always follow his bold plans with equally bold actions." Saint-Chamans suggests that his master's 'carefulness in action' was partly due to the great wealth that he had already acquired, although there is no hard evidence that by this time he had become richer than any of the other marshals. If, after his severe wound in the Genoa campaign, he *was* less bold than either Ney or Lannes, he was certainly a much more serious professional soldier than either of them. There were many ups and downs in Soult's relationship with young Saint-Chamans but, considering their quite different backgrounds, it was a credit to them both that it lasted so long. When, in September 1806, the young man watched his master sit down in a village barn and for many hours dictate precise and complicated orders to assemble at Ratisbon the whole of his corps, then scattered in bases all over southern Germany, he did not hide his admiration.[3] In this precise attention to detail Soult was more and more coming to resemble Napoleon himself.

The reason for this renewed activity was that Prussia, which had so far maintained correct relations with France, had suddenly begun to bestir herself. Napoleon's increasing dominance of western Europe had led Frederick William III's advisers, mostly aging Prussian soldiers who had learned their military art under Frederick the Great, to rally behind the beautiful Queen Louise in order to persuade the vacillating King to show more belligerence while the bellicose Hardenburg had replaced the more pacific Haugwitz as Foreign Minister. The immediate cause of Prussian indignation was a rumour that Napoleon was planning a secret bargain whereby Hanover, now occupied by Prussia, would be handed back to England.

Because of the threatening moves being made in Berlin, Napoleon considered that he must prepare immediately for war. By October 1806 the Grande Armée was ordered to advance to the Prussian border. It was some 160,000 men strong and probably in better shape than at any time in its history. Soult's IV Corps, numbering about 32,000 men, was still the largest in the army and was to form the right flank in any conflict with the Prussians. Indeed, when Napoleon took over personal command of the army again, he directed that Soult's corps should be the first to enter Prussian territory at Bayreuth. Ney's corps and the Bavarians, who now formed part of the Grande Armée, were ordered to follow behind: Davout's and Bernadotte's forces would occupy the centre with Lannes and Augereau on the left flank. These various military dispositions were made before the expected Prussian ultimatum was received. Soult, marching north, was required to ensure that the town of Branau on the River Inn should be turned into a strongpoint against any military resurgence by Austria. He had timber for its defences floated down the river from the Tyrol and a force of 5,000 men, with orders to hold the town at all costs, was left behind as a garrison.

From his headquarters at Würzburg Napoleon had decided to attack the Prussians at once, taking the initiative by marching through the Franconian forests and Saxony. Here the roads were better than those on a more westerly route and they provided the shortest route to Berlin. Russia was still at war with France and a march through Saxony would guarantee that a Russian army coming to the aid of the Prussians could be held in check more easily while a watchful eye could also be kept on the Austrians. Both these defensive tasks would be Soult's responsibility. Napoleon outlined his plan of operations in a long letter to Soult, again perhaps the 'first among equals'. The plan was then to be copied to the other marshals.[4] In this celebrated document he outlined his intention to turn the whole Grande Armée into a vast *bataillon carrée* in which two army corps would always be facing the enemy, two would be on the flank and two would be in reserve. Within the framework of this plan Soult was ordered to advance rapidly on the right flank while keeping his eye on the Russians and the Austrians. From October 9 to October 13, IV Corps pushed ahead, moving at the rate of some 30 kilometres a day, with patrols and flank guards marching even faster; the soldiers had no time for proper bivouacs or cantonments, sleeping in barns or village sheds whenever these could be found. Soult kept the Emperor fully informed of his movements and was bombarded in exchange by a torrent of instructions; he was ordered to make any prisoners march in front of his column so that they would bear the first impact of an enemy attack.[5] As the rest of the Grande Armée was advancing equally fast it was essential to discover the location and intentions of the Prussians. In fact, the elderly Prussian generals were in a state of some confusion – unable to decide whether to advance or to hold their ground. Had they moved further into Saxony, Soult, with instructions to make for Gera, would have found his corps forming the front face of the *bataillon carrée*. As at Austerlitz he would then have played the leading part in the impending battle. Indeed Napoleon had initially assumed that Gera would be the rallying place for the whole Prussian army, especially after the sharp encounters between the corps of Bernadotte and Lannes and Prince Hohenlöhe at Schleiz and Laalfeld.[6]

In the event Hohenlöhe's forces remained near the town of Jena while the King with the Duke of Brunswick and the largest part of the Prussian army retired northward to Auerstadt. Assuming wrongly that the whole army was still near Jena, Napoleon proposed to surround the Prussians there. The battles of Jena and Auerstadt took place on October 14. While the corps of Lannes and Augereau advanced upon Jena from the south, Soult's task was to attack the right flank of the Prussians across the River Saale. In the first major action of the battle Saint-Hilaire's division, supported by the cavalry of Soult's corps, had a fierce clash with a sizeable Prussian force under General Holtendorff near the village of Lobstadt. Although seriously outnumbered, Saint-Hilaire made good progress but his success would have been still greater if Soult had not been compelled to recall him to engage in the main battle against Hohenlöhe. Lannes and Augereau, supported now by Soult, were making headway but their advance was hampered by a characteristically rash and premature attack by Ney on the village of Vierzehnheiligen – an action that might have proved disastrous if Hohenlöhe had been bolder in counter-attacking. Brun de Villeret received his 'baptism of fire' at Vierzehnheiligen and he vividly recalls how the situation was fully restored by the joint efforts of Lannes, Augereau and Soult.[7] A victorious French advance then took place and the battle ended with a brisk encounter between Soult's cavalry and one of the few Prussian regiments that remained on the battlefield. Only at the end of the day did Napoleon learn that Davout had taken on the main Prussian army, led by the King and the Duke of Brunswick, at Auerstadt. Despite severe French losses the Prussians had been decisively defeated. The French victory would have been even greater but for the intransigence of Bernadotte who was nearly court-martialled for his inaction. Both he and Ney incurred the Emperor's fury. Davout's victory at Auerstadt had been unique but the operations of Soult and the other marshals at Sena were warmly praised in the 5th Bulletin of the Grande Armée.

After the twin battles of Jena and Auerstadt there followed one of the most famous pursuits in military history – the first example perhaps of a *blitzkrieg*. It was led by Murat's cavalry with the corps of Soult, Ney and Bernadotte. Soult's immediate objective was Magdeburg and he moved at his customary breakneck speed. On the way there was a characteristic incident. His corps came up with Field Marshal Kalkreuth in command of a Prussian force, some 12,000 strong, protecting the King of Prussia himself. Kalkreuth asked Soult for an armistice, saying that this request came from the King. Without consulting Napoleon, Soult turned the request down out of hand. He referred to the fact that Tsar Alexander had pretended that he had been granted an armistice after Austerlitz which had enabled his army to recover and to fight another day. It says much for Soult's professional relationship with the Emperor that he was able to reject forthwith this armistice plea. Afterwards Napoleon told Soult that he fully approved.

Soult was then ordered to leave Magdeburg to Ney, to cross the Elbe and to help pursue Blücher's army On the way he captured an entire squadron of Saxon cavalry, finding their horses much more useful than the men. Despite disciplinary problems during the hot pursuit, Soult continued to move very fast. Blücher, with the remnants of his army, had tried to escape from the north German coast on British ships but was cornered in Lübeck. Here Soult joined Murat's cavalry and Bernadotte's corps. Restraining Murat, with some difficulty, from launching an immediate attack on Lübeck, which might well have resulted in heavy casualties, Soult sent into the attack Legrand's division which had not been fully engaged at Jena. Having forced his way into the town, this massive man and his enormous horse could be seen on the ramparts "like a wizard in the middle of exploding fireworks". Soon the Prussians were in flight everywhere. Blücher and his army were taken prisoner.[8]

After this very successful operation Soult was in a sense 'upstaged' by Bernadotte who took great pains to ingratiate himself with the Swedish troops who were in Lübeck as allies of the Prussians. Making himself acceptable to foreigners was one of Soult's virtues, as he had shown in the Rhineland, in Switzerland and in Italy, but on this occasion Bernadotte's Gascon bravura and the fact that he was related by marriage to Napoleon's brother, Joseph, certainly carried greater weight. Five years later Napoleon reluctantly agreed to Bernadotte being chosen as Crown Prince of Sweden. Marbot describes the Lübeck events and deplores Bernadotte's later treachery towards France.[9] It might have proved better for the French Empire if Soult had been chosen instead!

After Lübeck, IV Corps moved briefly to Schwerin: the Hereditary Prince of Mecklenburg hung about at Soult's headquarters waiting to learn about the fate of his duchy but this time Soult was cautious and would say nothing until he had learned the Emperor's intentions.[10] The corps then moved on to Berlin where it was reviewed by the Emperor. Brun de Villeret met his wife's uncle, the *émigré* Comte de Bruges, who was to play an important part in Soult's life at the time of the Restoration, and the cheerful Saint-Chamans rather surprisingly found Berlin a more enjoyable place than Vienna. Soult himself was too busy for much relaxation.

IV Corps only remained in the city for about a week since Napoleon hoped to make contact with the Russians before winter made fighting impossible. If he could not bring them to battle immediately, he wanted to establish the Grande Armée in a strong position so as to surround and annihilate them early in 1807. Soult was ordered with the rest of the army to march to the banks of the Vistula, by way of Frankfurt-on-Oder and Posen. His corps remained the largest in the army, now numbering 22,000 men, but his most senior divisional general, the ill-tempered Vandamme, had departed to look after Napoleon's youngest brother, Jérôme, in the conquest of Silesia. He was replaced by General Leval. Once again, as at Austerlitz, the corps was virtually the central hinge of the Grande Armée, with Ney and Bernadotte on its left and Lannes, Davout and Augereau, based on Warsaw, on the right. At the beginning of December, Napoleon made a determined effort to surround the main Russian army, now commanded by Bennigsen, an ex-Hanoverian in the Tsar's service, at the River Narew north of Warsaw. Soult's corps played little part in the so-called Manoeuvre of Narew which involved bloody battles at Pultusk and Golynin because the Russians slipped away before Napoleon could bring the whole Grande Armée, including IV Corps, into action. These opening encounters of the terrible winter war in Poland were the first partial setbacks that the Emperor had suffered since the Grande Armée had left the Channel coast over a year before.

Like the rest of the army, Soult's corps now went into winter quarters for about a month, occupying a large area of Prussian Poland north of Warsaw. Headquarters were at the little town of Prassnitz and the base depot at Plock on the Vistula. Soult's responsibilities were for a desolate marshy area between the Narew and the Orzyc Rivers. Conditions in this part of eastern Europe were completely different from anything thus far encountered by the Grande Armée. In contrast to the reasonably civilized conditions and better roads of Germany, the roads here were nothing more than muddy morasses. Heavy rain in October had been followed by a fierce early winter and then by an unseasonal thaw. The failure of the Manoeuvre of Narew had partly been caused by these appalling weather conditions. "It was a nightmare of a battle," wrote one of the participants. "Horses were drowned in the mud and guns and ammunition wagons followed them without the drivers daring to help to extricate them lest they followed the same fate. Everywhere there were the debris of broken down vehicles and guns."[11] Under these conditions and so far away from home, morale faltered. Coignet reported the misery which began to spread among the old soldiers: there were many suicides and it was from this time that the word *grognard* came to describe the soldiers' constant grumbling until the word eventually became a term of honour.[12] It was nothing more than a foretaste of 1812. In theory at least, the French were serving in friendly territory. Soult made strenuous and not entirely unsuccessful efforts to keep up the men's morale, endeavouring to fraternize with the people from the surrounding countryside as well as the 'notables' of Prassnitz. But in this desolate region there was no possibility of the army living off the land. The various corps had to fall back on rudimentary commissariat arrangements that they had previously scorned. Food depots and base hospitals had been established on the Vistula and supplies were ferried somewhat haphazardly down the river. Soult, stationed furthest from the river, was especially hard hit. Geographically he was not far removed from the civilized pleasures and fleshpots of Warsaw, or from the agreeable castle of Finkelstein where Napoleon was entertaining his young Polish mistress, Madame Walewska, but in practice he might have been on another planet!

There was no loosening of the close professional ties existing between Soult and his master. Once when Saint-Chamans reported to the Emperor for an order, Napoleon remarked: "Your general and I work marvellously together!"[13] There was a rumour that he had even considered making Soult ruler of Poland. However, the best indication of Napoleon's feelings towards him was Berthier's jealousy, and Saint-Chamans comments openly on the detestation that Berthier had begun to feel for Soult. Soult himself, was too self controlled ever to refer to this but he felt it deeply. In another respect Soult was more fortunate than many of his comrades. The marshals who had become known in the army as 'the Italians' or 'the Egyptians', because they had accompanied Napoleon in his operations in those countries, seemed especially affected by the appalling weather conditions in Poland. Murat, Lannes, Augereau and several of the divisional generals fell ill, yet Soult, tough and dour as ever, never had a day's sickness, working unsparingly to maintain the discipline and uphold the morale of his widely separated corps. Saint-Chamans, whose occasional criticisms have been noted, described him at this time as fully meriting the high reputation that he had already acquired – absolutely tireless himself and keeping his staff officers and aides-de camp on the move with orders and reports day and night.

The chain of events that now led up to the terrible battle of Eylau was set in motion, as had been the case many times before, by rashness on the part of Ney. Faced with the same supply problems that confronted Soult and the other corps commanders, Ney had made some over-ambitious forays in the north almost as far as Königsberg. This had caused a quick reaction by Bennigsen who advanced rapidly, threatening Bernadotte's corps which was next in line to Ney's. In fact Bennigsen may have intended to take this action in any case; and Napoleon's impatience with Ney abated when he saw another opportunity of surrounding the Russians. Bernadotte was ordered to withdraw slowly in order to tempt Bennigsen further.[14] Then Napoleon embarked on a vigorous pincer movement near the village of Ionkovo, Soult's corps playing a major role. Legrand's division strengthened Ney's corps for a frontal attack while Saint-Hilaire's and Leval's divisions attacked Bennigsen in the flank, trying to cut his communications with Königsberg. However, captured French dispatches had informed the Russians of Napoleon's intentions and they began a hasty withdrawal. At first things went well for the French and, in close collaboration with Murat and Ney, Soult's cavalry moved up

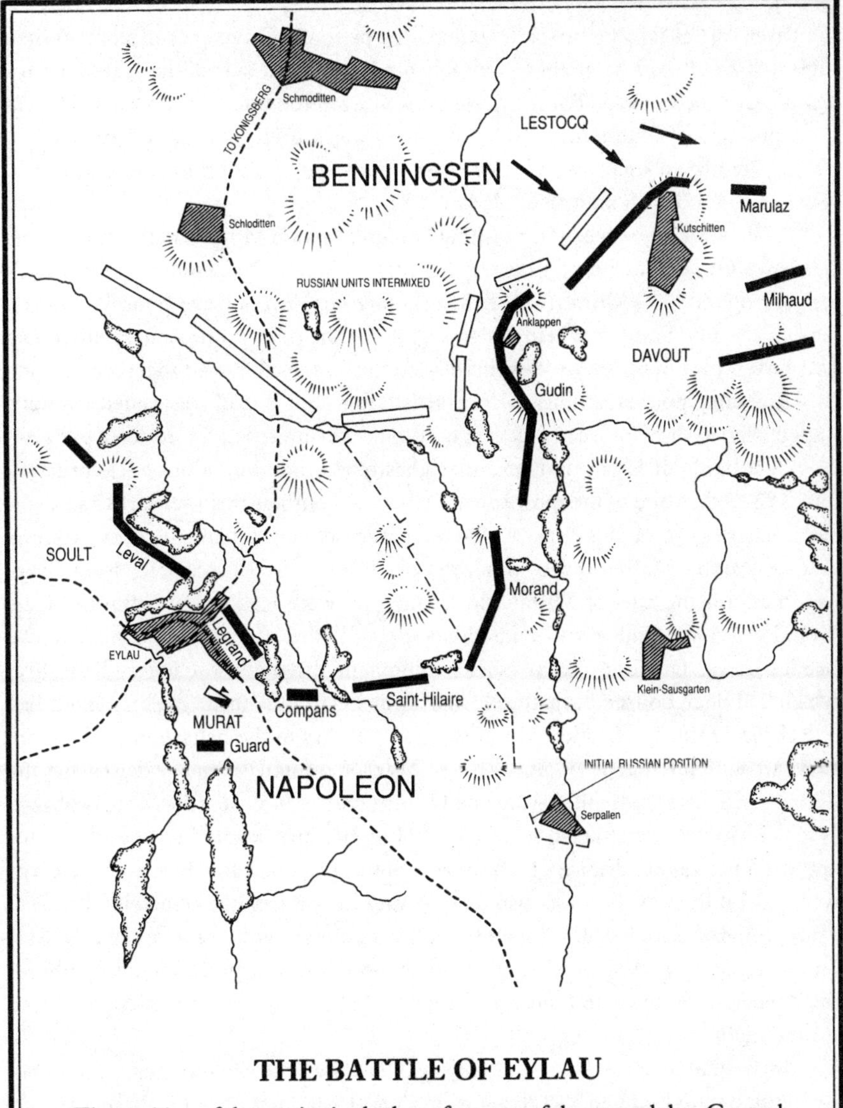

THE BATTLE OF EYLAU

The position of the armies in the late afternoon of the second day. General Bennigsen has fallen back after his violent encounter with Saint-Hilaire's Division of Soult's Corps, while Leval's and Legrand's divisions have resisted Russian attacks for the whole day. Compans commands the remnant of Augereau's VII Corps, which has almost been destroyed. Davout's III Corps is still strongly engaged with the Russians; with Murat's cavalry, it has saved the day. Lestocq's Prussians are just appearing as a reinforcement for Bennigsen. Ney is still some distance away.

the River Alle as far as Guttstadt, taking some prisoners, baggage and stores. When night fell Soult had been able to establish a bridgehead across the Alle but once again Bennigsen managed to extricate himself from the trap and slip away. He was hotly pursued by Murat and Soult, and there was a brief, indecisive battle at Hof before Bennigsen finally withdrew to take up a strong position in and around that village of ominous significance – Eylau.

Collaboration between the dashing but intemperate Murat and the more level-headed Soult, had by now apparently become an important element in Napoleon's military operations. Murat (who had little love for anyone save himself) did not particularly like Soult, but held a high regard for the dour professional soldier who had served him in southern Italy in 1801. With Lannes they had together pursued the Russians and Austrians before Austerlitz: Soult had restrained Murat's impetuosity in the capture of Lübeck; now they were united in the advance to Eylau.

The battle of Eylau, fought under ghastly weather conditions on February 7 and 8 1807, was one of the most appalling human conflicts that the world had so far seen. There is some doubt as to how the battle actually began. Augereau's young aide-de-camp, Marbot, who was present, claims that it resulted from over-eagerness on the part of Murat and Soult, who were leading the advance of the Grande Armée and who wanted to protect the Emperor's administrative headquarters, including his personal equipment, his field kitchen and the like, which had been housed prematurely in the outskirts of the town.[15] This sounds like a decision of the hot-headed Murat but it is contrary to the behaviour of the more cautious and intelligent Soult. Perhaps Marbot wanted to find excuses for the disaster which subsequently overcame his own master in the battle. More probably, Napoleon himself, wishing to seize Eylau before Bennigsen could escape again, fully approved the rapid advance of Murat and Soult. Davout's and Bernadotte's corps were still on the way: Ney was also far off trying to deal with the remaining Prussian army under Lestocq. Murat's and Soult's soldiers were desperate for at least temporary shelter from the hideous weather conditions, so, after a bloody conflict in the streets of the town and more gruesomely in the cemetery, they occupied Eylau for the night.

In certain respects the situation next day was not unlike Austerlitz – but Austerlitz without any of the glamour or glory. Once more Soult's three divisions held the centre with Saint-Hilaire out in front of the town. As at Austerlitz, Davout was pressing forward fast with orders to attack the left flank of the Russians: this time Augereau was on Soult's left while Ney and Bernadotte were still far away. As day dawned, the full fury of the Russian attack fell upon Soult's corps, especially on Saint-Hilaire's division, and his losses were heavy. Augereau's corps, launched into the battle to support Saint-Hilaire, was caught in a blinding snowstorm, lost its way and was almost entirely destroyed. Soult's two other divisions, which had been heavily engaged in the fighting the night before, were now confronting the Russian reserves: until Ney and Bernadotte arrived they could not advance to the aid of

Saint-Hilaire and Augereau without endangering the whole French position. Meanwhile Davout's corps and Murat's cavalry were fully engaged in the main battle and were making desperate efforts to restore French fortunes in a conflict which still remained undecided. The sour Thiébault, who hated Davout as much as Soult, asserts that Davout was 'carried' by his divisional generals – which is plainly nonsense. In fact Murat and Davout completely saved the day. Ney's belated arrival also helped to restore the situation but when night fell both sides still remained in the positions they had occupied during the afternoon.

Casualties had been heavy. Augereau's corps had been decimated and Saint-Hilaire's division in Soult's corps had suffered great losses. Everywhere there were heavy losses. "I have never seen so many dead gathered together on one piece of ground," wrote Saint-Chamans. "Whole divisions had been cut to pieces where they fought. For a quarter of a league one saw nothing but mounds of corpses."[16] Ominous cries of "Vive la Paix" were heard instead of "Vive l'Empereur".

In the midst of all these horrors Soult seems to have been the one person who really kept his head. Among his papers is the story of being summoned to see the Emperor in the middle of the night, finding him sitting alone in front of a miserable fire and visiting with him the ghastly shambles of Surgeon Larrey's various hospital depots with dead and wounded, limbs and blood, everywhere.[17] It was then that the Emperor seemed to have considered retreat while in response Soult made his celebrated remark that "French bullets were not made of cotton-wool either". Evidently, Soult argued strongly that retreat would mean abandoning the great number of French wounded as well as having a disastrous effect on the army's morale. Speaking from his recent experience of the battle, he advised that it would be prudent to wait until the much delayed corps of Ney and Bernadotte could play a full part in any renewed fighting. More importantly, the Russians themselves might retreat. When Berthier, Murat and the other marshals appeared, Murat at least favoured withdrawal. Napoleon, however, was now inclined to agree with Soult who was ordered to send out officers to investigate the enemy situation. At 5 a.m. his officers brought back the welcome news that the Russians were moving back. Soult's a.d.c., Saint-Chamans, was immediately sent to carry the great news to the Emperor. Despite the horrors and the heavy French losses, this Russian withdrawal proved crucial, and in the Bulletins the battle would even be described as virtually a French victory.

At another staff meeting held in the morning Soult's advice was altogether more cautious. Ney had recovered his natural élan and was now in favour of the Grande Armée pressing on to Königsberg as quickly as possible. Soult, with his own heavy losses in mind, suggested instead that the army should take up a strong defensive position on the River Passarge behind Eylau, allowing it time to recover from its battering, while it awaited reinforcements. Napoleon, who had been much shaken by the scenes of carnage and also by audible cries of "Vive la Paix", took this line too. Reorganization and recovery were obviously needed badly. So the army was ordered to retire from Eylau and align itself in cantonments along the Passarge. Given their conflicting advice to the Emperor, relations between Ney and Soult were once more at breaking point.

Both sides claimed victory at Eylau and manipulated the number of each other's casualties. Napoleon made much of the fact that the Russians had withdrawn from the battlefield but there was no avoiding the fact that Eylau had been the first major military embarrassment that he had suffered, and the moral effect throughout Europe was severe. In other ways too Eylau was a turning point. Of the great, well-trained army that had left Boulogne and the Channel coast, it was mostly the non-commissioned officers and the Imperial Guard that remained at reasonable strength. Of the reinforcements that began slowly to arrive, many came from the other countries of the Empire, and the proportion of French soldiers in the Grande Armée became progressively less.[18] Furthermore the morale of the entire army had been affected. The Imperial Guard was becoming increasingly disliked as a privileged formation and the young aristocratic staff officers and a.d.c.s were equally unpopular. Mutual jealousy among the marshals and senior officers had also continued, sometimes being encouraged by the Emperor on the 'divide and rule' principle. Although the battle itself was saved by Davout and the heavy cavalry reserve of Murat, much of the burden had fallen on Soult in the centre of the line. Augereau's corps was virtually destroyed; Ney had appeared almost too late and due to intercepted orders Bernadotte had not arrived at all.[19]

No sooner had Soult established his new headquarters at Liebestadt than (in anticipation of another more famous conflagration five years later) the little town, probably as the result of an accident, was totally destroyed by fire. Soult was obliged to take up his abode in the castle of Rosenau belonging to one of the Baltic barons, a strange ménage in which the baron's first wife lived in the back rooms of the castle as a kind of servant. It was a spartan dwelling with no heating and practically no furniture but Soult was better off than the officers and men of his corps who were spread around the neighbouring villages. The weather was still atrocious, the countryside had few agricultural resources and disease was rampant. The living conditions were terrible and many of the soldiers had not removed their uniforms for months. Soult and the others were frequently blamed for poor commissariat arrangements. Soult sent out foraging expeditions as far as the Vistula where the situation was rather better, and to evacuate his sick and wounded. A constant stream of orders and advice for all the corps commanders arrived from the castle of Finkelstein with optimistic instructions as to how to thresh corn inside their own cantonments, an impossibility in such frozen conditions. Restored now to a total of 30,000 men, Soult's corps, still the largest occupied the centre of the line, and he was soon having his new recruits licked into shape and getting them drilled and disciplined even in this appalling weather. As usual he continued working all hours of the day and night, reading the riot act to Saint-Chamans and some of his younger a.d.c.s when their noisy entertainments disturbed him, just like a strict schoolmaster.[20]

The Russians had also been reinforced. The Tsar, with the King of Prussia, had established headquarters at Memel and, at the beginning of June, serious campaigning began again. The Russians made a strong attempt to drive a wedge between the forces of Soult and Ney: Soult lost the small bridgehead that he had established over the Passarge while, to Napoleon's great annoyance, Ney also retreated, having lost most of his baggage and making a facetious request to Soult to lend him a pair of trousers! Within a few days Napoleon launched his own offensive, hoping yet again to cut Bennigsen off from his base at Königsberg. Once more it was Murat and Soult who led the attack on a greatly superior Russian force at Heilsberg. It was a fierce struggle in which the Russians fought back hard. At one point Murat, Soult and their staffs had to take cover in a wide square made up of Saint-Hilaire's and Legrand's divisions. "These redoubtable operations directed by Soult in person held the Russian attacks in check: the squares protected by French infantry and dismounted cavalry – and even by some of the Russian prisoners in French hands – formed by their matchless bravery an impenetrable barrier to the enemy's attacks."[21] French losses were heavy: Soult himself had two horses killed under him but, mainly as a result of fine supporting attacks by Davout and Lannes, the Russian offensive was checked and they eventually retired. The French remained in possession of the field but again Napoleon had failed to surround and destroy the Russians.

After Heilsberg the Emperor divided up his army. Murat, as usual with Soult and also with Davout, was sent against Königsberg, the capital of old Prussia, a city of 80,000 inhabitants and for so long Napoleon's goal. He assumed that it would be heavily fortified. Meanwhile the Emperor himself encountered the main Russian army near the village of Friedland. The preliminary moves against Königsberg followed a familiar pattern. As in the attack on Lübeck the previous year, Murat advocated an immediate all-out attack while Soult wanted a more cautious infantry approach. Then Murat's cavalry and Davout were called away to support Napoleon at Friedland, leaving Soult alone to deal with Königsberg and the numerous Prussian units trying to escape along the coast into the city. There were some sharp engagements but after a preliminary bombardment Soult launched a major attack on the city, resulting in an immediate request for an armistice. News had arrived of Napoleon's victory at Friedland and Königsberg at once surrendered with many prisoners, vast quantities of supplies and equipment of all kinds including a mass of English merchandise, much of it still in English ships. Soult was ordered to advance upon Memel but before he could do so peace negotiations had begun with the Russians.

It was perhaps rather an anti-climax, after all the great things that Soult's corps had achieved since leaving Boulogne, that they were not present at the final battle at Friedland. But Königsberg was a big prize and soon Soult was involved in the many military and political activities that followed the Treaty of Tilsit. Indeed the year and a quarter between June 1807 and October 1808 was an important divide in Soult's life. Prior to this time he had been one of the most successful and trusted of Napoleon's military leaders. Although he had been also involved in administrative and political problems in the Rhineland, in Switzerland, in Italy and in southern Germany, his main task had been to train the greater part of the magnificent army that had triumphed over the whole of Europe, and then to fight in almost all the battles himself. Now things would be different. For the next year or so he was to command a large army of occupation in northern Europe, with all the administrative and political problems stemming from that. There was then to follow his five and a half years' involvement (except for one short break) in the grim Peninsular War in which the political problems to be faced were as difficult as the military ones. Among all Napoleon's marshals, these experiences would be unique.

Soult's first area of responsibility, with his headquarters first in Königsberg, then in Elbing and then in Stettin, was the occupation of the whole of Old Prussia from Königsberg to the River Oder. Under the terms imposed on Prussia by the Treaty of Tilsit a French army was to remain in occupation of Prussian territory until the heavy financial burdens imposed on her had been liquidated. After the Emperor had reviewed IV Corps he emphasized to Soult the importance of his role. "You must keep a very firm hold on Prussia," he wrote.[22] Both in Prussia and later in Spain, Soult would discover that carrying out these simple directions was a good deal more difficult for those on the spot than for the man who issued them far away in Paris. One of his first problems related to Danzig which had been a hard nut to crack when Lefebvre, his admired old chief from the days of the 'Sambre et Meuse', had with difficulty captured it. Soult was sensible and tactful in his approach. There was no love lost between the Danzigers and the Prussians and on his various visits he was well received in the newly created Free City.

Soult had many other responsibilities. He was frequently in touch with the Emperor before Napoleon's famous meeting with Tsar Alexander on the raft in the middle of the Niemen. Together with his old adversary, Field Marshal Kalkreuth, and Marshal Davout, who commanded in Warsaw, Soult worked out in great detail the frontier to be established between Prussia and the new Grand Duchy of Warsaw created by Napoleon as an encouragement to the Poles. He also had personal dealings with Tsar Alexander himself. Whilst at Elbing he heard of a plot hatched by some Prussian officers against the Tsar and, with Napoleon's approval, he sent Saint-Chamans with a report of the matter to St Petersburg. Needless to say, the aide-de-camp was highly flattered by this mission and to be invited to dine with the Tsar, when Alexander presented to Soult a diamond studded portrait of himself as an expression of his thanks and admiration.[23]

The honours and awards given to Soult and to the other marshals at this time were well contrived by the Emperor to create a new imperial nobility that hopefully would be entirely dependent on himself. The marshals and certain ministers would be given titles which were supposed to match their achievements. The titles of some of the marshals came from battles in which they had particularly distinguished themselves – Rivoli for Masséna, Elchingen for Ney, Auerstadt for Davout. There were also 12 ducal fiefs which had been part of the Venetian Republic, the titles and revenues of which were available for distribution. One of these was the dukedom of Dalmatia which was awarded to Soult. Although he acquired this rather bizarre title he never set foot on the Illyrian coast. Much has been made of Soult's supposed annoyance at not being given a 'battle title' but the problem was that there was no particular action save for the great battle of Austerlitz in which Soult had distinguished himself more than any of the other marshals – and Austerlitz was reserved for the Emperor himself. Characteristically, Thiébault made the most of this. Having produced the ridiculous comment that the title of 'Duke of Austerlitz' was withheld from Soult because of his poor showing in the battle, he wrote about Soult's "plunder of usurped territories that nothing would justify. It is significant that the Dalmatians were drunken, brutal and addicted to theft!"[24] Thiébault, after some delay, became a baron – the lowest rank in the new imperial herarchy. It does not appear from his personal papers that Soult was at all aggrieved about the form of his title although the mischievous Saint-Chamans makes some snide comments about it. In any event it was much more important to him that he remained colonel of the Chasseurs of the Imperial Guard and therefore a member of the Emperor's military houschold. Honours were also given to his 'inner circle'. His brother, Pierre, became a general of brigade and the Legion of Honour was distributed among his aides-de-camp. Again, rather characteristically, Saint-Chamans remarked that Napoleon "could not give me a title more honourable than that previously acquired by my ancestors". This is a dilemma that has faced some of Soult's own very delightful descendants ever since!

Annual revenues and a little immediate cash accompanied these titles. Soult and some of the other marshals were also given estates in eastern Europe. Although Soult was among the most senior marshals, a careful analysis, which Thiers carried out, shows that he did rather less well financially than, for example Berthier, Masséna, Davout and Ney but better than some of the others.[25] Napoleon rewarded his successful generals well but the suggestion that at this time Soult was unbelievably wealthy and inordinately greedy is another *canard* that has become attached to him. Soult was much interested in the economic possibilities of his newly awarded estate of Raeconzeck on the Vistula. The land looked like producing a fair quantity of salt which was a comparative rarity in that part of Poland. Great quantities of wood for different estate purposes were obtained from neighbouring forests. With his customary energy and thoroughness, Soult had some artesian wells drilled and Brun de Villeret was sent off to get ideas on various aspects of estate management from the Prussian court and from Frankfurt.[26]

Amidst these preoccupations there was time for some relaxation. Soult was first quartered in a charming house in Königsberg belonging to the elderly Count

Schülenberg who lived in complete amity with his wife and her lover. From there he went boar hunting, a sport at which, according to Brun de Villeret, who was developing a pawky sense of humour, he was not very adept.[27] Indeed Soult was a notably unsuccessful huntsman: there was an unfortunate incident later, while stag hunting with the Emperor at Marly, when he and Berthier were involved in Napoleon being wounded in the hand. On his return from St Petersburg, Saint-Chamans showed a tendency to get too big for his boots. Soult effectively cured this by not speaking to him for several days. Eventually he seems to have been restored to favour by the tactful intervention of Louise, of whom the marshal still remained in considerable awe.

Some months later Soult succeeded Victor as military governor general of Berlin when the latter was posted to Spain. It was a critical moment in Prussia's history. After her shattering defeat in the war she had lost large amounts of territory to the new Kingdom of Westphalia (which had been created in favour of Napoleon's brother, Jerome) and to the greatly enlarged Kingdom of Saxony. Naturally Prussia also had to accept the provisions of the Berlin Decrees which forbade any trade with England and did great damage to her commercially. All this made for a very difficult atmosphere in Berlin. Soult was not directly involved in civil relations with the Prussian government but, because he was in charge of the considerable French military presence in the city, he had to use all his firmness and tact in order to make conditions tolerable. That famous group of reforming ministers, Stein, Scharnhorst and Gneisenau, were striving to introduce drastic reforms in the antiquated Prussian political system by abolishing serfdom and, of more immediate importance for Soult, in the Prussian army. All this reflected the dawning spirit of German nationalism which was beginning to become apparent even within the states of the Confederation of the Rhine. From Paris Napoleon treated these new developments with hostility and contempt. "The King of Prussia is to be pitied for having appointed ministers who are distinguished equally for clumsiness and perversity!" he remarked, and Stein had soon to be dismissed. Soult did his best to make the French army of occupation reasonably acceptable, adopting the same conciliatory tactics that he formerly used in the Rhineland – again assisted by the fact that he had a German wife. There was a good example of his generosity in his attitude to the Prussian Officers Cadet Corps in Berlin. They had no money and their morale was low, so Soult prevailed upon Daru, the French civilian administrator, to give them some financial aid. This was not obviously in French interests but Soult's concern, almost throughout his career, was where possible to create amicable international relations. The Germans did not forget Soult's comparatively brief rule in Berlin. As Louis de Saint Pierre writes in the introduction to his *Memoirs of the Spanish War:* "So generous was his regime in Berlin that when, eight years later, he was banished from France by King Louis XVIII he would find in Prussian Westphalia some very warm hospitality."[28]

As far as Napoleon was concerned the marshal still remained 'the faithful Soult.' In September 1808 he was summoned to take part in the great gathering at Erfurt were, in front of the 'parterre of kings', Napoleon and Tsar Alexander reaffirmed their friendship. Soult was in the imperial box in the Weimar Opera House when Alexander saluted Napoleon at the moment when the actor, Talma, pronounced the celebrated words, "The friendship of a great man is a gift from the gods!" He was also with Napoleon during the Emperor's famous encounter with Goethe although, alas, history does not relate what if anything Soult and the great writer said to each other. Afterwards he accompanied his master to serious political discussions with the Kings of Bavaria and Saxony. A long talk with the Emperor subsequently covered such matters as Tsar Alexander's ambitions in Turkey and Constantinople which Napoleon considered to be highly dangerous. But, ominously for Soult's future, the subject uppermost in the Emperor's mind was that of Spain. The gradual growth and development of the 'Spanish cancer' was probably to have a greater effect on Soult than on any of the other marshals and it was to change his role from a highly successful military commander into something between a general, a politician and a viceroy.

THE IBERIAN PENINSULA

6

"THE DUKE OF DAMNATION"

"EVERY BRITISH OFFICER, who had the honour to serve against him, had a great respect for him. If King Joseph had accepted his advice the fate of the War might have been different." This was the verdict on Marshal Soult by Sir William Napier, historian of the Peninsular War.[1] Napier is distrusted by Sir Charles Oman on the subject of Soult because he was so great an admirer of the Marshal and indeed was lent many of his papers for the purpose of writing his *History*. Modern historians regard Napier as out of date, inaccurate and writing too soon after the events that he records. But he writes vigorously of events in which he took a full part and his very detailed record of the Peninsular War should surely be regarded more generously.

How much did the 'Spanish cancer' contribute to Napoleon's eventual downfall or is this a case of obsessive British interest in the Peninsular War? Alternatively, have the French gone to the other extreme in not writing enough about it? Despite the number of French military memoirs covering the period it is interesting that Hector Soult, in the preface to his father's *Memoirs*, comments that the Spanish War remains one of the least well-known periods in French military history. Soult's own edited *Memoirs* were only produced by his great granddaughter, Antoinette de Saint Pierre, and her husband, Louis, as recently as 1955. These *Memoirs* have not received the attention that they deserve. They are an important contribution to the history of this very controversial period.

At a time when nationalism was not fully developed, the Peninsular War brought to a head the question whether much of mainland Europe could actually be ruled from Paris. In Napoleon's satellite kingdoms a king who had liberal advisers with ideas stemming from the French Revolution was often a great improvement on the national product. Few monarchs could have been worse than the Spanish or the Neapolitan Bourbons. However, in the end, it was the Spanish War that dealt one of the fatal blows at Napoleon's dictatorship. His brother, Joseph – 'the intruder king' as he was called – had far more liberal ideas than the Bourbons whom he temporarily replaced. But detailed research on the part that Spain played in her own War of Liberation makes it clear that, by and large, the Bourbon monarchy remained the focus of loyalty for the majority of Spaniards, including both the liberals and their conservative opponements whom they contemptuously called the 'serviles'.[2] For the French the problem in Spain, more than in any of the other satellite kingdoms, was that Napoleon was unwilling to give his brother any real independence. French power could only be maintained by armies led by strong-willed and able French marshals. The only two who really succeeded there were Soult and Suchet. Both of them had political awareness as well as great military skill.

The Peninsular War certainly harmed the military reputations of many of the marshals. Ney had to be sent home for gross insubordination. Lannes was only there for a short heroic period. Berthier as usual acted as the Emperor's mouthpiece, sometimes with surprising incapacity, and always, where Soult was concerned, with malevolence. Augereau, Gouvion St Cyr and Moncey achieved very little. Victor and Mortier, with varying degrees of unwillingness, came eventually under Soult's overall command. Of the 'three greats', as the Bourbons called them after the Restoration – Davout, Masséna and Soult – Davout never served in Spain while Masséna's great reputation was destroyed.[3] There remained Soult who for five and a half years was confronted by every kind of crisis in the Peninsula. Despite many hostile critics, his reputation stood high among most of his contemporaries both French and English. Suchet is often described as the marshal who did best in the Peninsula. He certainly succeeded brilliantly in subduing and then successfully administering Aragon and Valencia. But his operations on the east coast against Spanish armies and Spanish guerrillas, with some ill-timed and ill-led Anglo-Sicilian 'combined operations', had much less significance for the outcome of the war than the major operations elsewhere. Nor did it harm Suchet that he was the nephew by marriage of King Joseph Bonaparte while Soult's relationship with Joseph were often stormy and in the end disastrous. Also Suchet produced detailed *Memoirs* after the Restoration while Soult claimed that he was too busy to do so. Both of them had to grapple with Spanish regulars and endless streams of guerrillas but Soult had also to fight against important British forces led first by Sir John Moore and then by Wellington himself. In the end Wellington's Allied army proved to be the decisive factor in the Peninsular War. Wellington himself considered that Soult was a much greater soldier than Suchet – indeed, in his view, he was Napoleon's 'homme de guerre'. In the south it was to be Soult who built up the real French power base in the Peninsula.

Before Soult's arrival there had been dramatic events. Spain had been France's more or less faithful ally for over ten years but in 1808, partly to secure Spanish as well as Portuguese cooperation in the economic war against England and partly for aggressive territorial reasons, Napoleon had decided to intervene in the Peninsula. There was nothing very new in this. As long ago as the sixteenth century Henry of Navarre had said that France had always got Spain "inside her belly" while, 100 years before Napoleon, Louis XIV's grandson, Philip, had become King of Spain. Philip's pathetic descendant, Charles IV, Spain's present ruler, and his son, Ferdinand, were constantly at odds. Godoy, the chief minister, had failed in his efforts to restore Spain's political and military position. Despite a great uprising against the French in Madrid Napoleon had persuaded Charles IV and subsequently Ferdinand to abandon their rights to the Spanish throne in return for a comfortable period of exile. Napoleon had put his brother, Joseph, in their place. Joseph had some modest support among the Spanish 'establishment' and certain liberals but national feelings remained loyal to the wholly inadequate Ferdinand. By now there were plenty of French troops in the country although they were mostly young, second-line men. At first, with Spanish help, General Junot had seized Lisbon as the Portuguese royal family fled to Brazil in British ships. Suddenly there were popular Spanish uprisings against Joseph. A large French force surrendered at Baylen in Andalusia; the French were hard pressed everywhere and Joseph, abandoning Madrid, retreated to the line of the Ebro. Meanwhile the British, always anxious to gain a foothold in Napoleonic Europe, had landed a small army in Portugal under Sir Arthur Wellesley. Wellesley defeated Junot at the battle of Vimiero, forcing him to conclude a convention at Cintra which nevertheless allowed him to return to France to fight again with his whole army intact.

Baylen and Vimiero resounded like thunderclaps all over Europe. Napoleon took immediate steps to repair the damage. In October 1808 the Grande Armée was broken up into an 'Army of Germany' and an 'Army of Spain' to be commanded by Napoleon himself. Immediately after Erfurt the Emperor set off for Spain, ordering Soult and other marshals to join him there. With no time even to visit his family in Languedoc, Soult moved swiftly from Berlin to the Spanish border. The Emperor was dissatisfied with the lethargic performance of II Corps of the Army of Spain in front of Burgos, the capital of Old Castile and an important strategic centre. The corps was commanded by Bessières, an admirable cavalry commander and indeed a devoted admirer of Napoleon, but a poor commander of a unit comprising all arms. In Vitoria, that town of eventual ill omen for the French, Soult hardly had time to get off his horse before Napoleon ordered him to ride on and take over from Bessières. Soult appeared at his new headquarters in Brivesca at 4 am on November 4 and having outdistanced all his aides-de-camp awoke Bessières and told him that he had arrived to take over his command. Fortunately the two were friends. To the credit of them both the hand-over proceeded smoothly and Bessières became commander of the reserve cavalry.[4]

When Soult assumed command, II Corps consisted of three infantry divisions, commanded respectively by Mouton, Bonnet and Merle, Milhaud's dragoons and the light cavalry, commanded by Soult's former aide-de-camp and warm admirer, Franceschi. Merle had been his chief of staff in Germany but he did not know his other divisional commanders well. Several of those he acquired in the Peninsula were distinctly odd. Bonnet used to horsewhip his wife and make her ride behind his carriage instead of his valet when she had done something that displeased him. But of Mouton (afterwards the Comte de Lobau) it was said "This 'mouton' is much more like a lion."

Napoleon had sharply criticized the abandonment of Burgos. He regarded its immediate recapture as essential to the reconquest of Spain. Soult lost no time. Within a few hours of taking over from Bessières his cavalry were in close contact with a good-sized Spanish force – the Army of Estremadura – under the Conde de Belvedere near the village of Gamonal. Belvedere's army included the Spanish and Walloon Guards, some of the best troops in Spain who were to distinguish themselves later at Albuera, many volunteers of good family who had by this time rallied to the popular cause and thousands of peasant auxiliaries. The army was reasonably well armed and equipped mostly with English stores.[5] The Spaniards were consumed with a kind of Baylen euphoria. "We are obliged to our English friends," one Spanish general is reputed to have said. "We shall be pleased to escort them through France to Calais. It will be pleasanter than a long voyage. They need not trouble to fight the French. We shall be delighted to have them as spectators of our victories!" However, when Belvedere's army was attacked by Soult's veterans, expertly handled by the Marshal himself, they put up only a feeble resistance and, with the French cavalry cutting off their retreat, were totally defeated with over 3,000 casualties. Soult then seized Burgos. It was within 50 hours of his taking over command and it was his first of many victories in the Peninsula. True to his usual habit of underplaying the actions of his subordinates, Napoleon belittled this fine achievement by referring to Belvedere's army as a "cowardly babble of braggadocios who could not stand up to the charge of a single French brigade".[6] Then , despite all Soult's efforts to control his troops, the French sacked Burgos in the familiar pattern which was to be followed by both sides in the Peninsular War. There is a description from contemporary sources of Napoleon arriving in Burgos, early the following morning, to find half the city on fire, the churches desecrated and the whole place turned into a sewer with drunken soldiers reeling about the streets. These were already the realities of war in the Peninsula.[7] When the hard and sometimes dirty work had been done, King Joseph with his major general, Jourdan, in attendance arrived to express horror. Jourdan was Soult's former chief from the Army of the 'Sambre et Meuse'.

Elsewhere, quite unaware of the arrival of Napoleon with his reinforced Army of Spain, the Spaniards remained absurdly over-confident, thinking they were only facing some 80,000 starving and disease-ridden French. In the Asturias Blake, commanding the Army of the Left, was ordered to march along the north coast to Irun where he would join up with Castanos's Army of the Centre, completely surrounding the enemy in an even more magnificent 'Baylen'. The French reaction was swift and decisive. The victories of Soult and Victor at Espinosa and Reynosa effectively destroyed Blake's army which fled along mule tracks to the mountainous regions of the Asturias and León. Soult captured all his artillery and baggage while the half-famished French soldiers gorged themselves in a well-stocked Spanish depot. By November 17, in a headlong advance, Soult seized Santander on the northern coast, capturing a mountain of British supplies from seventeen ships of a

British flotilla, which had only just had time to put out to sea. In the whole of this operation he had covered 100 kilometres over appalling Spanish roads in a few days, a feat, according to Oman, rarely equalled in the whole of the Peninsular War. Santander was a most important base through which English supplies could reach the Spaniards and Bonnet's division was given the task of 'mopping up' so that the little ports all along the northern coast could no longer be used for bringing in supplies. With his main force Soult occupied Llanes, the chief town of the Asturias, where he was given a friendly local welcome.

He was faced, however, with two important new developments. The central junta in Seville had now given the Marquis de la Romana a kind of overall command of the Spanish armies in the north and he was soon to be made virtual viceroy of all the northern provinces including Galicia. Romana had commanded the Spanish contingent serving with Napoleon's Grande Armée in northern Europe as a result of an arrangement made with the Bourbon government. After the forced abdication of the Bourbons he had been brought back to Spain in a British ship. An ambitious, two-faced individual, who had earlier sent an unctuous profession of loyalty to King Joseph,[8] he continued to vacillate in his political loyalties until he was finally brought over to the nationalist cause by the rank and file of his army. His real ambition was to establish personal authority in northern Spain. In a short time he was to be the first Spanish general to develop the kind of guerrilla tactics which the French were to find impossible to combat.[9]

The second problem facing Soult and the other marshals was that the British had returned to the Peninsula in some force although their situation was somewhat confused. The Convention of Cintra which had allowed Junot's army to return to France and fight again had raised a storm of protest in London. Wellesley and the other generals who had been placed over him after Vimiero had returned home to face courts-martial. But the British government had stuck to its decision to help the Spanish and Portuguese with large subsidies and a fair-sized army. In command was the heroic but luckless Sir John Moore who had enjoyed a fine if chequered military career, but who was politically out of tune with some of the ministers at home. Half of Moore's army was already in Lisbon: half under Sir David Baird was coming out from England to land at Corunna in northern Spain. Campaigning in the wild Spanish mountains was quite different from fighting in any other part of Europe, as both sides were soon to discover. There was an almost complete intelligence blackout which at first affected both armies equally. For the British, information gradually seeped in from Spanish guerrillas, but Moore had to contend with continued Spanish over-confidence and with unrealistically sanguine reports from the British diplomatic representative in Spain. The French were in the dark, so far as intelligence was concerned, for more or less the entire war.

Encouraged by his over-optimistic information, Moore had decided on the risky strategy of advancing into Spain in the hope of uniting along the way with Baird's army from Corunna. He had quickly reached Salamanca while Baird had got as far as Astorga. Soult was much better informed than Napoleon of these potentially dangerous British moves. He also had a shrewder idea than the Emperor of the tough fighting qualities of the British and he realized that they needed to be attacked as soon as possible. Could they be destroyed while their two armies were still divided? According to his papers, he evidently considered this. As usual Napoleon underestimated the British threat. Anyway, for various political and strategic reasons, he considered that his first objective must be Madrid. There would be time to attack the British afterwards since he assumed quite wrongly that in the face of a large-scale French advance the British would retreat once again to Lisbon. Accordingly, after a dramatic crossing of the Somo Sierra, he marched on Madrid and recaptured it without much difficulty. There he spent a few days reforming and liberalizing the Spanish political system for the benefit of his brother, Joseph. In fact he was already considering a plan for dividing the country into a series of viceroyalties, as happened later. Commenting to Dr O'Meara years later at St Helena about the total ineffectiveness of his brother as a ruler, Napoleon said, "My brother was really too good to be a great man."[10]

After the capture of Madrid the Emperor had concluded that the remaining centres of resistance in the Peninsula must be Seville, to which the central Spanish junta had fled, and Lisbon. So while his main army was concentrated in the capital for its onward march, Soult's corps was ordered to destroy the other Spanish forces in the Asturias and León before advancing into Galicia and dealing also with any British forces which had arrived there.

Unfortunately for Soult, a dispatch from Berthier incorporating these orders and adding that the British were presumed to be retreating on Lisbon was sent by the hand of one unescorted French officer. The messenger, after using some abusive language to a Spanish postmaster, was murdered, and his important dispatch was sold to the British. This unexpected windfall, while giving Moore the gloomy news of the fall of Madrid, informed him that Soult had been ordered to march towards Galicia with his comparatively weak force of a single corps. Moore was thus given at least a fleeting chance to practise on Soult the same strategy that the marshal himself had thought of using on Baird, isolating him from Napoleon's main army, overwhelming him quickly and perhaps even bestriding the Emperor's main communications with France, potentially disastrous for the whole French position in Spain. It was the identical strategy that Blake's Spanish army had hoped to use earlier. By now Moore had at last linked up with Baird's army coming from Corunna and he marched rapidly northwards, heading for the River Carrión where there were advance units of Soult's II Corps.

It was a bold and risky move but it was even more dangerous for Soult. His corps was very much stretched, with garrisons in Santander and other towns, so that only 11,000 infantry and 1,200 cavalry were available for action against a reunited British army almost double its size. Urgent and dramatic steps were immediately taken to reinforce Soult with units from Victor's and Junot's corps which were already under orders from the Emperor himself to join him in Madrid for the march south to Lisbon and Seville "in order to end the war". According to Soult's own *Memoirs* – and there is no reason to doubt their accuracy – he himself took the decision to countermand the Emperor's orders by requesting General Mathieu Dumas, who commanded the rear echelon of Imperial Headquarters in Burgos, to direct General Lorge with some of the reserve cavalry and units of Junot's corps to reinforce him forthwith.[11] Again it testifies to the close professional relationship existing between Soult and his sovereign that he felt able to change Napoleon's express instructions in this way. Soult now established himself in a strong position at Saldana, some 30 kilometres from Moore's first objective at Sahagun. As King Joseph shrewdly commented at the time: "To have supposed that Soult would have allowed himself to be attacked by superior forces while Napoleon remained peacefully in Madrid would have grossly underestimated them both."[12]

In the contest that was now developing between Soult and Moore, first blood, nevertheless, went to Moore. In a brilliant little action the 15th Hussars routed a French cavalry force composed of chasseurs, dragoons and some Hanoverians in the French service. "There was scant firing of pistols and our lads made a good use of their sabres," wrote one of those taking part, who afterwards, incidentally, became a fierce critic of Moore.[13] Sahagun has been called by Oman the most brilliant cavalry exploit of the whole Peninsular War. Jomini, the French military historian, described it as a serious defeat. With a little more luck the 15th Hussars might have caused even greater losses.

Moore's triumph, however, was short-lived. As soon as Napoleon learned of the new situation, he not only praised Soult's initiative in obtaining reinforcements but immediately altered his own strategic objective. Instead of advancing on Lisbon and southern Spain, he decided that he now had a fine opportunity to annihilate the British. Preceded by Ney's corps, he turned north and made a spectacular crossing of the Guadarrama Mountains. His orders to Soult were explicit: "If the British attack you, retire a day's march. The further they proceed, the better for us. If they retreat, follow them closely!"[14] Napoleon was to be the hammer, and Soult the anvil. It was the same strategy that Napoleon had used, not always very successfully, against the Russians in the winter war in Poland.

Moore quickly became aware of the acute danger of encirclement. He began a speedy retreat, hotly pursued by Soult who had the satisfaction of being right in the centre of things again. The appalling winter conditions were equally serious for both sides and they prevented Napoleon from getting across Moore's line of retreat, first at Benavente and then at Astorga. However, there was a serious breakdown in the discipline of Moore's weary army as it slowly retreated towards the coast with the Light Brigade acting as a desperate rearguard. As Savary commented: "Soult pushed the English rearguard so hard that he often came up with them."[15] In Astorga there were terrible scenes. The remnants of Romana's army, defeated despite some obstinate resistance at Mansilla, were retreating fast with the French hard on their heels and they had consumed most of the provisions in the town. When the starved and weary British troops with their accompanying womenfolk found practically no food left in Astorga, they set fire to the town; but having discovered only well-filled wine cellars, they were soon sprawling dead drunk in the streets where they were an easy prey to Soult's pursuing cavalry. Napoleon, in his chagrin at failing to surround and destroy the British, made maximum use of their misfortunes for propaganda purposes. In a report to his brother, Joseph, he wrote: "The English are running away. They have mistreated and beaten many Spaniards. The newspapers should make the most of this. Insert in them some letters purporting to be written from monasteries where the English have turned out the monks. Have some pamphlets printed describing the state of Spain abandoned by the English."[16]

By the end of the year, always unwilling to be associated with failure, the Emperor had decided to give up the pursuit and to return to France. There was news of a possible Austrian resurgence and of another political conspiracy involving Talleyrand, Fouché and even Napoleon's own brother-in-law, Murat. Having told his brother, Jérôme, that the Spanish business was now at an end – the Emperor left the pursuit of the British to the marshal who he considered would be best able to operate on his own, informing Soult that he now "commanded from the Douro to the sea".[17] However, Berthier, emphatically no friend of Soult, was temporarily left behind to transmit the Emperor's orders on military operations. Moreover Soult's old enemy, Ney, who was furious at not being given sole charge, was ordered to move on parallel lines in Galicia in order to give Soult general support. Staff officers from Ney's corps were attached to Soult's headquarters to provide the expected liaison. Mermet replaced Mouton as one of Soult's divisional generals, and two other divisions, those of Delaborde and Heudelet, with Lorge's and Lahoussaye's dragoons, were formally added to Soult's corps. Bonnet's division was still holding Santander and Heudelet had not yet arrived. Some 50,000 men, including Ney's corps, were thus nominally available to fight the British; but because of Ney's refusal to cooperate effectively and the need to move fast without waiting for the reinforcing divisions, little more than half that number could be utilized for Soult's campaign of hot pursuit.

Some comparisons may be drawn between the two protagonists in this short but dramatic phase of the Peninsular War. Both Soult and Moore had spent an important part of their military career in training soldiers. Soult's major contribution to the training of the Grande Armée in Boulogne has already been described. Moore had also spent some time with a direct responsibility for military training. The 'Experimental Rifle Corps', formed in 1800, came under his direct command at Shorncliffe Camp in Kent. The aim was to create lightly armed units – very similar to the French *tirailleurs* – with the special task of covering the main army's advance or retreat. As has been noted, by a strange coincidence these men might have been the first troops whom Soult would have encountered if he had led the French invasion force from Boulogne in 1804. Now he was to meet them in very different circumstances, for it was to be this same rifle corps, soon to be called the 'Bloody Fighting Ninety Fifty' or the Rifle Brigade, which, with the 43rd and 52nd as part of the Light Brigade, formed the rearguard of the bedraggled British army in the terrible Peninsular retreat.

As Soult and Moore hounded their weary soldiers onward by the sheer force of their personalities, coping with an appalling mountainous terrain in the depths of winter, they had equally severe problems with their higher authorities. Soult was to suffer continuous interference and embarrassment from Napoleon throughout the Peninsular War, with Berthier often acting as the Emperor's watchdog. Indeed the French chain of command was by now unbelievably complicated – and must reflect seriously upon Napoleon's administrative gifts. Joseph was not only King of Spain but was also nominally in command of all the French armies, Soult having to keep him as far as possible fully informed. Berthier was the faithful transmitter of the Emperor's orders – sometimes with very troublesome additions of his own – but these were quite often out of date when they arrived. Nor had Soult any direct authority over those marshals who were supposed to support him – Ney and also Bessières who was now responsible for the lines of communication with France and took his orders directly from Paris. A most complicated chain of couriers was organized between Soult, Berthier, Ney, Joseph, Bessières and Paris which could not possibly keep pace with the rapidly changing events in the Peninsular War. Moreover they were constantly at the mercy of more and more active guerrilla bands. The communications system became even more 'Gilbertian' when Napoleon left Paris to fight the Austrians once again on the Danube so that reports often had to be sent on to him, taking weeks to be transmitted.

Moore's problems were rather different. He was reasonably independent but he had a government at his back which was very much aware that he was commanding Britain's only sizeable army. "There had been no such command for a British officer since the days of Marlborough," he recorded in his diary.[18] He was also disliked and distrusted by many of the Tory ministers.

Both Soult and Moore had trouble with their colleagues and subordinates. Ney's overall unwillingness to cooperate was already notorious in the army. Gruff old Marshal Moncey called him "a very bad bedfellow" and his general bloody-mindedness was one of the main reasons for the French failure in Spain and Portugal. Soult had other worries as well. He was mostly admired by his personal staff and by the rank and file of his army whom he was to lead through thick and thin over the next few years, but as usual he had problems with several of his divisional generals. These difficulties were soon to have serious consequences for him. This was partly due to his cold and even sour manner but it was also because some of his generals had served with Junot in the previous year's campaign and resented Soult as a newcomer. This applied especially to Loison and to Delaborde. Loison – 'le Tondu' or the 'one-armed one' – hated Soult as indeed he did most of his comrades. For his part, Moore had always to face the sulkiness and lack of cooperation of Sir

David Baird, described by Wellington as "lion-hearted but having no tact or talent". Alexander Gordon, one of the heroes of the cavalry action at Sahagun, was equally disloyal to his chief, writing back to his brother, Lord Aberdeen, the future Prime Minister, to describe the commander-in-chief's conduct as being "one continuous example of imbecility and folly".[19]

The Spaniards themselves were equally troublesome to both armies. On the one hand, Soult was treated in a civil manner by political and ecclesiastical figures in Galicia, some of whom were willing at first to accept the authority of King Joseph. But very soon he had to deal with increasingly fierce and effective guerrilla attacks. There is nothing very unusual in an incident described by Marbot in his *Memoirs*. Marbot was on his way to join Soult in Santander when he came across a young officer of the Chasseurs pinned upside down on a barn door with a fire underneath him, obviously burnt alive. In his turn, Moore found during his retreat that Romana was both uncooperative and obstructive. There are differing accounts of the Spanish attitude to the various foreign armies in this increasingly ferocious war. A dispatch from Soult to Berthier describes drunken British soldiers burning farms and pillaging the country folk who often handed them over to the French.[20] On the other hand Franceschi, Soult's cavalry commander, reported that the British were well supported by the peasants who warned them of impending French attacks and helped them when they were defeated. Probably the fiercely independent Galicians hated any intervention in their affairs whether by the French or the British. Certainly Romana was able to turn them into highly effective guerrillas and the French were eventually to find that Galicia was virtually ungovernable.

This was the background for the duel between Soult and Moore. Napier admired them both equally. "Moore's talents saved the British in the Peninsula," he wrote, while he described Soult as "superior to any of the French nation, if Napoleon can be excepted, pursuing Moore with a vigour that testified to his desire to finish the campaign in a manner similar to its opening at the victory at Gamonal."[21]

After Astorga Moore thought only of saving as much of his bedraggled army as he could. Of possible embarkation ports in Galicia, Vigo was favoured by the Royal Navy but Corunna was preferred by Moore himself since it had better defensive positions from which to cover the operation. Soult kept up the pressure all the time, earning a half-grudging admiration from the weary soldiers that he was pursuing. Instead of his brand new title, 'Duke of Dalmatia', they called him (in the 'Eatables' for Etaples and 'Wipers' for Ypres tradition of the British private soldier) 'the Duke of Damnation'. Inevitably the hot pursuit caused sharp French casualties too. Near Villafranca, where Moore took his final decision to make for Corunna, General Colbert, a member of the same family as Louis XIV's great minister and a brilliant young cavalry leader loaned by Ney to Soult, charged precipitately over a bridge and was killed by a sniper's bullet fired by Rifleman Tom Plunket. "I shall soon be decorating you," Napoleon had said earlier to the young Colbert. "Make haste Sire. I'm getting old!" was the reply. He was 29. Now it was too late.[22] Soult regarded his death as one of his most grievous losses.

On the high mountainous plateau of Lugo Moore finally turned and offered battle. It was January and at last it gave Soult a chance. He arrived at midday with his army in some confusion, partly because some of his older soldiers had dropped behind in the hectic onward march. With his habitual disregard of the problems of Spanish geography, Napoleon, writing to his brother Joseph at the time, remarked, "Soult ought to have reached Lugo long ago."[23] On arrival there and insisting as always on a personal reconnaissance, Soult advanced with some cavalry and artillery towards the British line hidden by mountains. When he opened fire with his field guns there was a sharp artillery response which confirmed that he was facing the British army in strength. After probing attacks on the enemy flanks he decided that he must await the arrival of Delaborde's division and, more importantly, for some support from Ney whose staff officers were still at his headquarters to provide the close liaison between the two marshals which the Emperor had decreed. Soult made a specific and urgent request to Ney to send Marchand's division to attack the British right. Soult's and Moore's armies were now about equal in strength but the British had the advantage of a strong defensive position and Soult, as has been said, was "certainly wise not to run his head directly against a brick wall".[24] All the next day he waited for reinforcements and for a supporting attack from Ney. But his old comrade was thoroughly uncooperative, alleging afterwards that Soult's request was not pitched strongly enough and that the roads were very difficult. On the following day Moore resumed his retreat. To have risked his whole army in an attack against the French would have been madness for him too. He left 500 wounded in hospital with some artillery and stores while many of his cavalry horses had to be destroyed. Describing all this in a letter to Ney, Soult still assumed that he would be reinforced by Marchand's division. He also suggested politely but firmly that the remainder of Ney's corps should make for Vigo, mopping up "the remnants of Romana's Spaniards", blocking the use of that port as a place of embarkation for the British and helping to guard the considerable number of prisoners that II Corps had already taken.[25] These various requests did not appeal to the prickly Ney.

For the British the last stage of the retreat from Lugo to Corunna by way of Betzanos was a real shambles. They lost in casualties and stragglers more than double the number of men that had fallen so far. Rifleman Harris describes an agonized exchange between a fellow rifleman and an officer as follows: "By Jesus, Musther Hills, where the divil are you taking us?" "To England," replied the officer with a gloomy smile. "That is if we can ever get there, Maclaughlin!".[26] Soult pressed the British hard but the pursuers were almost as weary as the pursued and Soult needed to bring up his whole available force with his artillery in order to try to destroy Moore's army before it could embark. In fact he was given four extra days

THE BATTLE OF CORUNNA

The scene at the height of the battle. The high ground from which Soult launched his artillery attack on the British ships during the following day is also shown.

1/1

Extrait du Registre des Batemes, mariages et enterremens de la paroisse de saint amans Labastide, District de Castres departement du tarn de l'année 1769.

Jean de dieu Soult, du present Lieu, fils du sieur jean Soult notaire [struck out] & de Demoiselle Brigitte de Granier mariés, a été Baptisé dans notre Eglise le vingt neuvieme de mars mil sept cent soixante neuf, etant né le meme jour, son parrain a été le sieur jean pierre Degranier son oncle & sa marraine demoiselle marie jeanne huc signés: jean pierre Degranier Mr. J. huc & Boubal curé signés au Registre.

Nous Secretaire-Greffier de la Commune de saint amans Labastide soussigné, Certifions avoir Extrait mot à mot Le Bateme ci dessus, sans y avoir Rien augmenté ni diminué, en foi de ce à saint amans le quatrieme janvier Mil sept cent quatre vingt treize l'an Second de la Republique française/

Gayzard sre greff.

Vu au directoire du district de castres [illegible] departement [illegible] le cinq janvier 1793 l'an second de la republique [illegible]

[illegible] Seyerac Olombelaine Rianly

Above: Soult's birth certificate. His baptismal name was Jean de Dieu; "Nicolas" was a rude nickname which stuck to him; it had no official authority.

Left: The stone house in the Grand Rue of St-Amans-Labastide where Soult was born. It was enlarged later and has now been divided into small apartments. (J. P. Escalettes)

Below left: Brigitte de Grenier, Soult's mother. The de Greniers were one of the celebrated families of "gentlemen glassmakers of the Tarn". Brigitte lived until her 90s and was much honoured by her son. There are numerous French and English descendants of the de Grenier family. (From "Sud", *Revue Mensuelle du Tarn* by Michel Bourgignon)

Below: Abbé Soult, the Marshal's uncle, an itinerant curé from whom Soult received his very modest book learning. (Michel Bourgignon)

Right: Soult as a young general in the Revolutionary armies.

Below, left and right: Louise Soult's parents. They had a respectable Rhineland industrial background. (The Stadtarchive of Solingen)

Left: Johanne Louise Berg, Soult's wife from the Rhineland. She was no great beauty, but Napoleon used to say that she "managed" her husband. Certainly she exercised much influence over him. (From *Rhein-Echo* of May 22, 1951)

Below left: Napoleon Hector Soult, the Marshal's only son, who succeeded him to become second Duke of Dalmatia. He was a distinguished diplomatist who edited his father's memoirs on the Revolutionary Wars. (Courtesy of the Comtesse de Guitaut)

Below: Hortense Soult, the Marshal's daughter. She married the Marquis de Mornay Montchevreuil. (Courtesy of the Comtesse de Guitaut)

Right: The château of Pont-de-Briques, Boulogne, Napoleon's headquarters. It has been said that "between the years 1803 and 1805 the heart of France beat within the walls of this small château". Now the Route Nationale, N1, sweeps past on either side of it. (From *Les Cahiers du Vieux Boulogne*)

Right: The Palais Imperial, Boulogne. Described as "a great lady in court dress adrift in a bourgeois environment", it was the home of the Vicomte Désandrouin, an enthusiastic supporter of the Revolution who willingly allowed it to be used as the military headquarters of Berthier and his staff. (From *Les Cahiers du Vieux Boulogne*)

Right: The Hotel Chanlaire, Boulogne, home of the Chanlaire family. This was Soult's headquarters, although he spent much of his time in the Pont-de-Briques and the Palais Imperial. The house has now been demolished to make way for a school.

Left: The old "fishermen's quarter" of Boulogne where the *camp droit* of Soult's army corps was established. It was badly damaged during the Second World War and demolished afterwards to make way for housebuilding.

Left: Models of the *chaloupes cannonières* in which Soult's army corps was to embark for its hazardous crossing of the Channel.

Below: A fierce engagement with a British naval squadron off Boulogne. (from the collection of P.-A. Wimet)

Right: The general-in-chief in Boulogne. Soult was made a Marshal of the Empire in the first promotion list in May 1804.

Below: The Chappe telegraph system. The end of the telegraph line in Boulogne after it was moved from the belfry tower to the city ramparts. Soult had to communicate with Paris at least twice a day in addition to the flood of written dispatches that he received from Napoleon.

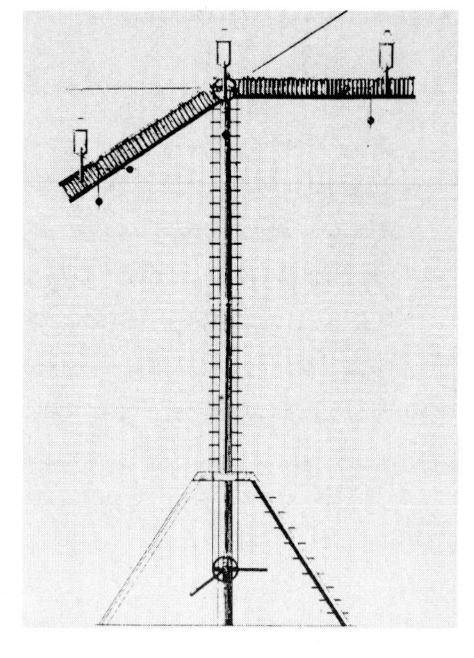

Below right: The Chappe telegraph system. The outside signal installation erected on Cap Gris Nez for transmitting messages to Dover Castle after England had been invaded.

Saint-Cloud, le 9 Floréal an 11 de la République française.

Citoyen général Soult, j'ai donné l'ordre au Ministre de la Marine de faire armer tous les bâtiments de transports d'avirons autant qu'ils peuvent en porter. faites moi connaître ce qui en est la quantité qu'il en faudra & les jours de travail qui seront nécessaires pour installer ces avirons.

Bonaparte

The avalanche of written orders, a high proportion of which came to Soult. Many of them are in Napoleon's published correspondence and there are other unpublished letters in the family archives or at St-Amans-Soult. Here are two typical letters in Napoleon's somewhat illegible writing.

Above: "St Cloud 9 Floreal Year XI, Citizen General Soult,
I have given orders to the Minister of Marine to equip the transport ships with as many oars as they can take. Let me know urgently how many are needed and how much work will be needed to provide them. Napoleon Bonaparte."

Below: "St Cloud 10 Germinal Year XIII, Cousin, [A]letter from Admiral Verhuel assures me that the port of Ambleteuse cannot take "sloop gun ships" because he claims that in[?] the inner basin[?] there is only five feet of water . . . Send me a report on this subject. There was certainly a tremendous "sanding up" this winter. I want everyone to work as hard as possible to dredge the harbour. Let me know how much "sanding up" there has been. It is infuriating that, six months ago, the harbour was full of water. God keep you in his holy care. Napoleon"

Mon cousin, une lettre de l'amiral Verhuell m'assure que le port d'Ambleteuse ne peut pas contenir de chaloupes canonnières, par ce qu'il prétend que dans les [illegible], il n'y a que cinq pieds d'eau. Transportez vous sur les lieux, & faites moi un rapport sur cet objet. Il y aurait donc eu un prodigieux ensablement cet hiver. mon intention est qu'on travaille avec la plus grande activité à creuser ce port. faites moi connaître de combien est cet ensablement; il me semble qu'il y avait beaucoup plus d'eau il y a six mois. Sur ce, je prie Dieu qu'il vous ait en sa sainte et digne garde. à St Cloud le 10 Germinal an XIII.

Napoleon

EMPIRE FRANÇAIS.

Au Quartier-général, à Calais
le 23 Germinal an 13.

SOULT, Maréchal de l'Empire,
Colonel-général de la Garde de S. M. l'Empereur, et Roi
Commandant en Chef le Camp de St.-Omer,

à Monsieur Devilliers commissaire Général de police
à Boulogne

Je vous envoye monsieur un raport qui vient de m'etre fait,
mettez du monde a la poursuite de l'individu qu'il concerne, nul
doute qu'il ne soit un agent anglais, depuis quelques jours
on remarque que beaucoup d'etrangers parlant cette langue —
sont passés par St Omer, ont pris la route de Gravelines, et se sont
ensuite rejetés sur Calais peut etre meme sur Boulogne. —
il convient de faire surveiller avec plus de soin que jamais
les environs du Port de Boulogne, envoyez aussi quelqu'un —
chez Sauvage à Neufchatel. Tout le monde est prevenu
à Calais, je donne le meme avis au commandant de la
Gendarmerie instruisez moi du resultat de vos recherches —

J'ai l'honneur de vous saluer

Soult

Above: Soult's Orders. These are equally numerous but are unpublished. Part of a typical order relating to a suspected British agent written from Calais, demonstrating that Soult's authority extended all along the Channel coast.

Above: The Column of the Grand Armée – a great public relations exercise. In the huge plaque on the base of the column Soult presents the design to the Emperor. (Claude Sarazin)

Left: "The first tactician in Europe." Marshal Soult at the time of Austerlitz, Jena and Eylau.

Right: A bust of Soult which did not in the end form part of the column. (Claude Sarazin)

Below: Unpublished letters from Napoleon to Soult testify to the importance the Emperor attached to the detailed information with which the Marshal supplied him and to Soult's administrative ability. A typical example: Military movements leading up to Austerlitz "Schöbrunn 24 Brumaire, Cousin,
I have had your letter. Continue to send me information. Strongly support the manoeuvres of Prince Murat. Bernadotte must provide support too. St-Hilaire [commanding one of Soult's divisions] must remain here until tomorrow. So as to lose no time I have sent Cafarelli's division to Stokerau. St-Hilaire's division must stay here until tomorrow. God protect you. Napoleon. St-Hilaire will arrive at the same time by a forced march."

Mon cousin, j'ai reçu votre lettre. Continuez à me donner des renseignemens. appuyez ferme les mouvemens du Prince Murat. Bernadotte doit appuyer aussi. St Hilaire restera ici que demain à midi. pour ne pas perdre un moment, j'ai envoyé la division Caffarelli à Stokerau; car il faudra que la division St Hilaire reste la journée de demain ici. Sur ce je prie Dieu qu'il vous ait en sa sainte et digne garde.

Napole

St Hilaire arrive à l'heure même à force de marche

Schonbrunn le 24 brumaire à 3 heures après midi.

Above: The capture of Burgos. Soult's first action in the Peninsular War, years after taking over command of II Corps. Soult is directing his troops with Lobau, one of his divisional generals. (Cover of the St-Pierres' publication of Soult's *Memoirs of the Spanish and Portuguese War*)

Below: The battle of Corunna from the French side. "Soult was always at the head of his troops". (From the portrait in the grand salon of the château of Soultberg)

Right: The battle of Corunna from the British side.

Right: The "Corunna Walk", 1983/4. This took place 175 years after Sir John Moore's famous retreat, hotly pursued by Marshal Soult. Beside Moore's tomb are Rifleman K. P. McNish, L/Cpl T. O'Meara, Captain C. D. Blackmore, Rifleman J. I. Hayward and Rifleman S. Pearce. (Major Blackmore)

Right: The plaque commemorating Sir John Moore unveiled by Captain Blackmore on a new building in Corunna in the presence of distinguished Spanish and British representatives. (Major Blackmore)

Left: Marshal Soult at the time of his invasion of Portugal; a print used 22 years later when he was King Louis Philippe's Minister of War.

Below: The storming of Oporto by Soult's army.

PORTUGAIS.

LEs habitans de la Province d'entre Douro et Minho viennent d'assurer leur indépendance, leur liberté et leur prosperité future; ils ont déclaré que la Maison de Bragance, qui depuis 17 mois a abandonné sa Patrie et l'a laissée en proie à l'anarchie et aux déchiremens d'une guerre civile, était déchüe du Trône; en même tems ils ont exprimé le voeu que S. M. l'Empereur et Roi, le Grand Napoleon designât à son choix un Prince pour regner en Portugal, sous sa Suprême Protection, lui jurant d'avance fidelité, obeissance et dévoûement, et promettant de faire, s'il le faut, les plus grands sacrifices pour obliger les autres Provinces qui ne se sont pas encore prononcées a adhérer à leur voeu et à se soumettre.

Il appartenait à la premiere Province du Portugal que la nature a si heureusement partagée, et qui forme à elle seule le quart de la population du Royaume, sur tout aux Villes de Braga et d'O-Porto, l'une la plus ancienne Métropole des Espagnes, et l'autre une de plus importantes Villes de Commerce, en même tems qu'elle est la Capitale des Provinces du Nord, d'exprimer les premieres un voeu si conforme aux interêts de la Nation entiere, et que de toute part on s'empresse d'imiter; ainsi leurs habitans acquérent la gloire d'être les liberateurs de leur patrie comme ils en seront toujours les plus fermes appuis. Portugais, hâtez vous de suivre cet exemple et unissez vous a eux d'actions et de sentiments pour que les contrées les plus éloignées du Royaume participent à cet heureux bienfait. Désormais plus de guerre, la paix doit regner par tout, et chacun reprendre ses travaux accoutumés; ce serait un sacrilege, le plus grand des crimes, s'il se trouvait encore des hommes assez aveugles et assez ennemis de leur Patrie qui voulussent perpétuer les troubles et tourner les armes contre leurs Concitoyens, qui sous la foi des serments les plus sacrés, renoncent sincerement à leurs erreurs passées, et veulent à tout prix soutenir le Gouvernement juste et libéral qu'ils ont reconnu, et qui seul peut et doit faire leur bonheur.

Portugais, je porterai au pied du Trône de l'Empereur l'expression du voeu que vous venez d'émettre, et vous ne devez pas douter que S. M. qui, en m'envoyant parmi vous, n'a eu en vuë que votre indépendance et la prosperité future du Portugal, ne le prenne en trés grande consideration; mais en attendant que ses Suprêmes intentions soient connûes, comme Gouverneur Général du Royaume, j'accepte en son nom les serments que vous avez faits et les obligations qu'ils vous imposent; malheur à celui qui y manquera: Je veillerai à votre bonheur, et je ne négligerai aucun soin pour que la tranquillité, l'ordre et la confiance se rétablissent par tout: + Notre Sainte Religion, qui est tous les jours insultée par des hérétiques, que ceux qui vous gouvernaient précédemment avaient appellés à leur secours et non au votre; + notre Sainte Religion qui a tant souffert pendant vos malheurs, sera particulièrement protegée et elle brillera d'un nouvel éclat: Des institutions bienfaisantes seront créées, et des Lois justes, mais sévères, que je saurai faire éxécuter, veilleront à la protection des Citoyens paisibles et bien intentionnés; elles encourageront les entreprises utiles, récompenseront les bons services, ainsi que les actions généreuses et méritantes, en même tems qu'elles assureront la punition des coupables qui porteraient le trouble dans la societé; mais à votre tour vous serez obéissants, fidéles et disposés à faire tous les sacrifices qui seraient nécéssaires pour assurer la prompte soumission des contrées où malheureusement il régne encore des troubles, et où il existe des rassemblemens, vous contribuerez enfin au maintien de la paix et à la répréssion du Brigandage. Vous défendrez de toute insulte les Ministres de la Religion et vos Magistrats; vous payerez les impôts avec exactitude, et vous ne tournerez vos vues que vers ce qui peut être utile à la Patrie, et approuvé par les Lois.

J'ai arrêté au Nom de l'Empereur que dans toutes les Villes du Royaume, il serait formé une Garde Nationale; son organisation ne saurait être trop prompte, puisqu'elle a pour objet d'assurer le maintien de l'ordre et le repos des familles: Portugais, vous montrerez du Patriotisme en vous empressant d'entrer dans les rangs de cette garde et en vous montrant toujours dignes d'en faire partie, des distinctions et des honneurs seront la récompense de ceux qui les auront mérités.

J'ai aussi arrêté qu'il serait formé des Légions pour la défense de la Patrie; la premiere doit s'organiser à O-Porto, sous la dénomination de *Legion du Douro*, et les autres successivement: Tous les Militaires qui servaient précédemment dans les Régiments de Ligne des trois Provinces du Nord, sont appellés pour faire partie de la premiere. Ce serait un crime qui emporterait punition exemplaire si on hésitait à s'y rendre; si malgré l'appel qui sera fait, il était des Militaires qui refusassent leurs services; à present sur tout qu'un nouvel ordre de choses s'établit, et qu'il s'agit de l'honneur, de la défense et de la prosperité de la Patrie; le Clerge, les Chefs de famille et tous les bons Citoyens doivent eux mêmes veiller à ce que cette disposition s'accomplisse, et assurer de notre part qu'il ne s'agit aucunement de porter des Portugais à s'expatrier; mais de les faire tous participer à la gloire nationale en assimilant ceux qui seront admis, aux mêmes honneurs et avantages dont jouissent les Troupes Imperiales Françaises, les premieres du Monde.

D'autres mesures seront aussi prises, j'ai la confiance que vous en serez les soutiens; aujourd'hui le regne des Lois commence, aussi plus d'anarchie ni d'excés quelconques, soumission, fidélité, dévouement et obéissance, voila vos devoirs; je les exigerai de tous avec la volonté determinée de les faire remplir.

L'Armée Imperiale que j'ai l'honneur de commander, que vous avez vue si terrible sur le champ de bataille, ne sera plus pour vous qu'une Armée amie, et alliée, protégeant vos personnes et vos proprietés, et respectant vos Lois, ainsi que vos usages. Vous n'aurez plus à craindre des vexations, du moment que la tranquillité sera par tout retablie, et que par vos soins la subsistance des Troupes sera assurée. Votre cause est la sienne; en entrant sur votre Territoire elle avait pour objet de vous rendre votre liberté et de vous préserver d'une ruine entiere, effet inévitable de l'état d'anarchie qui regnait parmi vous: à présent les intérets se confondent et nous devons tous marcher au même but; cette armée vous protegera contre toute aggression étrangere et contre vos ennemis interieurs. Vous devez la seconder et ne pas vous borner à une admiration sterile puisqu'il s'agit de vos interêts les plus chers. Elle devient aujourd'hui le *Palladium* de votre existence politique. Elle vous rendra parmi les Nations le rang que vous devez y tenir, et qu'ont voulu vous faire perdre ces auxiliaires impuissants, qui sous le saint nom d'alliés tiennent garnison dans votre Capitale et prétendent y faire la Loi; /mais ils ne perdent pas de vue et le Port et les vaisseaux, qui seront, comme à la Corogne leur dernier azile, quand ils auront répandu un peu d'or et beaucoup de maux dans votre belle Patrie; / que notre union soit leur desespoir, que le Prince qui le premier a élevé une barriere eternelle entre vous et lui, et vous a dégagé de vos serments, en portant sa nullité au de là des mers, apprenne qu'une Armée Française est en Portugal, une Armée de liberateurs et d'amis; qu'une réconciliation franche et loyale nous rapproche, comme des hommes qui n'ont pas cessé de s'estimer, et qui désormais confondent leurs interêts et leurs voeux.

On a commis contre des Militaires Français des assassinats et des horreurs inouies; mais a qui doit-on les imputer? C'est à des hommes qui dans tous les Pays sont la honte du genre humain; des vils scélérats, dont on avait brisé les fers, sans songer en leur remettant des armes, qu'il n'en fallait pas davantage pour déshonorer la cause qu'on voulait défendre; la justice en fera raison, les honnêtes gens les signaleront, les poursuivront comme des bêtes féroces: ils n'échaperont pas à leur destinée; partout ils trouveront des échafauds, le glaive de la justice et la mort. La Nation frémit des crimes qui ont été commis, elle les désavoue, mais pour s'en absoudre entierement elle doit elle même les prévenir par la suite.

Si les Militaires que je commande donnaient lieu à quelques plaintes, qu'on s'adresse avec confiance au premier Général, au premier Officier Français; les plaignants seront accueillis et ils recevront prompte satisfaction: Les habitants de Braga et d'O-Porto le savent, et se plaisent tous les jours à le repetter.

Mais, Portugais, gardez vous de vous rendre justice vous mêmes, le crime reçoit tôt ou tard la peine qui lui est due; je n'en laisserai point d'impunis; évitez de nouveaux malheurs; concourez vous même à l'ouvrage de votre prosperité dont je m'occupe sans cesse, et que nous achevrons ensemble si vous me secondez. Fait à O-Porto au Palais du Gouvernement le 26 Avril 1809.

(*Signé*) LE MARECHAL DUC DE DALMATIE.
De par S. E. Monseigneur le Gouverneur Général de Portugal.
L'Auditeur au Conseil d'Etat Secrétaire des Commandemens
Am. Taboureau.

PORTO: NA TYPOGRAPHIA DE ANTONIO ALVAREZ RIBEIRO.

Above: One of Soult's proclamations to the people of Portugal, unexeceptionable so far as Napoleon was concerned. (Archives of the château of Epoisses)

Ma Cousine, j'ai reçu votre lettre du 14 janvier. Je
suis faché des mauvais bruits que des avocats brouillons ont
fait courir sur votre mari. Je n'ai jamais eu qu'à me louer
du zèle qu'il a montré pour mon service et des preuves d'attachement
qu'il m'a données. La présente n'étant à autre fin, je
prie Dieu qu'il vous ait en sa sainte et digne garde.
À Paris le 20 janvier 1810.

N

À Ma Cousine
La Marechale Duchesse de
Dalmatie.

Above: Napoleon's letter of reassurance to Louise Soult over reports of her husband's alleged treason. "Cousin, I have received your letter. I was annoyed at the bad rumours which pedlars of mischief have circulated about your husband. I have never had anything but praise for the enthusiasm which he has shown for my service and for the proofs of loyalty which he has given me. I pray that God will keep you in his holy care. Paris 20 January 1810. Napoleon." (Archives of the château of Epoisses)

Below: Part of Jomini's letter to Soult's son giving his views on Soult after the Marshal's death. "I much regret never to have known the Marshal whom I saw for the first time at Lucerne in Switzerland when he was defending my country against the Austrians . . . of all the Emperor's lieutenants it was with him that I would have got on best (as well as Massena) and I would have been happy to have gained his confidence but chance separated us . . ." (Archives of the château of Epoisses)

J'ai beaucoup regretté de n'avoir pas été Connu de Mr le Marechal
que j'ai vu pour la 1ère fois à Lucerne en Suisse en 1799: alors
qu'il defendait mon pays Contre les Autrichiens. j'étais un
Chef de bataillon de 20 ans mais je songeais déjà aux grandes
operations de la guerre Car 3 ans après je Commençais mon premier
Traité. De tous les Lieutenants de l'Empereur C'était je crois
celui avec lequel je me serais le mieux entendu (ainsi que Massena)
et j'eusse été heureux d'avoir sa Confiance. Le Sort m'en a toujours éloigné

because unfavourable winds had delayed the arrival of the British transports.

Although the hills around Corunna offered strong possibilities for defence, some of Moore's generals were so dispirited that they suggested that the prudent course would be to reach a sort of embarkation truce with the French – a kind of Cintra Convention in reverse. But it is inconceivable that the realistic Soult would have accepted anything other than unconditional surrender. So a battle was inevitable. Again the full cooperation of one of Ney's divisions would almost certainly have resulted in the annihilation of the British. Assuming that this full support was being given – or perhaps even for more malevolent reasons – Berthier had held up the march of another of Soult's divisions, Heudelet's, while Bonnet's division was still stationed in Santander. The presence of these two divisions must have brought victory to the French since they would have greatly outnumbered the British. As it was, the two armies were about equal in strength.

Soult's expert eye had quickly seen that the French tactic must be to drive the British as far away as possible from the harbour of Corunna, their main embarkation point, and towards the River Brugo to the north. He therefore put his strongest forces – a mixed division of infantry and cavalry under General Mermet – on his left facing the village of Elvina, which was the obvious key to the whole British position. He had somewhat weaker forces under Merle in the centre while Delaborde's division, which had finally joined him at Lugo, was on his right.

Soult waited to open his attack until he had brought up his heavy artillery – a laborious task on atrocious Spanish roads. He had also to rebuild the bridge over the River Mero at El Burgo, heroically destroyed by a British engineer officer who blew himself up in the process. He then launched a heavy artillery barrage which caused considerable British casualties. Meanwhile his light cavalry, under Franceschi, ranged around the British positions on the right of their line. But the really decisive place of action was the village of Elvina. Its solidly built houses and church buildings offered the British strong defensive positions with an excellent field of fire. Preceded by their customary cloud of *tirailleurs*, Mermet's French division made a violent assault on the village. Charles Napier, the historian's younger brother, described the rapid advance of the French with their loud battle cries – "En avant! Tuez! En avant! Tuez!"[27] Using their system of attack which had been so successful against the Austrians and Prussians, the French suffered from the very accurate British musket fire poured into their compact columns from strong positions in the village. However, Mermet's division finally succeeded in capturing Elvina, enabling the French cavalry to spread out more widely, seizing the village of San Cristobal on the right flank of the British line. Moore ordered a vigorous counter-attack with his reserves under Lord Paget: Elvina was recaptured and a tremendous slogging match took place among the stone walls and sunken roads with which the whole area is covered. It was during these violent exchanges that Sir John Moore was fatally wounded. The village of Elvina was captured and recaptured at intervals during the day while the French divisions of Merle and Delaborde made strong supporting attacks on the remainder of the British line. By nightfall Elvina was still in British hands and, although casualties were about equal on both sides, the plain fact was that Soult had failed to destroy the enemy.

By now the rescuing ships had arrived and during the night of January 16 British embarkation slowly took place. According to the French military historian, Lejeune, never at a loss for a picturesque phrase, Corunna was "an ant-hill of indescribable confusion".[28] Thwarted in his main objective, Soult had some of his heaviest artillery dragged up on to the heights of San Lucia overlooking the harbour and opened an intense fire on the British ships. Four transports went aground but the troops were mostly rescued by the men-of-war. An indication of French annoyance at their lack of complete success was given by Brun de Villeret, Soult's aide-de-camp, who refers sardonically to the "magnificent sight" of the English rescue fleet sailing off while the efforts of the French artillery to stop them were "like La Fontaine's fabled hares squirting water on the millions of frogs in front of them!"[29]

Among the officers initially left behind was Charles Napier who had been wounded in the face at Elvina and left for dead. Soult saw him and had him put into a French ambulance to be looked after by his own doctor. When Soult left for the invasion of Portugal, he handed Napier over to Ney's corps and he was finally returned to England to fight another day.[30] From then onwards the three fighting Napier brothers developed a great personal regard for Soult.

Corunna surrendered immediately after the departure of the British and Soult followed this up by capturing the big Spanish naval base and arsenal at Ferrol. The British had hoped to hold on to Ferrol with a naval squadron but in the aftermath of Corunna the Spaniards surrendered to their old allies of Trafalgar, the French, and the admiral-in-charge became a supporter of King Joseph.

So ended the first campaign in Galicia. In the final stages Soult had led his army pell-mell from the Carrión to Corunna, a distance of 400 kilometres across terrible mountain ranges and in the most ghastly winter weather, in pursuit of an enemy army which had left desolation in its wake. In their retreat the British had lost over 4,000 men, most of their cavalry horses and artillery: 500 horses were captured but the remainder had had to be killed – a loss that was to be severely felt later in the Peninsular War. The army also lost most of its ammunition and stores. On the other hand, through Moore's skilful handling of the retreat and of the final battle, the British army had been saved.

How far should Soult be blamed for letting the British escape? Should he have pressed his pursuing veterans even harder than he did? Thiers, never his friend, concedes that he could hardly have moved faster but adds rather sourly that the Emperor's departure from the army to return to Paris, leaving Soult in charge, was a great misjudgement. However, given the difficulty of the terrain and the stalwart conduct of some of the British, it is by no means certain that Napoleon would have succeeded where Soult failed. In his *Memoirs* Soult, without any malice, takes the line that, deprived of effective support from Ney and in the absence of two of his divisions held back on garrison duties in Santander and León, he had no real chance of fighting a victorious campaign. He also claims that, in the circumstances, Corunna was more of an 'armed reconnaissance' than a full-scale battle. There is some special pleading here. In reporting the battle immediately afterwards to the Emperor, Soult gave a faithful account of what had happened, causing Jourdan, King Joseph's chief of staff, to observe spitefully that his dispatch was not that of a general who had been successful.

This was Soult's first major independent command. What were the immediate and the long-term results? It is sometimes suggested that Moore's advance and retreat had disrupted Napoleon's overall strategy of invading southern Spain and Portugal. Yet, within a year, Soult himself was to conquer most of southern Spain and had established himself as a virtual viceroy in the whole of the south. The rather pathetic 'Beau' Cradock still commanded in Lisbon, but it was Moore's own considered opinion before his death that further British military operations in the Peninsula were hopeless. Many of the political leaders in London agreed with him. Although the British army had been saved, it arrived home in a terrible state. A storm had scattered the fleet of transports so that the weary troops were landed everywhere on the English coast from Dover to Land's End. Their haggard appearance, ragged uniforms and filthy accoutrements were a kind of tribute to their heroism but there was no doubt they were a beaten army. At first sight, therefore, it seemed that, despite his ill success at Corunna, Soult's offensive had delivered the *coup de grâce* against the British. The operation had come at an important psychological moment for the French. Everywhere, in spite of the Emperor's departure, they had regained the initiative. Saragossa, despite its heroic resistance, was soon to be captured: Marshal Victor was thrusting south after his victory at Ucles; and slow if steady progress was being made on the east coast, with Suchet the most successful of the French commanders. The Spaniards felt that they had been badly let down by their British allies. Before he returned to Paris, Napoleon could claim that the disgraceful events which had begun with the surrender at Baylen had now been avenged. As Savary recorded in his *Memoirs*, the Emperor happened to hear the news of the British evacuation of Corunna just after he had had a very sharp encounter with some of the senior French officers involved in the Baylen affair. He grinned with sardonic satisfaction when he heard what Soult had accomplished.[31] In a letter to his brother, Joseph, he commented: "It is a good experience for the Spaniards to see an English army in such a state of disarray."[32] Now it simply remained for the rest of Spain and Portugal to be subdued against 'ineffective' national armies and for the small British force in Lisbon to be eliminated. Not for the first time, Napoleon had greatly underestimated Spanish and Portuguese national pride and the widespread activities of the guerrillas in both countries. Above all, so far completely unforeseen, there was to be the arrival of Sir Arthur Wellesley.

As a footnote to the hard fought contest between Soult and Moore it is right to record that there was much vocal criticism of Moore's generalship in London both in Parliament and even in the army itself. But his opponent, Soult, commented quite differently. He put up a memorial in Latin at the place where Moore was fatally wounded and, writing to his friend Napier years later, he said: "I should like to emphasize that Sir John Moore's military dispositions were the best that could have been made. Everywhere he fought me vigorously and skilfully, finding a glorious death in the midst of a battle which does honour to his memory."[33] In the contest between these two tough and rather similar adversaries it was the 'Duke of Damnation' who paid one of the most generous tributes to Moore's memory.

It is interesting to note that when in 1983-4 the Royal Green Jackets enacted in the full uniform of the period the famous march from Sahagun to Corunna they found conditions in the mountains of Galicia for both the pursuers and the pursued quite as severe as their heroic forbears in 1808-9.[34]

7

"KING NICOLAS" – FACT OR FANTASY?

THE NEXT FOUR MONTHS cover the first of many of the crises in Soult's military and political life. In January 1809 he was still 'the faithful Soult' who had not, admittedly, annihilated the latest British expeditionary force to the continent of Europe but had sent it packing with heavy losses and in total disarray. In May he was to lead his own army back from Portugal in similar disarray after being driven out of the country by a highly skilled opponent. He was also the victim of suspicion and calumny after a mysterious and potentially dangerous military conspiracy. It was an extraordinary transformation.

Immediately after Corunna he had received from Berthier very precise orders about the next stage of the campaign to conquer Portugal and the rest of Spain as well as to eliminate the remaining British forces in the Peninsula. "Let us carry our eagles to the Pillars of Hercules and get rid of the hideous leopard that contaminates the whole Peninsula" was Napoleon's euphoric description of what Soult and the other marshals were expected to do. At the moment it was Soult who was required to play the leading role. He was to conquer Portugal with a corps now numbering four infantry divisions commanded respectively by Merle, Mermet, Delaborde and Heudelet, two heavy cavalry divisions under Lorge and Lahoussaye, and light cavalry under Franceschi. This gave him a force of seventeen infantry regiments and ten cavalry regiments, nominally about 50,000 men. Taking account of losses in the Corunna campaign and the sick and wounded, his strength was between 20,000 and 30,000. They were mostly veterans of the Grande Armée – very different from the scratch force of second-line troops with which Junot, assisted by the Spaniards, had captured Lisbon the year before. In addition General Loison – the one-armed 'Le Tondu' – and some staff and engineer officers including thirteen Portuguese officers who had served with Junot were added to provide local experience. In the case of Loison this reinforcement turned out to be very much a mixed blessing. Soult was assured by Berthier that the Emperor had the fullest confidence in his ability to carry out this very important operation.[1]

His invasion force was part of a 'master plan'. Victor, the plump ex-sergeant major who had been made a marshal after Friedland, was to operate on the Spanish-Portuguese border in the Merida area so as to support Soult's advance on Lisbon. Victor was then required, with Soult's help, to march south and conquer all the rest of Spain. There was to be another diversion by the advance into north-east Portugal of a division commanded by Lapisse – part of Bessière's army that was now responsible for north-western Spain except for Galicia. In Galicia, Romana and the guerrillas were fighting an almost independent war; against them Ney struggled ineffectively. All these instructions came through Berthier from Napoleon himself. When, followed by Berthier, the Emperor left for Paris, King Joseph and his major general, Jourdan, had been given nominal command of all French forces in Spain but his responsibility for Soult's army corps in Portugal was ambiguous. This vague control from Madrid added to the many problems facing Soult and the other marshals.

Soult had been given a ridiculously tight timetable. He was expected to reach Oporto by February 5 and Lisbon by February 16, causing the publisher of Soult's *Memoirs* – but not Soult himself – to assert that Berthier had manufactured a totally unrealistic schedule which Soult could not possibly follow.[2] It seemed to be based on the assumption that he would have a mere military promenade. Jourdan commented that Napoleon "must have supposed that the road was as freely passable as that from Paris to Lyons!"[3] In the event it soon became clear that Soult would have to fight hard.

His first task was to give his desperately weary and often barefooted men a few days' rest for which there was no provision whatever in Berthier's timetable. Soult was a tough fighting soldier, not a superior staff officer like Berthier, and he had a lot of arduous work to do. After its hectic march to Corunna his army was very poorly clad and equipped. His munitions and supplies for the onward march into Portugal would have to come from British stocks captured in Ferrol and soon most of his army was clad in British army greatcoats. He finally cleared matters up in Ferrol and Vigo, handing over his conquests to the unappreciative Ney and only reaching the flooded banks of the River Minho, the frontier between Spain and Portugal, in the middle of February. By this time, according to Berthier, he should almost have reached Lisbon; but he knew enough about the realities of warfare and was confident enough of his own professional relationship with the Emperor to treat ill devised timetables in a practical way.

Almost at once he was in difficulties. He had hoped to cross the torrential Minho at the mouth since a reasonably good coastal road led from there to Oporto. He had brought fishing boats with him and he sent an advance party of men across the river as he had done so successfully across the Linth in Switzerland. The flooded river made this operation impossible. Several men were drowned and others were taken prisoner by a strongly entrenched Portuguese force of militia and armed civilians. There was now no alternative to a river crossing much higher up, which meant using the terrible mountain roads inside Portugal and leaving behind the heavy guns. It also entailed renewed fighting with the irrepressible Romana in Spain. Once more Soult tried to destroy Romana although the real responsibility for this was now Ney's. The guerrillas blocked the way to the Minho from the north. As

Franceschi, Soult's cavalry commander, commented: "Romana creates an army. When his voice is heard the whole population rises in arms. When one marches against him he escapes. When one returns he returns!"[4] Finally, leaving more of his heavy artillery and a small garrison at Tuy under Lamartinière, Soult got his army across the Minho near Chaves. He was entering Portugal again five months after Junot had left the country. At Chaves he established a base hospital and did his best to conciliate the townsfolk despite strong advice from Loison and the other 'old Portuguese hands' to take a strong line.

By now his timetable had slipped by over a month and marching south-west over narrow mountain roads to the old cathedral city of Braga he met with strong Portuguese resistance. Much to the surprise of the French, this came from some recently raised Portuguese units well provided with artillery and helped by swarms of militia and armed peasants. Mermet's and Delaborde's veteran divisions, with Heudelet marching on their right, and supported by Lahoussaye's dragoons and Franceschi's light cavalry, had great difficulty in forcing their way forward. When Soult finally entered Braga he found the whole city deserted. Freire, the governor, who was accused of being a French supporter, had been murdered and his corpse, half eaten by pigs, lay in the main square. Some of the Portuguese prisoners, who had been released carrying proclamations from Soult promising a new regime of freedom and reform, were similarly massacred. A *corregidor* from the neighbouring town of Barceles who had held office for some 30 years and was greatly respected, came to Braga assuring Soult of his own and the town's submission but he was promptly murdered by those whom Soult now described as the "fanatical leaders of the insurrection". All in all it took some days to restore a semblance of order in Braga. Characteristically – and for political rather than devotional reasons – one of Soult's first acts was to attend, with his whole staff, High Mass in Braga Cathedral – the primacy cathedral of the whole of Portugal.[5]

Obviously the French had seriously underestimated the scale of Portuguese resistance. Their lack of military intelligence in the face of an initially hostile population was threatening to be as serious in Portugal as it was already becoming in Spain. It was a sharp reflection on the advice given by Loison and the other so-called French and Portuguese 'experts' who had been with Junot's army the previous year. Particular blame attaches to 'Le Tondu' – or 'Maneta' (the 'one-armed one') as he was contemptuously called by the Portuguese – since it was the cruelties perpetrated by him personally and by his division which had aroused much of the hatred that the Portuguese country folk felt for the French. On the other hand, at least until they had served for some time in Wellington's Peninsular army, the Portuguese regulars were more enthusiastic than effective. Many of the senior officers had escaped with the Braganza royal family to Brazil. The army had lost many other men when Junot invaded Portugal and Junot had also succeeded in sending to France some of the best of those who remained in a force of three infantry and some small cavalry regiments which served in the French army for the rest of the war.[6] Ensign

Aitchison of the Third Foot Guards probably reflects first impressions by British officers of the Portuguese army. He wrote, "Their army consists of weak men and mere boys. In contrast to the peasantry who detest the French there is a great want of exertion in the army's higher ranks."[7]

Soult had quickly realized that the key to the Portuguese situation was not so much the regular army as the civil population. If, as he had tried to do in other countries, he could win over the official and wealthy elements, even some of the priests, he might be able to build up a sizeable French party in the country. The British connection remained important. Charles Beresford, the tough, one-eyed illegitimate son of an Irish peer, so cordially disliked by the historian Napier, had been given a Portuguese command and Robert Wilson, the "slippery fellow", as Wellington called him, had formed a Lusitanian Legion composed of Portuguese irregulars. But the Convention of Cintra, allowing Junot's army to return freely to France, had dismayed many Portuguese and the main British military presence in the capital was provided by the pessimistic 'Beau' Cradock whose orders were to service the British base until it was abandoned! Indeed he was in almost as isolated a position in Lisbon as Junot had been the year before. The British admiral in the Tagus was of the opinion that the British must evacuate the country as soon as the French had effectively occupied a large part of it.

It was against this background that Soult, as he advanced, inundated the country with proclamations of goodwill, promising happiness and prosperity once the country had been freed from the British yoke. Since the departure of the Braganzas independent juntas had been set up all over Portugal and Soult endeavoured to conciliate those in the north. The tenor of his proclamations would have been fully approved by Napoleon.

Leaving Heudelet to hold Braga, Soult now prepared to advance on Oporto. The bishop, Antonio de Castro, was virtually the city's ruler and a tyrant. He was a member of the council of regency which formally governed Portugal after the departure of the Braganzas but the royal family was not much loved in Oporto; there was intense rivalry between Oporto and Lisbon and, although the bishop appealed to the British for help after the fall of Braga, his own Oporto junta was not recognized even by the British despite their strong commercial ties with the city. In fact the bishop, whom Robert Wilson described as "an old woman", greatly disliked too much British involvement in the loyal Lusitanian Legion. All this gave Soult the chance to play some political cards.

He sent the bishop a long letter urging him to help calm down the popular excitement and discuss proposals which could turn him into one of the liberators of his country, ensuring the warm friendship of Napoleon. When no reply came he wrote similarly to the city authorities. General Foy, who could speak some Portuguese, was sent to act as intermediary but was taken prisoner and only saved himself from the death for which men, women and children clamoured by holding up both his hands to show that he was not the detested 'Maneta'. A Portuguese general who favoured negotiations was murdered by agents of the bishop so by now there was obviously no alternative to launching a full-scale attack on the city. Accordingly the divisions of Merle, Mermet and Delaborde – the same generals who had fought the English at Corunna – converged on Oporto and, with their loud battle cries of "Napoleon and Glory", fought slowly through the city street by street until they reached the big pontoon bridge over the Douro. Fighting their way across the bridge, they finally established themselves in the suburb of Villanova on the left bank. The bishop had fled and his cavalry, trampling a bloody pathway to the river as they desperately tried to escape, beat down and killed many Portuguese civilians who were also trying to cross the bridge. Some of the bishop's soldiers held out bravely in his palace for a time but when it was at last captured all resistance in the city ceased.

There followed a hideous wave of reprisals and counter-reprisals. General Foy was rescued unhurt but many French prisoners had been badly mutilated while pro-French Portuguese like the unfortunate General d'Oliveira had been torn to pieces in the streets. It had been a case of total conflict with even priests and consuls of neutral countries having to man the city's defences. Infuriated by the excesses committed against their own countrymen, the French soldiers avenged themselves upon the local inhabitants and, as Soult admits in his *Memoirs,* the 'sack of Oporto' became notorious.[8] It was again characteristic of both sides in this bloody war. Later historians have judged some of the stories to have been exaggerated; they certainly lost nothing in the telling by either side. However, despite the destruction, churches and monasteries were generally respected; there were many cases of French soldiers protecting the townsfolk or sharing their rations with them and it was certainly true that Oporto returned quite quickly to reasonable tranquillity under French rule.

Soult's victory had been overwhelming. The Portuguese had lost some 10,000 men, including those drowned in the river. Nearly 200 guns and vast supplies of ammunition were also seized. As French ammunition supplies had almost run out Soult simply had to win the battle. Additionally about 30 English ships loaded with wine and other supplies were captured in the harbour. In comparison, French losses amounted to no more than 80 killed and 300 wounded. A serious loss in the earlier fighting was that of General Jardan, a man – like the youthful Colbert – after Soult's heart, who practically lived with his brigade and whose family Soult at once commended to the Emperor in a personal letter.

Soult captured Oporto in March 1809. Then for the next one and a half months he was to be involved in some of the most dramatic and indeed mysterious events in his whole career.

An intelligence blackout had once more descended on him but with his customary energy he proceeded to make all the necessary military arrangements. He had the pontoon bridge over the Douro rebuilt and Franceschi carried out long-range reconnaissances in the direction of Coimbra, supported by Mermet's infantry division stationed on the left bank of the Douro. Meanwhile, anxious about his communications with the north, Soult ordered Heudelet to fight his way back to the Minho and re-establish links with Lamartinière on the Galician side of the river in Tuy. Soult had then to decide on his next move.

In his *Memoirs* he carefully analyzes three possible alternatives.[9] The first and most obvious choice was to march straight on Lisbon in accordance with his orders; there was a reasonable road along the coast by way of Coimbra. The regency council in the capital was a shambles; the British position in Portugal was highly uncertain with Cradock assuring Robert Wilson that the government would not send another army to the country; and in the aftermath of the courts-martial that had resulted from the ill-starred Convention of Cintra, government opinion in London was very much divided. Thiébault, Soult's incessant critic, who was now well placed as a malevolent observer and gossip dispenser as governor of the base headquarters in Burgos, was quite emphatic that Soult should have done this.[10] An unbiased commentator, the Portuguese historian, Pinheiro Chagas, described his delay as "inexplicable. If he had marched immediately on Lisbon he would not have encountered any Portuguese troops capable of resisting him and Cradock's forces would probably have embarked immediately."[11]

On the other hand, for a serious professional soldier with a considerable political flair the contrary arguments were strong. His orders to march on Lisbon had been given when Portuguese resistance was thought to be minimal. It was quite plain that this assessment was grossly mistaken. Nor was Junot's previous experience greatly encouraging. He had certainly occupied Lisbon but he had been virtually isolated there while the cruelties perpetrated by Loison and other generals inflamed the Portuguese against the French. Soult considered that to carry on south without leaving in Oporto, a city of 80,000 inhabitants, an adequate garrison would be madness. Heudelet's division was defending the lines of communication with Tuy, so that a strike force available for an onslaught on the capital could be far too small. He was also entirely without information about any supporting moves either by Victor or Lapisse which were essential parts of Napoleon's overall strategy. In fact no messages got through to him either from Madrid or Paris throughout his entire time in Portugal. His previous experiences of King Joseph and of Jourdan did not encourage him to believe that they would be very energetic in pressing Victor and Lapisse to support him. After his victory at Medellin, Victor did remain in the area of Merida as instructed but he made no attempt to move into Portugal in support of Soult nor did he communicate with him in any way. Yet it was understandably difficult, as Jourdan says in his *Memoirs*, for Victor or Lapisse to launch themselves into the unknown in Portugal without any information from Soult himself. There were many simple logistic arguments too. The huge amount of ammunition, stores and equipment captured in Portugal needed to be moved forward to Oporto if he was to make a serious advance on Lisbon. Chagas, the Portuguese historian, considered that the severe losses suffered by the French in northern Portugal, where initial resistance had been even more ferocious than anything that Soult's army had met in Spain, coupled with increasing French war weariness, contributed to his caution.[12]

But the conclusive decision to sit tight resulted from the rumour and then the definite information that, after hesitation and argument in London, a new expeditionary force under Junot's old opponent, Sir Arthur Wellesley, was once more landing in Lisbon. At this time – though not for long – Soult did not know Wellesley, but the British resistance at Corunna had left its mark. As a serious soldier enjoying a good professional relationship with Napoleon, Soult was quite ready to defy the Emperor's orders if he believed it to be justified. In his considered view, an onward march on Lisbon was not to be contemplated at the present time.

A second option was a retirement either northward to link up again with the uncooperative Ney or eastward to join Lapisse who was supposedly in the area of Ciudad Rodrigo. Strangely, the intelligent if wayward Saint-Chamans concluded in his *Memoirs* that after a short stay in Oporto his chief should have retired north, taking with him all the guns, ammunition and supplies that he had captured. He could then have secured an important area of northern Portugal as a kind of additional protection for the French forces in Galicia.[13] This was probably a case of wisdom after the event. In fact such pusillanimity was out of the question after the Oporto victory, especially as Soult might then have been accused of letting down both Victor and Lapisse.

For Soult the third alternative was the right one. This was to remain in Oporto and consolidate his position both militarily and politically in northern Portugal. Oporto was the second largest city in Portugal and in some respects as important as Lisbon itself. Then, hopefully after being reinforced, he could continue his march on Lisbon when he knew more about the military intentions of the new British expeditionary force.

His consolidation measures were to move Franceschi as far south as the River Vouga partly to test the seriousness of continued Portuguese resistance but mainly to assess the strength of the new British forces and to learn about Wellesley's intentions. Simultaneously, Heudelet's division, supported by Lorge's dragoons, had marched back to the Spanish frontier and relieved the hard-pressed Lamatinière in Tuy. Despite mutual jealousy between Heudelet and Lorge, this operation had been successful: frontier fortifications between Spain and Portugal which neither Soult nor Ney could maintain were destroyed, supplies were brought down to Oporto, and the northern provinces of Entre Minho et Douro and Tras os Montes were divided into two occupation zones. Soult's other military decision was the most important. He sent a good-sized force eastward so that he could secure a line of communication with Spain. He eagerly awaited news of Lapisse from that direction but Lapisse was still inactive, and his early death in the battle of Talavera has made it difficult to judge what he was actually intending to do. In any event this line of communication could be a valuable retreat route for Soult in case of emergencies. A strong Portuguese regular army formation under General Silveira was operating here, supported by the Lusitanian Legion with British officers, some militia forces and a good number of armed civilians. Unwisely as it turned out, Soult placed Loison in charge of the French. The obvious choice, as divisional general without a specific command and a reputed Portuguese expert, was 'Le Tondu'. In fact, although he does not say so in his *Memoirs*, Soult was probably glad to get rid of this obnoxious man from Oporto. He reinforced him temporarily with Delaborde's division and, after his successes in the north, with Heudelet's division as well. Despite the size of his forces, Loison enjoyed only a mixed success, finally establishing himself at the important village of Amarante on the River Tamega, which would protect communications with Spain.

This was the military background to the political steps which Soult believed were needed to secure the French position in northern Portugal – and to the two most controversial developments in his career so far. One was his effort to build up a French party in Portugal so that the country could be brought fully into the French system – leading to the claim that he tried to make himself 'King of Portugal'. The other, partially linked with this, was the mysterious Argenton military conspiracy. Some 180 years later it is still difficult to get these two events into correct perspective since accounts and assessments vary so much with the views of the commentators. Strong opinions are expressed in Soult's own *Memoirs*, by his personal staff, by his divisional generals, by his French enemies, by his British opponents, by more distant observers in Madrid and Paris and, more important than all, by the Emperor himself. Contemporary and later historians – French, English and Portuguese – have reflected these differences.

Certain facts are clear. Ever since the far-off days of the 'Sambre et Meuse', Soult, perhaps more than any of the other marshals, had developed a strong political sense in dealing with the occupied peoples of Europe. To Napoleon, he was still 'the faithful Soult' – in no way involved in internal French politics. But again and again in the past he had shown a genuine flair in dealing with the many different Europeans who were being brought under French control. However, coupled with this policy of moderation, he adopted, as already noted, a cold and distant manner to some of his generals which was to do him much harm. Nevertheless most of his personal staff greatly admired him. General Ricard, his chief of staff who came from Castres, only a few kilometres from Soult's own birthplace, was to be his most active assistant and all his aides-de-camp supported him, although the aristocratic Saint-Chamans finally turned against him when writing his *Memoirs* after the Bourbon Restoration. Of Soult's senior generals, Heudelet and Franceschi were firmly on his side.

As Napoleon's Empire extended its boundaries it was increasingly necessary for some of his marshals to be given independent commands which inevitably carried political as well as military responsibilities. Talking to Dr O'Meara years later in St Helena, the Emperor declared that to be a 'commander-in-chief' was the only real test of a soldier's full talents. But, as a total autocrat himself, Napoleon did not give his military leaders many chances of being really tested in this role. Masséna had enjoyed a free hand in Italy during the Consulate but was soon recalled for 'peculation'; Junot's brief period of isolated grandur in Lisbon hardly counted; and now in Portugal Soult was being given one of the most difficult political assignments of all.

Of course the Emperor had gravely misunderstood the situation in Portugal. Soult was now established in Oporto without any communication whatever either with Madrid or Paris. As Napoleon complained afterwards in a letter from Vienna, it was grossly culpable to have left Marshal Soult in that position for months. By now Soult had to decide what was best to be done in the French interests. As he wrote in his *Memoirs*: "An army chief who is not ready to act on his own initiative is not worthy of command. Of course the Emperor could always disclaim any action that I took afterwards."[14] However, these admirable sentiments were likely to have embarrassing consequences when he was confronting someone like Napoleon.

Installed in some splendour in the palace of Carrancas, Soult as usual quickly made up his mind what to do. In the country which was England's oldest ally, Oporto, more than any other city, had close political and commercial ties with London. There were numbers of British businessmen living there, many of them traditionally involved in the wine trade: British representatives in Portugal had done their best to encourage resentment against the French after the excesses committed by Junot's army the previous year and senior British officers in Portugal such as Beresford and Wilson were generally popular. An *Historical Record of the Port Wine Trade in Northern Portugal* paints a fascinating if somewhat highly coloured picture of the situation from the viewpoint of British business interests. The leading British port wine merchants had been placed in a most unenviable position as a result of the French invasion. They had to put their businesses in the hands of their Portuguese employees and usually they could no longer export any of their products. Their vineyards were left unattended since many of their workers had become guerrillas, and their business ledgers for the period were almost totally blank. "Meanwhile the French ate of the best and drank of the noblest giving themselves up to riotous living so that all that is held sacred by family ties was ruthlessly despoiled".[15]

On the other hand Portuguese opinion was notoriously volatile and, as recognized by some French and Portuguese historians, there was little basic ill will towards France which in the past had sometimes been regarded as a counterpoise to Portugal's great, sprawling neighbour – rather like the 'auld alliance' between Scotland and France. (Links between Portugal and France are still strong.) When he first entered the country Soult had utilized the political propaganda weapons employed with such effect in most of the rest of Europe first by the Revolutionary armies and then by Napoleon himself. His original 'freedom and good government' proclamations and his letter to Bishop Castro were entirely in line with this. But, by the time he was in full occupation of Oporto, a more sophisticated political policy was needed. With the bishop a fugitive in Lisbon and the Braganzas fugitives in Brazil, there was some chance of establishing a French party. Few people in northern Portugal wanted to be either a colony of Brazil or of England. Brun de Villeret, a sober commentator, records that some middle-class Portuguese were tired of British commercial domination and especially of their monopoly of the wine trade.[16] Perhaps few tears were shed at Portuguese employees taking over port wine businesses. Whilst not particularly liking the French, many people in Oporto got no satisfaction from the chaotic government in Lisbon so they were willing to accept a measure of French protection against the urban rabble who were the bishop's most vociferous supporters.

Far from being an oppressor, as he is sometimes described in Oporto folklore, Soult made serious efforts at conciliation. Chagas has given the most impartial view of him. He wrote: "Soult was very different from Junot who did not have the capacity for the important mission entrusted to him by Napoleon. The Duke of Dalmatia, on the other hand, was a political being and an intelligent man. He was better informed and much more suitable for a political mission than Junot. He thought mainly of gaining the loyalty of the Portuguese. They were, of course, unlikely to get true liberty from a French dictatorship but many people were better disposed towards the illustrious power of Napoleon and his revolutionary code than to the worn out 'old regime' of Portugal. Soult knew how to maintain a firm discipline protecting the lives and properties of the civilians and thus gaining a certain popularity."[17]

Soult concentrated especially on the church, the official classes and some of the businessmen including the considerable Jewish element. There were in Portugal a quarter of a million Jews who now hoped that the French would free them from their many restrictions. In the countryside it was not hard to find people who longed for a return to law and order in the place of the excesses of the various guerrilla bands. For the benefit of the church Soult made quite a show of sacramental devotion by regularly attending Mass in the cathedral. He also took special pains over a much venerated holy relic by presenting a silver lamp to the statue of Jesus Christ in the church of Matozinhos "as evidence of the veneration that French soldiers feel for our Holy Catholic religion". More welcome still, no doubt, he doubled the stipend of the rector of Matozinhos.[18] In using religion for unashamed political purposes he was, as usual, copying the behaviour of his imperial master. He attempted, too, to conciliate the younger, more liberal members of the Catholic hierarchy. On the civil side he followed Junot's example of maintaining himself in some ceremonial state. He assumed the title of governor general after he had captured Chaves but he went much further than his predecessor in filling the vacancies in the administration with reputable Portuguese and in trying to stamp out corruption. In the north Heudelet's division had brought almost the whole of the province of Entre Minto et Douro under French control. The rugged Tras os Montes was much less pacified but it could certainly have provided a French base in north-eastern Portugal had that been necessary. A naive report by a British officer described the French as "abandoning their usual system of terror, plunder and desolation by treating the Portuguese with feigned moderation and kindness". A dispatch from Cradock to Castlereagh contains the following gem: "It appears to be the object of the enemy to ingratiate himself with the populace of Oporto by even feeding them and granting them other indulgences."[19] On the military side Soult set up a Portuguese National Guard to help with security. No extra finance was needed: there was enough money in the treasury and indeed for various other relief measures that Soult organized.

None the less he considered, doubtless rightly, that these 'housekeeping' measures would not be enough in themselves to detach Portugal from her British connections and bind her more closely to France. Some clear political step was the only hope of achieving this. He was sure that Junot would have gained much more of a hold over the Portuguese if he had created a supportive political party. Accordingly he ordered his energetic and devoted chief of staff, Ricard, in conjunction with the French generals commanding in the two northern provinces, to find out as soon as possible how many people would be willing to break their links with the House of Braganza and join the French system. Ricard followed Junot's example in encouraging the sending of loyal addresses to the general-in-chief. The first such petition came from the municipality of Braga. A delegation of 36 prominent citizens declared they were willing to submit to Napoleon's rule and asked him to provide a prince of his blood to govern Portugal. Similar addresses with thousands of signatures came from most of the other towns in northern Portugal and in many cases it was suggested that as an alternative to a prince of Napoleon's family the chosen ruler should be the general-in-chief himself or "somebody else of his choice".[20] This proposal, as Brun de Villeret comments ingenuously, was to do his master much harm.[21] Soult, whose public statements were always more exuberant than his taciturn manner would suggest, told his various petitioners that he would "lay their representations at the foot of the Emperor's throne".[22] When he believed he was in the right he did not let the grass grow under his feet. A register of supporters of French rule, many of them calling for Soult himself to be their ruler, was opened in one of the municipal buildings; a newspaper, the *Diaro do Porto*, which advocated this idea, began publication and ran for a month; and an enthusiastic Jesuit, Father Veloso, harangued crowds in favour of Soult becoming at least king of northern Lusitania – i.e. northern Portugal.

The Marshal then directed Ricard to send a circular letter to all the divisional generals explaining the situation in the light of these "popular manifestations". The letter contained the sentence which was to cause Soult so much embarrassment later since it appeared to contain royal pretensions. "The Duke of Dalmatia would be begged to take up the reins of government – to clothe himself with supreme authority, the people to give him their loyalty and to support him with their lives and their possessions against all those opposing him and against those rebelling against him in the other provinces until the whole kingdom was brought into submission."

One of Soult's oft-repeated maxims was to do what one thought was right in all circumstances. No doubt, as he told Saint-Chamans, he genuinely felt that there was no alternative to trying to set up a satellite state under French authority which would encourage the church and the official and business communities to accept links with France and so protect the safety of the 20,000 French soldiers now in Portugal.[23] Everything would, of course, be subject to the Emperor's agreement and if, as he wryly comments in his own *Memoirs*, he was really trying to carve out a kingdom for himself without the Emperor's authority, he would hardly have used a circular to his generals to announce that fact![24]

It is easy to criticize Soult's methods as his critics have done over the years – to doubt the authenticity of addresses sent to a man whom Sir Charles Oman describes as having hands that were dripping with Portuguese blood, or to describe the hundreds of people addressed by Father Veloso and others as a mere 'rent a crowd' phenomenon. Certainly Ricard was zealous in prompting addresses from all the towns in northern Portugal. He would not have done this without fairly precise instructions from Soult. In fact he would not have had much difficulty in finding assistants for this task among the junior officers who were mostly well disposed towards the Marshal. He seems to have had little trouble in collecting signatures. After their initial fierce resistance to the French advance, the Portuguese army had been decisively beaten in Oporto. There was still plenty of guerrilla activity and there was another army under General Silveira, with British officers attached, south of the Douro. But by now there were many people in Oporto and in the north generally who only wanted peace and security. Lisbon was far away, the Braganzas even farther; the French were near at hand and obviously for the time in the ascendant.

What were Soult's real intentions in all this? A fair commentary comes from Marbot's *Memoirs*. Marbot had discussed the whole business with Soult's younger brother, Pierre, who was a close friend.[25] He had also studied the reports of Sir William Napier so that his *Memoirs* probably give the clearest assessment from contemporary sources. He points out that Napoleon had told Soult to use all means of detaching Portugal from England and binding her instead to France. Junot's previous invasion had failed. If the acceptance of a Portuguese crown was involved either for a member of Napoleon's family, or even for himself, this option should not be ruled out, subject always to approval by the Emperor. Soult was essentially a realist. Like Napoleon himself, he knew the value of ceremonial, whether in church or state, and a monarchical solution of the Portuguese problem strongly appealed to him as a 'political animal'. He was certainly ambitious – as were all the marshals – and his later behaviour as 'viceroy' in Andalusia shows how determined he was to rule any area that he conquered strictly and independently. Moreover he must genuinely have believed that a monarchy for Portugal, replacing the despised Braganzas, would be the best if not the only way of bringing Portugal into the French system. Even his old chief, Jourdan, who was not one of Soult's admirers, considered that his motives were not those of self interest.[26] The monarchical solution was the one that Napoleon himself had adopted in Spain, in Holland, in the Rhineland and in Italy. In northern Portugal there were, in addition, rather special considerations. Under the Treaty of Fontainebleau, signed a year previously with the Spanish Bourbons, Portugal was to be divided into three regions with the north, described as 'northern Lusitania', destined for military conquest. What was more natural, therefore, than that its present military conqueror should be offered a crown? The fact that all the kings on the satellite thrones were members of the Emperor's own family could not have seemed very relevant to the pragmatic Soult. Ever since Boulogne days he had known exactly what Napoleon thought of his elder brother, Joseph – and he was to have abundant evidence of this in the next few years in Spain. Moreover his own views of the Emperor's brother-in-law, Murat, must have been coloured by the many occasions in Germany and Poland when one of his own main tasks in military operations had been to prevent Murat from making a fool of himself. Above all, there was the evidence of impartial historical commentators such as Pinheiro Chagas, that there was plenty of Portuguese support for Soult's ideas.

Obviously any project of this kind, besides needing the Emperor's approval, required much time and energy. This meant that Soult had to remain in Oporto for three or four weeks instead of visiting his generals – a fact that was naturally criticized by his enemies and in the end had dire consequences for him in and around Amarante, east of Oporto.

The reaction of Soult's army to these activities was mixed. He had some support from a few of his generals. The peppery Heudelet makes no mention of the affair in his *Memoirs* and, as already noted, he generally admired Soult while the youthful Franceschi was devoted to him. Ricard, who was his right hand man all the time, was to suffer for it later in his career. Many of the junior officers and the rank and file probably favoured the initiative. Of his aides-de-camp the faithful Brun de Villeret saw the dangers and was appallingly involved later in explaining matters to the Emperor in Vienna. Saint-Chamans was characteristically cynical in his comments. He recounts ribald remarks made by some of the younger aides and even by the servants. The former began jokingly to decide what ceremonial offices they would hold at Soult's court! Saint-Chamans claims that, when his master asked for his views, he said plainly that "royal ambitions" would be much misinterpreted in the Tuileries.[27]

Of course it all provided a field day for Soult's critics and enemies both at that time and subsequently, especially when there followed two highly dramatic events – the mysterious Argenton military conspiracy and Soult's headlong flight from Portugal after the British capture of Oporto. Loison, commanding in the vital strategic town of Amarante, hated Soult. So did Quesnel, another old Portuguese hand who had been governor of Oporto under Junot and now held that position under Soult. Chagas has suggested that, to some extent, Soult's 'political activities' revived the old hostility between the Army of Germany and the Army of Italy which had been a feature of the Revolutionary Wars. This seems rather far-fetched but no doubt some of those who had the strong 'Republican' background of the 'Sambre et

Meuse' were shocked that one of their old comrades, Soult, appeared to have 'royal' pretensions. On the other hand, those with Royalist backgrounds, like Saint-Chamans, were not slow to misinterpret his political moves when they came to write their memoirs after the Bourbon Restoration. There were some who doubtless believed genuinely, if mistakenly, that Soult was being disloyal to the Emperor, but they were balanced by others who encouraged him along the hazardous course that he was pursuing.[28]

There was certainly a deterioration of discipline in Soult's corps which may well have reflected on general army discontent in which erstwhile Republicans dreamed about overthrowing the Empire – as General Malet was to try to do while Napoleon was in Moscow a few years later. There was discontent for other reasons among some of Soult's senior officers. While Napolcon's hard fought campaign continued on the Danube, some of the generals regarded the war in the Peninsula as a mere side-show. They were no longer fighting in the presence of the Emperor from whom all glory and honour flowed. Instead there was Napoleon's phantom elder brother in Madrid. In Portugal an aloof, tough and uncommunicative corps commander was admired by his junior officers and by the rank and file but jealously regarded by some senior officers who simply considered him as having been luckier than themselves in the promotion scramble. Moreover, if his plans for a satellite kingdom for Portugal were to be approved by the Emperor, they would be stuck in this backwater with no chance of earning promotion and rewards at home. Talking to French officers in Junot's army the year before, Wellesley himself had found that morale in this 'side-show' war was pretty low; and some of Junot's former generals such as Loison and Quesnel cordially disliked Soult also as a new and a strict disciplinarian who would stand no nonsense.

More serious, from the viewpoint of Soult's later reputation, were the slanders of his arch-critic, Thiébault, who was still military governor of Burgos. Reports from depots behind the lines lose nothing in the telling and Thiébault set to work exaggerating what passed between some of Soult's generals and himself after the Marshal's retreat from Oporto. One of them was Delaborde, an old 'Republican' of the Army of Germany who was shortly, in fact, only too pleased to become a count of the Empire, with Soult's full backing, and to succeed him in command of II Corps when Soult became 'Supremo' in north-eastern Spain. Thiébault also spread the *canard* that Soult expected Napoleon to be killed in the arduous Danubian campaign against Austria: then in the confusion he could mount the Portuguese throne. Some of this was a bit too much even for Thiébault's English translator, A.J. Butler, who dismisses his account of events in Oporto as being highly exaggerated.[29]

An even more bitter opponent of Soult was his old enemy, Ney. Their lifelong rivalry became even more acute when Soult was given the task of chasing Moore out of Galicia and then of reconquering Portugal. When Soult had later to abandon Portugal and return to Galicia, his rival was delighted. The ribald cries of 'Roi Nicolas' were first heard from Ney's army corps when the two marshals met again near Lugo, and a 'Roi Nicolas' jingle quickly spread to Madrid and to Paris. As already noted, Soult's name was never 'Nicolas'. It was a sort of French equivalent of 'Old Nick' and was used against Napoleon himself when he was on his way to exile in Elba. But the name has stuck to Soult ever since.

A true assessment of the whole Oporto episode, however, could come only from Napoleon. In May 1809 the Emperor was still fighting desperately against the Austrians on the Danube. Months were to pass before he heard much about events in Portugal and by then the military situation there and in Galicia had changed very much to the disadvantage of the French.

Towards the end of April, little more than a month after Soult captured Oporto, he had learned, as mentioned, the news that he most dreaded. Despite all evidence to the contrary from Cradock in Lisbon, the British government had decided to continue its involvement in the Peninsula and a new army of some 25,000 men under Sir Arthur Wellesley had landed in the Tagus. Wellesley had two immediate options. The first was to attack Victor who was still in central Spain making little effort to obey his orders to cooperate with Soult: the second choice was to march directly against Soult himself. Soult "was in possession of the most fertile province of Portugal and the favourite town of Oporto",[30] and also posed the more serious threat. He decided therefore on the second choice. Very soon he was in contact with Franceschi's cavalry patrols north of Coimbra. He also sent a secondary force under Marshal Beresford to join the Portuguese upstream beyond the River Douro towards Amarente. This move was specially important since he had received reliable information that Soult was about to evacuate Oporto, either retreating towards Spain or establishing himself in a strong defensive position in the mountains of north-eastern Portugal. He had indeed concluded that "Soult would probably not remain in Oporto once I cross the Mondego River".[31]

Wellesley's intelligence was quite correct. Soult had decided that, with the arrival of this new British army, it was no longer prudent to stay in Oporto. He intended to make a strategic retirement along the Douro valley so that he could join up with the long-awaited division of Lapisse. Thus reinforced, he could either maintain his position near the Spanish border or return to the attack from some base in the Portuguese mountains.

It was not surprising that Wellesley's intelligence was so good. Much of it had been provided by a French traitor, an ex-Jacobin named Argenton, who for the benefit of the supposedly aristocratic British officers, called himself the Sieur d'Argenton, a Royalist sympathizer. He was serving as captain in the 18th Dragoons. On the night of May 8, while Franceschi's cavalry, supported by Mermet's infantry, were falling back before the advancing British and Soult was busy with his preparations for evacuating Oporto, the Marshal had a visit from an agitated general of brigade, Lefèvre, with a dramatic tale to tell. Captain Argenton, who had once been his aide-de-camp, had given Lefevre the astonishing news that he had visited the British lines, ostensibly for amorous purposes, and that he had met Sir Arthur Wellesley and other officers who had provided him with British passports. Argenton had claimed that the French forces in the Peninsula were seething with discontent and that there was a plot to cooperate with the British in a march of mutinous officers and men from the French armies in Portugal and Spain to the Pyrenees. Here they would join with other disaffected French armies in an attempt to move on Paris and dethrone the Emperor. Argenton had even suggested that his former chief, Lefevre himself, would be sympathetic and that even Soult might join in the insurrection if it seemed to be gaining support. Another variation of his story was that there were actually two indignant factions in Soult's corps. The first of these was violently anti-Napoleon but there was a second group involving Loison and other senior officers who wanted to take action against Soult because of his alleged ambition to make himself a king. This faction would be greatly strengthened if the British were to encourage the Portuguese to support Soult's 'royal ambitions'. The French forces would then be hopelessly divided.

Argenton's allegations were greatly exaggerated and much distorted but they came at a crucial time for Soult who was in the midst of making his final withdrawal plans. It is naive to think that he was entirely ignorant of disaffection in his army but he had to find out more about Argenton's allegations without delay. The traitor was immediately arrested and brought before him. Despite a vigorous examination and a promise of mercy if he confessed, he refused to disclose the names of any senior officers involved except for his own commanding officer in the 18th Dragoons, Colonel Lafitte, and a certain Colonel Donnadieu who commanded the 43rd Infantry and had much distinguished himself in the capture of Oporto. Both these officers were somewhat 'cloak and dagger' figures. Lafitte was reputed to have been a kind of spy at Soult's headquarters on behalf of dissident elements in the army while Donnadieu was an inveterate conspirator who had begun his life as a fanatical Jacobin and ended up as an Ultra-Royalist after the Restoration.

After Argenton's 'revelations' Soult became intensely suspicious of those senior officers whom he disliked and distrusted anyway. He sent a highly confidential letter to King Joseph in Madrid accusing Loison, Lahoussaye, Mermet and Quesnel of disloyalty. Certainly their performance during the brief campaign that followed reflected either incompetence or treachery or both. Incidentally, there is no evidence at all that Soult himself was involved in any military conspiracy.

Over the Argenton affair Wellesley acted in a shrewd but honourable way. He naturally made full use of the valuable intelligence that the traitor brought to him about the morale and disposition of the French forces, also about Soult's ideas for the creation of a satellite state in Portugal with all the consequences flowing from that. But he had considerable doubts about the rogue's wilder statements and he flatly refused his invitation to encourage the Portuguese to offer a crown to Soult as a device for dividing and weakening the French army. He reported everything to Castlereagh who advised extreme caution. Wellesley affirmed that he would certainly not wait for any French army revolt but would use his own means of subduing Soult.[32]

The melodrama of Argenton's life continued. When the French had hastily to abandon Oporto he was still under close arrest. He had a strong military police escort during the retreat but succeeded in escaping from his captors on a narrow mountain path – a fact regarded with much suspicion by Soult's critics. He told the British in Oporto that the conspiracy had collapsed. Then he got away to England, returning heavily disguised to France to pick up his wife. He was captured and court-martialled when he made various scurrilous attacks against his corps commander, Soult, convicted of treason and shot. Of the other officers directly involved, Lafitte was finally allowed by Soult to return to his regiment as his guilt could not be definitely proved, but the conspiratorial Donnadieu remained in prison for several years.

Much concerned as he was over the Argenton affair, Soult was now fully engaged in preparing for the evacuation of his army eastwards to Spain. With characteristic energy he spent the day of May 11 supervising all the arrangements personally. After pulling back Mermet's and Franceschi's troops across the River Douro, he blew up the bridge. Then, convinced that the British would attack Oporto from the sea, he collected all available boats and either destroyed them or placed them under strong guard. He had no alternative to giving the disobliging Quesnel responsibility for this as governor of the city. Heavy guns, military equipment and stores were prepared for evacuation; everything that could not be carried away was destroyed. Mermet's and Delaborde's divisions were then ordered to prepare for their withdrawal along the banks of the Douro. Mermet was given the task of keeping a special watch on the river as his division moved slowly along the northern bank – a task which he conspicuously failed to perform. Tholosé, another of Soult's aides-de-camp, was sent off to the vital crossing place of Amarante, 65 kilometres upstream on the River Tamega, to ensure that it was firmly held by Loison's quite large forces, thus ensuring a line of retreat for Soult's whole corps. All this took time and it was not until 3 am the following morning, May 12, that Soult was able to snatch some rest.

Meanwhile Wellesley had been equally active. Argenton's information had made it clear that Soult was about to retire and that his army was in some disarray. Now was the time to strike if only he could find a way of crossing the Douro. As his biographer, Lady Longford, records, he "was on the threshold of the greatest adventure in the Peninsular War".[33] Despite Soult's careful preparations, not all boats on the Douro were under guard. He had been certain that any enemy attack would come from the sea and, under the towering walls of the bishop's seminary inside the city, there were moored some empty wine barges. Under cover of darkness an Oporto barber and some friends, having made contact with the British, brought these boats over to the south bank of the river. A small advance party of the

Buffs quietly and hazardously paddled their way across and, unseen by the French, proceeded to occupy the empty seminary. They were quickly followed by more troops until a force of several battalions was established, still unnoticed, inside the very strong building. Simultaneously a second force under Brigadier General Murray was sent across higher up the river in order to cut off the French withdrawal from the city – an even more important task.

It was not until 10.30 am on May 12 that General Foy discovered, to his horror, that the British were in full possession of the seminary. Earlier reports of redcoats being seen on the river bank had been dismissed as the men were thought to be Swiss troops in the French service taking a bathe. More seriously it was suggested in Soult's papers that General Mermet, whose division was passing along the river bank and had a special responsibility for guarding it, had a shrewd idea of what was happening but did nothing about it. Quesnel, as governor of the city, had also been appallingly lax, if not worse. However, in the general confusion there was no chance for Soult to investigate the two generals' conduct. Under his direction desperate attempts were made by Delaborde and Foy to drive back the British but by now they were far too strongly established and there was no alternative to a rapid retreat from Oporto. The only French success was to hold in check the second British landing higher up the river under the incompetent Murray. Had this succeeded, it would have been even more disastrous in cutting off a considerable number of Soult's forces.

In his *Memoirs* Soult describes the British capture of Oporto as more or less a rearguard affair with minimal French losses, only serious because of its effect on the army's morale and as demonstrating either laxness or treachery on the part of some of the generals. These comments are an absurd understatement, unworthy of Soult. In fact his veteran army had been the victim of a magnificent surprise attack and, as a result, he had been compelled to abandon his sick and wounded as well as much of his artillery. On their recovery, some of the French wounded made their homes in Portugal. The volatile citizens of Oporto, many of whom had been willing so recently to become subjects of a French satellite state, received the British with transports of joy, and the abandoned breakfast in Soult's headquarters was available to be eaten by Wellesley.

Even more serious for the French was the disastrous news that, attacked by a large force of militia and armed peasants supported by Beresford and the Portuguese army under Silveira, Loison had abandoned Amarante, retreating in flat contradiction to the precise orders that Soult had given him to hold this place at all costs. No doubt Loison could and should have stood firm. In the biography of his colleague, Heudelet, there is strong implicit criticism of Loison.[34] Relations between Loison and Soult had always been atrocious and Soult described the surrender of Amarante as a gross act of treachery.

Soult's position was now desperate. The main body of his corps was at Baltar on a narrow river road leading to Amarante, hedged in by the steep ridge of the

Sierra Catalina with the enemy occupying both ends of the road at Oporto and Amarante. His only possible line of retreat was northward across the mountains to Galicia again. At this critical moment he was thrown hard from his horse, falling heavily upon the leg where he had been severely wounded near Genoa nine years before. Lying in agony on a stretcher by the roadside, he formulated his plans. It was on occasions such as this that Soult showed himself to be one of the toughest and most resourceful of all the marshals. As his admirer, Napier, records rather sententiously: "Neither pain nor peril could shake the firmness of his soul."[35] Even the cynical Saint-Chamans says: "He rediscovered his greatness."[36]

A goatherd told him of a rocky track through the Catalina known only to country people. There was no other escape route. Immediately he ordered his troops to destroy the remainder of the artillery, to burn the baggage, to load the wounded and some ammunition on to the artillery horses and, simply retaining muskets, to make their way through the rugged and stony Catalina. He had sufficiently recovered to scramble along with them until they reached Guimaraes. Here they linked up with Loison's division and with Lorge's cavalry. A stormy interview took place between Soult and Loison in which the latter had the impertinence to suggest that Soult should offer another kind of Cintra Convention to the British. But Soult was made of different stuff. He placed Loison at the head of the retreating column, remarking that the hated 'Maneta' would never dare surrender to the Portuguese!

However, Soult's troubles were by no means over. Wellesley had moved as quickly as possible from Oporto to Braga while Beresford and Silveira already held the road from Braga to Chaves. Again it looked as if all routes back to Galicia were blocked. Once more Soult was unshakeable. He had now recovered from his injury and, halting on the road north while he checked the whereabouts of the various forces by which he was surrounded, he coolly held a review of his entire corps. It was a characteristic step to restore morale. Whatever may have been his relationship with some of his divisional generals, he had fully maintained his understanding with the lower ranks of his army. They still retained confidence in their chief and that saved them. Many were prepared to go through any hardship with him and, by and large, this loyalty continued until the end of the war.

The immediate problem was to get back to Galicia. The residue of Loison's artillery was now destroyed as well, and the army, travelling very lightly, moved quickly northward by narrow mountainous roads, having to cross two small bridges over rivers which had been turned by rain into raging torrents. Porto Nuovo on the Rio Cavado was seized from a strong force of Portuguese in a daring night attack carried out by a Major Dulong which has remained an epic in French military history. After crossing both rivers the army struggled onward, still pursued by Wellesley and the Portuguese. On May 19 Soult finally crossed the Spanish frontier near Orense, some three months after he had first entered Portugal. His army was now 19,000 strong: he had left 6,000 men behind, killed, wounded and prisoners; he was without guns, ammunition and stores; his soldiers were half dead with weariness, in tatters and many without their muskets. But they were all together and they had survived as an army. In effect they were in much the same state as Moore's army when it left Spain in January. Saint-Chamans described his chief during the memorable retreat as being "always at the front or the rear of the column, using resources that no one else would have done".[37]

Soult has been warmly praised by many historians for the way in which he handled the retreat and Wellesley was widely blamed at home for his failure to annihilate the French army. In fairness, Wellesley was hampered on several counts. The mountainous terrain had made it more difficult for the heavily equipped British to catch up with the unencumbered French: liaison with Beresford, and still more with the Portuguese, broke down and he was hindered by a general directive from London, in the aftermath of Cintra, to proceed cautiously and to limit himself for the present to freeing Portugal. Above all he was facing a resolute and skilful adversary in Soult. He reported that he had had "to stop his operations against Soult since there was no chance of impeding his progress".[38] Yet, all in all, Wellesley had achieved a very considerable success. Oman describes the Oporto campaign as one of Wellesley's strongest claims to fame. He had driven out of Portugal a veteran French army led by one of its most distinguished commanders with casualties of only a few hundred. Reporting on it to the Cabinet in London he described it modestly as "a pendant for the retreat to Corunna".[39] However, on this occasion, he tended to lose the subsequent propaganda battle. Moore's loss of 5,000 men from the small British army seemed to count for more in people's minds than Soult's 6,000 casualties, which were relatively low compared to the heavy losses in Napoleon's large-scale European battles. Wellesley took care to avoid further adverse publicity for the rest of the war.

So Soult's invasion, like Junot's first invasion and Masséna's third attempt later, had failed. The strong Portuguese resistance at the beginning, the mountainous terrain and the total failure of communication with the other forces which were supposed to have supported him had rendered his task too difficult. It is possible that, if he had pushed his veteran army relentlessly onward to Lisbon, where all was confusion until the arrival of Wellesley, he might have triumphed. Instead, as a good professional soldier, he opted for consolidation in Oporto and an attempt at a political solution. There were the added complications of the Argenton conspiracy and the disloyalty of some of his generals which contributed greatly to the difficulties of the retreat – difficulties which he partly overcame in masterly fashion. Once again it was the alert and articulate British army officer, Ensign Aitchison of the Third Foot Guards, who gave a good summary of Soult's operations. He wrote: "Nothing can palliate Soult's error in suffering us to force the Douro but it must be allowed that the manner in which he conducted his retreat will add to the high character as a general that he already bears."[40]

Finally, what of Soult's attempted political solution, provoking criticism of his alleged 'royal ambitions'? Napoleon's views on this affair must be recorded before returning again to the main story of Soult's career.

The Emperor had heard little or nothing about developments in Oporto until Soult had evacuated Portugal and then quarrelled violently in Galicia with his old enemy, Ney. Meanwhile Napoleon had issued one of his instant, long-distance orders requiring that the three corps of Soult, Ney and Mortier should now fight together as one unit under the command of Soult. For 'tactical' reasons this was said to be because Soult was the senior of the three but it was obviously yet another example of the high regard the Emperor had for Soult's professional skill. Napoleon, still fighting hard against the Austrians, had no time to spare for Peninsular problems. However, by the time of his final defeat of the Austrians at Wagram in July 1809, the very unpalatable news of events in Portugal was beginning to reach him, initially from English newspapers. Two of the principal villains, Generals Loison and Quesnel, had hastened to Vienna with poisonous accounts of Soult's ambitions, no doubt in order to cover up their own activities. When, after some delay, the faithful Brun de Villeret arrived, bringing Soult's dispatches covering his whole operation and including an account of the Argenton affair, he had to wait some time before being received by Napoleon. He then had a series of alarming interviews with the great man which he described graphically in his *Memoirs*.[41]

Although Brun was still a fairly junior officer, he had received no special briefing from his master who seemed to be quite confident that the Emperor would fully understand all he had tried to do in Portugal, including his attempt at a 'political solution'. With his customary habit of trying to intimidate those who brought unfavourable news, Napoleon first asked Brun whether from his name he was really a Frenchman at all! He then launched into a diatribe about Soult wanting to put a crown on his head and looking for support from a conquered people rather than from his Emperor. He declared that his marshals never became kings. (Murat was his brother-in-law which made him different and this was before Bernadotte!) If Soult had been an imbecile, said the Emperor, it might have been understandable but he had a calm head and broad vision. Had he been affected by the heat? There were dire references to rebellious Roman generals like Otho, Galba and Vitellius, who had made themselves emperors with fatal results. Soult and his agent, Ricard, must have been partly responsible for the serious upset that had taken place in the army. Anyway, why had the Marshal not made a dash for Lisbon or as an alternative remained with Ney in Galicia, which was still in a state of ferment?

Despite the avalanche of condemnation in Vienna, Brun kept his end up bravely. He stressed Soult's great military and political difficulties and he defended the case for some sort of political arrangement that would create a French party in Portugal as a means of bringing Portugal into the French system. With the French army surrounded in a potentially hostile country, unsupported by the other army units which were supposed to come to his aid and out of touch completely with both Madrid and Paris, he had really no alternative to acting as he did. In any case, proposals that he made for a satellite monarchy under a member of the Emperor's family – or himself – would be completely dependent on the Emperor's approval.

But Brun made little headway with Napoleon whom he later heard in conversation with Berthier, mockingly quoting Ricard's circular letter to the divisional generals. After several weeks spent "in a very hostile atmosphere" in Vienna, Brun finally returned to his master in Spain.

In September the Emperor at last sent Soult a formal letter. It is set out fully in his *Memoirs*. In this highly characteristic document Napoleon first expressed great displeasure at Soult's behaviour which, he said, amounted to high treason and had caused the various upsets in his corps. He criticized him in familiar terms for not marching straight to Lisbon or, instead, of helping to bring Galicia more effectively under control, and also for being caught napping by the British in Oporto, But finally, after referring to the great services that he had rendered at Austerlitz and elsewhere, he appointed him major general of all the French armies in Spain in the place of Jourdan. This meant being virtually commander-in-chief since his brother, Joseph, "had no experience of war".[42]

Soult's comments on this extraordinary letter are significant. "I understood my sovereign's letter perfectly and I never replied to it. I had no need to do so."[43] This was the considered comment of one professional about another. Napoleon knew very well that he had experienced a serious setback in the Peninsula. He had himself greatly underestimated the size of Soult's task partly due, as has been said, to "his amazing ignorance of climate and geography", and he was alarmed about the possibility of a serious army conspiracy directed against himself. His reaction had been to laugh off the whole affair, referring to Soult not as 'King Nicholas' but as 'King Nicodemus', little guessing that similar catcalls would later be directed against himself. Then, changing tactics when he found that 'cloak and dagger' events in Oporto might perhaps be more serious than he first thought, he described Soult's circular to his generals as treason, demanded the recall of the wretched Ricard and upbraided him in the Tuileries. But it was all 'shadow boxing'. Napoleon never changed his view of Soult as a great professional soldier. He was, no doubt, expressing his real thoughts to the Swiss General Jomini, then Ney's chief of staff, who had hastened to Vienna after Ney's bitter quarrel with Soult in Galicia – ostensibly in order to put his chief's side of the case to the Emperor. Napoleon commented on events in Oporto: "You have too much sense to believe stories. Soult had his reasons for acting as he did. He just had to build up a French party in Portugal!"[44] After Soult's death, Jomini wrote to the Marshal's son: "Of all the Emperor's lieutenants I believe that he was the one with whom I could have got on best (as well as Masséna) and would have been happy to have had his confidence. Fate always separated us."[45] As far as Napoleon was concerned, the 'Oporto affair' was soon forgotten. To Louise Soult, who was naturally very worried about it all, he wrote: "I have nothing but praise for the zeal your husband has shown for my service and the loyalty he has always given me."[46] Ricard was soon forgiven and served with distinction in Russia, being particularly well treated by the Emperor. Napoleon never referred to the affair again and was very non-committal when he was asked about it by Dr O'Meara in St Helena.

For a long time historians accepted at its face value the crude 'Roi Nicolas' story put around by Ney and Thiébault. Oman, a strong critic of Soult, admits that his reputation has suffered too much from the reports and diaries of men who disliked him even though his harebrained scheme would never have succeeded. More recently, Professor Tulard has commented that the 'Roi Nicolas *canard*' was mainly the result of the slanderous rumours put around by Soult's two particular enemies, Ney and Thiébault.[47]

All in all, it is reasonable to conclude that Soult's plan to turn Portugal or even northern Lusitania into a satellite kingdom was probably the best that could be devised to further French interests. It was always subject to the Emperor's approval and, had the plan been successful with or without Soult's personal involvement, Napoleon would probably have accepted it without much argument. Indeed Saint-Chamans wrote: "I have no doubt that the sign of the Emperor's confidence (in appointing Soult major general in Spain) meant that he had quite accepted Soult's activities in Oporto."[48]

The last words on this French invasion of Portugal must rest with the Portuguese themselves. Wellington, as a great soldier, created a formidable Anglo-Portuguese army which in the end played the chief part in winning the Peninsular War. But Pinheiro Chagas probably reflected contemporary Portuguese opinion when he wrote: "It is not surprising that, according to popular tradition, the arrival of the French and the English were seen at the time as two different invasions and were both equally detested. More than once in village wells, where the haphazard revenge of the countryfolk buried bodies of the invading foreigners, the red uniforms of the English intermingled with the hated uniforms of Napoleon's soldiers."[49]

8

SUPREMO IN WESTERN SPAIN

WHEN his tattered and exhausted army re-entered Galicia after evacuating Portugal, Soult found that once more he was expected to pull Ney's chestnuts out of the fire. Ney had failed completely to trap the ever-active Romana. Vigo had been recaptured by the British: Romana's training of the Spanish guerrillas had been highly successful and the whole province was in rebellion. The Spaniards were besieging a French brigade in Lugo. The first task of Soult's ragged army was to relieve Lugo. Pending fresh orders from Napoleon, who was still busy fighting the Austrians on the Danube, Soult was as always ready to use his own initiative to assist Ney to restore order in Galicia. He did not expect to receive any fresh instructions from the Emperor for some weeks. During this time the two marshals, operating together, should surely be able to subdue Galicia and to deal with the elusive Romana.

This was the prelude to another of those dramatic incidents involving Soult and Ney, which again, doubtless, has lost nothing in the telling. When Ney himself arrived at Lugo, high words were said to have been exchanged between the two marshals and there was even the threat of a duel. Certainly Ney's VI Corps greeted their ill-clad and exhausted comrades of II Corps with derision and contempt; much-needed artillery, equipment and supplies were withheld from them although there were plentiful supplies in Corunna which was still in French hands. Even Soult's great military critic, Thiébault, comments unfavourably on Ney's refusal to let Soult have even a few batteries of artillery.[1] Soult's aide-de-camp, Saint-Chamans, had no doubt where the responsibility for the difficulties lay. He considered that the ill discipline in Ney's corps was scandalous: if only his men had been as well organized as those of Soult or of Suchet the French would have been far better established in Spain generally.[2] It was then that the taunting cries of 'Roi Nicolas' were raised by both officers and men of VI Corps.

These bitter feuds could only be resolved by the so-called Convention of Lugo – almost like a treaty between two sovereign powers – laying down the respective responsibilities of the two marshals for waging war in Galicia. Under this convention Ney's responsibility, apart from trapping Romana, was to be the recapture of Vigo: he would also make available to Soult all the guns, ammunition and supplies of British origin which Soult had originally seized in Corunna and he was to remain in close touch with Soult. Soult himself, based further east in Monforte, would also try to capture Romana, but even more important, since Wellesley's future intentions were still unknown, he would watch the frontiers of Portugal and keep in touch with Victor's corps through Zamora. Ney totally failed to honour his part of the bargain. His advance to Vigo was blocked by a strong Spanish force entrenched on the steep banks of the river flowing into Vigo Bay and supported by the guns of British frigates anchored there. He therefore retreated on Corunna without either sending a force to link up with Soult or providing him with his badly needed guns and equipment. Soult was equally unsuccessful in capturing Romana but he did at least suppress some uprisings in eastern Galicia and in León. Having failed, despite various efforts, to maintain contact with Ney, he considered that he had an increasing responsibility to keep an even more careful eye on any advance that Wellesley might make into Spain. With this aim he marched his corps to Zamora in southern León. By June 21 Ney himself had given up all hope of retaining control of Galicia and had retired from Corunna to Astorga, that strategic town in northern León that had featured so prominently in Napoleon's and Soult's pursuit of Sir John Moore six months before.

There was intense mutual recrimination between Ney and Soult over the abandonment of Galicia. Soult had carried out his fair share of the bargain under the Convention of Lugo while at the same time scrutinizing the movements of Wellesley. The agreement, however, was supposed to remain secret so that Ney was able to trumpet abroad his accusation that Soult had deserted him and that as a result he too had had to abandon Galicia. In a letter to King Joseph he described Soult as having "left me with all his wounded and, having exhausted the supplies in all my depots, he abandoned me at the moment when I counted on his support". Similarly Marchand, one of his divisional generals, said that Soult's "defection" was "une atrocité inimaginable".[3] Ney's chief of staff, Jomini, was sent off to Vienna to put Ney's views to the Emperor without knowing the exact terms of the Convention. However, he had his suspicions and, when many years later he was in the service of the Tsar and Soult was one of Louis Philippe's ministers, he admitted that, according to the terms of the Convention, Soult had acted perfectly correctly.[4] Sent on a liaison mission to the angry Ney, Saint-Chamans also records a talk with another of Ney's generals, Lamartinière, the heroic defender of Tuy, who reported the shameful behaviour of Ney's staff in spreading stories about Soult's uncooperative conduct and even of his cowardice.[5]

In order to ensure that King Joseph received the correct account of what had happened, Soult sent General Franceschi to Madrid. Unfortunately the young cavalry general failed to protect himself effectively. He was captured by guerrillas and spent the rest of his short life being dragged from one Spanish prison to another until he finally died of yellow fever. Soult was desolate. He had lost a "dear and intimate friend who was always loyal to me". Franceschi was also a former aide-de-camp to King Joseph, and his young wife was Queen Julie's lady-in-waiting, so that he would have provided an excellent liaison with Madrid, preventing many of the serious misunderstandings that were to develop between Soult and the King.[6] Soult's younger brother, Pierre, took over Franceschi's light cavalry division. He was frequently wounded and much decorated but he was not in the same class as Franceschi.

Much of the argument against the war in Galicia was academic. These mountain operations were almost independent of the war in the rest of the Peninsula and the French could not conquer Galicia so long as Romana was at large. A recent historian has paid a warm tribute to his skill if not to his personality. He seems to have been the first Spanish general after the Baylen euphoria who really carried out a sensible defensive strategy. "He kept his army hidden in the shelter of the mountains ... (Its) mere presence prevented the invaders from applying all their forces against the insurgents."[7] Moreover, Galicia's long coastline was nearer than anywhere in Spain to England so that it could be constantly supported and supplied by the British fleet. On one occasion Romana was evacuated in a British warship when he was on the point of being captured. Jourdan commented wisely that Soult and Ney could not and should not stay on in Galicia if, as now seemed likely, Wellesley was moving towards the frontiers of Spain.[8] Long afterwards Wellesley claimed it it was he and not the Spaniards who had saved Galicia.[9] The truth seems to have been that, for the French, Galicia was unconquerable. "For months two whole army corps were tied down in a futile campaign that had no relevance whatever to the real French objectives."[10]

Cutting across these French disputes, there arrived at Zamora the long-distance instruction from Napoleon in Vienna ordering that the three corps of Soult, Ney and Mortier should operate together under the command of Soult, nominally on age grounds but clearly because he was by far the ablest of the three. This would provide a force of nearly 60,000 men which must work together as far as possible as one large army. Napoleon had already heard about some of the serious events that had occurred in Portugal, caused mainly by poor military cooperation. He had concluded first that the Portuguese invasion had failed largely because Soult had received no help either from Victor or Lapisse. He did not admit that his own original plan had been so loosely constructed that it was bound to fail. These cooperative failures had to be rectified in the face of Wellesley's latest moves. As he remarked, almost gleefully, to Ney's representative, Jomini: "While you have all been arguing, Wellesley is moving out of Portugal into Spain. However, if the three corps all operate together the English would be annihilated and the Spanish business would be ended."[11]

It was one thing for Soult to be nominated 'Supremo' by long-distance order, quite another to turn this order into action. His first problem was one of personalities. Despite tittle-tattle in Madrid to the contrary, he had little difficulty with the courteous and helpful Mortier commanding V Corps. Like Soult himself, Mortier had married a girl from the Rhineland: there were some misunderstandings between them later but he remained Soult's friend for many years until in fact he was killed in the royal assassination attempt during the reign of Louis Philippe. With Ney the position was naturally quite different. Ney was furious at Soult's appointment especially as General Delaborde, who had been earmarked to take over the command of II Corps from Soult, was away on sick leave and, on age grounds, it was Mortier rather than himself who was given temporary command of both II and V Corps. Naturally King Joseph had fully anticipated Ney's hostility. He had himself favoured a link-up of the three corps under one of the three marshals but had prudently suggested that, to prevent difficulties, the other two should be sent home.[12] He cannot now have been surprised to receive a letter from Ney saying that he could not possibly serve under a comrade who had been guilty of "such perfidy". Ney had already written to Soult directly saying that he had no confidence in his actions. For the time being he threw up his command in favour of Marchand.

With his usual thoroughness, Soult had reorganized and re-equipped his own II Corps while it was at Zamora, although it was still very poorly supplied with artillery. Having gathered the three corps together, as the Emperor had directed, his strategic intention was to lay siege to Ciudad Rodrigo as a preliminary to another invasion of Portugal. At the moment the destruction of the British army was his paramount aim. Even if Wellesley had already advanced into Spain, a fresh invasion of Portugal by an army three times as large as his own would dangerously threaten his communications and probably defeat him outright. These constant movements on or near the Portuguese border were to be features of the Peninsular War for the next few years with Soult, Masséna and then Marmont all adopting this strategy with greater or less success while Wellesley countered them with equal effectiveness. On the present occasion, with so great a numerical superiority, Soult had a good chance of avenging the disaster of Oporto. But the problems of cooperation remained acute. As a first step he ordered Ney's corps to move from Astorga to Benavente, sending his instructions to Marchand instead of to the absent Ney. However, arguing that an expedition into Portugal would be a disaster and that he would rather be shot than take part in it, Ney strictly forbade Marchand to cooperate. Soult had even more difficulty with King Joseph who was intensely preoccupied with the defence of his capital and giving full protection to all parts of the country that were now under his control. Joseph had at his disposal not only Victor's I Corps but Sebastiani's IV Corps as well as many garrison troops in Madrid itself. Nevertheless, deeming these forces insufficient, he ordered Mortier's corps to move away from Soult towards Avila while some of Soult's other units were sent off to deal with guerrilla activities in Old Castile. Nor was the King averse to adopting his brother's policy of 'divide and rule', having told Napoleon earlier that Ney "continue à ne point obéir ni Soult ni moi même!"[13] He later offered him the command of I Corps instead of Victor, an offer which Ney had the grace to refuse. These were the beginnings of the complex relationship between the King and Soult. The relationship was sometimes covered with a veneer of friendship but for the most part it resulted in downright hostility. It remained an important element in French operations for most of the war.

Initially Soult had some success with the King. He won back control of Mortier's corps which returned to Valladolid. The King also promised artillery reinforcement and some financial support. But none of this ever arrived. In any event, Joseph had no money available since he had already begun to spend his meagre resources on trying to rule as a real king and on supporting an extravagant Spanish court. As regards Soult's major strategic plan of attacking or outflanking Wellesley rather than simply protecting conquered Spanish territory, the Marshal recalled the campaigns of Philip V, Louis XIV's grandson and successful contender for the Spanish throne in the War of the Spanish Succession a century before. Philip had twice evacuated Madrid in the face of the enemy, only to return to it in triumph a little later. Soult recognized the political importance now of holding on to the capital but, in sending to Jourdan, Joseph's major general, his plan for attacking the British with his combined army of three corps, he emphasized that it would compromise everything if French troops simply tried to protect all the territories that they had occupied, including even the capital. Once the British had been driven out of the Peninsula these territories could be quickly recovered. He was to use similar arguments on other occasions during the war. Meanwhile his major offensive could be supported by Victor's corps acting both as a protection for Madrid and as a *corps d'observation* between the capital and the Spanish border. His plan was sent to Madrid on July 1. In place of the captured Franceschi, Soult's emissary was General Foy who had been sent on similar representative missions before, notably to the bishop of Oporto. Foy, who was able and intelligent, was to end up as a leader of the Liberal opposition under the Bourbons. But he was not nearly as effective a representative as Joseph's old aide-de-camp Franceschi would have been.

Initially the King and Jourdan accepted Soult's plan but three weeks were spent in exchanges between them. Meanwhile Wellesley had been very active. After bundling Soult out of northern Portugal he considered that Victor's corps which was now at Plasencia, north of the Tagus, posed the most serious threat. If he could attack Victor successfully he might even threaten Madrid. There was the usual intelligence blackout affecting both sides. Victor was ignorant of Wellesley's rapid advance across the frontier from Portugal while Wellesley was unaware of the serious danger to himself from Soult's three army corps in the Salamanca area.

The King and Jourdan were then guilty of a series of blunders. Instead of insisting on Victor remaining in his strong defensive position at Plasencia, where he would have been in close touch with Soult, they ordered him to withdraw along the Tagus to Talavera. There were rumours, but no confirmation, of an advance by Wellesley into Spain. However, the main reason for Victor's retirement was the threat of an attack on Madrid by the Spanish army of General Cuesta. Still intensely preoccupied with the defence of his capital, Joseph also summoned Sebastiani's corps to his direct assistance. He made similar rather hectic demands for Soult to join him as well. From far away in Vienna – and without any knowledge of events on the spot – Napoleon gave contradictory orders which served only to confuse matters. On June 30 he had sent Soult a dispatch saying that, if Sir Arthur Wellesley advanced along the Tagus to Madrid, Soult should fall upon his flank and rear and crush him. But shortly afterwards, perhaps in order to justify himself after hearing the results of Talavera, he blamed Soult for not having joined up directly with the King in Madrid, so that a combined army of 100,000 men could have annihilated the English.[14]

In fact Soult's strategic instinct was perfectly sound. He was now aware of Wellesley's advance along the Tagus valley. For the present his projected advance into Portugal by way of Ciudad Rodrigo had to be postponed. Instead he planned to move his three army corps to Plasencia and then to the Tagus. This would be quicker and had greater strategic possibilities than a far longer march to join the King in Madrid as Joseph – and apparently the Emperor – wanted.[15] Although it was unfortunate that Victor had retired from Plasencia, Soult informed Joseph, through Foy, that a combined operation between his own army and the King's could fall upon Wellesley on the Tagus and annihilate him. All that was needed was some careful timing. The royal army must stand firm in a defensive position until Soult could attack the flank and rear of the Allies.[16]

In the event, the battle of Talavera on July 28 1809 was fought by the French at quite the wrong time and in quite the wrong place. It effectively put paid to Soult's overall strategy to attack the flank and rear of the Allied army while King Joseph's army held them in check frontally. Foy had returned to Soult with Joseph's agreement in principle to Soult's plan but the King completely failed to play his part. Victor and Sebastiani had already routed a force of 6,000 Spaniards at Santa Ollalla, causing the Allied army to retire behind the River Alberche and take up a position on the banks of the Tagus at Talavera. King Joseph then called a council of war to decide on future action. Jourdan, whom Napoleon, and indeed Soult too, constantly denigrated, strongly supported Soult's recommendation that the King's army should stand fast in its defensive position until Soult was also ready to attack Wellesley. If Soult moved fast and a combined assault were then to be made by both armies, the effect on the Allied forces would be disastrous. However, buoyed up by their recent success against the Spaniards, Victor and Sebastiani simply could not wait and urged upon the King the need for an immediate attack on the Allied position. Victor himself was intensely ambitious. Having received his marshal's baton he had recently won a spectacular if rather empty victory at Medellin. But after failing to cooperate with Soult during the invasion of Portugal, he had been unable to carry out the Emperor's overall directive to conquer southern Spain at the beginning of the year. Now there was a chance to cover himself with glory in the presence of Joseph and before Soult's large army arrived on the scene to steal his thunder. Sebastiani, not to become a marshal until much later, was equally anxious to prove himself. Victor and Sebastiani could reinforce their arguments by claiming that Soult's approach march was being too slow since he could not reach Plasencia until the first days of August. In the bitter exchanges that took place later, Soult was much criticized for not arriving earlier. The criticisms were unjust. Soult was determined to follow the Emperor's original instructions to keep his three corps as close together as possible. Ney had returned with a bad grace to command VI Corps and no doubt deliberately delayed his march south while Soult needed to bring a fair proportion of his artillery with him over difficult mountain roads.

So the fatal decision was taken for the French to launch their attack on Talavera without waiting for Soult's arrival. As Saint-Chamans commented: "The speed with which the King's army engaged ruined Soult's excellent strategic plan."[17] Although there were the usual problems of Allied cooperation with the Spaniards and faults on both sides, the fierce attacks of Victor's and Sebastiani's corps, outnumbering the British by almost two to one, were beaten off and the French had to retreat behind the River Alberche. Wellesley had won the battle but in strategic terms the honours were about equal. On the one hand, the French had been forced to retire from Talavera; on the other, any possible advance by Wellesley towards Madrid had been thwarted. Emphatically the British won the propaganda battle afterwards. Jourdan on Joseph's behalf, put out reports claiming a victory; there were even suggestions among the King's entourage that he had performed better than his brother had done in the drawn battle against the Austrians at Aspern-Essling. But the English newspapers, which Napoleon read avidly, told a different story and Wellesley was made Viscount Wellington of Talavera: The Emperor did not hide his displeasure at what he called Jourdan's "inaccuracies and falsehoods".[18] It was another bad mark for the King's unfortunate major general. In a twisted kind of way it may have suited Napoleon, as much as Wellington, to see Talavera as a French defeat. At least that was the view of the embittered Jourdan afterwards. In his *Memoirs* he wrote that, "pour flatter la passion de l'Empereur", his elder brother and most of the marshals acting on their own in Spain had to be described as quite ineffective.[19] From time to time Soult suffered from this treatment.

Within a few days of Talavera Wellington came very near to disaster. Soult's three corps were now fully engaged in the mountainous area on his left flank. Mortier scattered a Spanish force commanded by Robert Wilson in the Banos Pass and then entered Plasencia where Wellington had had to abandon his sick and wounded. Realizing that he was in great danger from Soult's large army which was now massed near the Tagus, Wellington had no choice but to retreat hastily across the river by the bridge of Arzobispo. Shortly after he had crossed, Soult seized the bridge from a strong force of Spaniards. With skill and rapidity Wellington then moved his army by difficult mountain roads away from the Tagus to Truxillo. Truxillo was only a short distance from the river and, if Ney had been able to find the ford at Almarez, Wellington might still have been surrounded and overwhelmed. As Napier recorded: "The fate of the Peninsula hung by a thread."[20] Despite poor cooperation with his Spanish allies, Wellington managed to lead his army back across the frontier into Portugal. Soult had tried to persuade Victor to harass him on the left bank of the Tagus while he pressed forward north of the river towards Alcantara and Portugal. But, with his constant preoccupation with the safety of Madrid, the King soon ordered Victor to disengage and march off to fight another Spanish army in La Mancha. One more chance of surrounding Wellington had been lost.

In reporting his enforced retirement, Wellington praised Soult's strategy and blamed a total lack of cooperation from the Spanish army led by the elderly and ailing Cuesta. Describing these events, he wrote: "The enemy introduced a large army corps in our rear. As a result of this and mismanagement by the Spaniards we have been obliged to withdraw."[21] Later he referred to "the accurate knowledge the French have of our movements through their spies in the Spanish army. Soult has said that we are covered in glory, but if we had remained two days longer we must all have been prisoners or have been destroyed."[22] Soon Wellington was back on the River Guadiano between Badajoz and the Portuguese frontier with an army of little more than 17,000 men. In these circumstances he concluded that for the present he must stay in Portugal. His army evidently shared this view. As he commented: "There was not a man in the army who did not wish to return to Portugal."[23] He remained based in Portugal obstinately and wisely for the next two years.

All this inevitably caused a serious crisis in Anglo-Spanish relations. Once again the Spaniards felt, however unjustifiably, that they had been badly let down by their British allies especially when Wellington advised them that for the present they should adopt a defensive strategy.[24] Soult must have known from his spies of this Anglo-Spanish disarray and he appreciated that this was a real moment of crisis. As his admirer, Napier, records: "With the eye of a great commander Soult was the only Frenchman who really understood things."[25] The French forces still under Soult's command numbered over 70,000 men with 17,000 cavalry. As Wellington commented to Castlereagh: "We have in Estremadura the whole gang of marshals – Soult, Ney, Mortier, Victor and King Joseph."[26] Now was the time for them to attack Wellington, to march on Lisbon and to avenge Oporto by driving a second British army from the Peninsula. Soult would surely have been able to achieve this especially as the lines of Torres Vedras, which so baffled Masséna later, had not yet been built. If it were not possible to advance on Lisbon now, at least Ciudad Rodrigo should be seized as a base for further operations. This was the burden of all Soult's recommendations to King Joseph during these critical days.

The King's flat refusal to accept these recommendations was one of the great disappointments of Soult's career. Indeed everything conspired against him. Joseph could argue about the difficult mountainous terrain of Portugal which had deterred Victor at the beginning of the year. He referred to artillery and even cavalry inadequacies. In fact he was quite content that the British had retired into Portugal and he had little interest in pressing them further. His concern, as usual, was with the various Spanish armies operating in different parts of his kingdom, especially in the south which was still under the full control of the central junta in Seville and with the guerrilla bands which were increasingly active everywhere. Rather surprisingly, he was supported in his views by the Emperor who now directed that there should be no further invasion of Portugal during the remaining hot months of the summer – indeed until the following spring. After his victory at Wagram, which had ended the war against Austria, he was obviously contemplating a major invasion of Portugal next year, probably led by himself.

It is hard to understand why Napoleon supported Joseph in holding back Soult. No doubt he thought that a third attempt to invade Portugal needed much more elaborate preparation and, the following year, this proved to be the case. Moreover, if the Emperor was to lead the invasion army which he evidently contemplated at this time, he did not want Soult to spoil things by making a successful attack beforehand.

For the time being Joseph was justified by the Emperor's approval in insisting on a purely defensive role for Soult and his three corps. Much to Ney's satisfaction, he was moved back to Salamanca with the task of holding down León. Mortier was also given purely defensive duties and Soult had to remain strictly on the defensive in Plasencia. By now, with only II Corps again under his direct command, he was obviously too weak to launch a full-scale attack on Portugal. Nevertheless, when he was asked in September by the Ministry of War in Paris for operational proposals for the month of September, he insisted obstinately on the idea of an attack on Ciudad Rodrigo as a preliminary to an advance into Portugal. But this was not approved.

Meanwhile there came from the Emperor in Vienna a stream of long-range, 'wise after the event' invective which Napoleon showered on his subordinates when things had gone wrong – and they had often gone very wrong in Spain. Weak direction from Madrid, jealousy and poor cooperation between the various marshals, fierce Spanish resistance with an ever-increasing number of guerrillas and the skilful leadership and determination of Wellington's small army had been the main causes of the French failures. Having accepted the fact that his elder brother had no aptitude for soldiering, the Emperor directed most of his strictures at his major general Jourdan. Nevertheless, Napoleon certainly considered that this was the end of an important phase in the Peninsula War, with decisive possibilities for the future. On September 24 he wrote to Clarke, his Minister of War: "I rejoice to see England making efforts beyond the capacity of its population. Every big British expedition leads eventually to a general peace! Ministers who preceded the present British Cabinet were convinced of this truth. They were wary of engaging in an unequal struggle. Spain and Portugal will be the tombs of this brave people and their losses will finally lead to a great desire for peace!"[27]

These were sonorous if misguided sentiments. For the immediate future they had no direct consequences for Soult. He had spent most of 1809 fighting Moore and Wellington: now he was to be mainly concerned with the quite different problem of conquering and then administering a large part of the rest of Spain, with only occasional if fierce contests against his old foes, the British. This phase was to last over three years.

9

KING JOSEPH'S "COMMANDER-IN-CHIEF"

IN HIS MEMORABLE LETTER from Schönbrunn of September 20 1809, in which Napoleon first accused Soult of high treason and then made him King Joseph's major general in succession to Jourdan, he emphasized that because his brother had no experience of war Soult must "look after everything".[1] Jourdan had been blamed rather unjustly for the year's disasters. He had been in a thoroughly false position. This old Republican was genuinely fond of King Joseph whom he had served faithfully in Naples. It has been well said that he "made Joseph feel he was a man of war while King Joseph made Jourdan feel he was a man of spirit!"[2] They were both wrong. In fact Jourdan rightly assessed his master's military position. He wrote: "Napoleon's orders were obeyed unquestioningly: the King's orders were discussed, criticized and often ignored by his military chiefs."[3] Despite his past Republican principles, he would dearly have loved to have been made Duke of Fleurus to commemorate his victory in the Low Countries during the Revolutionary Wars, but he was never ennobled by Napoleon and he did not even appear as a marshal in the Imperial Almanac from 1809 to 1811 on the grounds that he was only on the strength of King Joseph's Spanish army.[4] Disillusioned, he had several times asked to be relieved of his post on health grounds, not really expecting to be taken at his word. Disgusted when the Emperor finally agreed to his request, he was convinced that his former general of brigade from the 'Sambre et Meuse', Soult, had been intriguing against him. There is no evidence for this. The old 'Anvil' was not unintelligent: but he failed completely to carry out his master's commands, such as they were. Furthermore he subscribed to some of the King's 'Spanish nationalist' ideas. Joseph might safely pose as a 'Neapolitan nationalist' in Naples. But to be a 'Spanish nationalist' in Madrid was much too dangerous.

Soult was expected to change all this. Forceful and capable, he was unlikely to be sympathetic to what the Emperor already considered were his brother's anti-French sentiments. He had tried for a 'political solution' in Portugal and had burned his fingers in the process. He arrived in Madrid as very much the Emperor's man and someone whose orders were likely to be obeyed. From time to time these orders would inevitably be given in Joseph's name and would reflect his views. This double loyalty obviously had its dangers.

In his brilliant study of Joseph Bonaparte's kingdom of Spain, Michael Glover describes Marshal Soult as an unpleasant man who was "ambitious, avaricious, suspicious and friendless".[5] This is surely too harsh a verdict. It is based to an extent on the views of Soult's aide-de-camp, Saint-Chamans who, as has been noted, was partly critical and partly admiring. There were also the opinions of Joseph's entourage in Madrid, called by some French historians the "ci-devant français".[6] These included Miot de Melito who had accompanied Joseph from Naples, and Bigarré, his principal aide-de-camp. Both Miot de Melito and Bigarré left voluminous *Memoirs* which were naturally very critical of Soult. Soult had little in common with the easy-going Jourdan. Nor, as the direct military representative of the Emperor, was he likely to find many friends at Joseph's court. He was certainly ambitious and not over-scrupulous; some described him as a *condottiere!* As such he had little affinity with the philosophical side of Joseph's nature. Though avaricious, he was never among the wealthiest of the marshals. As a collector of loot in Spain he probably acted no worse, and displayed better taste, than many others who soldiered in the Peninsula. His 'artistic acquisitions' will be discussed later. Despite his abrupt and dour manner, his immediate circle, as distinct from Joseph's courtiers, admired him greatly. Neither a Bayard, like Lannes or Oudinot, nor a 'yes-man' like Jourdan, he was wiser, stronger willed and therefore more valuable to the Emperor than any of them. His professional relationship with Joseph was also quite different from Jourdan's. It has been described as being more like that of a Prussian field marshal with his monarch – winning the battles himself and giving the King the necessary amount of glory afterwards.[7] In fact for some months he was genuinely Joseph's commander-in-chief.

Due largely to the operations of Soult, a second British army had now retired rather speedily from Spain. But the French situation in the Peninsula was still serious. Two invasions of Portugal had failed and the whole of southern Spain as well as Galicia was under the control of the central junta now established in Seville or of semi-independent Spanish generals. A great number of veteran French soldiers were serving in Spain and the drain on French military manpower was becoming alarming. As a result of the fighting up to 1809, probably as many as 75,000 men never saw France again and in the years that followed several hundred thousand more would share the same fate.[8] It has been said that over half a million Frenchmen had been or would be killed, disabled or more or less permanently tied up in Spain and Portugal. This compares with an almost equal number of casualties in Napoleon's Russian campaign but many of these latter casualties came from satellites of the French Empire or from countries that were temporarily allied to France.

This was the gloomy background against which Soult and the other marshals fought. There were now three major tasks facing the French – to conquer the whole of Spain, to conquer Portugal and to drive out the British. For the next few years Soult was mainly concerned with the first of these tasks. In Spain the situation varied greatly in different provinces. French armies, acting more or less independently, with little direction from Madrid or Paris, fought Spanish generals who were virtually autonomous, uncontrolled by the central junta in Seville. In Catalonia, Gouvion St Cyr and then Augereau fought against Spanish regulars and guerrillas. Most of the province was gradually brought under control except for the town of Gerona, but neither St Cyr nor Augereau were likely to take many orders from King Joseph. Suchet had embarked on his successful operations in Aragon and Valencia which were to earn him a marshal's baton. His aunt by marriage, plain little Queen Julie, the merchant's daughter from Marseilles, had, like Louise Soult, prudently stayed in Paris; and Suchet was no more willing than the other French generals to take orders from his wife's uncle in Madrid. In the north strong French forces faced weaker Spanish regular armies but roaming guerrilla bands were posing an ever more serious threat to communications with France. In the province of La Mancha hard fighting continued while Andalusia south of the Sierra Morena was under the haphazard control of the central junta which, surprisingly, was still bubbling with confidence. At first the intention was that Soult, as major general, should control all the French forces and he was urged to take personal direction of one or two corps operating together.[9] The Emperor had been more explicit to Brun de Villeret before Brun finally returned from the drubbing that he received in Vienna. Soult must draw up an overall plan, protect communications with France, establish fortified posts everywhere and so have the honour of ending the war in the Peninsula if Napoleon did not return in person.[10]

With characteristic concern for outward appearance, Soult made his headquarters in a fine palace that had belonged to Godoy. He first had to win the trust of his new master. For reasons already described, their relations had been strained as far back as Boulogne days when Joseph had served briefly as a colonel in Soult's famous IV Corps. Their sharp differences on operational matters when Soult was 'Supremo' in western Spain had left both men sore. Moreover, King Joseph was still smarting over the departure of his favourite, Jourdan. Also his whole concept of kingship in Spain was quite different from his brother's. Conveniently forgetting that he only ruled in Spain because there were French soldiers all over the country, he really believed that he could reign as 'His Catholic Majesty, King of Spain and the Indies' by winning the loyalty of his subjects through conciliation. Soult certainly did not underestimate 'conciliation', as he had shown in Oporto, but, as an able professional soldier and the Emperor's lieutenant, he also understood military realities. However, as his main task was now to conquer Spain rather than to fight directly against the English, there was at last some common ground between him and the King. He worked hard to get on reasonable terms. The King reciprocated and according to Soult's *Memoirs* they reached a fair *modus vivendi.*[11]

Soult had hardly assumed his command, with no chance yet of exercising his authority over any of the other semi-independent armies in the north and east, before he was confronted by an unexpectedly serious threat from the south. The over-confident central junta had ordered General Areizaga, an elderly, inexperienced but brave soldier, to launch a direct attack through La Mancha on Toledo and Madrid. Wellington, still based on the River Guadiana and firmly committed to a defensive strategy, flatly refused to have anything to do with this rash undertaking. At the beginning of November Areizaga, at the head of the largest Spanish army still operating, numbering about 60,000 men, thrust confidently through the passes of the Sierra Morena towards Madrid. Victor's I Corps in La Mancha fell back slowly before the Spanish advance. Two other French formations, Soult's old II Corps, now commanded by Heudelet, and Mortier's V Corps were on the Tagus near the area where the French had tried to surround Wellington after Talavera. Sebastiani's IV Corps, was between Aranjuez and the village of Ocaña. Soult, with the King in tow, took full direction of the impending battle although orders were of course given in Joseph's name. II Corps was ordered to guard the line of the Tagus in case, after all, an Anglo-Spanish army came to the help of Areizaga, while Victor continued to retreat slowly along the left bank of the Tagus. The large Spanish army reached a hill called Santa Cruz de la Tarza on the river bank and Areizaga sent cavalry patrols across the Tagus ranging as far as Aranda, only some 30 kilometres from Madrid. Meanwhile Soult was marshalling his forces behind the river. Mortier and Sebastiani were in the neighbourhood of Aranjuez, reinforced now by a division from the Madrid garrison under General Dessolles. Suddenly aware of this concentration of French military strength, Areizaga withdrew to the village of Ocaña where he drew up his large army in the flat plain around the village, and awaited the French attack.

As Areizaga was commanding the last considerable Spanish army that operated independently in the Peninsular War, this is a convenient opportunity to comment on Spanish regular armies against whom Soult and the other marshals were fighting. The soldiers were brave, obstinate in defence – as they were to show later at Albuera – and sometimes capable of marching directly on defensive positions. The exasperated Wellington often described them much more harshly. For instance he wrote that "the Spaniards do nothing but stand still. Indeed we consider ourselves fortunate if they do not run away."[12] Later in the war his views were more favourable. Spanish army drill was certainly very poor: the soldiers found it difficult to manoeuvre; their skirmishes were not comparable to the French *tirailleurs* and their cavalry was also very weak. Wellington used to say that the Peninsula was the graveyard of horses and certainly the Spanish cavalry horses as well as the draught horses for the artillery were poor and undernourished. The quality of Spanish generalship, with notable exceptions such as Romana, was ineffectual and, more significantly, the generals, again with certain exceptions, were gradually becoming political pawns of the central junta.[13]

It was an army like this that faced King Joseph and Soult at Ocaña towards the end of November 1809. The French numbered some 30,000 men, little more than half the size of the enemy. But Areizaga had made some foolish dispositions. His left

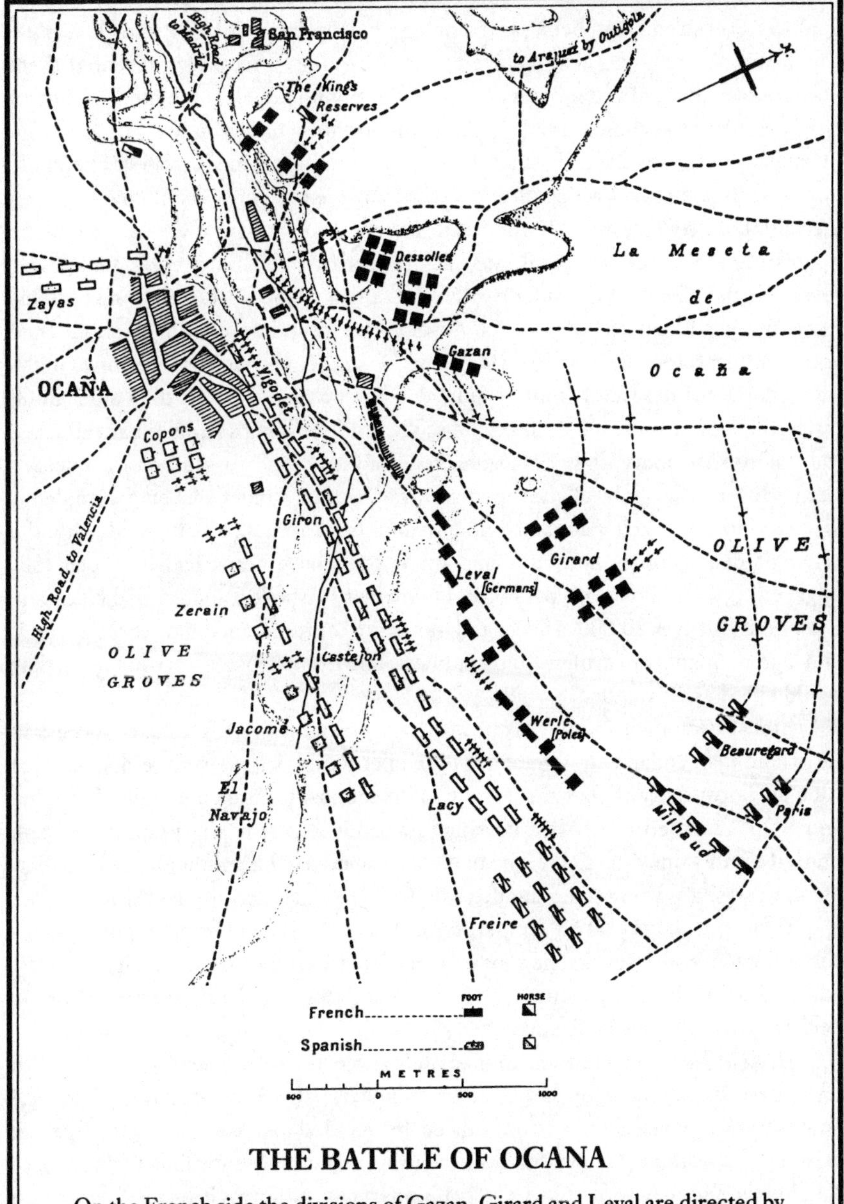

THE BATTLE OF OCANA

On the French side the divisions of Gazan, Girard and Leval are directed by Mortier, while the cavalry under Milhaud and Beauregard is directed by Sebastiani. Soult, acting in King Joseph's name, is in supreme command. On the Spanish side, Zayas's division is so placed that it can take no part in the battle at all.

flank, 15,000 strong, had been placed behind a deep ravine, the Ravin de la Canda, which was the only physical feature in the area. This effectively prevented them from taking any part in the battle. On his side, Soult had taken the unusual step of giving Mortier the command of the four infantry divisions from his own and from Sebastiani's corps while Sebastiani commanded the combined cavalry. The battle began with a heavy French artillery bombardment. This was followed by an onslaught of French cavalry on the Spanish right flank, moving diagonally along the Spanish line of battle. As usual, the magnificent French cavalry carried all before them. Meanwhile Mortier's infantry divisions attacked the Spaniards frontally. This was a more difficult operation since the Spanish troops were strongly entrenched and fighting ferociously in the village of Ocaña. Both Mortier and one of the divisional generals, Leval, were wounded. This was the crisis of the battle. Soult ordered up infantry reinforcements. Dessolles and the King's Royal Guard attacked the Spanish left flank while Sebastiani renewed his cavalry assault on the enemy's right. By now the bulk of the Spanish army was in danger of being completely surrounded. Areizaga had had enough and fled from the battlefield with the remnant of his forces hotly pursued by Victor whose corps had not been fully engaged. It was a disastrous battle for the Spaniards who lost some 5,000 killed and wounded. But over 20,000 officers and men were captured, including three generals and a great quantity of artillery and supplies. The French losses were not more than 1,700 killed and wounded.

Soult's victory at Ocaña was probably the greatest French military success in the whole Peninsular War. Coupled with Kellerman's victory over the Spaniards at Alba de Tormes near Salamanca, it gave a great boost to French morale. The King and Soult returned to Madrid in triumph. In his report to the Emperor, Joseph praised Soult's fine direction of the battle but, again like his brother in trying to play off the marshals against one another, he was later inclined to give Mortier chief credit for the victory. The Emperor disliked receiving glowing reports of his subordinates' successes and he sent no congratulations for Ocaña which has hardly featured at all in Napoleonic mythology. Yet Napoleon had never won such a decisive victory in the Peninsula.

Back in Madrid, Soult was immediately subjected to very unwelcome political pressures. Encouraged by his Spanish ministers, the King declared a general amnesty and, against Soult's strong advice, he decided to enrol some of the Spanish prisoners captured at Ocaña into his own army, while those unwilling to enlist were sent home. These new recruits were given smart new uniforms instead of their usual tattered clothing, as well as arms and equipment. But they often deserted back to the enemy later, usually to the guerrillas. Soon King Joseph was mockingly described as the central junta's 'quartermaster general'. Soult was powerless to prevent this foolish if well-intentioned initiative. In fact, in a much more careful and restrained way, he was able to raise a fair number of effective Spanish recruits for anti-guerrilla operations when he himself later ruled southern Spain. At this time he did arrange for various German and Swiss soldiers originally serving in the French army, captured at Baylen and then recaptured at Ocaña, to be formed into labour battalions where they provided excellent auxiliary services. However, as he had expected, the incorporation of Spaniards into Joseph's army at this time provoked furious comments from the Emperor. "Spaniards should never be allowed to join our army," he wrote. "They are habitual traitors. It was monstrous having them serving with French troops when they were stained with French blood!" He also insisted that Spanish flags captured at Ocaña should not be retained in Madrid but should be sent at once to Paris.[14]

Meanwhile, as 'Napoleon's man' in Madrid, Soult faced an increasingly hostile attitude at court not only from the Spaniards but even more from the King's French adherents, who were sometimes more Spanish than the Spaniards. The King had created his own order of chivalry to be awarded in addition to the Golden Fleece and instead of the Legion of Honour. French officers at his court – but certainly not Soult – were given estates and titles of nobility: General Bigarré, the chief aide-de-camp, was made a Spanish marquis and was given a large pension. He and Miot de Melito, who was also much honoured, were increasingly hostile both towards Napoleon and Soult. Indeed Soult and Sebastiani had some difficulty in getting these renegade Frenchmen to treat the Emperor's name with any respect; some of them felt that it would not have mattered if the Emperor had been killed in the Austrian campaign. Of course there were endless grounds of dispute between Paris and Madrid. A major reason for the invasion of Spain had been to strengthen the Continental Blockade against England. This meant that customs officers who carried out their duties efficiently – and not all of them did – seriously damaged the Spanish economy: indeed Spain suffered from the ill effects of the Continental System as much as any other country in Europe. Again the proceeds from captured British goods had to be sent to France or made available to the French armies in Spain rather than benefiting the Spanish economy. Napoleon was treating his brother Louis, King of Holland, in much the same way. Joseph received far too little money from his French subsidy to meet his many expenses, including his elaborate court, and he even had to pay off the debts of his Bourbon predecessors.

Against this difficult background Soult was trying to exercise, in the King's name, overall command in Spain. He sent orders to Suchet to press on with his advance towards Valencia: he tried hard to persuade his old enemy, Ney, to attack Ciudad Rodrigo and he made strong efforts to curb the increasingly active guerrilla bands operating in the north. Given a little time, he might have been able to wield some real authority over the semi-independent French generals now caught in the middle between the two quarrelling Bonaparte brothers. But by now the Emperor had begun issuing a stream of orders to French generals in the north without any reference whatever to Soult, apparently as preliminaries to his projected invasion of Portugal.[15] To make matters worse, as from December 1 1809, Berthier was given the rank of major general of the Army in Spain in order to act again as Napoleon's intermediary, while Soult, nominally with the same powers as before, merely became Joseph's chief of staff. Once more Brun de Villeret was posted off to Paris, ostensibly to offer the Emperor Soult's felicitations on his approaching marriage to the Austrian archduchess, Marie Louise, but in fact to test the waters. Despite a 'reassuring' letter from Napoleon about the new command arrangements,[16] Brun did not in the aftermath of the Ocaña victory find the Emperor at all well disposed either to his brother's court or to Soult himself. Ney had gone to Paris full of recriminations against Soult while Loison – Maneta, 'Le Tondu' – who had behaved so treacherously to Soult in Portugal – had been given another important command in Spain. It was significant that when Kellerman, the victor at the battle of Alba de Tormes, wanted to express his anxieties about military problems he wrote to Berthier and not to Soult.[17]

It was soon clear that the veteran army which was now available after the end of the war against Austria would be used mainly for a third and definitive invasion of Portugal, perhaps led by the Emperor himself. Berthier's reappearance seemed to confirm this while some of the Emperor's personal equipment and his travelling carriage arrived in Burgos. King Joseph sent two of his Spanish ministers to greet his brother at the frontier. However, Joseph and Soult saw no reason why the Emperor's preoccupation with Portugal and the destruction of Wellington's army should interfere with preparations for a fresh initiative of their own. The results of the decisive victory at Ocaña were being felt all over the south. Despite fierce Spanish patriotism there was strong dissension in the central junta between those with more liberal views and the conservatives. There were many conflicting local interests: some people had doubts about Ferdinand and the royal family as symbols of loyalty; some would settle for peace at any price; and some were even attracted by the liberal principles of Joseph and his government. The central junta was widely accused of corruption, incompetence and megalomania. Indeed Ocaña and Alba de Tormes virtually brought it to the end of the road.[18] In the circumstances it would have been inexcusable on either political or military grounds for the French not to have taken advantage of the chaotic situation in Seville to march south.

Joseph himself must have remembered Napoleon's words after he had been brought back to Madrid more or less in the Emperor's baggage train at the beginning of the year: "The invasion of Andalusia will finish the Spanish business. I leave the glory to you!"[19] After Ocaña he need no longer be simply part of his brother's baggage. With Soult's help he could become far more independent of the Emperor. Andalusia was the richest province in Spain and his Spanish ministers assured him that he would find many supporters there.

Soult has been much criticized for encouraging the King in all this for reasons of personal ambition and private avarice. The displaced Jourdan was strongly opposed to a wide-ranging operation. He affirmed in his *Memoirs* that the British were the real enemies and it was a mistaken strategy "to garrison the whole surface of Spain".[20] Later historians, who have sometimes tended to regard the Peninsular

War as primarily an Anglo-French conflict, have also asserted that the conquest of the south was a calamitous waste of French military manpower which should have been used for the destruction of Wellington's army. Sir Charles Oman takes this line when he sharply criticizes Soult for the great harm that he did to the French cause in the Peninsula.[21]

These seem to be mistaken arguments. There were strong military as well as political reasons for the dramatic initiative now undertaken by the King and Soult. When Napoleon had ordered Soult to conquer Portugal in January 1809 it had been part of an overall operation to invade southern Spain too. As recorded, Brun de Villeret had only recently brought back a message from Napoleon in Paris to the effect that Soult should have the honour of ending the war in Spain if the Emperor did not return himself.[22] If the veterans from the Austrian campaign were to be used in Portugal this left Joseph and Soult with more troops to march south.[23] Soult certainly believed that the conquest of the south could only assist the invasion of Portugal and would put an additional strain upon Wellington and the British. Indeed this is just what happened. Of even more importance, Soult had undoubtedly realized by this time that the French could not possibly win the war until they had occupied the greater part of the country and until they had virtually crushed Spanish resistance. Of course this never happened. But Soult did succeed in one of his ambitions. He established in the south the main French power base in the country for a period of more than two years. When he was forced finally to abandon Andalusia, French rule in Spain was doomed.

During the last weeks of 1809 the realistic Soult did not allow silence in Paris to deter his preparations for invading the south. In the middle of December he told Berthier that at no time since the beginning of the war were conditions so favourable and he put forward several alternative plans. The main problem was that the direct route through the Sierra Morena by way of Carolina meant traversing the narrow and heavily fortified pass of Despeña Perros. An alternative route which Victor favoured would have meant a long detour through the province of Estremadura and would have brought the French to within striking distance of Anglo-Spanish forces in the area of Badajoz. A final plan, taking account of these various considerations, was sent to Berthier at the beginning of January. Having still received no reply, Joseph and Soult left Madrid on their own initiative on January 7 1810, advancing south at a rapid pace. Again Soult had shown he was no mere servant of the Emperor, like some of the other marshals, once he believed he was taking the right course. He ordered Mortier to make a speedy advance through the narrow passes of the Sierra Morena to Carolina, leaving his artillery to be brought along by a more circuitous route: Victor was to proceed by way of Almaden towards Cordoba while Sebastiani's IV Corps advanced on the left flank towards Linares. Meanwhile II Corps was to remain on the Tagus to guard against a possible British attack: Suchet was to operate aggressively in Valencia to keep the Spaniards busy there and there was to be another offensive move towards Ciudad Rodrigo. Only after the King and

Soult had left Madrid did a grudging approval come from the Emperor.

Soult's various operations were triumphantly successful. The French armies marched quickly through the narrow passes of the Sierra Morena. Well fortified as Despeña Perros and the other passes turned out to be, they had too few defenders and these had little heart for a fight. About 6,000 prisoners and a sizeable amount of artillery and stores were captured. An 'Order of the Day' dated from Baylen, the town of France's great humiliation, announced the victories and the cities of Jaen and Cordoba opened their gates without resistance to Sebastiani and Victor respectively. A fair number of Andalusians rallied to the King and gradually the 'invasion' became more of a peaceful perambulation.

One of the few Spanish generals who kept his head was the Duke of Albuquerque. He hastened south by way of Badajoz and clashed with Victor's advance guard at Ecija not far from Seville. He then retired towards Cadiz. The central junta fled from Seville to Cadiz. Most of them had sent their families there already. Seville, the seat of government of the whole of unoccupied Spain, was wide open to French attack.

There was now another of those controversies that have so dogged Soult's career. On military grounds there was no doubt that Victor's I Corps should have marched straight on to Cadiz, leaving Seville to fall into French hands afterwards. At the time Cadiz was poorly defended and in a state of great confusion. A determined French attack could easily have captured it. In the event it was decided to enter Seville first and to seize Cadiz afterwards. By then it was too late. The defences had been hurriedly repaired. Spanish and British reinforcements were arriving and the city was too strongly defended for an immediate assault to succeed. In fact Cadiz never was captured and an entire French army corps wasted the next eighteen months investing it although they achieved the negative success of keeping a large Allied force blockaded there.

Soult has been blamed by some writers for advising King Joseph to enter Seville first and thus to delay the march on Cadiz. It was not surprising that the dismissed Jourdan took this view, saying that the King must have felt bound to accept Soult's military advice. Joseph's 'military intimates', Bigarré and Miot de Melito, adopted the same line in their *Memoirs*. The real explanation must be that the shortest way to Cadiz lay through Seville and, in his dispatch of January 26, Soult gave Victor the most precise instruction to enter Seville, to leave a few regiments there in order to retain possession of the city and then march straight on to Cadiz before the enemy had time to organize its defence.[24] Understandably, the King wanted to make a safe and splendid entry into Seville so that he himself delayed the onward march of the main body of Victor's corps. This was certainly the view of Napier who, as always, has made a careful study of all the available documents.[25]

Apart from this blunder, the march into Andalusia had been a real triumph for the King and for Soult. Despite some hectic, last minute attempts at resistance by an armed mob, Seville quickly surrendered and on February 1, three weeks after he had left Madrid, the King, accompanied by Soult and a glittering array of generals, entered the city in triumph, installing himself in the Moorish palace of the Alcázar. The 'rebel capital' had fallen, causing a moral repercussion throughout Europe. Then, as was the case after Soult had captured Oporto, the volatile Andalusians hastened to welcome Joseph. Indeed there were said to be more 'Josefinos', as his adherents were called, in Seville than in any other city of Spain. In a vivid passage Bigarré describes the welcome that Joseph received. "Every morning priests and monks came to kiss his hand telling him that he had been sent by God. The nobility did everything in their power to please him. One grandee presented him with twelve magnificent bulls, another with some splendid Andalusian horses. Others placed their wives and daughters at His Majesty's disposal! In scenes of indescribable enthusiasm the populace prostrated themselves before him!"[26]

Despite this euphoria, Soult and his generals had more serious tasks. Sebastiani, on Soult's orders, had marched quickly through Granada and had reached the Mediterranean coast, capturing the wealthy city of Malaga. But this was a difficult campaign. Sebastiani had to operate against the Spanish general, Blake, with a mixed force of Spanish regulars and armed guerrillas. Aided by British officers and units from Gibraltar, the Spaniards seized the town of Ronda and briefly reoccupied Malaga. The difficult south-eastern campaign which continued for some two years was fought to enable Sebastiani to join up with Suchet in Valencia. At first Sebastiani was handicapped further by having to provide protection for Joseph's various 'victory progresses' in Granada which included a state visit to Malaga, a period of residence in the Alhambra and a splendid occasion when in one small town the King insisted on receiving a band of hostile guerrillas and won them round completely to his side.[27] Soult accompanied the King on some of these progresses but he spent much time in Seville turning to good use the considerable defence resources that he found there. There was a big military arsenal and a large arms foundry. Provided already with the great quantities of guns, gunpowder and ammunition that he had captured in the Sierra Morena, he soon had a fair quantity of ammunition and a small siege train that could be used against both Cadiz and Badajoz.

The most urgent problem for the French was the capture of Cadiz. Here strong defences had been built to protect not only the rocky promontory of Cadiz itself but the large marshy area around Cadiz Bay known as the Isla de León. Various forts and strongpoints had been renewed and reinforced so that Victor's army corps faced a defence line which extended for some 40 kilometres. The new regency council, which had replaced the old central junta, was supposed to be acting in the name of King Ferdinand but Ferdinand himself was living in comfortable captivity in France and was soon begging Joseph to allow him to marry one of his daughters. The council was as quarrelsome and corrupt as the old central junta: it had foolishly got rid of its saviour, Albuquerque, by posting him as ambassador to London and there were a number of French sympathizers in Cadiz. But there were plenty of patriotic

Spaniards, too, who were determined to resist while, for political and strategic reasons, the British simply could not afford to allow Cadiz to be captured. In many respects it was even more important to them than Lisbon. There were strong anti-British feelings in the city where a French naval squadron had sheltered for some time after Trafalgar, and earlier Wellington had commented: "Britain will not be admitted to Cadiz at the present time."[28] However, the Spaniards now had no alternative to accepting British help. British reinforcements arrived with some Portuguese units, bringing the total garrison in the city up to 30,000 men. British raiding parties also carried out harrying operations along the coast from Gibraltar to Tarifa. During the first few months of 1810 the French, under Soult's overall direction, did achieve two useful successes. Despite strenuous efforts by British engineers to strengthen it, the French captured the important fortress of Matagorda which enabled them to use heavy artillery against the remaining defences of the Isla de León. Again French soldiers and sailors, most of them survivors of Trafalgar, confined in ghastly conditions in two old hulks, succeeded with the help of the besieging army in floating a ship across Cadiz Bay to freedom. The memoir writer, Admiral Grivel, who was involved in this operation, describes dining with Soult afterwards and finding this dour man so charming that he would have been prepared to carry out any hazardous operation that he demanded.[29]

Meanwhile, Mortier's corps was operating under Soult's command against stiff resistance on the lower reaches of the River Guadiana near Badajoz. But Soult must have realized that by this time other orders which he was continuing to send as Joseph's chief of staff to Suchet in Valencia or to Bonnet in Santander were only for show. There is an ironic comment in one of his papers, noting that "by a coincidence" his orders coincided with similar ones sent out in the Emperor's name by Berthier.

In fact, while King Joseph was being received with such enthusiasm in the main cities of Andalusia, very different developments were taking place in the north. Under an imperial decree of February 8 1810 the provinces of Catalonia, Aragon, Navarre, Biscay, Burgos and Valladolid were in future to be administered by the military commandants who were occupying these provinces. The generals were empowered to raise taxes, make local appointments and take decisions quite independently of the King who was left to administer only Madrid and New Castile. The situation in the south, where he was now residing and ruling, and where Soult commanded his armies, was left in temporary abeyance.

The reasons for this new decree, which preceded by only a few months the total annexation of Louis's kingdom of Holland, were clear enough. They were at once political, economic, military and personal. The public reasons were that the Emperor could no longer tolerate the enormous expenses of his armies in Spain: other ways must be found of financing military operations there. Of course, on purely political grounds, the highly successful occupation of Andalusia had increased Napoleon's suspicions of his brother's ambitions. When the advance into

Andalusia had begun, Joseph had issued a proclamation in which his brother's name was not mentioned. "Rally round me, Spaniards," he declared, "and a new era of glory and happiness will begin." He added that Spain must not lose one acre of its territorial sovereignty.[30] Since Joseph and Soult had left Madrid, Napoleon had alternated between treating the Andalusian expedition with ignorance, jealousy or contempt. His first specific reference to it came in a letter to Berthier of January 31 in which he insisted that only forces that were basically necessary should travel to the south, adding that "only the English are to be feared. The Spaniards are mere partisans who can never keep the field."[31] Napoleon's views about the Spaniards were now not far removed from Wellington's!

Of course Napoleon continued to feel that the French occupation of the south was a distraction from his main thrust into Portugal. No doubt he had intended at first to command this third invasion himself. However, his marriage to Marie Louise and his increasing concern over Russia's future intentions led him to entrust the command to Masséna, who had so recently achieved glory in the campaign against Austria. Perhaps, at the back of his mind, also, was a reluctance to be involved in an operation which had failed twice before and posed so many serious military and logistics problems. More and more orders poured out from imperial headquarters without reference either to Joseph or to Soult, organizing into three corps, commanded by Ney, Reynier and Junot, the great army which was now to invade Portugal under Masséna. All military dispositions in northern Spain were subordinated to this major operation, particularly to ensure that the lines of communication with France were guarded as far as possible from such Spanish regular forces as still existed and more importantly from the swarms of guerrillas that abounded in the mountainous north.

Soult's position at this time was particularly delicate. On the one hand he was a French marshal owing his allegiance to the Emperor and, especially after the recent events in Oporto, determined that his French loyalties should not be called in question. On the other hand, as chief of staff to His Catholic Majesty, he had just occupied almost the entire southern part of the kingdom. Napoleon's decree of February 8, relating to northern Spain, was naturally most embarrassing to Joseph, who, in a letter to his wife, Julie, in Paris, discussed abdication, not for the first time. "If the Emperor wishes to disgust me with Spain," he wrote, "I want nothing better than to retire immediately."[32] Meanwhile he was acting out the charade of being a real king by issuing a decree on April 17 laying down various long-term administrative measures such as the abolition of Spanish provinces in favour of 38 prefectures with elected councils, cantons and communes. In the confused state of the country and with the military governments in the north, these reforms only functioned half-heartedly around Madrid and spasmodically in the south.

To a great extent the King was deceived by the initial fervour with which he was received in Andalusia. Soult, who was much more realistic, tried hard to moderate his enthusiasm. He continually urged Joseph not to accept too readily the specious promises of those who agreed to support him and then abruptly changed their minds. The city of Malaga was typical. It joyfully celebrated Joseph's arrival one day and a few days later opened its gates to the guerrillas once more, destroying among many other buildings the house and property of the American consul who had recently entertained the King.[33] Guerrilla warfare, blood feuds and contraband trading were the normal way of life in southern Spain and these were precisely the problems that Soult himself would have to face when, for the next few years, he himself was virtually the viceroy of Andalusia.

For the present, despite pressures from the Emperor, his relations with Joseph remained at least 'correct'. On the King's departure from Seville – never to return – at the beginning of May, he told Soult that his absence would be short. He asked the Marshal to keep in close touch with him, especially over taxation and economic problems, and "in a free and easy manner" emphasized the confidence and respect that he had for him.[34] These polite relations were not to last long.

The first few months of 1810, when the French occupied virtually the whole of Andalusia except Cadiz, was indeed a real turning point in the Spanish War. It has been well said that "Spain had been reduced to such a state of prostration that she could do no more than survive until she could be liberated by the Anglo-Portuguese army of the Duke of Wellington".[35] The establishment of a French power base in the south represented the best chance, however brief, of a full French conquest of the country.

10

"VICEROY IN THE SOUTH" – THE FRENCH POWER BASE IN SPAIN

FOR OVER TWO YEARS, from the time when King Joseph departed for Madrid in May 1810 until Soult himself was compelled to leave southern Spain in August 1812, the Marshal reigned over Andalusia as viceroy in everything but name. The patriot cause was in a state of paralysis, with only Cadiz, Galicia, parts of the east coast and Catalonia free from occupation. There was, indeed, a real possibility of a complete French conquest. The 'regency' established in Cadiz as a council of five remained as hopelessly divided between the conservatives on one side and the opposing liberals, intent on sweeping away all forms of absolutism. As one British representative had told Wellington, he now had "only five blockheads to deal with instead of thirty four".[1] A 'National Cortes' had been convened but it was highly unrepresentative since so much of the country was under French control.

This state of paralysis had various consequences. Spanish regular armies were much reduced in size and effectiveness so that the patriotic cause had to be upheld more and more by the guerrillas, not always with beneficial consequences for Spain. Indeed the country was increasingly to be determined by foreign intervention – on the one hand by Wellington's Anglo-Portuguese army, which was Spain's ultimate saviour – on the other hand by the French army of occupation. Napoleon's Russian campaign and the great military skill of Wellington were the main reasons why a 'French alternative' became impossible. That it was ever a starter was due not so much to King Joseph Bonaparte as to two forceful and capable French marshals, Soult and Suchet. As Owen Connelly writes, the architects of the 'Napoleonic legend' pay far too little attention to the great 'marshal administrators' like these two men.[2] Above all it was in southern Spain, where Soult ruled with a fair degree of acceptance by the Andalusians, that there was ever a chance of this 'French alternative' succeeding.

Soult administered the south whilst engaged in continuous operations around Badajoz and the Portuguese frontier, against Cadiz, along the south-east coast, in the mountains of Granada and Murcia and against guerrilla bands everywhere. Before examining these operations, it is important to consider the measures that he took internally to administer and to stabilize this French power base.

Soult's military independence from King Joseph was not officially confirmed until a decree was promulgated by the Emperor on July 14 1810 making him commander-in-chief of the 'Army of the South'. In fact he had been operating as an independent administrator in Seville from the beginning of May. In a letter informing him of this new decree, Berthier emphasized his overall command of the three army corps of Mortier, Victor and Sebastiani. The army was to be paid and properly equipped on the old principle that 'war supported war', so that it must have first call on the resources of southern Spain. Soult must continue to respect King Joseph but – writing no doubt with his tongue in his cheek – Berthier affirmed that it all showed the "high confidence" which the Emperor felt for Soult.[3] A shorter letter to the King stated that these arrangements were made "for operational reasons".[4] It was all too clear to Joseph that Soult's position had become as independent as that of the generals in the north. Again he considered abdication and the new situation did nothing to improve his relationship with his nominal chief of staff.

Naturally Soult's first concern was with his three army corps numbering, according to the imperial muster rolls, some 100,000 men under arms,[5] although Soult asserted that the three corps were much under strength. Almost at once he began quarrelling with Madrid about financing this large army. He insisted that all monetary contributions levied in Andalusia were needed for his military operations. A long correspondence with the Treasury ensued in which Soult expressed much respect for the King but made the position quite clear. On one occasion he told Victor that he had prevented six royal prefects from the new 'departments' created by King Joseph from sending ten to twelve million rials a month to Madrid as this money was needed "for urgent military necessities".[6] There were also difficulties over army pay with the Emperor himself but in July the Ministry of War in Paris decreed that money sent to the Army of the South must proceed under a strong military escort to protect it not only from guerrillas but from Joseph's government as well.[7] Officers on their way to or from Soult's army were also ordered to proceed through the capital without stopping. This did not prevent the King from trying to coerce entire units to join him. Napoleon's insistence that his brother had no rights to merchandise captured from the British must have been particularly riling to him.[8]

In organizing his army to defend the whole area of southern Spain with a coastline about 1,000 kilometres long from the frontiers of Portugal to the borders of Valencia, Soult was faced with an administrative task after his own heart. He was far away from Paris in a part of Europe where Napoleon's interest was only spasmodic, so that he was continually obliged to improvise. Inevitably he was becoming involved in civil administration, although Napoleon had warned him against this. But Soult, who was in any case a compulsive administrator, had little alternative. His ideas were succinctly expressed in a letter to Berthier on August 18 1810: "I have for His Catholic Majesty all the respect that is due to him but it is difficult to feel the same about his ministers. The King announces his intention of returning to Andalusia but I have to say that I do not think that his presence is necessary here. Inevitably it will lead to a different kind of administration which will not lead to the pacification of this part of Spain. It will take away part of the resources which the army needs and it will make through his ministers an explosion of opposition which cannot be avoided."[9] A few days later he was telling Berthier that the army headquarters for the whole of Spain should be moved to Seville, leaving Madrid as little more than an administrative district. This was creating a power base in southern Spain with a vengeance! These were no doubt sincerely held views of a determined and able man who knew a lot about administration and who intended to do things in his own way.

Ultimately, of course, French rule depended on the effectiveness and determination of Soult himself and of his subordinate generals. Naturally it was easier to use strong-arm measures when Joseph was far away in Madrid. Law and order posed the most serious problem and at first guerrilla bands were as active in the south as elsewhere in Spain, especially in the Sierra Morena and in the mountains of Granada. Recent studies have closely examined the major contribution which the guerrillas made as symbols of Spanish patriotism in the War of Liberation, while underlining their limitations when faced by determined military force.[10] In order to combat the *partidas* in southern Spain, Soult, like many other military leaders both then and now, adopted a mixed strategy of fast-moving army columns coupled with a series of fortified strongpoints. As in Piedmont in 1800, where he had continued to use some of the more villainous Barbets to police the mountains against their former comrades, he created special Spanish units under French leadership, the 'Guides de la Sierra Morena' based on Jaen and Cordoba, which he employed against the guerrilla bands. He also organized in Seville a sizeable civic guard – the 'Escopeteros' – for internal police duties made up mainly of Spanish and French civilians.[11]

After defeats in battle Spanish regulars often slipped away to join the guerrillas or, as after Joseph's amnesty, they returned to their own homes. Charles Cocks, Wellington's brilliant intelligence officer, referred in his Diaries to the great number of ex-soldiers "dispersed during the war and glad to join any army that would pay and feed them". He advocated enlistment in the British Army.[12] Soult was well aware of all this and made his local commanders keep a watchful eye on those ex-soldiers. Then, on the principle that they were less dangerous anyway when they were in uniform, he succeeded in re-enlisting some of them into the French army. They were mainly used for local defence but two regiments of Spanish *chasseurs à cheval* fought well on the French side at Albuera. This was of course in flat contradiction to the instructions of the Emperor who had refused, for example, to allow the Régiment Joseph Napoléon, made up of Romana's old division still serving with the French army, to return to Spain at all.[13] Many area commanders recruited local counter-guerrilla units, but as Soult's recruitment schemes seemed to be the most successful, Napoleon wisely left them alone. Once again Soult had defied the Emperor's orders when he considered himself to be right.

Another vigorous measure that he took against the guerrillas was to impose double or treble taxation on villages which had paid them ransoms.[14] A special watch was also kept on horse and mule transport, and an attempt was even made to introduce some form of personal identification in the south. Some of Soult's generals were just as ruthless as himself, especially Sebastiani who became, like Soult, a 'church despoiler'. Dessolles, who was briefly under Soult's command, was an excellent administrator but some of his senior officers had little administrative experience which meant that Soult himself had to intervene personally in various parts of Andalusia.[15]

To an extent the activities of the guerrillas themselves played into Soult's hands. Their chiefs were often petty dictators, uncooperative with one another and indeed sharply hostile to rival bands which entered their own 'territories'. Often their taste for pillage far outweighed their desire to fight the French. Nor did the Spanish country folk benefit greatly from their operations since any goods seized from the French became the guerrillas' personal property. Of course their widespread activities compelled Soult, like the other military leaders in Spain, to mount continuous attacks on them with his regular forces at a time when he was fully engaged in military operations elsewhere. They also provided diversionary tactics, gave valuable intelligence to the allied armies and, to an extent, interfered with French military communications. But in the south, at least, they were poorly provided with equipment and they had no artillery so that they could never attack strong military bases. Nor could they resist any but the weakest French counter-attacks. In general, they could never form the nucleus of a Spanish national army: indeed their very existence made recruitment to the regular army more difficult.[16]

The situation in the north was much more serious for the invaders. Here the *partidas* disrupted large parts of Navarre and of the Basque country, seriously threatening lines of communications with France itself. By 1812 the famous guerrilla chief, Espoz y Mina, had established a local administration with sizeable military armaments, some artillery and even with military hospitals.[17] In southern Spain things were different. It certainly cannot be claimed that Soult had actually won the war against the guerrillas. Units of Sebastiani's IV Corps had regularly to operate against them in Granada, and the Sierra Morena was never completely cleared, but some regions of Andalusia became relatively peaceful as did parts of Aragon and Valencia under the control of Suchet; the transport of supplies was rarely interrupted and couriers could travel virtually without escort. Evidence of this comes from Soult's own papers and from the *Memoirs* of Brun de Villeret, but there was much additional evidence. Years later, when the great Espoz y Mina visited Joseph Bonaparte in exile in America, he said that Soult's name was especially execrated in Spain.[18] Surely this was a tribute to the Marshal's ruthlessness and effectiveness. Again General Lejeune, who was sent to the Peninsula on an investigation mission, gave a full if highly coloured picture of southern Spain at this time. He had a gloomy interview in Madrid with King Joseph who told him that Andalusia had originally submitted voluntarily but was now greatly oppressed by Soult. However, he found that everything was very peaceful in the south: he could even indulge his passion for nature study while crossing the Sierra Morena, admittedly with a strong escort. It was only when he returned north again that he was captured by the Spaniards and held as a prisoner of war first in Spain and then in England at Ashby de la Zouche.[19] Saint-Chamans recorded that he could usually travel with dispatches anywhere in Andalusia without an escort and later when he took part in the Russian campaign he compared the Grande Armée's state of confusion when it set out on its long march to Moscow with the firm discipline of Soult's armies in southern Spain.[20]

It is an exaggeration to claim, as some French historians have done, that when governmental burdens had to be endured in Spain a French yoke was probably the easiest to bear. It is also hard to assess the loyalties of Soult's Spanish auxiliaries. Certainly this loyalty cracked as soon as he was compelled to withdraw from Andalusia in August 1812. On the other hand, it is clear that his effective occupation of most of the south prevented any real progress being made in the War of Liberation until Wellington led his army of veterans across the Spanish frontier in the summer of 1812.[21] It is understandable – and not, as it is sometimes described, an act of villainy – that Soult at that time offered Joseph a safe haven as well as a base for further operations in relatively tranquil Andalusia.

As regards general administration, Soult wrote interestingly in his private papers about conditions that he found in southern Spain. He described the country as having existed under a 'rather detached' monarchy with a series of foreign dynasties but depending upon an older and stronger form of local government. Of course the officials now appointed by King Joseph for the recently created 'departments' would certainly have to 'play themselves in'. Many of them were quite inexperienced and they could not operate at all without the protection of French arms.[22] Soult recorded that he had a strong ally for his civilian administration in the royal commissioner for Andalusia, the Conde de Montarco, who vetted his various ideas on reform and with whom he collaborated closely.[23] His senior officers were strictly ordered to maintain good relations with the civilian authorities and with the population in general. A useful function was also performed by Brun de Villeret who continued the work on civilian affairs which he had begun when he was on Soult's staff in Madrid. Among his reforms in Andalusia, Soult tried to eliminate, as far as possible, the ruinous system of land requisition, which in a country often so poorly administered from the centre usually resulted in much unfairness. It had caused large areas to remain uncultivated because the poorer farmers wanted to avoid requisitioning. Instead, after consultation with the Conde de Montarco, he devised a land tax payable either in money or in kind. A high proportion of the land was actually owned by the church and, by arranging a simple form of taxation for church lands and regularizing the collection of tithes under the close supervision of Spanish or French officers, he earned the gratitude of the church and her support against the guerrillas.[24]

In fact, despite the plundering activities both of himself and some of his generals, the church as a whole accepted French rule because it provided at least a measure of stability. But Soult did not hesitate to take sharp action against the church whenever he considered it necessary. When the Seville chapter tried to oppose a royal decree, four of the canons were immediately arrested and the chapter was fined two million rials.[25]

Unlike most of the other marshals, Soult was greatly interested in economic and commercial matters. This was primarily for military reasons but it was also for the economic benefit of the whole of Andalusia. He made full use of the big military arsenal and foundry in Seville; Granada could supply him with small arms and gunpowder; lead came from the mines of Linares and Almaden, copper from the Rio Tinto, sulphur and saltpetre from Buenamaurel. Three years previously he had endeavoured to introduce improvements in the estate that he had been awarded in eastern Europe after Tilsit. He was to do the same in the Midi when he was a minister under Louis Philippe. Now he was similarly active in Andalusia, embarking on negotiations with the commercial houses of Xeres and Haurie, and bartering supplies of their wine, dried fruit and other commodities, which could no longer be exported overseas, for the benefit of the army and the civil population. He became even more commercially adventurous in Malaga, building up a modest seaborne trade in foodstuffs with Morocco and, through the good offices of the French consul in Tangier, d'Ornano, with other small North African ports. He even appointed unofficial consuls of his own there. Additionally, he equipped some privateers in Malaga, in which Brun de Villeret was involved, in order to acquire more foodstuffs for Andalusia by fair means or foul. British naval operations in the Mediterranean prevented any major expansion of the coastal trade and Tangier was effectively blockaded by the British navy but, when the serious crop failure in 1811 led to great food shortages, he had to take greater risks and to adopt more drastic economic measures.[26] Part of the trouble in feeding the civilian population was caused by transport difficulties. Soult gradually improved the transport system for both military and civilian traffic. He enlarged and made navigable the River Guadalquivir as a main transport route from Seville to Cordoba. This was done in the teeth of strong opposition on grounds of cost from both Madrid and Paris.[27] But it all ensured that, at least for the first half of his period of rule, the people of Andalusia were reasonably well fed.

During General Lejeune's visit of inspection he stayed for three days in Seville under Soult's direction examining all the civil and military establishments, the hospitals, the arsenals and foundries. Everywhere he found intense activity and excellent order. He then went on to visit Victor's siege works around Cadiz and also Cordoba and Granada. Obviously Soult was very much in charge of this well-ordered province but, letting his hair down during a visit to the theatre on his return to Seville, the Marshal complained about his problems in keeping at bay his many enemies, British, Spanish and Portuguese. He was also faced with the same difficulty that he had experienced in Oporto – his senior officers were thoroughly discontented. This must have been partly due to his constant inability to get along with his generals despite being admired by his personal staff, his junior officers and the army rank and file. Soult told Lejeune that officers of high rank serving under him simply did not obey his orders. He had a special problem because two of them were also marshals – his friend Mortier and the highly disobliging Victor. Sebastiani, commanding IV Corps in Granada, was also very difficult. Again, too, it was partly because they were all serving in this remote corner of the Empire far away from true military glory and from that fount of honours, the Emperor himself.

Despite these problems Soult knew as well as Napoleon the value of military display. General Apollinaire Fée, the chief army pharmacist, describes Soult at the height of his authority. "After King Joseph's departure he became the 'King of Andalusia' himself. As with Homer's Zeus, Olympus trembled at his nod! Never was a monarch supported by such pomp. He was always surrounded by a dazzling entourage. On Sundays the élite troops would line the route to the cathedral for the general-in-chief's arrival. He would appear followed by a brilliant staff. He made a smiling response to all this magnificent ceremonial while preserving a cool, formal dignity. He had learnt a lot in this respect from the Emperor."[28] None of the marshals knew as well as he did how to follow Napoleon's example in well organized ceremonial and in punctilious attendance at Mass on the right occasions.

By now French power in Andalusia looked stable. The intellectuals who had some qualified admiration for the ideals of the French Revolution and the nobility in Seville, Cordoba and elsewhere had gone over to the French in considerable numbers. In the country districts French rule offered stability against the violent activities of the *partidas*. As the British intelligence officer, Charles Cocks, reported: "The landowners, the great farmers and the townspeople are tired of the war and would be very glad to put an end to it in any way."[29] Except in Cadiz and a few other areas, the Spanish regular army was gradually being squeezed out of existence. Everywhere there seemed little to be gained from resistance.[30]

Not surprisingly, Soult's relations with King Joseph had begun greatly to deteriorate. This was partly due to Soult's military operations but mainly because Joseph regarded him increasingly as his brother's representative or as a virtually independent ruler. In either case he was devoting all his financial resources to the payment of his armies or for the benefit of the people of Andalusia, so there was nothing whatever to be spared for Madrid. From the beginning there had been minor pinpricks. On his return to Madrid, the King had complained that Soult's artillery stationed at Aranjuez to cover his crossing of the Tagus had caused death and injury to some of the prize herds in the royal parks. There were rows over relations with Spanish newspaper representatives. More importantly, the King had refused on financial grounds to allow Soult to build a strong fortress in Seville which would be the base for French power in southern Spain; this reflected Soult's idea that Seville would be a better capital than Madrid itself. As the months passed, Joseph felt an increasing sense of isolation as all effective power in occupied Spain except around the capital passed into the hands of Soult and the other military chiefs. He continued to talk about abdication. Soult incurred most of his wrath since the Marshal now had such a firm grip on the south – that part of Spain which seemed to be so full of *afrancasados*, as French supporters were called. "If Andalusia is taken from me," Joseph had written to his brother, "I shall be nothing more than a hospital porter or prison gaoler in Madrid."[31] In May 1811 he made a hasty if forlorn visit to Paris nominally to attend the baptism of Napoleon's newly born son, the King of Rome. Here, his open hostility to Soult came to a head. According to Soult's information he did not allude to him by name but "he could not restrain his malevolence and he spared no statement or insinuation that would harm me".[32] Naturally Soult, as a mere viceroy, could not attend the baptism but Louise upheld his interests well. As a prominent member of the imperial court she held the 'baptismal cloth' at the ceremony and later received a magnificent *parure* of diamonds to commemorate her part in the baptism.[33] King Joseph got little comfort from his journey except that Napoleon graciously allowed him to have back his beloved Jourdan as chief of staff instead of the all-powerful Soult. This did not improve relations between Madrid and Seville. In April 1812, on the eve of his departure for the invasion of Russia, the Emperor once more made his brother commander-in-chief of all the French armies in Spain. But, two months later, Jourdan wondered whether Soult was ready to acknowledge this fact. With fresh problems in the military and political field, relations between Soult and the King were nearly at breaking point.

Meanwhile, in the first half of 1811, Andalusia, like other parts of Spain, faced a serious economic crisis. Half the harvest crop in the south had failed and the price of corn rose alarmingly.[34] This was made all the worse because the Continental Blockade had prevented the export of products on which southern Spain largely depended, including wine and fruit. Agriculture had been much impeded by the war and some of the leading landowners in the south had departed. How was the army now to be fed and how was a famine among the civilian population to be prevented?

Soult could take comfort from the fact that he had already done much to develop Andalusia's economic resources. But there were terrible transport problems which required draconian solutions. Grain was brought, often by force, from isolated farms in military vehicles and under police or military guard to be stored in safety and then to be distributed to the army or to the people in the large towns or villages. More and more special barges were used on the widened Guadalquivir between Seville and Cordoba and the modest coastal trade between Malaga and Morocco as well as privateering activities were increased. This did something to alleviate the situation but the famine continued until there were actually dead lying in the streets of Seville. Soult presided daily over an emergency committee to distribute soup and foodstuffs to the starving inhabitants.[35]

As another desperate measure, while continuing his never-ending military operations to capture Cadiz, he engaged in some quite different activities there. The French attitude to the regency council and to the embryonic Cortes had been somewhat ambivalent. At one time Napoleon had urged his brother to open secret negotiations with the Cortes in an attempt at damage limitation. This idea came to nothing but under the spur of urgent economic necessities Soult himself engaged in private negotiations with traders inside the besieged city. Under these exchanges Andalusian products such as lead from the Linares and Almaden mines, wine, dried fruit and other commodities would be exchanged in Cadiz for supplies of flour, rice, linen and medical equipment for the use of the French military and the Spanish civilian population.[36] This involved serious breaches in the Continental System, similar to so many others occurring all over Europe. Of course Andalusian products found their way to England but Soult considered that his actions were fully justified by the emergency.

Napoleon himself had little idea of what was going on in this remote corner of Europe. He was much displeased with Soult for failing to capture Cadiz, for taking so long to master Badajoz and for allegedly giving little direct help to Masséna before the lines of Torres Vedras. From August 1811, with his own economic problems and with his major preparations for the invasion of Russia the following year, he stopped the financial subsidy to the Army of the South altogether. "How is it," he is supposed to have commented to Berthier, "that the most fruitful part of Europe cannot support the army? It is France that ought to get help from Andalusia!" In an attempt to tell the Emperor the true facts, Brun de Villeret was sent to Paris on two separate occasions. Despite the sharp criticism of the Marshal's military operations in some of Napoleon's letters, Brun was received by the Emperor in a friendly fashion – very different to the 'alarms and excursions' during his memorable visit to Schönbrunn in 1809. According to Brun, Soult was virtually instructed to maintain himself in Spain until further notice.[37] However, by the time the aide-de-camp returned from his second visit in 1812, Soult had been forced to abandon Andalusia altogether. Meanwhile Soult's intendant general, Mathieu Faviers, had been carrying on a long and ineffectual correspondence with Berthier about financial support for the Army of the South. One result was that Faviers was downgraded in rank. Later, with little available evidence, he was accused of bribery, partly perhaps as an element in the smear campaign against Soult himself. Characteristically, Thiébault called him Soult's "head peculator" and expressed spurious indignation that he was made a peer of France when Soult was a minister under Louis Philippe.[38]

Despite all these economic problems, the military operations and the guerrilla activities in the mountains, Andalusia – that easy-going land with nearly a million inhabitants – remained relatively calm throughout Soult's viceroyalty. Brun de

Villeret, the unemotional memoir writer, describes a busy but tranquil existence in Seville with much hard work being relieved by frequent balls and bullfights and by playing chess. The high-spirited Saint-Chamans contributes a more vivid picture of the ladies of Seville among whom Soult and his officers could relax. He describes them as being "large, tall and handsome without being regular beauties. They are piquant and voluptuous. They are shockingly ignorant and read very little except religious books and perhaps *Don Quixote*. They are devoted to pleasure and to love in particular. Those who have known them and are now far away will miss them forever."[39]

A.G. Macdonnell, whose book, *Napoleon and His Marshals*, probably introduced many of us to a study of this fascinating group of men, describes Soult marching out of Seville for the last time when he was compelled to abandon southern Spain with a gigantic train of wagons carrying the spoils of his viceroyalty. In a magnificent coach rode "les maréchales", two beautiful sisters, one of whom had been Soult's mistress and the other married to a Spanish colonel who had been Victor's mistress. Officers of senior rank were followed in the cavalcade by a mistress on horseback escorted by a cavalry trooper![40] This vivid pointer to some of Soult's off-duty activities was probably not much exaggerated. Louise had never joined her husband in Seville, and Soult, like Joseph, certainly enjoyed the charms of beautiful women. He seems to have had a natural son born to one of his lady friends but the youth died unmarried. Unlike the King, Soult's mistresses exercised no influence whatever on his policy except perhaps to give him a real affection for Andalusia and its people.

What are the facts about Soult's plundering activities and his wholesale removal of pictures and art treasures from monasteries all over Andalusia? Perhaps rather surprisingly, he had developed an excellent taste for pictures, and in the church buildings of Andalusia there were hundreds of works by the great Spanish painters, Murillo, Alonso Cano, Francisco de Zurbaran and many others. It was a common practice in wartime, particularly in this most ferocious of wars, for works of art to become the spoils of the victors. King Joseph's decree for the dissolution of Spanish monasteries provided great opportunities for plunder. At the Treaty of Paris, ending the war in 1814, it was specifically provided that art treasure acquired during the fighting all over Europe need not be returned. The situation was changed in the Peace that followed Waterloo but this had only a limited effect on art treasures acquired by the French in Spain. Napoleon, who frequently complained about the conduct of his marshals in the Peninsula, once asserted that he ought to make an example of Soult by shooting him "since he was the worst plunderer of all".[41] This may have been true. But the Emperor himself saw nothing incongruous in asking his brother in Madrid, on behalf of Desson, the French director general of museums, for a present of fifteen masterpieces from private houses or suppressed monasteries.[42] Wellington also described Soult and his officers as great plunderers but the British themselves were not backward in acquiring loot. Probably Soult's greatest sins were in the scale of his plunder and in his continued retention of his art collection rather than handing it over to the state. The sale of his pictures after his death in 1851 made nearly a million and a half francs, which was a very large sum of money in the middle of the nineteenth century. In fact he had saved a great number of masterpieces from destruction, such as those, for example, in the Casa de Ayuntamiente in Seville. By far the largest number of pictures remained in Spain and, when King Ferdinand returned at the end of the war, they were as usual in the most deplorable condition. Those that Soult took away have ended up in art galleries or private houses all over Europe. A list of the pictures that he acquired, with some indication of their eventual destination, is given in the Appendix. It is hardly a conclusive argument but, all in all, Soult's wartime acquisitions were probably no worse than Lord Elgin's 'capture' of the Parthenon statues nor than the German removal to the Pergamum Museum in Berlin of the Ishtar Gate from Babylon. Nor do Soult's buccaneering activities seem to have affected the relative contentment with which many Andalusians regarded his viceroyalty.

No doubt Napier exaggerates outrageously when he claims that Andalusia under Soult's administration – like Aragon and Valencia under Suchet – "was as submissive as any department of France".[43] Certainly, when he was finally compelled by King Joseph to abandon Andalusia there were hundreds of Spaniards who wanted to go with him and others who regretted his departure. The military commentator, d'Espinchal, sums up his effect on the army and on civilians alike at this period: "Marshal Soult, like all men of great ability and talent, had many jealous enemies who were not worthy to come up to the top of his boots. But one cannot deny that he was one of the most remarkable soldiers and administrators of the Empire. His presence always had a spontaneous effect on the energy and cheerfulness of the French troops in the Peninsula."[44] Soult himself used to say long afterwards that Seville was almost his second home. A Spanish businessman said rather surprisingly to his biographer, Anarchasis Combes, "Your Marshal made us in southern Spain what we are!"[45]

This was the successful administrative background for Soult's incessant military operations to defend the French power base in Spain.

11

DEFENDING THE FRENCH POWER BASE IN THE WEST

SOULT'S MILITARY OPERATIONS in southern Spain covered three main areas – Estremadura to the Portuguese frontier and beyond; Cadiz and the south coast; and the mountainous regions of Granada and Murcia. All these operations were interdependent and had to take full account of the constant security actions against the guerrillas. Compared with the huge army which Masséna was to lead into Portugal, Soult's Army of the South was, as has been noted, much under strength and nowhere near the constantly changing number of effectives which appeared in the imperial muster rolls.

In the summer and autumn of 1810 the operations in the west were mainly the responsibility of Marshal Mortier's V Corps. Originally Mortier had been well supported by II Corps under General Reynier which had played an important observation and protection role on the River Tagus. In July 1810, after heavily defeating a Spanish force under General Mendizabel, Reynier was suddenly ordered to cross the Tagus and to come under Masséna's command for the invasion of Portugal. Spanish armies were by now ragged and starving, disease-ridden, ill-equipped and unpaid, with soldiers having to be sent home for want of food and clothing.[1] But Romana remained a formidable opponent. While Soult was busy elsewhere in Andalusia, Mortier's weak corps had to keep an eye on Seville itself, and it was diminshed still further when Soult withdrew Girard's division to meet some Spanish military activity in the mountainous region north of Gibraltar. This was a good example of the interdependence of all Soult's operations. The weakening of his command caused even the fair-minded Mortier to complain to the Emperor that his forces were being scattered all over Andalusia. Soult had consistently warned Berthier that this was the inevitable result of his three army corps being so much below strength, especially as King Joseph continued to intercept for his own use units that were being sent as reinforcements for the Army of the South. Having seen Mortier's letter to Napoleon, Soult sent him a reassuring reply.[2] This difference of opinion, unlike Soult's subsequent quarrel with Victor, did not last long. On the other hand, Soult's basic aims were quite different from those of his three corps commanders. They wanted to win battles in their own areas. Soult had to see that a victory in one place did not lead to a total defeat elsewhere. Despite all his problems, Mortier did well when Girard's division returned to him.

He attacked and defeated Romana's Spaniards at Villa Garcia, forced a small maritime invasion force to re-embark at Moguer near the Gulf of Cadiz and operated with success between the Rio Tinto and the Portuguese border. For the first time Seville itself was left to be defended mainly by Spanish troops in Soult's service.

So far these operations had at least kept Romana's Spaniards fully occupied. Meanwhile the Emperor was concerned almost entirely with Masséna's slow but methodical invasion of Portugal. Masséna regarded it as essential to capture the fortresses of Ciudad Rodrigo and Almeida before attempting to march on Lisbon. The defensive British victory of Busaco had briefly held up his advance and soon there was pressure on Mortier to march along the Tagus in the direction of Lisbon. Romana had now withdrawn into Portugal to support Wellington. Why, demanded the Emperor, was Mortier not hard on his heels?[3]

Soult's alleged failure to cooperate closely with Masséna is a constant criticism levelled at him. In a recent study on Soult it has been said quite flatly that "he did not lift a finger" to help his comrade.[4] Much of the contemporary criticism came from Soult's vituperative old enemy, Thiébault, first from his base headquarters in northern Spain and then as chief of staff to another of the many generals that he despised, Drouet d'Erlon. "Nothing," he wrote, "could be expected from Soult on the score of obedience or patriotism. In the course of his years as a marshal he never succeeded in doing honour to his profession by any feat of arms."[5] Inevitably some of this mud has stuck. How far is criticism justified?

It is certainly true that Soult was in no way jealous that Masséna – without any experience of fighting in Spain – had got the command of the Army of Portugal rather than himself. His old chief in Switzerland and Italy had been responsible for first introducing him to Napoleon and under the Emperor he regarded him as the greatest strategist in the French armies.[6] Soult's overall aim – the building up of the base in southern Spain – was quite different from Masséna's objectives. Nevertheless, Soult had shown on many occasions that he too fully appreciated the great importance of driving the British out of Portugal. Earlier, in correspondence with Berthier, he had referred to the need to capture Badajoz and then to occupy the Portuguese province of Alentejo which would have posed an even more direct threat to Lisbon than Masséna's long and difficult march across Portugal. But this would only have been possible with II and V Corps operating together. The removal of II Corps to march with Masséna left Mortier's corps far too weak to move across Portugal as far as the mouth of the Tagus, passing by the strongly fortified strongholds of Badjoz, Olivenza and Elvas. Mortier would also have had to take on both Romana's Spaniards and the British forces under Hill. Even the capture of the key fortresses would be difficult since Soult could not get hold of the large siege equipment which had been used with such effect during the French storming of Ciudad Rodrigo. The Emperor continued to hold exaggerated ideas of the numbers of troops at Soult's and Mortier's disposal. He seems to have thought that any moves to cooperate with Masséna would still leave Soult with some 30,000 men to defend Andalusia and to act as a general reserve, especially as Joseph could always reinforce him from Madrid. Napoleon never realized that Joseph's only concern was the defence of Madrid and the countryside around it.

The real answer to the criticism of Soult's lack of cooperation is that he *did* make a major effort to support Masséna. This was despite all the problems that faced him in the south – the siege of Cadiz, then at a critical stage, mountain operations against Spanish forces in Granada, the danger of Anglo-Spanish seaborne landings on the coast, and security operations against the guerrillas. In the autumn of 1810 he began preparing for an advance in strength towards Portugal. As a thoroughly professional soldier, he was quite satisfied that he must first capture Badajoz and the other frontier forts, just as Masséna had insisted on first seizing Ciudad Rodrigo and Almeida. Since Soult received no help either from Madrid or Paris, he had to make preparations from his own resources. As usual, they were very precise indeed. Guns, gun carriages and armaments in general came mostly from the foundry in Seville and wagons for the transport of artillery and engineering equipment, as well as supplies for the troops, had to be collected from all over Andalusia. There was little to be found in poverty-stricken Estremadura where so much fighting had already taken place. It had taken nearly half a year, under the personal supervision of the Emperor himself, to prepare Masséna for his great invasion of Portugal. Soult had only a few weeks, with no help from anyone.

His expeditionary force finally set out towards the end of 1810. It comprised all the resources of V Corps, two regiments of infantry, two of cavalry and light artillery borrowed from Victor, and some cavalry from Sebastiani with accompanying artillery and light siege equipment. Merida, in front of Badajoz, was quickly occupied but an appeal to the King to guard the expeditionary force's right flank was abruptly turned down. At the turn of the year the important stronghold of Olivenza, defended by some 4,000 Spaniards, was captured after a short investment. Based on Olivenza, Soult with his small force was now ready to lay siege to Badajoz itself. Badajoz had a garrison of some 8,000 men and was well provided with artillery, munitions and supplies. Soult's army was too small to surround the city completely but Latour-Maubourg's cavalry division manoeuvred on the right bank of the River Guadiana while Girard's and Gazan's divisions began operations against the fortress. Gazan, who had served Soult well before, now became his chief of staff. Later he was to be his successor in Spain and finally his chief of staff once more in the Pyrenees campaign. Already these manoeuvres were having an important strategic effect in Portugal. A somewhat bedraggled Spanish army had hastened back from Lisbon. It was commanded by Mendizabel as successor to Romana, who had died of a heart attack. Before a full assault could be made on Badajoz, a sharply fought battle took place on the banks of the River Gebora in which Soult and Mortier decisively defeated the Spaniards, inflicting up to 2,000 casualties and capturing 5,000 prisoners as well as much artillery. This victory did not lead to the immediate fall of Badajoz but a much feebler Spanish general, Imaz, succeeded as governor when his predecessor was killed. Then, after a breach in the fortifications and an urgent request from the inhabitants to yield, Imaz surrendered. This was a major French success. Many prisoners were taken as well as 200 guns and a large quantity of ammunition. In under two months Soult had captured the two main strongholds near to the Portuguese border and had destroyed or dispersed the army that had marched to their relief. Wellington had sent Beresford unavailingly to save Badajoz. This important stronghold remained in French hands for a year – a continuing menace to the Allied armies in Portugal.

These actions naturally did something to relieve pressure on Masséna but by now the latter could no longer maintain himself before the lines of Torres Vedras. He had heard the sound of the French guns outside Badajoz but then there was silence so that he assumed that the attack had failed. In fact the bombardment of Badajoz had temporarily ceased while the battle of Gebora was fought. If Masséna had known that Badajoz would fall four days after he began his retreat, things might have been different. There was obviously no effective liaison between Masséna and Soult and, despite the difficulties of sending messages through strongly held enemy country, this is a serious criticism of both of them. On the other hand, Soult had made a genuine attempt to help Masséna, albeit too late. By now serious developments had taken place in Andalusia. A British landing at Algeciras was menacing Victor's army besieging Cadiz, and another Spanish army, led by the energetic Ballasteros, was threatening Seville so that, if it *was* too late to join Masséna, Soult simply had to return there.

How was Soult's support operation assessed at the time? The Emperor himself was at first highly critical, although in the end he seems to have accepted philosophically Soult's inability to march to the Tagus. As usual he had first heard about the fall of Badajoz from English newspapers. At once he dictated another 'long-distance memorandum congratulating Soult on capturing Badajoz but then criticizing him for not advancing at once into Portugal with an army drawn from the whole of Andalusia. In his view the only places in the south that were at all important were Seville and Cadiz. He referred to "the mania of trying in a moment of crisis to hold every place in Andalusia". By reducing his forces everywhere Soult could leave enough men to hold Seville, where all the sick and wounded could be concentrated, and to continue besieging Cadiz. The rest of Andalusia could be reconquered later. Meanwhile, Napoleon insisted, it was not too late for Soult to march into Portugal, cooperating with the King and with Masséna who, Napoleon understood, was still based on Coimbra in the centre of the country. King Joseph's predatory interferences with reinforcements for the army of the South were also sharply condemned. The 5,000 men presently seized by the King must be sent south and a fresh reinforcement of 8,000 infantry and 2,000 cavalry forming the army corps of Drouet d'Erlon were also to be sent to join Soult.[7] Of course these long-distance orders were quite unrealistic; Masséna could no longer maintain himself in Portugal at all; the King was only interested in the defence of Madrid, and Soult was certainly not going to abandon the whole of Andalusia. It was quite contrary to his whole philosophy of maintaining French power in southern Spain. Masséna was also angry at Soult's failure to join him in Portugal, but in due course the two Marshals resumed their old friendship and, when Soult was Minister of War under Louis XVIII, it was at his table in Paris that Wellington was finally introduced to his old opponent in Portugal.

Perhaps the best general comments come from Soult's sharp critic, Oman. Oman thought that no blame should be attached to Soult on this occasion. He quotes Napoleon's letter of January 25 1811 to Berthier in which the Emperor assumes quite plainly that Soult had to capture Badajoz first. He then emphasizes that the Emperor's orders usually arrived much too late and were quite of date when they did get there.[8] In short, Soult did not march on Lisbon partly because, with his relatively small army, he had first to capture Badajoz and partly, with Napoleon's orders arriving much too late, there was muddled coordination between him and Masséna. Ultimately it is highly doubtful whether, even with Soult's help, Masséna would have been able to break through the defensive area of Torres Vedras.

When Soult returned to Seville, Mortier was left in charge of operations. Solid, dependable Mortier remained very active around the border, capturing and demolishing several other forts and reprovisioning the garrison of Badajoz under the able General Philippon. With the retreat of Masséna from Portugal he was faced with a considerable Allied army, composed of British, Spanish and Portuguese troops commanded by Beresford and four times the size of his own V Corps. He had withdrawn from the frontier area and remained based at Llerena. Soult had no idea when his promised reinforcement – the new corps under d'Erlon – would arrive. As usual no help was forthcoming from the King even to the extent of protecting an urgently needed food convoy proceeding from Cordoba to Badajoz. Much is said by King Joseph's biographers about the 'bloody mindedness' of the various French marshals and of Soult in particular but the marshals could certianly complain also of a total lack of cooperation on the King's part. As Mortier was one of the King's few favourites, this inactivity was especially mean. However, greatly to Soult's distress, he now had to relinquish Mortier, who, weary of the Spanish War, had been granted some leave in Paris before being sucked, like so many of the other senior officers, into the great invasion plans for Russia. The able cavalry leader and ex-aristocrat, Latour-Maubourg, who got on well with Soult, temporarily took Mortier's place as corps commander.

By the beginning of May 1811 Beresford's military operations became bolder and he began to lay siege to Badajoz. It was high time for Soult to take some vigorous action in the west once more. According to his own papers, the move to relieve Badajoz could be the first step in yet another invasion of Portugal along the left bank of the Tagus. He set out these proposals in a memorandum to Berthier.[9] Although he was now faced with a serious economic crisis in Andalusia, while his relations with the King were at a low ebb, he still wanted to maintain the initiative in the Peninsula. But first he had to confront Beresford's army, some 20,000 strong, investing Badajoz. A Spanish army under Blake, of about the same size, was hastening to join him. As Soult marched west, Beresford quickly raised the siege of Badajoz and withdrew to the village of Albuera in order to block the French advance. It was May 2 1811. Soult's immediate aim was to defeat Beresford before Blake's Spaniards could join him. At present his army was larger than Beresford's but if Blake arrived he would be greatly outnumbered. His tactical plan was to make a determined diversionary attack on the village of Albuera itself before launching his main assault on the Allied right wing. This vigorous left hook was to be carefully concealed by hilly ground and was intended to take place before Blake appeared. In the event, with the usual fog of war affecting the French fighting in a hostile country, Blake's forces had already arrived, giving Beresford a marked numerical superiority. Nevertheless, aided by Godinot's feint attack on Albuera, Soult made his massed infantry assault on Beresford's right flank, strongly supported by Latour-Maubourg's cavalry. He achieved complete surprise, suddenly appearing on the plateau held by the Allies with four-fifths of his entire army. The French cavalry took over 1,000 British prisoners. Discussing the battle with his British doctor, O'Meara, at St Helena years afterwards, Napoleon said that he had greatly blamed Soult for not pushing right home his cavalry attack, which would have cut the Allies to pieces.[10] However, to their surprise, the French now found themselves fighting Blake's Spanish army as well. This included some of the famous Walloon Guards and the Irish Regiment, recruited from all over Europe, containing some particularly tough and resourceful men. A tremendous dogfight ensued, with the Spaniards fighting obstinately, as they usually did in defence. British action took time to develop but soon the accurate fire of the brigades of Cole and Colbourne began to have its effect, while with his greater numbers, Beresford was able to launch a sharp flank attack of his own. Soult brought up all his reserves, making Albuera probably the bloodiest battle in the whole war. Several generals on both sides were killed or wounded, including Francis-Jean Werlé, commanding the French reserves, who had been with Soult since 'Sambre et Meuse' days and whose death was a great blow. At last, heavily outnumbered, the French were driven back off the plateau. Soult maintained his position overnight on the flatter ground below, and Beresford was certainly in no condition to attack him again. By next day Soult learned that Wellington himself, with a still larger army, was advancing towards the Portuguese frontier after his hard-won victory over Masséna at Fuentes d'Onoro. Accordingly he had to abandon any hopes of advancing into Portugal for the present. Reverting to a defensive strategy, he slowly, perhaps over-prudently, withdrew to the east, covered by his cavalry.

The losses by both sides in this terrible battle were between 6,000–7,000 killed and many more wounded. The casualties were more serious for the French because of the smaller size of Soult's army. Soult is supposed to have exclaimed angrily after

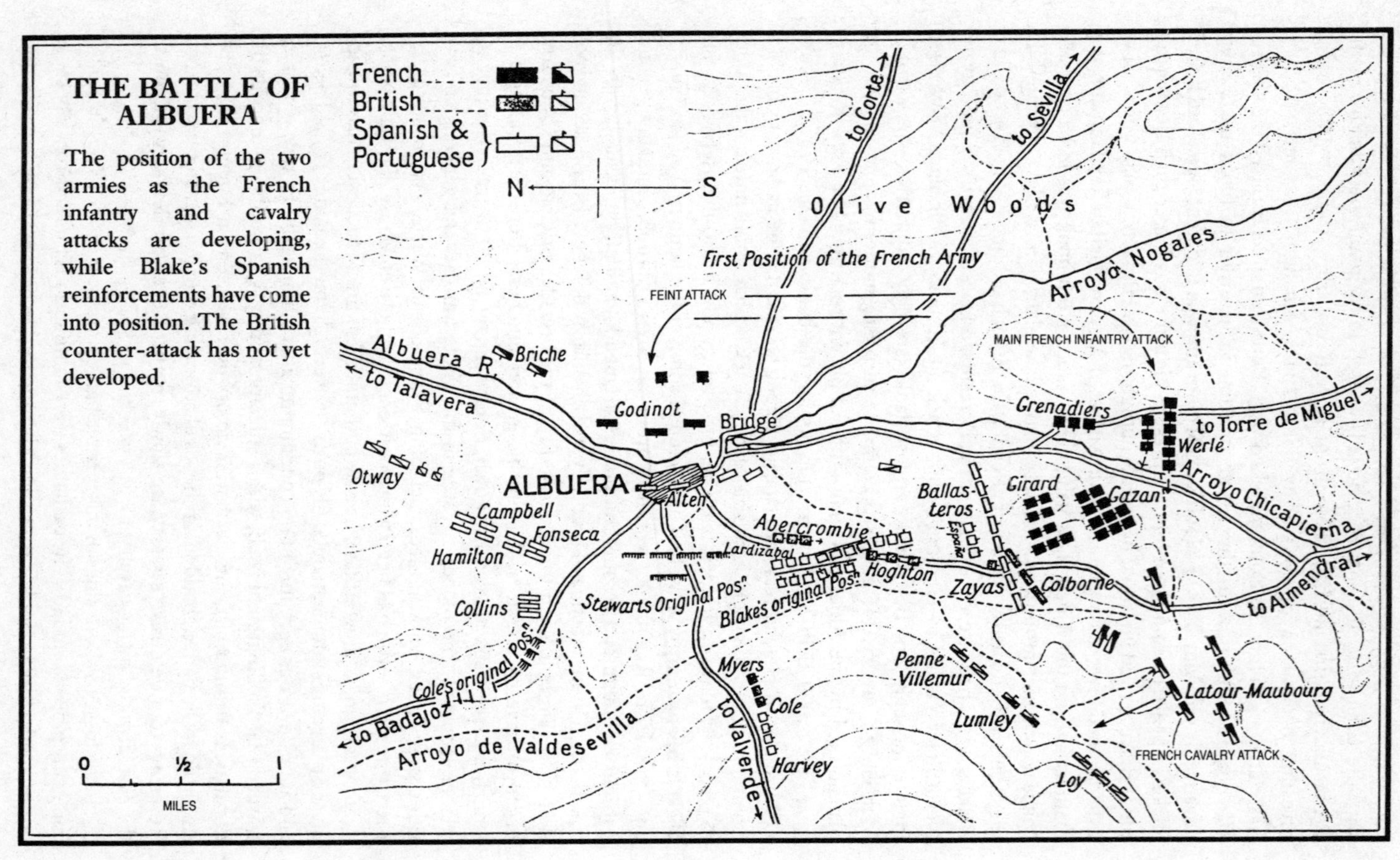

THE BATTLE OF ALBUERA

The position of the two armies as the French infantry and cavalry attacks are developing, while Blake's Spanish reinforcements have come into position. The British counter-attack has not yet developed.

the battle, "The enemy was completely beaten. We had won the day but they did not know it and would not run away!" Beresford was as horrified as Soult by the carnage and his first dispatch on the battle had to be rewritten by the more realistic Wellington, who had learned his lessons from the public criticisms levelled at him following the Convention of Cintra and over Soult's escape from northern Portugal after Oporto. Albuera became not only a British military victory but a public relations victory as well.

Why in the end was Soult defeated? It was partly because Godinot's attack, although successful at first, was broken off too soon. Certainly Soult rebuked him afterwards. Did this failure contribute eventually to poor Godinot's suicide? The following year, after another reprimand for ineffectiveness, he was to use a sentry's musket to blow out his brains. The strain of this ferocious war was having its effect on many senior officers. At Albuera Godinot's indecisive attack enabled Allied troops to be transferred more quickly to the main battle on the plateau. In fact, the French were worsted because the Spaniards were much better fighters in defence than some of their critics have allowed, and the Portuguese units did even better. Partly, too, the usual French columns of attack, although very successful against continental armies, were once more excellent targets for the sustained and deadly musket fire of the British infantry: Girard's division, fighting in more open order, held its own and inflicted higher casualties than some of the other French troops. Ultimately, however, Soult, having achieved a remarkable tactical surprise, was outnumbered and overborne by the Allies, so that he could not maintain himself on the battlefield. There is also something in the criticism often made of him that he was best at drawing up battle plans beforehand and that once the plan was finalized it became like "an immutable decree from heaven and only rarely to be changed".[11]

After the battle Beresford was temporarily if unjustly relieved of his command and Wellington resumed the siege of Badajoz himself. Soult returned to Seville, again leaving a covering force at Llerena. The Seville hospitals were full of wounded from Albuera; boastful notices about a French defeat appeared even in this relatively friendly city where there was much distress and almost famine conditions caused by the bad harvest. Nevertheless, aided by his devoted chief of staff, Gazan, who had himself been wounded at Albuera, Soult slowly restored the situation. D'Erlon's reinforcing IX Corps had at last arrived, less 4,000 men who had been 'borrowed' by the King's Army of the Centre. If only he had arrived earlier, the result of Albuera might have been very different.

There followed a series of manoeuvres by both sides around the key fortresses of Badajoz and Ciudad Rodrigo, still firmly held by the French. Both had to be captured by Wellington if he was to make a major advance into Spain. With Masséna's departure from Portugal, Soult believed that the main weight of Wellington's attack might well fall upon him in the south since he was convinced that the British could make little progress in invading Spain while he maintained his firm base in Andalusia. Meanwhile Wellington embarked upon a second siege of

Badajoz. But this proved a slow business. As always in the Peninsula the British had poor siege equipment and Philippon, the French governor, defended the city with great skill. Meanwhile Marshal Marmont, who had succeeded Masséna in command of the Army of Portugal, was ordered by Napoleon to reinforce Soult. Soon after Albuera Soult had received a letter announcing Marmot's forthcoming arrival. It was one of the only communications that he ever received from the Army of Portugal. The two Marshals met at Merida and advanced, 50,000 strong, to the relief of Badajoz. Wellington quickly withdrew to Elvas in Portugal. Re-entering Badajoz as a welcome relief force, Soult warmly congratulated Philippon on his defence.

This rapid concentration of forces was, said one commentator, "a good lesson for all French leaders in the Spanish war".[12] It led to the immediate raising of the siege of Badajoz. Should not the two Marshals then have made yet another attempt to invade Portugal? A recent historian has written: "Neither of them dared to push forward against a markedly inferior force."[13] In his own *Memoirs* Soult contends that Wellington's army still outnumbered the French. He was well aware of Wellington's carefulness in not fighting a battle unless the odds were definitely in his favour. Both Soult and Marmont were afraid of being lured into the heart of Portugal and brought to battle in difficult conditions before they could get near Lisbon. As was customary, their intelligence was poor and they were unaware that Wellington had many political and military problems of his own with the Portuguese, the Spanish and his own government at home. Of course the two Marshals had their own problems too. As usual, Soult had constantly to look over his shoulder at what was happening behind him in Andalusia. Suchet's forthcoming conquest of the whole of Valencia had meant that the Spanish forces there had retreated into Murcia which posed difficult military problems in the south-east. Marmont was concerned with the dangers of an attack on Ciudad Rodrigo and on the whole French position in the north. Neither of them had had any orders to invade Portugal nor had they made any preparations for an invasion. But the plain fact was that Wellington had seized the initiative. Albuera and Fuentes d'Onoro had given the French a very healthy respect for the Allied armies and the marshals preferred to fight Wellington if possible on a ground of their own choosing. So they decided on the unadventurous course of remaining on the defensive in the west throughout the hot summer months. Yet another chance of attacking the Allies and invading Portugal had been missed. For this Soult, as the senior Marshal of the two, must bear much of the blame. Even his great admirer Napier admits this.

This was the moment when after "eight years hard labour" young Saint-Chamans left Soult's service to command a cavalry regiment. Again he had spoken out of turn to his chief as he had done once or twice before. This time it was about some triviality over feeding the servants. The plain fact was that occasionally Soult, the *petit bourgeois* who used to say he was his own ancestor, lost patience with some of his aristocratic aides-de-camp, particularly with the outspoken Saint-Chamans.

Afterwards Saint-Chamans wrote about his service with Soult, using his usual mixture of praise and venom. "I served him with delight and I left him with equal delight," he wrote, describing his chief as unpleasant, hard, egotistical and suspicious, taking too little interest in those who served him, and adding that he had spent countless days and nights without any rest at all. The plain fact was that this young man had never had to work so hard in his life. Also, as he generously admits, without the things that Soult had done for him his military service would have been completely forgotten.[14] Saint Chamans's last duty was to conduct Marmont around the field of Albuera.

Then Soult and Marmont began to quarrel. Soult had reverted to his strongly held conviction that his main responsibility was the defence of the French base in Andalusia. As he had so many problems elsewhere in the south he argued that, for the present at least, Marmont should take over responsibility for the defence of Badajoz since its occupation was even more important for the Army of Portugal than for the defence of Andalusia. There was a lot in this argument. However, Marmont flatly refused and the Emperor had to deliver a 'Solomon's judgement' by insisting that Marmont should at least remain based on the Tagus, able to go to the help equally of Badajoz or Ciudad Rodrigo, while Soult left d'Erlon in command in the Estremadura between Seville and the Portuguese frontier.

The main interest in the 'Andalusian War' now switched away from the 'western front' to the many other operations taking place on the south-east coast and in Granada. But there were still plans in the air for a fresh invasion of Portugal, perhaps even led by Napoleon himself if, after all, he could reach an accommodation with Tsar Alexander. There were also reports of projected attacks by Wellington on Badajoz or Ciudad Rodrigo. All this kept Soult and the other French military leaders guessing. Hill remained in command of the British forces in southern Portugal, facing d'Erlon in Estremadura. One disaster befell the French in October 1811. A division of d'Erlon's corps commanded by Girard was surprised and surrounded by Hill at Arroyo dos Molinos with a loss of 900 killed and 1,500 prisoners. Soult did not excuse failure. Girard and his second in command were sent home to France in disgrace. As one British soldier commented after the battle: "The 'parlez-vous' were badly trounced."[15] Girard was to expiate his 'disgrace' four years later when, mortally wounded at Ligny just before Waterloo, Napoleon created him 'Duke of Ligny' on the field of battle.

But the most serious disaster for the French was the loss of Badajoz in April 1812 after its third and last siege by the British. As Napoleon was to say later, "Not only the fate of Badajoz but of the whole Peninsula was decided during those days of blood." It was another turning point in the war. While Soult was busy in Andalusia Marmont was much preoccupied in the north. Wellington had recaptured Ciudad Rodrigo and his skilful, quick-moving strategy had totally confused the French. Soult was now compelled to disengage from other operations to march for the third time to the relief of Badajoz. On April 8 he had reached a village a few leagues away only to learn the dread news that Badajoz had fallen. The fortress had been seized after a violent and prolonged assault ending the night before and then the city had been sacked while the gallant Philippon was taken prisoner. In the recriminations that followed there were suggestions that, after a year of French occupation, the defenders had become over-confident; on the other hand, there were complaints from the defenders that they had run out of ammunition and gunpowder too soon because these had not been fully provided. This accusation was hotly denied by Soult's artillery and engineer officers who claimed that they had poured all available supplies from the Seville foundry and from other army sources into Badajoz while they could still do so. Soult, naturally and not unreasonably, blamed Marmont and the King's Army of the Centre for giving him no help. Of course he recognized how serious was the loss of Badajoz for the whole French position in Spain. But he had other worries. Andalusia was still threatened from Murcia and by the Spanish forces of General Ballesteros. General Rignaud, the French governor of Seville, had only a small French force to hold Seville, many of them hospital patients. Ballesteros, whose ragged army, like most of the Spanish forces, had been reduced by the French occupation to little more than a division, was well provided with British equipment; he also counted on a general uprising in the city against the French. But nothing of the kind emerged. Most of Seville's inhabitants remained passive under Soult's rule and Ballesteros retired in some confusion.

Meanwhile Drouet d'Erlon was left in charge in Estremadura. Wellington made no further advance into southern Spain, switching his main operation to the north again, leaving Hill in command in the south while he brought Marmont to battle at Salamanca, soundly defeating him. All this had a most serious effect on Soult, especially as Napoleon, on the eve of his departure for Russia, had reinstated his brother, Joseph, at least formally as commander-in-chief of all the French armies in Spain. Jourdan, the King's reappointed chief of staff, doubted whether Soult would acknowledge these changes. However, Soult was even more affected by the constant drain of his senior officers to meet the increasing demands of the Russian invasion. More serious still, Soult was soon fully engaged in a fantastic internecine quarrel with King Joseph which could only have taken place within the French imperial armies in Spain at that time! A major contention between Seville and Madrid was the operational control of Drouet d'Erlon's army corps. This was a prelude to Soult's enforced relinquishment of the fine French base in the south.

On the Allied side there were also some fundamental changes. Of course the *partidas* were still upholding the patriotic cause even in southern Spain, but with the capture of Badajoz and Ciudad Rodrigo, and with Wellington's victory at Salamanca, the decisive leadership in the war could only come now from his Anglo-Portuguese army which was becoming more and more of a match for France's veteran armies. This was a fact which Soult fully recognized.

Meanwhile some account must be given of the continuous operations on the south coast of Andalusia and in the mountains of Granada and Murcia.

12

OPERATIONS IN THE SOUTH AND SOUTH-EAST OF SPAIN

THROUGHOUT THE PERIOD of Soult's rule in Andalusia the capture of Cadiz certainly remained his most urgent problem in the south. Victor's army corps was mainly responsible for the siege. Like Lisbon, its capture or defence was equally important to both sides. It was now the capital of 'independent Spain' and a large Anglo-Spanish-Portuguese force held it – or was partly bottled up in it. Within the city the incessant quarrels, primarily between the liberals and the conservatives in the regency council and in the cortes, went on as fiercely as ever. Nor were the British any more loved than when their first reinforcements appeared. These forces, now under General Graham, varied greatly in size: sometimes men were withdrawn for the defence of Lisbon, being replaced by drafts from Gibraltar or Sicily. Indeed, there was permanent close inter dependence, both militarily and politically, between Cadiz and Lisbon. Much depended on Graham's Anglo-Portuguese forces but the Spanish troops were good at defending fortified positions. Less useful were the 'Voluntarios Distinguidos de Cadiz', a regiment which was considered by the liberals in the Cortes to be a model for a new Spanish national army, but they had a firm guarantee that they need never serve outside the walls of the city.[1]

All in all, however, an Allied army of up to 30,000 men defending a large area that was strongly fortified presented the French with a much more difficult problem than it seemed to Napoleon far away in Paris when he enquired indignantly why "10,000 miserable Spaniards were still holding out there".[2]

That shrewd military commentator, Marshal Jourdan, always jealous of his successor, Soult, records in his *Memoirs* that Cadiz could never be captured now without full command of the sea – and this was impossible since the British navy dominated the eastern Mediterranean.[3] Soult was rarely discouraged by unfavourable strategic theories. Soon after King Joseph's departure for Madrid he intervened personally in the siege operations, much to Victor's chagrin. The chain of French forts all round Cadiz and the Isla de León were completed and by October 1810 Soult had collected a little fleet of some 85 pinnaces and gunboats together with military transports capable of carrying in all some 10,000 men. Two battalions of sailors and skilled shipwrights, long held up in Madrid, had also arrived. The whole armada was based in the Guadalquivir River which reaches the sea only a short distance west of Cadiz. By the beginning of November a good part of this fleet of little ships had slipped down the river, successfully avoiding Allied warships and being transported as necessary overland on rollers rather like the *portage* system in Canada. Soon there was a considerable concentration of French shipping near the Trocadero Canal between the Isla de León and Cadiz itself.[4] It was like Boulogne and the projected invasion of England all over again.

Soult was as much alive to the importance of artillery power as the Emperor and the force contained about 200 guns of all sizes. Soult and his excellent group of artillery advisers had to rely mostly on their own resources – the foundry in Seville, gunpowder from Granada and lead from Linares. The armament included some huge, newly invented pieces built in the Seville foundry called 'cannon mortars' which could hurl a projectile a distance of 5,000 metres right over the city of Cadiz. To achieve this range the shells were filled with lead, and although they had little explosive power they had a considerable effect on morale. Soult's next objective was to batter down the fort of Puntales with this concentrated artillery fire and to establish his besieging army firmly between the Isla de León and Cadiz itself before capturing both of them in turn. Recognizing the danger, General Graham, with a mixed force of British, Spanish, Portuguese and German troops, had heavily reinforced Puntales and the neighbouring redoubt of Cortadura, bringing in additional shipping and reinforcements from Gibraltar. But some of the troops guarding the forts were of poor quality and a determined attack by Soult at this stage might well have succeeded. Preparations were almost completed for the assault.

However, as a graphic illustration of Soult's problems in the south, it was just at this time that he was ordered by the Emperor to march to the help of Masséna in Portugal. The expeditionary force for this new operation had necessarily to include some of Victor's infantry and Latour-Maubourg's cavalry from the army surrounding Cadiz. While Soult marched east, Victor was again left in charge of the siege operation. This had been probably the nearest that the French ever got to capturing Cadiz. It was much closer than Masséna ever got to Lisbon!

Meanwhile, in charge of IV Corps, Sebastiani had been carrying on a kind of independent war in Granada with the object of quelling the guerrillas, occupying as much of Murcia as possible and extending French control of the coastline between Malaga and Cartagena in order to link up with Suchet in Valencia. Based on Cordoba, he made a series of punitive strikes although he was constantly hampered by demands from the King to help deal with guerrilla bands in La Mancha, which was outside his operational area. In October, backed by the British navy, a small Allied force from Ceuta in Morocco, commanded by Lord Blayney, had landed at Fuengirola. The operation was badly mismanaged; the force was driven off and Blayney himself was taken prisoner. Sebastiani then resumed his operations along the Mediterranean coast, almost reaching Cartagena. Wellington was strongly critical of these pinprick coastal operations which achieved very little and were often at the expense of his own military activities in Portugal. Such 'combined operations,' usually mounted from Sicily against the French forces of Soult and Suchet, certainly made a surprisingly ineffective use of British naval power.

However, at the beginning of 1811, with Soult fully engaged near the frontiers of Portugal, there was an excellent opportunity for the Allies to launch a more ambitious operation which would threaten the French siege positions around Cadiz and menace Seville itself. Some rather confused planning took place in Cadiz. The Spanish General Ballesteros, one of the more successful Spanish commanders in the south, was ordered to advance upon Seville; the guerrilla bands based in the mountains of Granada were urged to keep Sebastiani busy and a combined Allied force of 4,000 British and 12,000 Spaniards, drawn mostly from the Cadiz garrison, were transported by sea to land at Algeciras and march from there westward to take Victor's much weakened army in the rear. The valiant old British General Graham yielded up his command to the Spanish General La Pena since the latter had much the largest force, and together they advanced upon Chiclana, one of the French fortified positions around Cadiz. There they were attacked vigorously by Victor who had seized the initiative. La Pena gave little help to his British allies and a short but exceedingly bloody battle took place at Barosa in which the French could not overcome a vigorous British resistance. Casualties were about equal but the Allies had the best of the battle. The Cadiz defenders took back some strongpoints captured by the French and Victor's attempt to destroy the British force failed. In the end both sides returned to their positions in and around Cadiz.

After Barosa there were bitter recriminations on both sides. There was a major Anglo-Spanish quarrel, caused mainly by Spanish jealousy, over the increasingly dominant part that the British were now playing in the war.[5] As Wellington commented trenchantly to his brother, Marquess Wellesley, "I am convinced that the majority of Spanish officers would prefer submitting to the French to allowing us to have anything to say to their troops."[6] General Graham resigned his command in disgust. There were similar dissensions on the French side when Victor openly complained that Sebastiani had done nothing to help him. If Sebastiani had abandoned his mountain operations in Granada and had marched south, Victor believed that the Allied army would have been annihilated.

Soult's troubles with two of his corps commanders now came to a head. Victor blamed his commander-in-chief for drastically weakening his forces around Cadiz in order to go to the help of Masséna. When Soult hurried back to defend Seville, Brun de Villeret was sent to calm down Victor. Compared with his famous, rampaging interview with the Emperor at Schönbrunn after Soult's Oporto adventure, Brun might have expected a fairly easy ride with Victor, especially as he had a brother serving on the Marshal's staff. Instead he was treated to a two-hour tirade from the red-faced Victor lying sprawled out in bed complaining about being totally starved of troops and of provisions. His invectives were so violent that he could never finish a sentence and he ranted on until he was completely exhausted. Only then did he calm down and describe his problems more rationally. Brun realized that he was getting rid of his frustrations but it showed how bad were his relations with Soult. Victor was no good at administration and many of his complaints were due to his own hopelessly inefficient staff duties. Brun did his best to put some of these matters right.[7]

Trouble also developed with Sebastiani who, when ordered to take more action against the Spanish forces in Murcia, likewise complained about severe manpower shortages, adding that he was a sick man, and finally asked to be relieved of his post. Soult accepted his resignation and appointed in his place General Leval who had commanded a division in the famous IV Corps in the Grande Armée and had fought well at Ocaña. He was an able, well-disciplined soldier. But there were troublesome take-over problems. Sebastiani changed his mind and refused to go and there was some confusion until Leval finally assumed command.

Quarrels between French marshals and generals were an endemic disease in the Peninsula and indeed throughout the Napoleonic wars, but Soult's cold and abrasive manner undoubtedly contributed to these troubles as it had done in Oporto and elsewhere. Also both Victor and Sebastiani were equally cantankerous – and the war in Spain had gone on for a very long time.

Hearing the results of Barosa, as usual from the English newspapers, Napoleon continued to make long-distance criticisms of French operations. Once again, he underestimated Soult's problems. By the second half of 1811 Soult had under command a nominal force of some 60,000 men for the occupation of the whole of the south. A third of this army was around Cadiz, the remainder in Estremadura and Granada, leaving Soult himself with only a small mobile reserve. With these forces he was fighting for Badajoz, defending Seville, trying to capture Cadiz and combating the guerilla bands in the Sierra Morena. Yet he gave his armies no rest. In the late summer of 1811 he collected a mixed force of French regulars with a small number of his own Spanish units to help Leval quell an insurrection in Ronda and to carry on operations into Murcia. Suchet had made great headway in Valencia and a major attack in Murcia would obviously be very helpful to him. Although it was impossible to coordinate action directly with Suchet over hostile country, or alternatively through the futile royal headquarters in Madrid, Soult attacked the Spanish General Freyre at Bazan in Murcia and, but for a poorly coordinated flank attack once again by the unfortunate Godinot, he might have annihilated the whole Spanish army. As it was, the Spaniards retired to the plague-stricken city of Cartagena and Leval was left, with his cavalry commanded by Soult's brother Pierre, to keep control of the mountains of Granada and Murcia as well as the Granada coastline.

By now Soult's relations with King Joseph had become very strained and, surrounded by hostile forces in Portugal, Badajoz, Cadiz and south-eastern Spain, he was becoming increasingly isolated both from Madrid and Paris. But he relished his 'independence', feeling that he had really become the Emperor's 'prefect' in this remote part of the French Empire. Napier comments euphorically on his hero at this time: "Few men could have stood firm in such a whirlwind as Soult did, not merely holding his ground but planning other great offensive enterprises. He was always to be dreaded. Who can deny his firmness, vigour, foresight and admirable arrangement?"[8]

Always restless, and continuing to 'think big', Soult now embarked on another ambitious operation which he really believed would ensure his full control of the south. This was his proposal to capture Tarifa on the extreme southern point of Spain and indeed of Europe. It was one of the places where the invading Moors had landed in AD 700. Despite all his other preoccupations and constant demands from Paris that he should finally capture Cadiz, Soult asserted that the loss of Tarifa would be more injurious to the Allies than the retaking of Badajoz. It was amazing and perhaps rash to embark on a totally new operation at this stage of the war, but the imaginative Soult considered that by seizing Tarifa he could make a much more effective onslaught on Cadiz, which had been greatly strengthened since his last major offensive against the city in 1810. He would also be able to threaten Gibraltar; he could menace British naval communications with the eastern Mediterranean, and he could increase the commercial and political ties which, not without some success, he was building up with North Africa.

Despite continuing problems in the mountains of Granada and in Murcia, as well as the disaster which had befallen Girard's division at Aroyos Molinos in Estremadura, Soult ordered Victor to seize Tarifa forthwith. It consisted of a small fortified town and harbour connected by a narrow neck of land to an island. The French expected only weak opposition but, when they launched their assault just before Christmas 1811, they met with surprisingly fierce resistance from a mixed Anglo-Spanish force reinforced by troops and ships from Gibraltar. In fact the French attack was driven back with heavy losses. Tarifa was then blockaded and continued to be hemmed in for months. Indeed no serious attack could be made on it again before Soult had to begin preparations for abandoning Andalusia. General Campbell, the governor of Gibraltar, must be given the credit for defeating this first attack which was in a sense the high-water mark of Soult's offensive operations in southern Spain. Yet Campbell was actually reprimanded afterwards for putting British troops at too great a risk.

During the Tarifa operation relations between Soult and Victor reached breaking point. Soult reported the situation to the Emperor, commenting with surprising mildness that it was awkward to have two marshals operating together in a relatively small area. He offered to resign in favour of Victor. Of course Napoleon had no doubts which of the two to choose and Victor was permitted to return home on health grounds. Like many others, he was soon absorbed into the invasion army against Russia.

Despite all these problems, Soult sincerely believed that his strong hold over the south, while Wellington was operating against Marmont, placed him in an excellent position to strike against the flank and rear of the Allied army. Moreover, if he could seize Tarifa and with Suchet's help capture Cartagena, his position would be secure enough for him to contemplate a sudden attack on Portugal which would force Wellington to retreat from Spain once more. At least, while Napoleon was away in Russia, the Allies would be kept at bay in the Peninsula. Fresh insurrections on the south-east coast, the reappearance of General Freyre in Murcia and a new threat by General Ballesteros to Seville itself were all developments which Soult handled with his customary resolution and dexterity. Hill, commanding the British forces in the south, had again retired to Portugal although the Allies remained in firm occupation of Badajoz.

Throughout the early summer of 1812 Soult remained in a bouyant mood, but events then built up leading to his bitter quarrel with King Joseph in August and finally to his enforced abandonment of the whole of southern Spain.

13

THE ABANDONMENT OF ANDALUSIA AND WAR IN CENTRAL SPAIN

WHEN IN MARCH 1812 on his departure for Russia Napoleon gave his brother once more the full military and political control of Spain, Joseph's devoted chief of staff, Jourdan, prepared an appreciation on future military policy in the Peninsula. Jourdan concluded that the French armies in Spain, still numbering over 200,000 men were greatly overstretched in having to hold down a largely hostile country. He had not changed his views on this since he sharply criticized the invasion of Andalusia in 1810. Nor had he ever visited the south where the guerrilla bands had been at least brought under control. He and King Joseph judged Spanish nationalist fervour partly from the quarrelsome debates taking place in the regency council in Cadiz but more from the turbulent and highly effective operations of Mina and the other *partidas* chiefs in the north. However, much the most serious threat to French rule in Spain came from Wellington's Anglo-Portuguese army, especially after his capture of Ciudad Rodrigo and Badajoz. Indeed, despite all the guerrilla activity and the operations being carried out by the diminished Spanish regular forces, the Spaniards themselves, to their dismay, had already begun to play a secondary role in their own national war. The liberation of Spain, like that of Portugal, could now be won only by Wellington's army. In the spring of 1812 Wellington could strike either at Marmont in the north or at Soult in the south. In Jourdan's view the most serious threat must be to the north and this was soon to be confirmed by Marmont's defeat at Salamanca. Moreover, by this time, both Jourdan and the King greatly disliked and distrusted Soult. So Jourdan's main proposal was that the whole of southern Spain should be evacuated. Such a major decision needed confirmation by the Emperor. On the other hand the intermediate step of moving d'Erlon's corps northwards from Estremadura to reinforce Marmont against an attack by Wellington could be ordered forthwith.

The appreciation recommending the total evacuation of Andalusia crossed a dispatch from Napoleon stating categorically that French forces in Spain should be quite large enough to hold Wellington in check; the invasion of Portugal could be postponed but all conquests in the Peninsula should be preserved and extended. The Emperor considered that 40,000 English should not be allowed to spoil all that the French had done in Spain. These final instructions from the Emperor, sent off just before he travelled east, confirmed Soult's view that it would be politically disastrous to abandon Andalusia. He has been accused in the polemics of his enemies of being unwilling to leave the 'fleshpots' of Andalusia. But his intensely busy life over the last two years left him little time for any such luxuries. He remained convinced that, if the French preserved their base in the south, they could always present a serious threat to any attack that Wellington might make in the north; inevitably, indeed, the British would have to march south later. Soult also remembered how the French defeats at Baylen and Vimiero four years before had had a tremendous political effect throughout Europe. The total abandonment now of southern Spain when the Emperor was fully engaged in Russia would shake the fabric of the Napoleonic Empire.

The immediate dispute between Soult and the King related to the operations of Drouct d'Erlon's corps. At the beginning of May this corps was, on the King's orders, to be detached from the Army of the South to support the Army of Portugal north of the Tagus. In a sharp letter to the King dated June 8, Soult declared that the Anglo-Portuguese army was still a serious threat to Andalusia; it would be most unwise to weaken his forces. D'Erlon's corps was needed to keep in check Hill's sizeable army in southern Portugal. Anyway it was wrong for orders to be sent over the army commander's head to one of his own corps commanders. In the circumstances Soult offered his resignation.[1] This was strong stuff and it was so reported in indignant terms to General Clarke, the Minister of War, in Paris.[2] The King had also learnt through one of his most zealous staff officers, Colonel Desprez, who had recently visited Seville, that the irrepressible Soult pretended not to realize that he had been once again appointed commander-in-chief; in any event he ignored the fact and certainly did not inform his various corps commanders.

In the immediate dispute much now depended on the personality – or lack of personality – of d'Erlon. General Jean-Baptiste Drouet, Comte d'Erlon, had begun life as a dedicated Republican and had then become, like so many others, a fervent Bonapartist. Largely because of his patent anxiety at this stage to conciliate King Joseph, Soult seems to have regarded him as something of a 'palace general', usually addressing him mockingly as 'count' rather than 'general'. D'Erlon's latest biographer describes how the general's frequent *'atermoiements'* or changes of mind first appeared in famous circumstances when, under conflicting orders from Napoleon, Soult and Ney, he marched uselessly to and fro during the manoeuvres leading up to the battle of Waterloo.[3] In fact these *atermoiements* seem to have begun much earlier when he was also harried by conflicting orders from Seville and Madrid. D'Erlon's later career was much entangled with Soult's not only in Spain but in Restoration France and in exile in Germany. When d'Erlon died after being made, at his own urgent request, a marshal by Louis Philippe, Soult presided over a memorial ceremony in his honour in his native Rheims.

By now, with Wellington seriously threatening the Army of Portugal, the King's relations with the obstreperous Soult over both the control of d'Erlon's corps and the future of Andalusia had become so bad that he decided to accept the Marshal's resignation. On June 30 he addressed the first of a series of letters to him in the following terms: "Torn between the alternatives of losing your talents and military experience or allowing to break up in my hands the power with which the Emperor has entrusted me I have no alternative but to accept your resignation." Soult was ordered to hand over his command to none other than d'Erlon, his senior corps commander.[4] But it does not appear that the King seriously believed that Soult would resign because further military orders followed requiring him to send 10,000 men to the defence of Toledo with the proviso that the safety of Spain and the honour of the Emperor's arms depended on these orders being obeyed promptly.[5]

The whole miserable relationship between the King and Soult had now come to a head. On the King's side feelings understandably went very deep. His dream had been to rule over a peaceful and contented Spain. All this had been set at nought for many reasons and principally, in his view, because of the behaviour of the various French marshals and generals. Soult was the worst villain of all. He had been the King's major general and had conquered virtually the whole of southern Spain for him. But then he had proceeded himself to rule Andalusia in all but name. Now that King Joseph had once more been appointed commander-in-chief, the day of reckoning with this intolerable man had surely arrived. All the time that he had reigned in Madrid he had been obsessively concerned with the protection of his capital. Now there were cogent strategic reasons for reinforcing the Army of Portugal and, while defending Madrid, for evacuating Andalusia completely. On the political side Joseph, with his brother's approval, was in discreet touch with both Cadiz and with King Ferdinand in his comfortable captivity in France. In Cadiz the liberals in the council of regency and the cortes were soon to promulgate the constitution of 1812 which, it was said, would represent "the most formidable army that the French had had to face for it had transformed what they regarded as a horde of savages into a nation of free men."[6] But there were some 'conservatives' prepared to make a deal with King Joseph who could then get rid of Soult's rule in Andalusia. On the other hand Ferdinand seemed only too willing to accept one of King Joseph's new orders of chivalry and to marry one of his daughters.

Soult had strong feelings too. As a professional soldier he had the greatest contempt for King Joseph and, rather unjustly, for Jourdan as well. The failure to support him in Oporto; the disastrously premature attack at Talavera; the refusal to allow him to invade Portugal afterwards were events that certainly rankled. There had been the period of polite restraint in Madrid and in the invasion of Andalusia. Now Soult possessed strong strategic and political reasons for staying put in the south. He had kept Andalusia reasonably tranquil and with Napoleon on his way to Russia he wanted to hold southern Spain in trust for his imperial master. In a letter sent to King Joseph on July 16 he refused categorically to raise the siege of Cadiz or to evacuate Andalusia. He then suggested for the first time that, as an alternative, the King should join him in Andalusia where he would be much safer in this bastion of French power.[7] Reporting this to Clarke in Paris, Jourdan described it as "an extraordinary proposition".[8]

Events now moved quickly. Following Marmont's defeat at Salamanca on July 22, the King commanded unequivocally that Andalusia be abandoned "in order to save Madrid", but almost at once he himself decided to evacuate his capital and to retreat to Valencia with the whole heterogeneous circle of his Spanish and French court. Soult was ordered to join him forthwith in Valencia with the Army of the South.

But Soult remained obstinate and the rather melodramatic events that followed have been well recorded by himself. First there were his two strongly worded letters of August 12, one to King Joseph and the second, on no account for the King's eyes, to Clarke as Minister of War, to be passed on to the Emperor in Russia. Both these letters have been strongly criticized by Soult's enemies. La Forêt, the French ambassador in Madrid, who was certainly no friend of Soult, gave a highly coloured account of Soult's letter to the King, describing it as an offer to him "to cross the Rubicon and enjoy the abundant sources of the south". La Forêt recorded that the officer bringing the letter had said that the Marshal "had tears in his eyes when he professed his devotion to the King". However, in the opinion of some of his French advisers in Madrid – "les centaines de vampires françaises", as La Forêt called them – the King seemed actually to have feared for his personal safety if he joined Soult.[9]

La Forêt often jumped to hasty conclusions and, whatever Soult may have thought of Joseph, he certainly would never have been so foolish as to take violent action against the Emperor's brother. Nor was he so much interested in Andalusian 'abundance' as La Forêt suggests, although he would certainly regret the loss of power if he were no longer to rule over his 'nation'. Actually his letter to Joseph was much more sober. It contained neither tears nor threats. It is a well-reasoned defence for maintaining the French position in the south. After bewailing the defeat of Marmont at Salamanca, Soult roundly declared that this certainly did not mean the end of French rule in Spain. Instead the Armies of the South, of the Centre and even the Army of Valencia should be concentrated in Andalusia. If the Army of Portugal remained in the north the enemy would be caught between two large French army groups and both would also be a potential threat to Portugal. The defeat of the Army of Portugal was only an incident in a military duel; the raising of the siege of Cadiz and the loss of Andalusia would be a disaster for the whole French Empire, perhaps even causing the United States now at war with England to conclude peace![10]

In the event, the effects of the French withdrawal from southern Spain were submerged in the far greater disaster in Russia, but there is little doubt that at this time Napoleon himself would have agreed with Soult's arguments. Joseph, however, was solely concerned with the preservation and then the recovery of his capital, with maintaining an escape route to France and, understandably, with the obstinacy of a very rude lieutenant who continued to disobey his orders. The active Desprez was posted off to Paris to pour out his troubles to the more than receptive Minister of War, General Clarke. Clarke, the Duke of Feltre, was one of the least attractive of the Emperor's servants. His real administrative talents were coupled with a toadying manner which preserved him in his very hot seat. He cordially disliked Soult. He was, incidentally, one of the first of Napoleon's generals to adhere firmly to the Bourbons and the first to be made a marshal by Louis XVIII.

Soult was originally deceived by Clarke's ingratiating manner and did not appreciate his enmity. As he was the Minister of War he had in any case to send through him his second letter of August 12, which was intended for the Emperor's eyes. This letter reflected Soult's genuine anxiety about the conduct of Joseph himself. He had always been disturbed by the King's ultra-Spanish sympathies, had learned of his secret links with some members of the cortes in Cadiz and probably did not realize that Napoleon had more or less authorized these approaches. However, unlike his own secret trade talks with Cadiz, the papers were full of the King's 'secret' discussions and, in Soult's view, this was very harmful to the French cause in Spain. There were many other spicier details in the Cadiz papers. These asserted that King Joseph's ambassador in Moscow had joined the Russian army in the field against Napoleon and, which was true, that the King's brother-in-law, Bernadotte, now Crown Prince of Sweden, had not only concluded a secret understanding with England but had welcomed the French traitor, General Moreau, to Stockholm. It was also reported that Bernadotte had asked for an élite force of Spanish regulars to be provided by the Cadiz Cortes to act as his personal bodyguard. While still serving as a French marshal in Swedish Pomerania in 1809, Bernadotte had commanded Romana's Spanish division. Now he wanted some of these Spaniards back. There were more serious rumours spread by word of mouth. One was that Joseph was in secret correspondence with his brother-in-law about the withdrawal of all French troops in Spain, whilst staying on as an independent Spanish king, and that he was also in touch with his brother, Lucien, now living in exile in Worcestershire, about Lucien's proposal to Lord Castlereagh for a total French evacuation of the Peninsula.

Having made his own views known to his generals on some or all of these subjects, Soult's second letter of August 12 described in detail the stories now appearing in the Cadiz newspapers, although he did not at this stage refer to the darker rumours of Joseph's other alleged perfidies. Soult also complained that he had been kept more or less in the dark about the various military events that had been taking place in northern Spain.[11] This second letter, sent to General Clarke from Malaga, fell into Joseph's clutches as the ship carrying it to France was blown by a storm into the harbour at Valencia.

There was then a real storm. Soult was commanded to leave Andalusia at once and to join the other French armies in Valencia. This time he simply had to obey. Until the last moment he had kept up a brave show of activity in Seville so that Wellington was still uncertain whether he could safely move north from Madrid or whether he would first have to confront Soult in the south. In the event, the King's peremptory orders settled the matter. At long last the Marshal was compelled to destroy the great siege fortifications around Cadiz which had been in place for over two years and then withdraw slowly northwards from Seville. As a good professional soldier he timed his departure to begin at 2 am and he was accompanied by a number of sympathetic Spanish families – not to mention the *maréchales* – the two young sisters who were his own and Victor's mistresses. A final order to his armies was characteristic: "I want no damage to be done. Private property must be scrupulously respected. The country should remain in good order and should preserve the memory of an excellent French administration so that if, later on, our armies return to Andalusia we will receive a warm welcome. We must also provide for and protect the emigration of those people compromised by the French cause whom we cannot abandon."[12] Cynics reading this military order might comment on the artistic masterpieces and other plunder with which Soult's wagons were fully laden. Predictably, the fickle inhabitants of Seville turned against him at the end. Even his faithful *escopeteros* fired on the French army as they departed "while tiles, flower-pots and even furniture rained down on their heads like hail".[13] Because of the large number of civilian families accompanying the army, progress northward was slow, but with characteristic thoroughness Soult had established a well-stocked transit base at Cordoba which was also the rallying place for the many different French army units spread out all over southern Spain. Soult then had to make a cautious and difficult march through the mountains of Murcia, avoiding the fever-ridden coast and being harassed by numerous small Spanish forces. Perhaps not surprisingly, the Spanish troops who had served him so well for the last two years gradually deserted him.

It took him 37 days to cover the 160 leagues to the borders of Valencia. Here at the end of his long march he had a dramatic encounter with King Joseph at Fuente la Higuera near the frontier. The King was accompanied by Marshals Jourdan and Suchet but Soult and the King had a private talk which seems to have passed off surprisingly well. Was it, as Du Casse suggests, that the generous Joseph was always ready to forget the past? Alternatively, were Soult's suspicions about his conduct too near the truth for him to behave other than generously, as has also been suggested?[14] The most likely explanation is that the King was simply biding his time until he received his brother's support for his bitter complaints against Soult and his strident demands that he should be punished. This is Soult's own opinion and he adds that they simply discussed "military matters".[15]

Clarke's response in Paris was naturally very satisfactory to Joseph. He assured the King's fleet messenger, Desprez, that the Marshal's behaviour in Andalusia had been as disgraceful as his conduct in Oporto three years earlier. Desprez was then posted off with indignant letters from Joseph to be delivered to the Emperor in Moscow. The zealous colonel covered the whole distance from Paris to Moscow in the record time of 38 days, only to be sharply snubbed when he was eventually received by Napoleon. Understandably, the Emperor told him that he was far too busy to be concerned with these trifling matters. Anyway he had heard about them "from another source" – perhaps even in Russia from English newspapers? The Emperor commented that Soult's views about his brother's strong pro-Spanish sympathies were shared by all the other French generals. He went on to say that the King might be French at heart but one could not guess that from his language. He added that Soult had "the best head in Spain" – and to dismiss him now would be to insult the army. Desprez was sent away with a flea in his ear. As he was an engineer officer, he was told to go and make himself useful to Marshal Mortier with the proposed destruction of the Kremlin when the French left Moscow.

With Wellington occupying Madrid, future policy had now to be decided. The angry King had offered the command of the Army of the South either to Suchet or Jourdan but they both refused. He then demanded written advice about the future from all three Marshals. As the most experienced fighting soldier, Soult's views prevailed but his relations with the King remained very strained. His plan was really an extension of the proposals he had made so often from Seville whereby the enemy occupying the centre of Spain should be attacked by two sizeable French forces – the Army of Portugal, now firmly reconstituted on the Ebro after the defeat of Salamanca, and a strong army group consisting of two fast-moving columns converging from the south. The larger of these two columns would move along the line of the Tagus while a secondary force thrust straight towards Madrid. As Soult was not slow to point out, the Army of the South, which was to form the major part of the Tagus column, had lost nearly three months in marching round via Valencia instead of, as Soult had so often recommended, threatening Wellington directly from Andalusia.

As usual the King was mainly concerned with the future of his capital and, while paying lip-service to Soult's strategic plan, he began making modifications, supported by Jourdan who usually fell in with his wishes, whatever were his own ideas. Soult had counted on an important reinforcement from the Army of Aragon but the King dared not press his nephew, Suchet, to agree to this since Suchet claimed that he was still being threatened by an Anglo-Sicilian force that had landed at Alicante. This was another of the rather futile maritime operations carried out by the Allies on the east coast of Spain which had little effect on the course of the war except as an encouragement to Spanish morale. Anxious not to give Soult too much power anyway, the King strengthened d'Erlon's Army of the Centre, which was to march directly on Madrid, at the expense of the Army of the South. This was despite a conciliatory gesture by Soult suggesting that the King should personally 'command' the Army of the South. The Marshal's attempt to create a 'mass of manoeuvre' on the Tagus on Napoleon's model was largely foiled by Joseph's determination to recapture Madrid at once.

There were also constant administrative disputes between Soult and the King. It was only thanks to Suchet's helpfulness, and not at all to Joseph, that Soult's army received some much needed stores and ammunition following its long march from Seville, and there were all the usual wrangles over pay. Again, after the march towards the Tagus had begun, Soult was compelled, to his fury, to provide escort for a big convoy of Spanish families from Joseph's court, "the useless mouths", as Brun de Villeret describes them, who were returning from Valencia to Madrid. For his part, the King strongly objected to Soult sending campaign reports direct to Clarke in Paris instead of through himself as commander-in-chief.

Despite these various problems there was now a real chance for the French to recover their position in Spain. In September Wellington, besides commanding his Anglo-Portuguese army, had also been given supreme command of all Spanish forces. But there were many in Cadiz who were intensely jealous of the British, wishing desperately to regain their own primacy in the War of Liberation. The liberals were thinking in terms of a *levée en masse* of the population but several of the 'conservative' generals were pursuing their own private paths. The ambitious Ballesteros, for example, was creating a kind of petty dictatorship in some of those parts of southern Spain which Soult had relinquished.[16] Against this disturbed political background Wellington had made his disastrous attempt to capture Burgos. He had hastily to retire, pursued by the regenerated French Army of Portugal, while Hill's army also retreated, continually harassed by Soult who was rapidly advancing along the Tagus. King Joseph re-entered Madrid on November 2, to be greeted by a sullen population which had so warmly welcomed Wellington a few weeks before.

Soult was immediately summoned to Madrid by the King to advise on future operations. Despite their intense mutual dislike, Joseph still regarded Soult as his chief military adviser and the remainder of this winter campaign was carried out under his overall direction. Taking advantage of Wellington's military embarassment and his political problems with the Spaniards, this was really Soult's last chance to win the war.

Wellington had by now retired beyond Salamanca towards the Portuguese border. Indeed Salamanca itself had changed hands so many times that the graffiti in the soldiers' cafés were in French and English, thickly plastered on top of each other. Probably both nationalities were equally detested by the inhabitants. Wellington had taken up a strong position on the River Tormes near Alba in the area in which he had defeated Marmont a few months previously. But he only had 68,000 weary soldiers while the French forces moving against him under Joseph's nominal command were some 80,000 strong. During the 'operational conference' before the battle Jourdan advised an immediate frontal attack against the dispirited British, using some narrow fords across the Tormes. This would have had the advantage of bringing Wellington to battle immediately. Soult, supported by Clausel, the most successful of the generals commanding the Army of Portugal, was characteristically in favour of a more cautious left-flanking attack where the river crossings were better, possibly enabling him to surround and annihilate the British. The disadvantage was that Wellington, if he was quick, could escape completely by retreating on Ciudad Rodrigo. The King accepted Soult's plan and, after a feint frontal attack, Soult sent his cavalry and the rest of his army across the river against the British right flank. He had lost none of his skill in tactical manoeuvring and, not for the first time, he earned the admiration of that alert British observer, Ensign John Aitchison of the Third Foot Guards. Aitchison wrote: "Marshal Soult with that spirit of enterprise that distinguished him above all the French generals passed a great part of his force over the River Tormes by night and by noon the next day, despite a cannonade from 14 of our pieces, the whole army was on the left of the Tormes."[17] Unfortunately for Soult, a torrential storm helped Wellington to make a quick and well organized retreat towards Ciudad Rodrigo and the Portuguese frontier. As Jourdan commented bitterly and perhaps unfairly: "Wellington was allowed to escape in the face of 80,000 of the best troops in Europe."[18] The cavalry pursuit under Pierre, Soult's brother, was less vigorous than it would have been under his old cavalry leader, Franceschi, and Wellington got clear away. Soult was at first inclined to continue the pursuit so as to achieve a real revenge for Marmont's defeat at Salamanca, although, according to Oman, he did not want to invade Portugal again.[19]

Soult in his own papers contended that it was the King who decided that it was now too late in the year for further operations and the latter returned with the Army of the Centre to Madrid while Soult established his winter headquarters in Toledo.

It was for the French a disappointing end to what had been a successful campaign. They had indeed lost their last chance of winning the Peninsular War. Again Soult was entitled to feel that an all-out attack mounted from Andalusia might have had a quite different result. Now, because of the King's timidity and obstinacy, the whole of southern Spain had been lost. However, short of winning a complete victory, Soult had achieved something. All the territory – and more – lost by Marmont had been regained. In their rapid retreat British casualties, killed, wounded and prisoners, numbered some 5,000 in addition to their sharp losses in the abortive attack on Burgos. A mass of arms and equipment had been captured and once again the British had been cleared out of central Spain. They would not return for another six months. By then the responsibility of fighting them was no longer Soult's. It was only after he departed that Joseph lost his kingdom altogether in the disaster of Vitoria.

The Marshal spent the last winter months of his long sojourn in Spain living in characteristic splendour in the Archbishop's Palace in Toledo. Amid the celebration of carnival and various public festivities he worked as hard as ever. His army had still not recovered completely from the long march from Seville, followed by its vigorous operations along the Tagus and the Tormes. In Toledo he carried out a major reorganization, seeing that his troops were properly clothed, fed and paid, dealing with cavalry remounts, artillery reconditioning and hospital building. By the middle of February he could tell the King that he was ready to take the field again.

All this time the disputes with Madrid had continued, mostly concerning the respective responsibilities of King and commander-in-chief on the one hand and army commander on the other. Soult complained that he could not carry out his military duties because of constant interference; there were still frequent disputes over the troops' pay and the Marshal rightly suspected that the King was sending to Paris malicious reports about his failure to annihilate the British on the Tormes. In fact Joseph had gone much further. He had now developed an *idée fixe* about Soult claiming that, but for him, he would have been able to pacify the whole of Spain. While Napoleon was still in Russia he suggested almost hysterically that Soult was spreading rumours to the effect that the Emperor had been killed and that he was involved in the famous Malet conspiracy which had provoked a short-lived but serious crisis in Paris. Despite all Joseph's efforts to stop him, Soult continued to correspond directly with Clarke, so that the Minister of War found himself in a quandary; he much preferred Joseph whom he could manipulate, but he was of course fully dependent on the Emperor's overriding directions.

Napoleon himself had far more pressing problems than the affairs of Spain. The 29th Bulletin of the Grande Armée had described the Moscow disaster, but the Emperor's health was said to be excellent. In the light of all that had happened in Russia, Napoleon wanted a situation in Spain whereby the north of the country and the Pyrenees would be protected from enemy attack while he was fighting his next desperate campaign in Germany. There was not much value in his brother continuing to reign in Spain unless he could reach an accommodation with some Spanish leaders in Cadiz behind the backs of the British. On the other hand, if his brother abdicated and returned to France, there was a danger that he might threaten the regency of the Empress while Napoleon was away. Marie Louise's regency was of considerable importance for Napoleon's future relationship with his father-in-law, the Emperor of Austria.

In response to yet another frantic demand for the removal of Soult, Clarke so far forgot his natural caution as to write to King Joseph: "If Soult's conduct is so two-faced and crafty, the Emperor, remembering his conduct in abandoning Portugal after taking Oporto, may punish him but it is not a good time when Napoleon is away and rebellious ideas are in the air. So do not push things too far!"[20] This was a strange letter for the Minister of War to write about the senior Marshal in the French service in Spain.

In fact, things came to a head between Soult and the King in rather a different way. At the end of 1812 Soult had informed the Emperor that if the crisis with the King made his future in Spain impossible he would prefer to resign and take up another command in Europe. The demands from Joseph for his removal had now reached such a pitch that he actually told his brother that he would forego his next financial subsidy if he could get rid of Soult. He also requested the removal, among others, of General Cafarelli, who was commanding in northern Spain and was equally obnoxious. In the event, handing over the command of his army to General Gazan, Soult was able to depart on leave honourably, on the understanding that he would soon be given another important appointment. As an additional snub to Joseph, Cafarelli, who also departed, was immediately awarded the prestigious post of commander of the Empress's bodyguard. Soult had a frigid farewell audience with the King on March 2. He was not invited to dinner.

Yet, even at the last moment, the relations between the King and Soult remained curiously ambivalent. To provide for a more effective defence of northern Spain, which was what mattered most to the Emperor now, he ordered his brother to remove his headquarters from Madrid to Valladolid. Joseph immediately made use of a chance remark of Soult's to oppose this demand. This was to the effect that the day the King left Madrid he would have renounced Spain completely. If this was really Soult's view it was a rather surprising change of mind. But, with or without Soult's supporting argument, the King was compelled to leave Madrid for Valladolid towards the end of March 1813 and he was to lose his whole kingdom three months later at Vitoria.

Soult left Spain at the beginning of March 1813, no doubt imagining that he would never return. If he had remained, there would probably have been no Vitoria. This was the strongly held view of Marbot and other contemporary memoir writers. Soult was far too much of a professional soldier to have got into such an operational mess as that of the King and Jourdan. He would certainly have kept the various corps commanders in better order as he was later to do in the campaign in the Pyrenees and southern France. Had he stayed, French rule might have lasted at least north of the Ebro until the Emperor's abdication the following year.

The debate about the effect of Soult's prolonged occupation of Andalusia has long continued. Some historians, like Thiers and Oman, consider that it was a factor that contributed as much as any other to France's *débâcle* in the Peninsula. On the other hand, there is much to be said for Soult's own view as set out in his *Memoirs*. He obviously enjoyed the panoply of power in Seville and he certainly brought a measure of peace and good order to southern Spain for two and a half years. He also believed firmly that to maintain Andalusia as a French power base was the right military strategy. In August 1811 the British intelligence officer, Charles Cocks, had referred to the danger of advancing far into Spain "because Soult could, in that case, penetrate with a corps to Lisbon".[21] In the summer of 1812 Wellington himself also referred to Soult's obstinate refusal to leave southern Spain. "Any other but a modern French army would have left Andalusia but I suspect that Soult will not stir until I force him out. I must think of making that movement as soon as I can take my troops there without injuring their health."[22]

These comments put in a nutshell the dilemma that faced Wellington so long as Soult remained in Seville. By staying on in Andalusia, Soult forced Wellington after Salamanca to march on Madrid and central Spain instead of making a quicker and more dangerous advance upon the Ebro. All this was ruined by the King's fateful direction to evacuate southern Spain. Even Oman admits that "while sooner or later this was bound to happen the whole fabric of the French occupation of Spain was dashed to pieces by the abandonment of Andalusia".[23] Soult himself would have quite accepted this summary of his whole political and strategic policy.

14

INTERLUDE IN SAXONY

FOR A SHORT four months from the beginning of March to the end of June 1813 Soult was not directly involved in the affairs of Spain. After four and a half years in the Peninsula partly as a fighter, partly as an administrator and partly as a politician, Soult reverted to his normal role as a highly skilled professional soldier in the French army in Europe.

Louise Soult was told by her old ally, Brun de Villeret, who was in France already, that her husband had at last obtained leave and was due home in March. He went straight to St-Amans in the Tarn to greet his wife and children as well as his old mother whom he had not seen for several years. But his period of leave was short. With France now in serious danger after the disaster in Russia, he was impatient to return to active service. He was soon back in Paris being received by the Emperor whom similarly he had not seen for a long time. Judging by the atmosphere that Brun de Villeret describes when he himself was at the Emperor's dinner table a short time previously, with the Empress also present dandling the infant King of Rome on her knee, Soult was clearly in favour again. Among the family archives there is a detailed memorandum from Brun de Villeret to his master about his interview with Napoleon. Brun told the Emperor how excellently Andalusia had been administered and what a cruel blow it was to the French position in Spain when Soult was forced to abandon the south. He also provided Napoleon with a detailed résumé of his master's viewpoint in his many conflicts with King Joseph in every field, including military operations.[1] The Emperor fully agreed with Soult's opinions, as reported by his chief aide-de-camp, not only over his brother's dangerous 'Spanishness' but also over his obvious incompetence. Old contentions about Oporto, jealousy over Soult's victory at Ocaña and strongly expressed criticisms of many of the Marshal's military operations seemed to have disappeared. Once more he had become 'the faithful Soult', "the best head among all the Frenchmen in the Peninsula" and a stalwart defender of the imperial power there.

But Spanish affairs were certainly not in the forefront of the Emperor's thoughts. He was facing a desperate military campaign in Europe. After all that had happened in the retreat from Moscow Prussia was adopting a much more hostile attitude. The Prussian contingent under General Yorck which had formed part of Napoleon's invasion army had proclaimed its 'independence' and then events had moved quickly. Something akin to nationalist fervour was sweeping over Prussia and spreading to other parts of Germany. After some wobbling even the feeble King Frederick William had become openly belligerent and in the middle of March he had concluded a treaty of alliance with the Russians. Many of the rulers of Napoleon's Confederation of the Rhine, including the King of Bavaria and even the King of Saxony, had become lukewarm towards France while Metternich, the astute chief minister of Napoleon's father-in-law in Vienna, was obviously hoping to become a kind of arbitrator.

Faced by yet another coalition which, of course, was fully supported by the British, the Emperor considered his brother's throne in Madrid was now expendable. All he wanted from the French armies in the Peninsula was for northern Spain to be defended as a barrier against any invasion of France. Once he had defeated the Allies in Germany he looked ahead to a solution of the Spanish problem whereby Ferdinand, married to a Bonaparte princess, would be restored, perhaps in agreement with some of the Spanish generals who might be willing to defy the great majority of the Cadiz cortes and to break ties with England.

Meanwhile the Emperor's first task was to take the field once again in Germany. He was woefully short of senior officers, of veteran soldiers and of cavalry. The corps commanders, Bertrand, Lauriston and even Oudinot were not really comparable with marshals of the first rank. Of these Davout was fully occupied with operations on the Lower Elbe; Masséna was old and ill; Ney, Marmont and Macdonald were there but Ney, who had covered himself with glory during the retreat from Moscow, was as rash and as disobliging as ever. Soult was fully available but Napoleon was partly holding him in reserve for possible re-employment in Spain. Initially he was appointed as a kind of alternative chief of staff under the direct orders of the Emperor to assist Berthier whose constant state of overwork was beginning to create embarrassment. Since Berthier was intensely jealous of Soult, this must have caused problems.[2]

Soult was also available for other special tasks. Characteristically Thiers does not refer at all to his active participation in the campaign in Germany except to suggest that Napoleon brought him along to prevent him from allying himself with Fouché and others in some conspiracy in Paris directed against Marie Louise's regency. This is nonsense. Having worked his passage back into the Emperor's favour, it is impossible to believe that he would have been engaged in such a political conspiracy. Later, after Napoleon's own abdication, loyalties among most of the marshals and the political leaders became confused but Soult, with Davout, was to be the last of the marshals to hold out in defence of France even after the Emperor had abdicated.

The first of Soult's special tasks was to take under his immediate orders the Imperial Guard commanded by General Roguet. The initial encounter with the Russians and Prussians was at Lützen in Saxony on May 2. It was a hard fought battle which was only transformed into a French victory when, in response to the famous order – "la garde au feu" – the Young Guard, supported by the Old Guard and the Guard Cavalry, "moved inexorably forward" and the entire Allied line began to retreat in growing confusion.[3] It was not a total victory: the Allied army was certainly not encircled and destroyed, which was Napoleon's original intention, and a vigorous pursuit was impossible because of the inadequacy of the French cavalry. After Lützen the French crossed the upper Elbe and entered Dresden; the King of Saxony was brought back to heel and Napoleon took up a strong position along the River Spree which at that point flowed through the town of Bautzen on the borders of Silesia. The various formations of the Imperial Guard, which had Soult in general command, played an important part in the victory.

Brun de Villeret had by now briefly rejoined his much respected chief although he arrived just too late for Lützen. But no sooner had he arrived than Napoleon, who had formed as high an opinion of him as Soult, sent him off to reconnoitre a section of the Spree. On his return he reported to the Emperor who was in conference with Berthier and Soult. The clarity of his report, following his long period of devoted service to Soult, led the Emperor to promote him to general of brigade, although, to his regret, no longer under Soult but in Oudinot's much less hospitable XII Corps on the right of the French line.

Napoleon's intention in the battle of Bautzen, which took place on May 20–21 was for Marmont, Macdonald and Oudinot to launch a strong attack on the Allied left flank, and for Ney and Lauriston to make a secondary attack on the enemy's right. Then, when the Allied reserves were exhausted, the crucial attack would be carried out by Bertrand's IV Corps, under the general supervision of Soult, against what was hoped would be the weakened right centre of the enemy line. Blücher was defending a plateau there, covering the key villages of Pliskowitz and Krechwitz.

The main strategic objective would be to encircle the enemy, driving him away from Silesia and placing him fully at the mercy of the French. But as so often in this campaign, the French troops were young and inexperienced – in quality nothing like the veterans of the old Grand Armée, so many of whom were still serving in Spain. Nor was corps leadership nearly as good as in the past. The initial attacks on the Allied left were fairly successful and the town of Bautzen was captured, but the approach march of Ney's left wings on the other flank was much too slow so that the Emperor had to confine the first day of the battle to fierce attrition tactics, delaying the final attack until the following day.

Soult was evidently delighted to be given overall command of his old IV Corps, even if its composition was now quite different. Bertrand, although relatively inexperienced as a corps commander, had served under him before when he had been responsible for some of the major port construction in Wimereux and Ambleteuse during the abortive preparations for the invasion of England in 1804. In his supervisory role Soult was really in his element. He had spent part of the first day of the battle having an elaborate earthwork built up on the east bank of the Spree, partly in the area which Brun de Villeret had reconnoitred. This made an excellent cover for the sappers of IV Corps to construct pontoon bridges across the river. He must have recalled his daring crossing of the Linth in Switzerland, which had made such an important contribution to Masséna's victory at Second Zürich in 1799. More importantly he hoped to repeat, under the eyes of the Emperor, and again with IV Corps, that famous storming of the Pratzen plateau which had been the decisive operation in the battle of Austerlitz.

It was not Soult's fault that Bautzen was no Austerlitz. In the fierce fighting that occurred the following day Ney's and Lauriston's corps were again very slow in coming into battle, partly through stupidity and partly through dilatoriness, so that the Allied reserves were not drawn away from the centre as Napoleon had planned. Although Soult's forces and the three French corps on the right smashed their way doggedly forward, their troops were nothing like the veterans of 1805 who had stormed the Pratzen. In what the Grande Armée bulletin described as the critical phase of the battle Soult captured Blücher's key fort but he then got bogged down with heavy losses because he could not effectively deploy his corps artillery. It was only when the Imperial Guard was brought into the battle that the enemy were driven from their defensive positions and forced to retreat – once again in fairly good order since the French were so weak in cavalry. Casualties were about equal on both sides but it was a clear French victory.[4] However, after some more indecisive fighting, the Emperor, at the beginning of June, concluded with the Allies a brief armistice, ostensibly as a prelude to negotiations for a settled peace but actually in order to get his army into better shape. It was a development that was to prove fatal to him.

This temporary cease-fire, during which Napoleon used Dresden as his base, gave him an opportunity to consider problems in other parts of the Empire. Of these one of the most urgent was the future of Spain where King Joseph and Jourdan had now been decisively defeated at Vitoria, so that Wellington's army was likely soon to pose a serious threat to France's Pyrenean frontier. It was in this vital area that the Emperor must all along have considered that Soult had the key part to play.

In his admirable *Memoirs* Caulaincourt comments as follows on Soult's 'Saxon interlude': "Napoleon, observing the weariness and the lowering of Berthier's mental powers, recalled Soult, who, he considered, had the most talent and capacity of all the marshals, to assist Berthier. But the disaster in Spain including the follies, as he called them, of Marmont compelled him with great regret to relinquish Soult so as to send him to restore the situation in Spain. The Emperor affirmed that he was the only one capable of bearing this burden."[5]

15

THE LAST OFFENSIVE IN SPAIN

SOON AFTER he had received news of Vitoria the Emperor gave Soult dramatic orders. He was to leave Dresden at once, travelling under the pseudonym of one of his own aides-de-camp, and reaching Paris in three days. There he was to get an up-to-date briefing from Arch-Chancellor Cambacérès. He was to stay in Paris for only twelve hours and then go on to Bayonne to take over command of the French armies in Spain and the Pyrenees with the title of 'Lieutenant General of the Emperor'. No doubt in the light of past problems this was intended to be a purely military appointment, whereby Soult communicated with the Ministry of War and did not assume any title such as Regent. His first task was to re-establish the French position in Spain after the recent disasters and to relieve San Sebastian and Pamplona, which were the only places of importance still left to the French in north-west Spain. His next objective was to drive Wellington back across the Ebro. He had a free hand to get rid of any senior officers that he wanted and this would no doubt include Marshal Jourdan.[1] He carried with him a letter to King Joseph ordering him to hand over his command.

Soult welcomed this new and difficult challenge. His one regret was that he was not allowed to take Brun de Villeret with him as his chief of staff. A decision to appoint Soult was quite natural. The Marshal had had more experience of fighting in the Peninsula than any other Frenchman and, as Napier records, "He was one of the few leaders whose indefatigable energy rendered him a worthy lieutenant of Napoleon."[2] His opinions of Joseph were well known but there is no evidence, as some have asserted, that he actively intrigued against him. As regards a future ruler of Spain, the favoured suggestion continued to be that Ferdinand should return married to a Bonaparte princess and under French auspices. Soult was required to give advice on this when he arrived. Already his role seemed likely to be morc than 'purcly military'. Although he had thus been given the overall command, nothing specific was said about Marshal Suchet whose forces were still holding parts of Aragon and Catalonia. Presumably Suchet was formally under Soult's orders but, as will appear, he was no more cooperative with his fellow Marshal than he had been with his wife's uncle when Joseph was ruling in Madrid.

One sharply dissenting voice was raised. Louise Soult with her two young children, Hector and Hortense, had joined her husband in Dresden and she was looking forward to a long stay with him at last. She protested loudly to the Emperor about him being sent off once more to Spain. Napoleon had a high regard for Louise and he was amused by the strong hold that she exercised over her forceful husband. But he was also displeased that she had never joined him in Spain and he was certainly not going to let her win this battle. He is supposed to have told her that he would not tolerate these vociferous protests: the duty of wives was to "ameliorate their husbands' misfortunes" and she should trouble her husband no longer. Some of this comes from the highly coloured *Memoirs* of Fouché but it is probably not far from the truth. It was one of the few encounters with the Emperor in which Louise Soult came off second best. She had to leave Dresden again four days after her husband's departure. Such were the rigours of married life under the Empire.

Soult arrived in Paris "as fast as and as straight as an arrow".[3] After talking to Cambacérès, he went on to Bayonne. Within eleven days of leaving Dresden he was taking over from King Joseph. Whatever the result of the future contest with Wellington, the long struggle with Joseph had been decided with almost embarrassing finality in favour of Soult. The Emperor's views on the matter had been caustically expressed: "I should have sent Soult back to take command at Valladolid. I do not like having my affairs handled by imbeciles who are neither soldiers, politicians or administrators. The King has neither military nor administrative talent. He cannot command an army: he can only prevent more competent people from doing so."[4] Clarke, the Minister of War, who had been so firmly on King Joseph's side, tried to put the best face on things by telling the King that the Emperor thought it "impolitic and disturbing for a prince of the blood to be responsible for the difficult events that Vitoria might bring in its train. That was why a marshal was being made the Emperor's lieutenant."[5] In fact Napoleon was still worried about his brother returning to Paris and upsetting Marie Louise's regency, so his first idea was that he should remain in northern Spain or in Bayonne. However, the King resolutely refused to stay there, as he said, "to be bullied more or less as a prisoner by Marshal Soult". Once again he became almost hysterical over Soult but, from the comments of Count Roederer who acted as an intermediary between them, they eventually arranged a calm and civilized hand-over. Instead of exacting some form of revenge, which the King feared, Joseph was astonished at the speed with which Soult took steps to pull together the heavily defeated French army.[6] In response the King at once put at his disposal all the personal troops that he had left – the Royal Guards, three infantry battalions, a gendarmerie company, some light horse and some artillery. Then, after wishing Soult all success, he left in a very dispirited state for his house at Mortefontaine near Paris, commenting in a letter to his friend, Clarke, that it was "his sincerest wish that a greater experience of war than I have ever been able to offer will enable the new commander-in-chief to re-establish affairs in the Peninsula but I fear that this is a vain hope."[7] He and Soult did not meet again until the Hundred Days.

On paper the French 'Army of Spain', as it was now called, was still quite large. Under Soult's direct command there were nine infantry divisions with light cavalry, two heavy cavalry divisions and several battalions of Spanish, German and Italian troops. Including the garrisons of San Sebastian and Pamplona, this amounted to some 100,000 men, of whom 85,000 were operational on paper. In addition Suchet had another 66,000 troops although they were not, of course, under Soult's direct control. Wellington had indeed done very well in keeping so many French veteran troops more or less permanently tied up in the Peninsula.[8] In fact to call Soult's new forces the 'Army of Spain' was largely a misnomer. Apart from Santona on the north coast and the strongholds of San Sebastian and Pamplona, still in French hands, the whole army was now on the Pyrenean frontier or had crossed over into France. Administration was in chaos with the army bogged down with a mass of camp followers, servants, muleteers and other non-combatants. Already there was a stream of French refugees fleeing northward from the frontier area. Soult's major problem was one of morale. The veterans who still formed a high proportion of the army were as good fighters as their opponents; yet they had been heavily defeated. From their long experience of the war in the Peninsula they recognized that the high command leadership, particularly in the summer of 1813, had been very bad. On the other hand, many of them had served under Soult. Indeed he had been soldiering in the Peninsula as long as most of them. Despite his many ups and downs, including serious problems with several of his senior officers, he was admired by the juniors and by the rank and file who served under him. On the other hand, some of the troops had been commanded by generals who were much more lax disciplinarians than Soult and did not take kindly to his strict administration. But, all in all, most of the army expected something better than the feeble leadership of King Joseph and Jourdan.

Wellington's Anglo-Spanish-Portuguese army was somewhat larger than Soult's and it had won a spectacular victory at Vitoria, but Wellington faced many problems. He had incessant difficulties with the cortes in Cadiz where there was intense jealousy of Britain's increasingly predominant role in the war and plenty of anglophobia. Indeed, later in August, he went so far as to resign his appointment of commander-in-chief of the Spanish forces, only to be reinstated a little later.[9] He was greatly concerned about Spanish discipline if and when he invaded France. On the political side he was determined to move cautiously while negotiations between Napoleon and the Allies continued at Dresden. Concerning the future of Spain, he was aware of French ideas to make use of the exiled Ferdinand and he suggested to London that it might be preferable to have Joseph Bonaparte as King of all Spain rather than envisage Ferdinand as a French protégé ruling a puppet state north of the Ebro.[10]

Soult's sudden and dramatic appearance at Bayonne was just what was needed to pull the French army together – at least on the surface – and, on July 23 he issued a characteristically forceful 'order of the day' declaring that the recent disasters were

Mon Cousin, je reçois votre lettre que m'apporte votre aide de camp. cet aide de camp me dit que la nomination du Prince de Neufchatel a mis de l'incertitude sur la confiance que j'aurais en vous. ma confiance en vous est entière. J'ai nommé le Prince de Neufchatel major général parce que j'ai voulu que la Correspondance passât par lui, comme devant être plus expéditive que par le Ministre de la guerre, et parce qu'il y a à faire une foule d'états dont il a l'habitude. vous devez prendre le même titre que celui qu'avait le M.al Jourdan, pendant tout le temps que j'étais en Espagne. Je suis très fâché de connaître la peine que cela a pu vous faire et surtout de l'influence que cela a pu avoir sur mes affaires, qu'on ait laissé de l'incertitude là dessus. Sur ce je prie Dieu qu'il vous ait, mon Cousin, en sa sainte et digne garde.

A Paris le 14 janvier 1810.

Napoléon

Au Maréchal Duc de Dalmatie.

Above: Napoleon's letter of reassurance to Soult when Berthier (Prince of Neufchatel) was again made major-general in Spain. It did not reassure Soult! "Cousin, I received your letter that your aide-de-camp brought me. The aide-de-camp told me that the Prince of Neufchatel's appointment has cast doubts on the confidence which I have in you. My confidence in you is complete. I have made the Prince of Neufchatel "major general" because I wanted correspondence to pass through him which would be quicker than through the Minister of War – and because[?] there are many things that he is used to doing.[?] You must take the same title that Marshal Jourdan had during the time that I was in Spain. I am very annoyed[?] . . . [?] and at the effect that this has had on your affairs since you have been said to have been uncertain [?] of my plans [?]. God protect you. Paris 14 January 1810. Napoleon." (Archives of the château of Epoisses)

Above: The battle of Ocaña, November 1809. The greatest French victory in the Peninsular War, Soult directing operations.

Below: Soult leading the French forces at the battle of Toulouse.

VINGT-DEUXIÈME TABLEAU.

BATTLE OF TOULOUSE,
10th of April, 1814.

Marshall Soult having entrench'd himself in Toulouse, and fortified the heights at the east of the *Canal du Midi* is attacked by the English Army, which successively carries the five Batteries, and invests the Town. The French evacuate Toulouse in the night, and on the 12th, the Duke of Wellington makes his solemn entry.

BATAILLE DE TOULOUSE,
le 10 Avril 1814.

Le Maréchal Soult s'étant retranché dans Toulouse, et ayant fortifié les hauteurs à l'Est du Canal du Midi, est attaqué par l'Armée Anglaise qui s'empare successivement des cinq Batteries, et cerne la Ville. Les Français évacuent Toulouse dans la nuit, et le 12 le Duc de Wellington y fait une entrée solemnelle.

Left, top and bottom: British infantry attack near the bridge over the River Garonne.

Above: The scene on the Calvinet heights with a description of the battle.

Above: Wellington's triumphant entry into Toulouse. J.-P. Escalettes, the Toulouse historian, has commented: "The French women's clothes are typical Toulousian but the buildings are not Toulousian. Also, Wellington is in a hunting coat, not in his red military jacket."

Opposite page, top: The original grand design for a memorial.

Opposite page,centre: The more modest column that was eventually built.

Right: The question of who won the battle is still in doubt. "Was the battle of Toulouse on April 10, 1814 a French or an Allied victory? This is a question on which one can share Honoré de Balzac's reflection on Marshal Soult, the Duke of Dalmatia: 'When he is a hated minister [under Louis XVIII] he has lost the

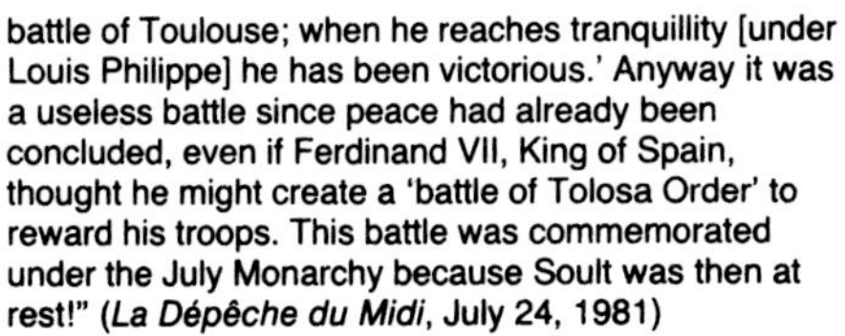

battle of Toulouse; when he reaches tranquillity [under Louis Philippe] he has been victorious.' Anyway it was a useless battle since peace had already been concluded, even if Ferdinand VII, King of Spain, thought he might create a 'battle of Tolosa Order' to reward his troops. This battle was commemorated under the July Monarchy because Soult was then at rest!" (*La Dépêche du Midi*, July 24, 1981)

La bataille de Toulouse, le 10 avril 1814, fut-elle une victoire française ou une victoire des alliés ? On peut se poser la question et réfléchir avec Honoré de Balzac, à propos du maréchal Soult, duc de Dalmatie : **« Tant qu'il est ministre, il a perdu la bataille de Toulouse; dès qu'il entre dans le repos, il l'a gagnée ».** Ce fut, en tout cas, une bataille inutile : la paix était signée. Et même si Ferdinand VII, roi d'Espagne, crût bon de créer un ordre de **« la batalla de Tolosa »** pour récompenser ses troupiers.

Cette bataille, Soult étant au repos sous la monarchie de juillet fut honoré.

Above: Marshal Soult at the time of Waterloo.

Above right: The Vicomte de Lescure. He led the Royalist group who harried Soult on his flight home after Waterloo.

Below: The safe haven which became a comfortable if undistinguished house: a contemporary print of the château of Soultberg in the nineteenth century.

Opposite page, top: The château of Soultberg today. (J.-P. Escalettes)

Right: The fine view of the Black Mountains from the château. (J.-P. Escalettes)

Left: Romance? The Napoleon legend under the July Monarchy. Marshal Soult supplied many of the ingredients. In this engraving he is standing at his Empire-style desk at Soultberg. The indistinguishable portrait over the desk is of Napoleon. On the desk is a bust of Louis Philippe. A "goddess of victory" and a laurel wreath complete the ensemble. Steel engraving from an exhibition catalogue about the "Napoleonic legend"; the exhibition was held in a Toulouse Museum in 1969.

Left: His home in Paris.

Right: One of the longest serving heads of government in French history: Marshal Soult as a civilian minister.

Far right: "Ambassador Extraordinary". Marshal Soult in London at the time of Queen Victoria's coronation.

Right: Reality? According to a hostile caricaturist in 1836. Marshal Soult, as a tough Minister of War, takes turns with King Louis Philippe in beating France about the head.

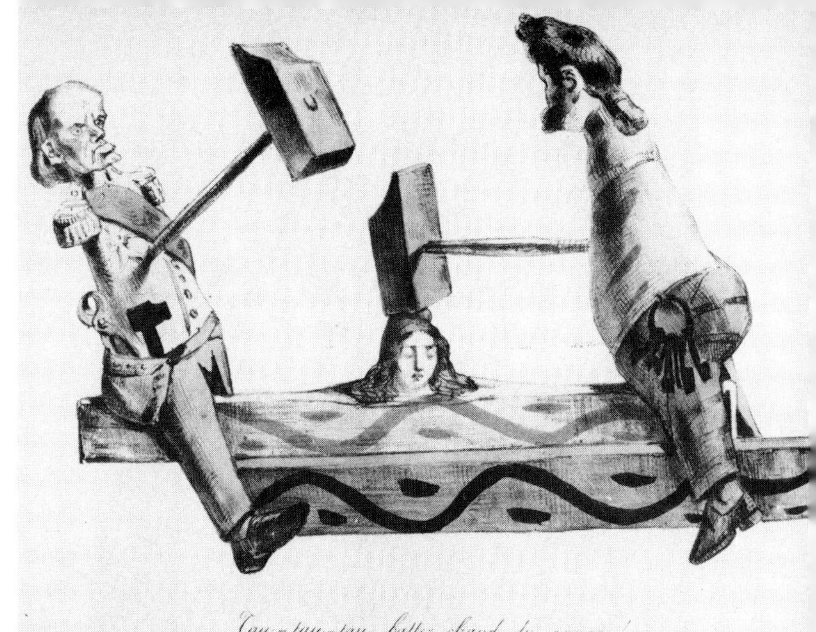

Left: Marshal Soult on his retirement. From the painting by the American artist, Peter Alexander Healy, for the American minister in London, Andrew Stevenson, who described Soult in London as "the observed of all observers". The picture is understood now to be in the possession of a family in Charlottesville, Virginia.

Above: Marshal Soult in old age, from the portrait in Apsley House. (Victoria and Albert Museum)

Left: The tomb of Marshal Soult in the family mausoleum at St.-Amans-Soult, Tarn. The following are the victories and events in his career inscribed on the tomb: Fleurus, Stockach, La Linth, Glavus, Gênes, Monte Creto, Turin, Tarente, Camp de Boulogne, Landsberg, Ulm, Austerlitz, Jena, Lübeck, Eylau, Heilsberg, Königsberg, Burgos, La Corronne, Braga, Oporto, Baltas, Ocaña, Seville, La Gebora, L'Albuera, Lützen, Bautzen, Bayonne, Toulouse, Waterloo, Ministre de la Guerre 1814, 1830, 1840, Ministre des Affaires Etrangères, Président du Conseil, Ambassadeur en Angleterre.

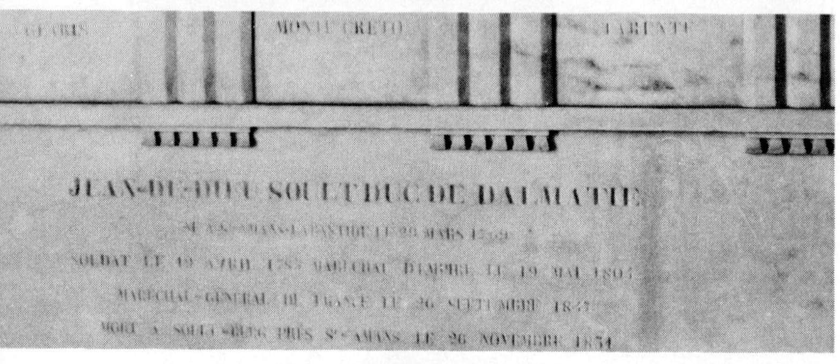

Left: Marshal Soult: coat of arms on his tomb.

Right: Many other descendants of the Marshal are commemorated in the mausoleum. They continued to serve France as shown, for instance, in the memorial to the brothers Reille-Soult de Dalmatie, the victims of the two World Wars.

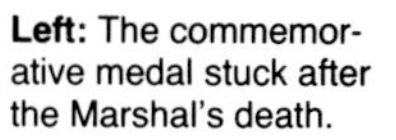
Left: The commemorative medal stuck after the Marshal's death.

due to the incompetent and faint-hearted counsels of the late high command – by implication Joseph and Jourdan; they were in no way caused by the weakness of the troops who must now, with their accustomed skill and bravery, repair these disasters.

It said much for Soult's uncompromising nature that he was ready to criticize the Emperor's brother like this; few of the other marshals would have dared to do so. Clarke, never missing an opportunity for attacking Soult, said that the enemy would use this 'order of the day' to increase the divisions between the army and the imperial family; Oman has called it the spiteful comments of an unamiable man. Be that as it may, Soult's directive provided just the right amount of shock treatment that the army needed. He followed it up with some root and branch reforms. Instead of the existing corps with large, unwieldy staffs he now created three groups or 'wings' under lieutenant generals and with much smaller staffs, rather like Masséna's organization of the Army of Italy in 1800. Each of the three wings which were now on the French side of the Pyrenean frontier were composed of three infantry divisions with supporting cavalry. Reille commanded the right wing based on Vera near the River Bidassoa: Drouet d'Erlon commanded the centre and Clausel the left wing. Gazan, who had succeeded Soult in command of the old Army of the South, reverted to the position of chief of staff and Villatte took charge of the reserve which, with a stiffening of French troops, included former Spanish supporters of King Joseph, Germans and Italians. Reille and Clausel had at different times commanded the former Army of Portugal and, with d'Erlon, had been involved in the recent disasters, but they were able soldiers of the newer generation and all three of them ended up as marshals of France under the Bourbons. Despite the insubordination that Reille was to display later in the Pyrenean campaign, his family were in the future to have close family ties with younger members of the Soult family.

Soult's shock tactics cured the army of its immediate state of nervous exhaustion and there was a great improvement in morale and discipline. Soult strongly fortified army headquarters in Bayonne but would have liked a little more time for reorganization. Napoleon, while fully approving all that he had done so far, was constantly pressing him to take immediate action. His complex negotiations in Dresden would be greatly helped by a quick victory in northern Spain. As usual in the Peninsular War, military decisions were ultimately determined by political needs elsewhere. When Soult arrived he found that Jourdan had been dithering between three strategic alternatives – to raise the siege of San Sebastian, to relieve Pamplona or to march eastward and join Suchet. Sending a copy of Soult's order of the day to London, Wellington considered that the Marshal was 'sanguine' in believing that he could do much more than try to relieve San Sebastian and Pamplona.[11] Of these alternatives Wellington thought his most likely preference would be an attempted breakthrough to San Sebastian and so, on July 25 he made a determined effort to storm the city before Soult could get there. However, partly due to the constant inadequacies of his siege train, partly to the feebleness of the naval blockade, but mainly to the skill of the French governor, Emanuel Rey, the attack failed.

In fact Soult had no immediate intention of relieving San Sebastian. He had confidence in Rey's ability to hold the city and to keep open his sea communications. Instead he determined to move in force to the relief of Pamplona, which he understood, wrongly as it happened, was in serious straits. If he succeeded in this surprise manoeuvre he could then march westward, attack the main body of Wellington's army from the rear, relieve San Sebastian and either press on towards the Ebro or join up with Suchet.

Soult ordered Reille to lead his forces quickly and quietly along the French side of the Pyrenees in order to join Clausel's in the neighbourhood of St Jean Pied de Port. Villatte's small reserve corps would take his place and keep watch on the British forces around San Sebastian. Thus the greater part of Soult's army had taken up its position on the French side of the mountainous Pyrenean frontier preparing for a march through the narrow mountainous defiles towards Pamplona. Clausel's and Reille's wings were to take the lead while d'Erlon on their right was to give full support. Pouring rain and narrow, muddy mountain roads would make an operation with such a large concentration of troops slow and difficult, However, the rapid transfer of Reille's wing from right to left had been carried out unobserved by the British and, given the chaos in the army when Soult arrived, it was, as Oman says, "a marvellous illustration of the Marshal's drive and ability that he could launch a dangerous surprise attack on Wellington's army only thirteen days after his arrival".[12] A British military commentator wrote: "He is one of the first generals of the French army and better able to cope with his Lordship than any other!"[13] It was to be a real 'do or die' march for the French, with the army only taking four days' supplies so that it was essential to reach Pamplona very soon.

The series of hard-fought battles which now took place – Col de Maja, Roncesvalles and First and Second Sorauen – are known collectively as the battles of the Pyrenees. One of the first encounters occurred in high mountain country that had a rather ominous past history for the French. It was here that Charlemagne, returning from an expedition of his own against Pamplona, had been defeated and his greatest paladin, Chevalier Roland, had been killed. Indeed Roland's bones lie buried in the monastery of Roncesvalles. As a paladin of the new Charlemagne, the realistic Soult was unlikely to be much affected by ghostly memories and at first things went pretty well. D'Erlon had the better of a fierce encounter in the Col de Maja. Meanwhile Clausel and Reille were advancing slowly southward through mountainous ravines. Clausel went by the more direct route towards Pamplona while Reille had to move along almost in Indian file by a kind of smuggler's path to the village of Linduz. Having caught Wellington unawares, the two French columns, each numbering some 17,000 men, greatly outnumbered the British forces opposing them since the bulk of the Allied army was still in the San Sebastian area. Soult has been criticized for dividing his army in this way but in such a mountainous region it is hard to see what else he could have done. However, as a result, the French could make little use of their numerical superiority. Clausel was first blocked by a mixed Anglo-Spanish force under Cole at Altobiscar and Reille similarly by British forces at Linduz. Hampered by fog and greatly outnumbered in a combat near Roncesvalles, the British had to continue their retreat. Clausel also pushed on but again thick fog prevented him from bringing the British to battle and encircling them as he had hoped.

By this time news of Soult's bold offensive had reached Wellington in the neighbourhood of San Sebastian and he hastened over to take command of the Allied forces, almost being taken prisoner in the process. Soult also had assumed personal command of Clausel's and Reille's divisions. The French seized the village of Sorauen only a few miles from Pamplona. Indeed the French defenders of Pamplona could hear the guns and see the campfires of their advancing comrades. It was near Sorauen that for the first time Wellington set eyes on his formidable opponent. Osire, a Frenchman acting as a double agent, pointed out the tall figure of the French Marshal directing the movement of his troops with his baton. "Yonder is a great commander," Wellington is supposed to have said, "but he is very cautious and I shall beat him."[14]

Soult had sent off optimistic reports to the Emperor in Dresden. Napoleon 'translated' these messages into the successful raisings of the sieges of San Sebastian and Pamplona. But the actual situation was very different. The first battle of Sorauen was fought on July 28, the fourth anniversary of Talavera. Soult made desperate efforts to seize the 300 metre high ridge near the village of Oricain which alone barred his way to Pamplona. The divisions of Clausel and Reille still outnumbered the British and several times they managed to reach the summit of the ridge, sometimes with the officers pulling the weary men upward by their belts. However, so strongly positioned were the British, assisted by some very active Portuguese units, and so accurate was their fire that repeated French attacks finally failed and Soult's forces had to retreat down the hill again to Sorauen.

Meanwhile, at Soult's urgent command, d'Erlon's wing had fought its way south against rather lighter opposition and by July 30 it had reached the village of Buenza, threatening communications between Allied forces surrounding Pamplona and San Sebastian. But the French got no further. A second battle at Sorauen, fought two days after the first one, resulted in a sharp French defeat. By now Soult had begun to overestimate the size of the forces opposed to him and he was afraid that he might be encircled in the mountains and annihilated. Accordingly he could do no more than order a general retreat of the whole Army of Spain to the Franco-Spanish frontier. His bold offensive had failed and it had cost him some 12,000 casualties.

Was Soult's Pyrenean offensive realistic? He had taken Wellington completely by surprise and it is arguable that he might have succeeded if he had been given a little more time for his preparations instead of having to get going instantly because of Napoleon's political requirements. There was also the appalling mountainous terrain which greatly reduced his temporary advantage in manpower. This type of warfare called for any army to be in excellent physical shape with a high state of morale. Despite the transformation that Soult had achieved in a very short time, the Army of Spain was not really in that state at all. He described the situation in a frank letter to his old enemy, the Minister of War. "I deceived myself when I told you that the army's morale was intact: I mistook for steadfastness the men's feelings of shame for recent disasters. They started off in a furious rush but showed no power of resistance – reminding me of the Revolutionary *levée en masse* in 1792. Later some of them were overheard saying that it was better to get back to the frontier rather than to fight once more in the middle of Spain."[15] In a second letter he emphasized that for political reasons he had had to act "too precipitately".[16] The fine French army, which over the last five years had done so much in the Peninsula, was beginning to become weary and disillusioned – and to run out of steam. Yet it was with these weary and discontented men that Soult was to succeed in holding Wellington at bay in the south of France until after the Emperor had abdicated.

At this stage it is possible that an immediate advance against Soult's disheartened army might have enabled Wellington to defeat and destroy it. But Wellington's natural caution was increased by the fact that he still knew so little about current events in Germany. There was always the danger that Napoleon might make peace with the Allies and then pour fresh reinforcements into Spain – perhaps even crossing the Pyrenees with himself again in command. So he settled down to reduce San Sebastian and Pamplona. Both cities posed problems and Soult was determined to make a last desperate effort to relieve San Sebastian, using once more Reille's weary divisions, with Clausel giving him flanking support. But the French were unable to break through a strongly held Allied position at San Marcial in which a sizeable Spanish force under General Freyre played the major role. Finally the French had to give up their attacks. "I despair of relieving San Sebastian," wrote Soult to Clarke, "and, if I do, I may well be cut off from Bayonne."[17] After a fierce battle around and inside the city San Sebastian was at last stormed and then sacked with particular violence. Pamplona held out for many more weeks. Meanwhile Reille's and Clausel's dispirited divisions had retired back into France. Thus ended the last major offensive that the French were to carry out in the Peninsula.

16

THE DEFENCE OF SOUTHERN FRANCE

WELLINGTON crossed the River Bidassoa into France on October 7 1813. As Captain William Bragge reported, his army "impinged upon the Sacred Territory at last!"[1] Soult was astonished that more than a month had passed after the battles of the Pyrenees and the storming of San Sebastian before this advance took place. But Wellington was still cautiously awaiting reports of events in Germany. Also he knew little about the scale of popular resistance he would find when he invaded the French homeland.

Soult had used the time to build entrenchments and other defence works along the frontier. Following the battles of the Pyrenees he expected that Wellington would attack his left flank in the mountains around St-Jean-Pied-de-Port and defences there were greatly strengthened. D'Erlon's wing of the army now held this part of the French line with additional forces under Foy around St-Jean-Pied-de-Port itself. Clausel was in the centre of the line with Reille defending the right flank as far as the sea. There were foothills and rather flatter ground around the Bidassoa. This made the area more difficult to defend, and Wellington had heard from Spanish fishermen that there were some low-tide fords near the estuary of the river. Wellington's personal appearance and a feint attack in the region of St-Jean-Pied-de-Port served to distract Soult. Covered by a heavy artillery barrage and supported by a vigorous diversionary attack on Clausel's forces in the mountains, the Allies finally crossed the Bidassoa. Reille's division, commanded by Maucune, was taken completely by surprise and beat a hasty retreat with sharp losses. Had Soult been able to mount a vigorous counter-attack the Allied army would have been in great difficulty because the fords were tidal and it would have been hard for them to withdraw. But he had no reserves available and Wellington could consolidate his position. Soult severely criticized both Reille and Maucune, who was soon transferred to the Army of Italy. As usual Soult put the best interpretation on these events. In a letter to Clarke at the Ministry of War he suggested that it was "advantageous rather than the reverse to lose the hills along the Bidassoa: the army now had its right wing resting in a much better position close to the sea."[2] Again Wellington could probably have pushed right on to capture St-Jean-de-Luz but he remained cautious while Soult continued to strengthen his fortifications in the mountains and along the River Nivelle that flowed into the sea there. His report to

Lord Bathurst in London was laconic. "Having deemed it expedient to cross the Bidassoa with the left of the army I have to inform your Lordship that that object was effected on the 7th instant."[3]

Soult has been criticized for concentrating too much on linear defence, which enabled Wellington to attack him whenever and wherever he wanted, although in order to hold the Allied army in check he had no alternative but to use all available natural obstacles. Meanwhile, however, he was devising an ambitious plan for crossing back into Spain in force. This would require the active cooperation of Suchet, his fellow marshal, who was still heavily engaged in Catalonia. Soult would maintain a screen against Wellington on the French frontier and would then concentrate the bulk of his forces in France together with those of Suchet, who would also retain certain strong points in Catalonia. Their combined army of some 60,000 men would march to relieve Pamplona, reconquer Navarre and Aragon and advance westward to attack Wellington's army on the banks of the Ebro. As Soult wrote to Suchet: "Dire neccessity demands that a combined army should make a big diversion in order to bring back operations from the Bidassoa to the Ebro." But Suchet was totally uncooperative, describing the proposal to Clarke as "useless and potentially dangerous". Clarke, never sympathetic to Soult, agreed that for Suchet to retire in order to regroup in France would make him look as if he were retreating with a beaten army. Suchet admittedly had difficulties of his own, being harassed both by guerrillas and Spanish regular forces in Catalonia. However, he exaggerated the seriousness of yet another ineffectual Anglo-Sicilian expedition led by Lord William Bentinck, which had landed on the coast. Wellington, who always had a poor opinion of Suchet, commented briskly that there was little to prevent him from "tumbling Bentinck back to the river where he landed". In fact Suchet's counter-proposal was even more unrealistic. Apparently ignorant of the crisis facing the Emperor in Germany, he proposed that a new army should be sent to the Pyrenees to cooperate with himself and Soult in a fresh invasion of Spain.[4]

Soult and Suchet were not on good terms. In Spain Soult had always been irritated by Suchet's 'special position' as nephew by marriage of King Joseph. There had also been earlier problems. According to his personal papers, Soult still remembered Suchet's conduct during the Genoa campaign of 1800, rightly or wrongly considering that he had imperilled both Masséna and himself by separating from them much too soon. There had also been differences when Suchet was one of Soult's generals of division in the Boulogne invasion army. The challenge which Soult now faced, opposed by Wellington's Allied army, was far greater than anything Suchet was experiencing in north-eastern Spain. Since, as now seemed probable, Soult would have to go it alone, he must have been encouraged by the Emperor's words at this time: "I have given you my full confidence and I can add nothing to your instructions or to the measures you have taken."[5] The arguments between Soult and Suchet were reported to the Emperor but they were quite lost among the disastrous events taking place in Germany which culminated in Napoleon's decisive defeat in the battle of Leipzig.

In the midst of this hotly contested campaign, both Wellington and Soult were much concerned, too, with political problems. Wellington was still having difficulties with the Spanish cortes. The quarrels in Madrid between the liberals and the conservatives continued. The supporters of the exiled King Ferdinand ... the *fernandinos* ... were opposed by generals such as Ballesteros who were mainly concerned with building up their own power. Beneath the surface politeness towards Wellington, their British commander-in-chief, there still lurked strong Spanish feelings of anglophobia. The sacking of San Sebastian after its capture provoked additional hostility: many civilians had been killed in the assault and some Spaniards even believed that the sacking had been a deliberate punitive action by the British because it was one of the chief Spanish ports for trade with France. Wellington was equally at odds with his Spanish troops. He had already reported to London that he would have to leave some of them behind, "otherwise their pillaging would turn the French peasants against him".[6] After six harsh years of French rule, it would be no surprise if the Spaniards decided to revenge themselves on civilians in France. Many of the Spanish regulars could in any case only maintain themselves by pillage and Wellington was soon forced to make a public example of one of his Spanish divisions. Marauding bands of Spanish guerrillas also invaded French villages, and Spanish muleteers serving with the British army often had to be severely disciplined or returned to Spain. By and large, however, the Spanish regulars fought well during the later battles in southern France.

Soult, with his political instincts, naturally sought to take full advantage of Wellington's difficulties. In a subsequent letter to Beresford, Wellington commented that Soult must have known through his spies of this Anglo-Spanish disarray.[7] Indeed, Soult considered that this might be the moment to make good use of the apparently subservient King Ferdinand, still living in comfort as a French protégé in the château of Valencay. When Napoleon returned to Paris after Leipzig he found a letter from Soult sent from St-Jean-de-Luz on November 3. The letter evidently recalled the conversations in Dresden between himself and the Emperor about the future of Spain. With pardonable exaggeration, Soult wrote: "It would only need a pretext for the Spanish nation to turn their arms against the English and become Your Majesty's allies. If the Prince of the Asturias (Ferdinand) could form an alliance with a member of the Imperial Family and then return to Madrid the English would have to retreat once more to Portugal enabling your armies in Spain for the most part to be used in the north."[8] The princess that Soult and the Emperor had in mind was Joseph's daughter, Zenaide. She was only thirteen but she had been described by that zealous go-between in Spanish affairs, Count Roederer, as a "plump little person, perfectly formed, who speaks with a good deal of sense and 'aplomb'". She had been called "a little Southern beauty, half Corsican, half

Marseillaise who, like most Mediterranean girls, matured quickly".[9] (Madame Mère, Napoleon's mother, had in fact been married at fourteen.) Napoleon had begun to have doubts about the value of marriage alliances with foreign royalty after his own father-in-law, the Emperor of Austria, had joined in the war against him. Nevertheless, La Forêt, former French ambassador in Madrid, was sent to Valençay to discuss with Ferdinand a possible plan for his return to Spain under French auspices. Much of this was no doubt wishful thinking on the Emperor's and Soult's part, and Joseph was sure that the plan would do no good, although determined to seek some compensation if anything came of it. The so-called Treaty of Valençay was actually concluded the following month. Ferdinand was to return to Spain with French help provided that his senior adviser, the Duke of San Carlos, managed to sell the idea to the Spanish people. Zenaide, however, was not included in the bargain: Ferdinand said he could only make up his mind about her when he had actually got back to Madrid. As it turned out, Soult was to get no benefit from this initiative – in fact quite the reverse.

Inevitably, these political manouevres were overshadowed by the fighting, and in November Wellington's army, with greatly superior numbers, proceeded to storm the strong fortifications erected by Soult over the previous three months along the River Nivelle. The main British attack this time fell on Clausel's divisions holding the mountainous Lower Rhun in front of the river. It was led by the Light Division and, as a famous rifleman wrote later: "We went through the redoubts of Soult's fortified lines as if they were a screen of reeds."[10] Supporting attacks were made on d'Erlon's division holding the river itself. The British soon carried the important strategic bridge at Amotz while the French forces based on St-Jean-Pied-de-Port failed with an ineffective counter-attack. Wellington had hoped to roll up the whole French line by attacking Reille's divisions on the French right but Reille succeeded with some skill in retreating in good order, destroying the defences of St-Jean-de-Luz and taking up another defensive position between there and Bayonne.

Once again Soult had been defeated despite all his careful defence preparations. But the truth was that passive defence was no substitute for first-class soldiers. French military coordination was not as bad as it had been at Vitoria but it had so far deteriorated that all three wings of the army were virtually fighting different battles. Clausel complained bitterly that he had fought for five hours without getting any help at all from Reille. It was amazing, in fact, that Soult still kept his army going at all. In this battle he lost another 4,000 casualties including some 1,400 prisoners and a fair quantity of artillery.

Soult now withdrew his forces to high ground in front of the River Adour and its tributary, the Nive, with his right flank resting on Bayonne, which he intended to turn into a *place d'armes*. Determined to try one more offensive in the difficult terrain between the Nive and the Adour before winter conditions suspended operations, he attacked all along the line from Bayonne to St-Jean-de-Pied-Port. The tactical plan was to hold Wellington in check on the left bank of the Nive while he tried to overwhelm Hill's forces which had already crossed the river. This separation of forces had dangerous possibilities for the British. As Soult commented, "The enemy is divided on the two banks of the Nive; he has, for the present, lost his numerical superiority by extending himself in this way. I shall attack him hard."[11] General Abbé, commanding one of d'Erlon's divisions that had fought under Soult in Andalusia, at first made excellent headway against Hill. Some of the fiercest fighting of the whole campaign also took place around St-Jean-Pied-de-Port. But the divisions on Abbé's right gave him little help and made slow progress against much larger British forces. Meanwhile Beresford had built a pontoon bridge across the river, restoring communications between the two halves of Wellington's army. Clausel, commanding the centre of the French line, should have been urged to attack much more vigorously but his advance was too slow and finally, in drenching rain, Abbé's attack also petered out. Soult's last major offensive operation of the campaign had failed.

Winter conditions caused both armies to remain virtually static from December 1813 to February 1814. Once more political issues dominated the actual fighting. Negotiations between Napoleon and the Allies were taking place at Châtillon and both Soult and Wellington awaited the results. Meanwhile Soult's problems were legion. The morale of his army was continuing to deteriorate: in the fighting on the Nive casualties among the officers were nearly a third as high as those of the rank and file; this had a serious effect on the cohesion of the whole army. Also, with the worsening military situation, there were frequent quarrels among senior officers; many who had not previously served with Soult resented his stern discipline and were repelled by his aloof manner; lapses of discipline, even among officers, were frequent and there were numerous desertions. Later there was to be a gross act of insubordination when Reille quarrelled in Bayonne with the able but comparatively junior officer, Thouvenet, who had been made governor of the town. Reille left Bayonne in disgust.

Soult received other body blows in quick succession. With the collapse of the Confederation of the Rhine after Leipzig, his German brigade, consisting of battalions from Frankfurt and Hesse Nassau, deserted to the enemy. Its commander, General Krause, even had the sauce to ask that his baggage, his military band and his female camp followers should be allowed to join him. Soult had to take immediate steps to imprison his remaining German troops as well as most of the other foreigners, including the Spanish Guards and the other Spanish soldiers that he had inherited from Joseph. Even more serious was the Emperor's demand that two of his best divisions should be sent off to join him for the last famous campaign in eastern France. Napoleon's excuse for this was the recently concluded Treaty of Valençay. Ferdinand's emissary, the Duke of San Carlos, had hardly begun trying to sell to the Cortes the proposal for Ferdinand's return before Soult was required to dispatch Leval's and Bayer's fine divisions with supporting cavalry to join the Emperor. So the whole plan discussed between Napoleon and

Soult to relieve pressure in Spain by returning Ferdinand rebounded much to Soult's disadvantage. He had also been told not to waste his cavalry in too many operations since it was badly needed by the French army elsewhere. His lack of cavalry hampered him for the rest of the campaign, notably for intelligence gathering, before the battle of Toulouse.

As happened so often in the Peninsular War, Napoleon in Paris was completely out of touch with the local situation. In the departments of the western Pyrenees Soult was faced with serious local problems, particularly over the 1814 'call-up' under which new recruits from the region were supposed to be drafted directly into his army. General Harispe, a native of the region, had been transferred from Suchet to Soult's army specifically to help with some of these local military problems, but the prefect of the Basses Pyrenées was soon reporting that most of the Basque country folk wanted to serve in free, undisciplined companies of *chasseurs basques* rather than to be conscripted into the regular army. Most of the local national guards were quite useless. Pau was guarded fairly adequately by the Hautes Pyrenées legion but conditions in the Landes department were as bad as those in the Basses Pyrenées. To compound these problems, indicating how little he understood what was going on, Napoleon had ordered the creation of a 'Reserve Army of the Pyrenees', based on Bordeaux and Toulouse, into which newly conscripted French recruits were now to be drafted instead of going directly into Soult's forces. Soult strongly criticized this decision. He had no direct control over the new Reserve Army: it removed potential recruits from his own forces and, in addition, he had to provide twenty cadres of officers and nco's to train and form the nucleus of the new army. As he complained with surprising mildness to the Ministry of War, having lost Germans and Spaniards, cadres for the new Reserve Army and regular divisions for the Emperor, "I really cannot create miracles and multiply the size of my army at will!"[12] Then, as a further illusory attempt to help things along in the south, Napoleon was to order a *levée en masse* like those that had taken place in the Revolutionary Wars, sending senators and counsellors of state southwards to supervise it. Churchill once said that it was an obscenity to compare the great Emperor with Hitler but, despite Napoleon's own brilliant military successes against the Allies in eastern France, these desperate measures in the south bore some of the marks of the military extravagances during the last days of the Third Reich!

Poor Soult had one more cross to bear – a burden to be shared almost equally with Wellington. (Indeed their political problems were often very similar.) On February 1 1814 Louis XVIII's eldest nephew, the Duke of Angoulême, had landed at San Sebastian and proceeded at once to Wellington's headquarters. Because this 'nothing man', as he came to be called in France, was married to the only surviving child of the martyred Louis XVI, and this part of France had been the home of his great Béarnais ancestor, Henry of Navarre, his arrival was intended to have a dramatic impact. However, against the background of continuing negotiations between Napoleon and the Allies, Wellington doubted whether there was much of a future for the Bourbons. Indeed, at this time, he considered that Bonaparte, if he were to listen to reason, would probably be the best sovereign for France. Soult, too, would have agreed strongly with the Royalist Chateaubriand, that in these early days of 1814 the Bourbons were as unknown to the younger generation in France as the children of the Emperor of China! When, with some lukewarm British support, Angoulême issued a proclamation to the French people calling on them to follow the "spotless white flag of their forefathers", Soult, who could produce fiery proclamations to order whatever the circumstances, countered with a tirade of his own. "The English general has shamefully provided an opportunity for sedition against us. The English have no other object than to destroy France. Let us fight to the last for our august Emperor. We will die under arms rather than live in dishonour!"[13]

Despite this typical rhetoric, Soult was in a dreadful situation. Apart from the poor morale of his army, his defeats in battle and the losses he had suffered for various reasons, he faced the increasingly sullen hostility of the people of his own native Midi. Indeed he derived very little material or psychological advantage from fighting in his home region. The Basques had their own ideas about the government in Paris: everywhere there was weariness and disillusionment after so many years of continuous war; and although the country people were much more anti-war than pro-Bourbon, Royalist propaganda was beginning at last to make some headway with a group called the Chevaliers de la Foi, in which Louis XVIII's future minister, Vitrolles, was prominent. A few white Bourbon flags began to appear in some southern towns.

Nevertheless, Soult continued to hold his army together. He never despaired although at one time he did suggest he might help the Emperor more if he gave up his command and joined him in eastern France, leaving Clausel to fight a partisan war against Wellington, but Napoleon flatly refused this offer. Soult's role in the south was indispensable. Gradually the Marshal retreated under the impact of Wellington's attacks. However, the Allied advance was equally slow and Wellington was still confined to this small corner of south-western France. The legendary Hoche, one of Soult's heroes, once said during the Revolutionary Wars that it took him seven days to cover 24 leagues. It was about 24 leagues from the River Adour to the Spanish frontier: with all his own problems and Soult's resistance it had taken Wellington nearly seven months to cover this distance.

By February, despite the very wet weather, it was time for both sides to get going again. As usual Soult was full of resource. The amphibious tactics which he had used fifteen years ago in Switzerland, then in the invasion preparations in Boulogne, and finally in attempts to capture Cadiz were once more employed in his defence of the Adour. Twenty gunboats with sailors and marines from Rochefort were engaged in operations on the river. Soult's continued defence of Bayonne, on Napoleon's instructions, was more open to criticism. It meant that the French battle line had to be extended more and more as he was driven eastward. Some called

Bayonne a 'shackle on his leg', but after it had been completely surrounded and the Allied armies had advanced far beyond it towards Bordeaux, it proved a real impediment to Wellington. It was also the scene of the last brilliant French operation of the whole campaign. After a series of engagements in the hilly area west of the Adour in which one village, St-Boes, was taken and retaken by both sides, the Allies crossed the Adour between Bayonne and the sea; the French line was turned and Soult retired to another strong position at Orthez.

The battle of Orthez, fought on February 17, began well for the French. They were greatly outnumbered but a strong British attack led by Cole on the French right wing, consisting of Taupin's and Roguet's divisions under Reille's command, was a costly failure and Picton's assault on d'Erlon in the centre was also held up. Then the Light Division, following a ferocious charge by the 52nd regiment, renewed the attack on Reille's divisions which slowly gave way until the French retreat became something of a rout. At one point newly arrived 'Marie Louises' – as the new recruits were named after the Empress – stood almost unarmed and practically untrained against the advancing British. One of Harispe's National Guard divisions surrendered almost *en bloc* and finally Soult had to abandon Orthez having lost 4,000 men and over 13,000 prisoners. By far the greatest number of casualties was among the infantry. Wellington's losses were only half that number. It is arguable that if Soult had used his reserves at the beginning of the battle, when things were going well for the French, he might have won: on the other hand he may well have considered Orthez to be no more than part of a fighting retreat.

After Orthez Soult was faced with a strategic dilemma. Should he retire towards Bordeaux, maintaining his defensive position in Bayonne, or instead retreat east towards Toulouse? He received the usual 'delphic' instructions from the Emperor via the Ministry of War. He was ordered to "attack the enemy in the flank when he would be able to defeat an army twice his size. He has talent enough to know what I mean!"[14] In fact, this was exactly what Napoleon was doing in his brilliant campaign in eastern France, but Soult was not fighting a number of ill coordinated Allied generals: he was fighting Wellington.

In the end he decided to retire to the east, leaving Bayonne to be surrounded. He wanted to avoid the sandy area south of Bordeaux where campaigning and even food supplies would be difficult. This meant leaving the Gironde and Bordeaux itself at the mercy of an Allied advance. He told L'Hullier, the military governor of Bordeaux, that he must somehow find the means of defending himself. Soult's decision to fall back to the more fertile land around Tarbes and Toulouse has often been criticized but it forced Wellington to divide his army while keeping his own forces more or less intact, so that he was no longer greatly outnumbered. He was also moving closer to Suchet and still clung to the hope of finally joining up with him.

Events in the Gironde did not turn out as he had hoped. Napoleon's *levée en masse* in south-eastern France was a total failure: indeed Napoleonic support in

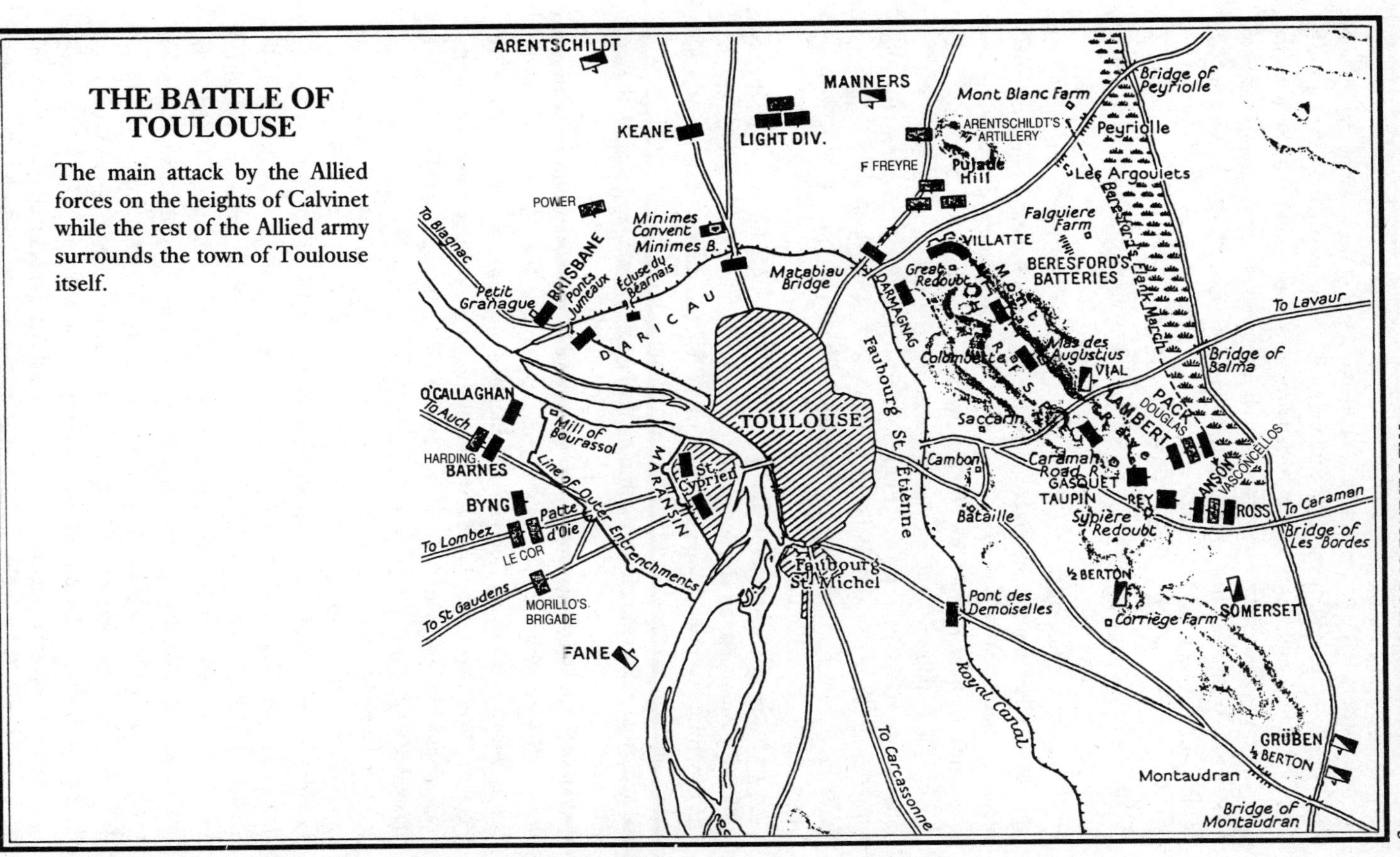

THE BATTLE OF TOULOUSE

The main attack by the Allied forces on the heights of Calvinet while the rest of the Allied army surrounds the town of Toulouse itself.

Bordeaux, where trade had greatly stagnated as a result of the Continental System, was seriously weakened by the drafting of recruits from the city to join the army in eastern France, while Lynch, the Irish-born mayor, considered to be a strong imperialist, proclaimed his support for the Bourbons and begged for Allied help. Accordingly Wellington had to send an army north towards Bordeaux, and the size of his main force was further reduced by having to contain both Bayonne and St-Jean-Pied-de-Port which was still held by the French. Soult's army had now been reduced to about 25,000 infantry and some 3,000 cavalry while Wellington's army was not much larger.

There were some brisk encounters in the region of Tarbes. A daring French raid on an Allied unit at St-Sever led to the capture of some wounded British infantry. Then, west of Tarbes, there was a fierce engagement that was mostly a Rifle Brigade affair in which the 95th showed how expert they had become since they had first opposed Soult so vigorously during the retreat to Corunna. "They were as much superior to the French *voltigeurs* as the latter were to other skirmishers," wrote one military historian.[15] In the event, Wellington's attempt near Tarbes to drive back Soult towards the Pyrenees failed and the Marshal managed finally to retreat on Toulouse.

The battle of Toulouse, fought on April 10, was almost, but not quite, the last Franco-British encounter during Soult's remarkable defence of southern France. The two armies were fairly equal in numbers. French casualties were about 3,200 against Allied losses of some 4,000. The battle was actually fought after Napoleon had abdicated although neither Soult nor Wellington was aware of this. Both sides claimed to have won but there seems little doubt that Wellington was the real victor. Soult fought at Toulouse because it was probably the best strategic centre in southern France, protected by the broad and fast-flowing Garonne, and reasonably close to the ever elusive Suchet. He knew the whole area since it was only about 100 kilometres from his own birthplace St-Amans-Labastide; and remaining loyal to the Emperor at least until 'many minutes beyond midnight', he wanted to keep his army reasonably intact for as long as possible.

Knowing the country well, Soult gained an immediate tactical advantage by using his small remaining cavalry force to entice Wellington towards Toulouse through the very muddy Gers region, which was also intersected by small rivers, while he himself took a longer but better maintained road from Tarbes through St-Gaudens. He thus gained an invaluable two days before Wellington's advance guard began to catch up with him. He needed every moment of this time. He found the town by now very hostile to the imperial cause. There were some actual Bourbon sympathizers but the feelings of the Toulouse townsfolk were, like the rest of the Midi, more anti-war than pro-Bourbon. The mayor of St-Jory, where Wellington was to establish his headquarters, complained of the hardships of constant conscriptions: moreover, news about the English had spread all over the south where they had become more popular than the French army, partly because they could pay more for the farm produce and provisions that the local people had to sell. There would be an increasing number of 'collabos' as Wellington continued his advance. For his part Soult found it more and more difficult to get provisions for his army and even food and wine for his own table. Nor did he obtain much military help from the townspeople. There was a wholly useless 'Garde Urbain' while many of the local 'Marie Louises' in his army, although often as brave as their comrades fighting with the Emperor in eastern France, had received practically no military training and were not equipped for war at all. However, popular ideas about the Bourbons in Toulouse remained fairly vague and it was not surprising that in a thanksgiving service after the battle a priest called for prayers for the long life of Louis XVIII and of his deceased wife.

Soult was always fated to fight battles in the teeth of serious difficulties and Toulouse was no exception. However, as usual, he did his utmost to safeguard the French position. Apart from defending the town of Toulouse itself he needed also to hold the Calvinet heights that dominated the town from the east. These had been skilfully fortified by his chief engineer, Michaux, but Soult had characteristically endeared himself to the rank and file of his army by taking off his tunic and helping to build the entrenchments too.

The British advance guard was in contact with the French a good fortnight before the battle took place. Wellington had two options – either to cross the Garonne below the town and establish himself in the comparatively flat ground to the north, or to cross the river above Toulouse so as to prevent any link-up between Soult and the army of Suchet which was now between Perpignan and Narbonne. Wellington believed, as it happened quite wrongly, that Suchet would now hasten to his fellow Marshal's support: Soult had done his best to conceal from the British the embarrassing rift between them. Hill was quickly ordered by Wellington to cross the Garonne and its tributary, the Ariège, above Toulouse. This seems partly to have been a feint attack to distract Soult from activities taking place to the north of the town and partly a genuine attempt to prevent reinforcements coming from Suchet. In the event the river crossings proved to be difficult and the marshy ground in that area made Hill's progress almost impossible. Wellington finally withdrew his division to its original starting place where it faced Maransin's troops defending the town in a corner between the ramparts and the Garonne. However, Soult, with his customary caution, had missed a good opportunity of pouncing on Hill's forces while they were still in some confusion between the two rivers.

By now, with some difficulty, Wellington's main army under Beresford was crossing the swollen waters of the Garonne by a narrow pontoon bridge downstream from the town. Quite soon the bridge was broken down by the violent current of the river, leaving some of Beresford's forces dangerously isolated on the right bank. Again Soult missed an excellent opportunity of swooping down on this fairly small force and annihilating it. There were various explanations for this second missed opportunity. Soult's cavalry had now been reduced to under 3,000 men so that his reconnaissance capabilities were strictly limited, he got no intelligence help from the basically hostile Toulousians and, in any case, since he was commanding one of the few remaining imperial armies he was apparently determined to continue fighting a defensive battle.

Accordingly he made no attempt to attack while the pontoon bridge was being repaired and Wellington's army was soon established in strength to the north-east of Toulouse. Preparations were then made to storm the Calvinet heights as a preliminary to an attack on Toulouse itself. The main battle was soon raging all around Calvinet which was attacked by three British columns and also by a Spanish force under General Freyre, whose Spaniards were twice driven back by Villatte's division and they retreated back down the hill in some confusion. But the three British columns led by Douglas, Lambert and Pack, attacking the heights from all sides, were much more successful. General Taupin attempted a counter-attack with characteristic bravado and was killed: many of the defenders were untrained 'Marie Louises' who fought bravely but ineffectively, while the British employed with some success the noisy thunderblast weapon, the Congreve Rocket, which had earlier been used in an attack on Boulogne. Finally, after much fierce fighting, Soult, fearing that he would be completely surrounded, withdrew his battered forces into Toulouse itself. All this time, on the other side of the town, Hill had been keeping the French defenders under Reille's general command fully occupied while the main battle was being fought out on the Calvinet heights. British losses in their various attacks were even heavier than those of the French.

As night fell it became clear to Soult that he could no longer hold his position inside Toulouse since the British were now in possession of the dominating Calvinet heights. There were said to have been unofficial contacts between French and British staff officers, all of them doubtless trying to find out about the latest situation in Paris. In a letter to Clarke, Soult reported that he would have to evacuate Toulouse; the fighting had been bloody; Wellington had suffered great losses but he had gained the main position outside the town. So, during the night, Soult made a skilful and unobserved evacuation, retiring to the distant town of Castres where he established his headquarters in the local hotel. [16]

Right up to the last, there were strange developments in this curious campaign. During his triumphant entry into Toulouse, Wellington was as sharply critical of the Toulousians sporting the white cockade as was Soult with the noble ladies of Castres who similarly bedecked themselves in order to give a premature welcome to the British cavalry of Lord Fitzroy Somerset. Meanwhile General Thouvenet had made a daring sally from Bayonne, killing one British general and capturing General Hope, the British commander. Soult himself flatly refused to accept a message announcing the Emperor's abdication sent to him by the miserable Dupont (of Baylen ill fame) who had just been made the Royalist Minister of War. He insisted on waiting for a properly drafted message from Berthier, brought to him by one of his former staff officers, the Marquis de Saint-Simon, who had lost little time in switching allegiance.

When at last it was all over, Soult, accompanied the Duke of Angoulême in an inspection of his army. Immediately Suchet, who had had no scruples about acting on the surrender message from Dupont, took over the command both of his own army and Soult's forces, becoming at once the Royalist commander-in-chief of the south. Soult himself had maintained for far too long a fighting loyalty to the Emperor to be immediately acceptable to the Bourbons.

As usual, falsehoods have clung to him over the battle of Toulouse. On the one hand he has been accused by some of having kept his army together for reasons of personal ambition – perhaps to play the role of a General Monk in the Bourbon Restoration. But there is no evidence for this and anyway the Restoration had already taken place. Nor is there a shred of evidence for the other *canard* put around by his Royalist enemies that he fought the battle in a vengeful spirit, well knowing that Napoleon had already abdicated. He denied this vehemently in his *Justificatory Memoir*, published in 1815 just before his exile in Germany,[17] and Wellington generously confirmed this view in a debate long afterwards in the British House of Lords.

What should be the final verdict on this whole campaign? Despite all his losses and all his problems, Soult did succeed in keeping his army intact so that he would still have been ready to resist the British if Wellington had carried out his avowed intention of advancing northward to the Loire. If Suchet had cooperated with him the campaign might have taken a quite different course. As it was, with an increasingly dispirited army, soon containing almost as many new recruits as veterans, Soult had fought a long rearguard action in an absolutely war-weary part of France, confining the greatest of all France's opponents to a relatively small area of the Midi until a final decision was taken elsewhere. As Oman commented: "No general, save William III, ever won so much from a series of defeats as Soult did from 1813 to 1814."[18]

Soult's own view on the battle of Toulouse is quite clear. In the display of his military exploits which Louis Philippe was to organize for him, as his 'illustre épée', in the Palace of Versailles in the 1840s, he chose Toulouse as his finest battle since, as he said, he was there fighting against three Allied armies, the British, the Spanish and the Portuguese and against the greatest of all the Allied commanders.

17

LOUIS XVIII'S MINISTER OF WAR

MOST OF NAPOLEON'S MARSHALS, generals and senior officials belonged to what could be called irreverently 'the weathercock school' – 'la Collège des Girouettes'. Many of them, including Soult, Ney and Suchet, switched their loyalties twice between Louis XVIII and Napoleon; some only once, and a very few, notably Davout, not at all. But every one of them would have claimed quite seriously that they had remained throughout loyal to France. As the commander-in-chief of the army which fought for Napoleon to the last – indeed 'after the last' – Soult was likely to be one of the most difficult of the Emperor's former servants for Royalists to accept. He had been replaced briefly in command of his army by the more amenable Suchet, and Wellington later gave an account of Soult returning rather pathetically to Toulouse to stare disconsolately at the carriage as his old opponent passed through the town on his way to Madrid in order to try to knock some sense into the head of the restored King Ferdinand. Soult had now to maintain a very low profile in Toulouse whereas Ferdinand had earlier been cheered enthusiastically on his way back to Spain.

Many of Soult's comrades-in-arms quickly accepted the new regime but after the fierce fighting that had taken place so recently at Toulouse it was obviously impossible for him to get one of those glittering commands in the household troops – joining the 'Company of Judas' – as the old *grognards* called Marmont's company of the Gardes du Corps. Nor, like eight of the marshals, did he become a peer of France. He was now living in his big Paris house in the Rue de l'Université and he was certainly more than willing to make his peace with the new Royalist government. Vitrolles, who had been such a nuisance to him as one of the leaders of the Chevaliers de la Foi in the south and who was now one of the King's leading advisers, described him cynically as attending a memorial service for the 'royal martyrs', Louis XVI and Marie Antoinette, "with tears streaming down his face and turning round repeatedly to make sure that his deep emotion did not escape public notice".[1] In fact some of the King's advisers had already turned appraising eyes on him. His kinsman and biographer, Louis de Saint-Pierre, claimed with some justification that, with Davout and Masséna he was reckoned by the Royalists to be one of three 'greats' among the marshals.[2] Of these Davout had refused to serve the Bourbons while Masséna had become old and weary. That left Soult who loved hard work and in any event could not bear to be left out in the cold. But how could he be reconciled to the new government?

An intermediary was obviously needed. This was forthcoming in the Comte de Bruges. Bruges was an unusual kind of Royalist *émigré* with – in the snobbish words of Madame de Chastenay – "a very mediocre social background".[3] While in exile he had commanded black troops in British-occupied San Domingo where he was said to have made a lot of money using his soldiers as cheap building labour. He had also inherited much money from his brother who was involved in property sequestration. He mixed assiduously in *émigré* circles in Berlin where he met his young nephew, Brun de Villeret, Soult's aide-de-camp, and in Vienna he had ingratiated himself with the King's brother, the Comte d'Artois. Although cordially disliked by the rest of Artois's entourage as a gloomy 'pen pusher', he was soon involved in the inner circles of the government. It was partly through his influence that, two months after his ignominious dismissal from the command of his army in the south, Soult was appointed to be the general commanding the XIII Military District with headquarters at Rennes in Brittany. Dupont, the Minister of War, after his own controversial past, was very willing to give this testing political post to Soult, whose only previous experience of northern France had been as commander-in-chief in Boulogne for the invasion of England ten years before. Then his main security task had been to suppress or arrest all the *chouan* or Royalist spies that came his way. Now in Brittany he was surrounded by a population that was for the most part Royalist.

Almost at once the new district commander was confronted by one of those awkward political problems which were continuous features of the whole Restoration period. The Duke of Angoulême had made an official tour of western France accompanied for some of the time by the duchess, that imperious daughter of Louis XVI. The duchess was determined that a memorial should be built to commemorate the victims of the Royalist landing at Quiberon which, despite British naval assistance, had been decisively defeated by General Hoche during the Revolutionary Wars. This proposal, which was strongly supported by local politicians, placed Soult in a dilemma. Hoche was one of his heroes but he had resolutely refused to serve under him at Quiberon because he was unwilling to fight against other Frenchmen. On the other hand he wanted to make himself acceptable to the Royalist government and to local Royalists, while the Duchess of Angoulême could either be a powerful friend or a dangerous enemy. He did not, as has been suggested by Thiers and others, take the initiative in the affair but as an 'act of state' he accepted the presidency of the committee to deal with the whole business. The bones of some of the Royalist victims were gathered together; a small memorial stone now stands near one of the expedition landing places and a much larger monument – the Chartreuse d'Auray – commemorating also one of the great Royalist leaders was designed by the artist and sculptor, David. It was inaugurated many years later in the presence of the Duchess of Angoulême while Soult himself was out of favour with the government. It was all rather awkward from Soult's point of view and it set people guessing about him. But it is unlikely that his old hero, Hoche, who was a political realist himself and whose vigorous personality is vividly displayed today in his statue in the main square of Quiberon, would have blamed his former admirer for his forced political involvement.[4]

More seriously than preoccupations with war memorials, Soult, with all his customary energy, concerned himself with the training of his troops. He also had built, near Quiberon and at other places along the Brittany coast, a series of fortifications to guard against future enemy landings. Some of these still exist. But Soult could not escape from the political problems of Brittany. Later, when he was Minister of War, he was involved in the notorious 'Rennes affair'. Under strong government pressure, he had appointed a well known *chouan*, Pecquet de Boisguy, as one of the King's commissioners in Brittany. Boisguy had been accused of various horrible crimes including the burying alive of a number of Republican soldiers during the Revolution. On the day when the King's new commission first met in the prefecture in Rennes, Boisguy only saved himself by rapid flight from being torn to pieces by the infuriated townsfolk.

By now Soult himself had become much more closely involved with the new government. Everywhere political intrigue was rampant, in which returning *émigrés* and former Imperialists were equally concerned. It has been well said that 1814 was the most explosive year in France's history since 1572 when Henry IV and Marguerite de Valois brought Catholics and Protestants together after the Wars of Religion.[5] Soult's future colleague, Guizot, who was now a junior minister, described Blacas and the Abbé Montesquieu, who acted as the King's chief ministers while Talleyrand was away at the Congress of Vienna, as being completely out of touch with the serious problems of the Restoration. The King, who usually presided personally at the meetings of his ministers, welcomed the divisions between them since they strengthened his own power.

In this maelstrom of intrigue the 'capitulé de Baylen', as the wretched Dupont was called by Napoleon's veterans, cut a poor figure. After Baylen Napoleon had forbidden him ever to wear uniform again and 'the man in the black suit', as he was also described, although well regarded by the King and not without talent, was far away from the centres of power. The future of the old Imperial army, along with France's serious economic problems, were the most important difficulties that confronted the new ministry. Baron Louis wrestled tenaciously with the financial problems but Dupont was on the whole content to be 'all things to all men', leaving his entire department in total administrative chaos with, as Brun de Villeret records, at least 35 portfolios of papers unconsidered and most of his major problems unresolved.[6] The actual cause of Dupont's downfall was the discovery of a plot to kidnap the King and the royal family, but in any case a more considerable personality was obviously needed to deal with the serious problems of the French army. The cautious Suchet was the candidate to replace Dupont favoured by

Fouché, among others, but a much bigger prize for the Royalists was Soult, whose appointment was strongly supported by Artois acting on the advice of the attentive Bruges, by the Duchess of Angoulême and by the King's close adviser, Blacas, who thought, quite wrongly as it turned out, that Soult would be completely dependent on him. Asked to choose between Soult and Suchet, Talleyrand from Vienna shrewdly affirmed that Soult would be much the stronger man.

On December 3 Soult became Minister of War, a portfolio which he held for three crowded and dramatic months. Brun de Villeret, who had worked so well with him in an administrative capacity in Spain, became secretary general of the ministry; Bruges was rewarded for his services by becoming chancellor of the Legion of Honour for which, as Minister of War, Soult had become responsible and into which, incidentally, he introduced some much needed reforms. However Bruges's appointment infuriated the Napoleonic veterans since his only military experience had been the command of his black troops in San Domingo!

Soult's many critics – and they include Thiers and the historian Henry Houssaye – admit that he was on the whole a good Minister of War. Even the sharp-penned Royalist diarist, Madame de Chastenay, after calling him "cold and calculating", said that he "combined the flexibility of a politician with the prudence of a skilful soldier".[7] Dupont had departed, leaving the French army in a state of great confusion. The efforts that had already been made to substitute a volunteer army to replace the 'blood tax' which had made Napoleon's rule so hated in various parts of France had not really begun to work. The situation was also much complicated by the fact that many men who had been called up under the 1813 and 1814 conscriptions had never joined the colours at all or had quietly returned home when the Emperor abdicated. Then there were the veterans of the Grande Armée, who had come streaming back in their thousands from the great fortresses in Germany and eastern Europe which had held out until the end. In addition there were the numerous Royalist *émigrés* who felt that they had sacrificed everything for their King and who now demanded some plum appointments in the army as their reward. The conflicts between these various groups of indignant Frenchmen were endless. In Paris half-pay officers thronged the cafés to sip pernod and talk of the good old days. Some would chuck passing aristocrats under the chin with such ribaldries as, "Hey Marquis, why aren't you back in your headquarters in Coblenz where the King will be waiting for you?"[8] In Montluçon a hussar colonel complained to a hotelier about the price of his dinner, remarking, "It's much cheaper in Paris – there, for a 'napoleon', we've got a great, fat pig!"[9]

This was the background for the serious tasks that confronted Soult. The 1813-14 conscripts who had never reached the colours had been described during Dupont's term of office as being 'on limited leave'. Soult sent much stricter orders to the prefects to try to get these deserters recalled but the prefects' efforts were strongly resisted in some departments. When they were successful and managed to get other recruits, the embodiment of some 50,000 extra soldiers presented further major administrative problems.[10] Within the army itself Soult set on foot numerous reforms. New bombardier and fusilier companies were created in many regiments; attempts were made to reorganize regimental headquarters as a means of reviving army loyalty; artillery and engineer services were reorganized; and the man who did more than anyone else to train and discipline the Grande Armée in the camp of Boulogne, ten years before, endeavoured to reintroduce proper military training in this new Royal army. Soult also took steps to ensure that France's frontier fortresses were properly equipped and provisioned; the still numerous foreigners serving with the colours were reorganized in special regiments – for instance a Spanish-Portuguese regiment was based at L'Orient – while Soult made efforts, despite France's parlous financial state, to deal with the never ending problem of soldiers' pay.

All this involved concentrated and incessant hard work. Brun de Villeret describes a typical working day. It began at 5 am during the depths of winter when he received detailed instructions from the Minister with discussions lasting for about two hours. Afterwards Soult and Brun worked in their respective offices with very little time for lunch until the latter part of the afternoon. Then the real turmoil began with distinguished officers and civilians from both the old and the new regimes asking for all kinds of different posts. Hardly was this hurly-burly over before Brun was summoned to dinner with his Minister when everyone present seemed again to be requesting this or that military preferment. After dinner Soult, often accompanied by Brun, had an audience with the King which Louis himself began to value more and more. As Wellington, now British Ambassador, reported to Castlereagh, the King greatly appreciated his military and administrative talents. He also provided the King with a full weekly summary of all his work. He and Brun returned to the ministry afterwards and the wretched Brun was not allowed to depart until about 11 pm to snatch a few hours sleep before beginning all over again next morning. He was soon exhausted but Soult seemed to be able to stand the pace easily.[11]

In trying to deal with all the army problems of the past and present regimes, the unfortunate Soult could not possibly win. The Royalists were indignant that more commands did not come their way; that Soult tried hard to limit their freelance 'Compagnies Rouges' and that he turned down Artois's dangerous proposal to bring back the old Imperial Guard from eastern France for a parade before the King in the Champs de Mars, which would have been madness. The Napoleonic veterans were furious that 700 of their officers were placed on half-pay while *émigrés* were given 'undeserved promotions' in the army; dozens of disgruntled officers defied the order forbidding their presence in Paris, marching to the Ministry of War still wearing the Napoleonic eagle on their uniforms, which they refused to remove until their pension demands were met.[12]

By far the most explosive issue was the continued presence in Paris of these former officers of Napoleon's armies. Dupont had persuaded the well-disciplined

Davout and even the vile-tempered Vandamme to depart to their country homes, but among his 35 unresolved portfolios in the ministry was the much more awkward case of General Exelmans. Rémi Isidore Exelmans, presently the inspector general of cavalry, was no great military genius; indeed he had been sharply rebuked by the Emperor for his rash conduct at the battle of Dresden. But his dashing personality seemed clearly to personify the vanished glories of the Empire. He had been one of Murat's senior aides-de-camp and, very unfortunately for the harmony of the First Restoration, an English francophile, Lord Oxford, visiting Paris en route for Italy, was caught carrying a letter in which Exelmans more or less offered his services to his old master, Murat.[12] King Joachim Murat was soon to make his bid for the crown of a united Italy which was to be so embarrassing to Napoleon himself. The Royalist government in Paris was not actually at war with Murat but one of the axioms of Louis XVIII's foreign policy, for which Talleyrand was labouring hard in Vienna, was that Murat should be turned off his throne in favour of the Neapolitan Bourbons. When Exelmans's letter fell into the government's hands, Dupont had contented himself with reprimanding the young general and then leaving his case well alone. By the time Soult succeeded him, Exelmans had become leader of the discontented Napoleonic ex-officers who still thronged Paris and Soult was not a man who left awkward cases on one side. He relieved Exelmans of his cavalry command, put him on half pay and ordered him to retire to his home at Bar-sur-Ornain. Given his prominent position among the disaffected officers, this was a reasonable step. However, the Exelmans case quickly developed into something more serious. Indeed it turned into a minor version of one of those 'affairs' which have been such frequent elements in the history of modern France. Claiming that he should be free to choose his own place of rural exile, and because his young wife was expecting a baby, Exelmans refused Soult's order. By this time the King and the royal family had become involved. King Louis, with his customary prudence, commented: "Let us go no further than justice."[13] But Artois was all for tough measures and his son, Berry, raged against Exelmans at dinner parties. On the other hand, there was strong army and popular support for him and Lafayette offered him asylum in his château. Being openly defied by a man who had become a symbol of discontent, Soult had no choice but to have him arrested in front of his swooning wife, and he was taken under military escort to Soissons. From here the excitable young general, now a father, succeeded in escaping; and he sent a message to Soult that he would only appear at a properly constituted military tribunal.

Soult would certainly not duck this challenge and Exelmans was brought before a military court martial at Lille in January 1815, accused of defying the King, of disobeying a military order, of breaking his oath to the Royalist order of Saint Louis (to which so many Bonapartist generals now belonged), of spying, of offering his sword to 'the general who ruled Naples' and for refusing to stay at his own home when he left Paris. Most of these accusations were justified, including the requirement to remain at home, since it was probable – and so it proved – that the half-pay officers might need to be called up soon for active service. But Exelmans conducted his own case with surprising skill and calm. He was very respectful about the King, made much of the fact that France was not formally at war with Murat, and that having to notify his place of residence was tantamount to foreign exile. Greatly to the embarrassment of Soult and the government, he was unanimously acquitted. Trying to make the best of a bad job, the government-controlled *Journal des Débats* suggested that such fair play would never have been tolerated in Bonaparte's time.

Soult's discomfiture was by no means distasteful to most of the other ministers who had become increasingly jealous of him. He was on excellent terms with the King himself and he was indeed virtually the only one of the ministers, apart from Baron Louis at the Treasury, who put devotion to duty and hard work above court intrigue. He was vilified in letters by his colleague, de Jaucourt, addressed to Talleyrand in Vienna. These were masterpieces of spiteful invective. In one letter he wrote about "the duplicity into which Soult's ambition had led him ... this coarse soldier's evil actions were a revelation of perfidy, hypocrisy and an imbecile anxiety to please. His speech is of the military type, vain, coarse, artful and fawning: his wife is his double."[14] On the other hand the old Imperial officers, who had found that there was now a much stronger personality at the Ministry of War than the embarrassed Dupont, began to fear and distrust Soult, who was caught between two fires.[15] Meanwhile the small group of dedicated supporters of the fallen Emperor – Davout, Lavalette, Bassano and others – bided their time and the old King not only enjoyed his evening sessions with his formidable Minister of War but also read with cynical delight copies of Bassano's pungently written Bonapartist publication, *Le Nain Jaune*, which was edited by Bory de Saint-Vincent, one of the clerks in Soult's own ministry.

With the King's full support, and impervious to the barrage of criticism from his colleagues, Soult lived with his family in considerable affluence in the big house in the Rue de l'Université and also at his country property in Villeneuve L'Etang near St-Cloud. Soult himself had hardly stayed in Paris for more than a few months at a time since he had first acquired his properties in 1803 but Louise lived there with the two children, Hector, now aged twelve, and Hortense, aged ten. Critics refer to his "dishonesty and avarice" which enabled him to live in such comfort. As already noted, a sober estimate of the revenues of Napoleon's marshals, prepared for the Vienna Congress, shows that Davout and Berthier were much the richest of the marshals with Ney and some of the others below them in wealth.[16] Of course they had all been generously rewarded by the Emperor and had acquired enough money and 'resources' during their campaigns to enable them to live in style on the rare occasions when they were able to stay at home. In fact Soult lived no more splendidly than many of the others but, in addition there was his famous collection of pictures which was the subject of much speculation and criticism.

The combination of First Empire style, the florid Germanic tastes of Louise and Soult's love of classical grandeur was unlikely to make the house in the Rue de l'Université very comfortable. There were fluted columns and allegorical figures of nymphs and shepherds everywhere. Some were already there; others added by the Soults – all over the house. The centrepiece in Soult's bathroom was at once ornamental and useful. It was a large clock adorned with swans and other decorative birds and animals surmounted by a powerful water jet – a kind of clock-cum-shower-bath – as if the Marshal did not want to waste a minute of his time when he was bathing! Later, when Soult was a very active Minister of War under King Louis Philippe, the 'workaholic' Marshal's house was enlarged to accommodate some of the departments of his ministry. But at this time it was simply used as a home and as a place for entertaining.[17] Both Soult and his wife entertained lavishly. At one of their first dinner parties, Soult brought together the British Ambassador, Wellington, and his former opponent Masséna in order to fight out old battles together.

In the last month of his term of office as Minister of War Soult was confronted with a much more serious problem than the 'Exelmans affair' – indeed with the dramatic events which swept away the First Restoration altogether. In the middle of February 1815 he had been fully engaged in meeting a request from the King, forwarded from Talleyrand in Vienna, for a force of some 30,000 men to be sent to the Lyons-Chambéry area as a potential military threat to Murat's Kingdom of Naples. The Austrian government was as anxious as King Louis to get rid of Murat but this whole move had to be kept secret so as not to cause any immediate embarrassment either in Vienna or to the new Piedmontese government in Turin. The ensuing troop movements were to prove very helpful to Napoleon on his dramatic return from Elba and correspondingly embarrassing to Soult. Also in February Soult arranged another potentially troublesome troop rearrangement. As a contribution to calming down the bitter feud that continued to exist between the ex-Imperialist officers and the Royalists, he moved out of Paris two of the most virulent Royalist regiments, the Régiment du Roi and the Régiment d'Orléans, which had been making a thorough nuisance of themselves under the military governor of Paris, General Maison, an ex-Bonapartist but now even more Royalist than the King. This move prompted further Royalist accusations of treachery against Soult.

In the aftermath of the 'Exelmans affair' Bonapartist feelings, especially in the army, were becoming more and more excited. In Elba Napoleon was well aware of this ferment. But although a Bonapartist agent, Fleury de Chaboulon, had visited him, it was clear that the Emperor was acting entirely on his own initiative when he made his famous landing at Golfe Juan at the beginning of March. A Bonapartist military uprising which occurred at about the same time in the north was quite a separate business. This was led by General Lefebvre-Desnouettes, who commanded the Guard Cavalry, and two dashing Lallemand brothers with general support from Drouet d'Erlon who was in charge of the Lille military district.

News of the 'Flight of the Eagle' from the Provençal coast northward took several days to reach Paris. Masséna, commanding in Marseilles, had sent an immediate report to his old comrade, Soult, but it had to be carried on horseback as far as Lyons since the newly installed Chappe semaphore system had at this date only been completed as far as there. It was then transmitted at once to Claude Chappe himself. He sent it immediately to the King by the hand of Vitrolles. King Louis's reaction was instinctive. He remarked placidly that the message should be passed at once to Soult who would know what to do about it. As it was Sunday, Artois and some of the other ministers were at vespers, but the agitated Vitrolles found Soult marching with his customary firm step across the Pont Royal on his way to a meeting of ministers. The King was quite right; Soult kept his head and knew exactly what to do. That evening he told his colleagues about the troops already sent to Lyons to meet Talleyrand's request. Later he announced that the King and the royal princes had approved an outline plan which he had evidently prepared already. Artois was to leave for Lyons at once to command an army mainly composed of those units which were already in position there as a potential threat to Murat. Berry, Artois's son, was to command a sizeable force collected in Franche Comté and based on Besançon. Angoulême would command on the right with his headquarters to be established at Nîmes with orders to attack Napoleon's rapidly advancing little column from the rear. Soult had no illusions about the military capacities of the royal princes but, from the political point of view, it was obviously essential that they should seem to be in command. However, to fight their battles for them, Ney was to be allocated to 'advise' Berry; Marshal Macdonald was given the key post as military adviser to Artois; Gouvion St Cyr also had an advisory role, and Soult communicated with all three of them immediately. Having come to Paris to receive orders from his old enemy, Soult, Ney insisted on seeing the King too. It was then that he is supposed to have made his celebrated boast that he would bring his old master, Napoleon, back to Paris in an iron cage. There were some last minute royal exchanges which did not matter very much: the sensible Duke of Orléans, the future Louis Philippe, with whom Soult was already very friendly, joined Artois in Lyons while Berry stayed behind at the King's side.

Meanwhile Soult was busy with military preparations that really did matter. Long afterwards Thiers, his enemy when they were both ministers under Louis Philippe, wrote critically of these preparations. But the plain fact was that with national, and especially military, feelings alienated from the Bourbons, Soult had to make the best of an almost impossible task. A reserve army of some 120,000 men was to be formed at Melun south of Paris and the half-pay officers were ordered to rejoin their regiments immediately in order to command units of newly recalled soldiers. Other new recruits were drafted into battalions of the National Guard. The half-pay officers were, to say the least, very ill disposed but Soult hoped that regimental loyalty as well as the return to full pay might influence them so that a reasonably well disciplined army could be provided. After all, he had fought an uphill battle ten years before in the camp of Boulogne, but in the end the Grande Armée was created. Now there was no time at all and very little inclination but, at the end of it all, Soult was surely, if unknowingly, beginning to create the splendid if ill-starred army that appeared at Waterloo. A royal ordinance calling for the creation of a National Guard was little more than a gesture. The cavalry officers of the National Guard were Royalist and loyal to the King, but the infantry were thoroughly discontented and often unwilling to serve. The prefects were ordered to form 'Conseils Généraux' to encourage recruitment into mobile National Guards but all this would be a slow progress and there was no time to spare. Napoleon's meteoric advance was continuing. There was a muddle over providing artillery for the forces already in position near Lyons but this was irrelevant since the regular troops were offering no resistance – indeed they were going over to Napoleon in their thousands. Additionally there was no 'clear the line priority' for military traffic on the Chappe semaphore system which was by now choked with messages from panic-stricken prefects. Indeed some Royalists, who had no doubt that Napoleon had returned as the result of a Bonapartist conspiracy, believed that the communication system was being deliberately sabotaged.

In the general confusion the King and Soult were among the few people in Paris who kept calm. Against the advice of Soult, Blacas and some others, who thought that action rather than deliberation was needed, the Chambers were reconvened and were addressed in dignified terms by the old King, while, inevitably in the circumstances, Soult produced in the *Moniteur* a proclamation in suitably vitriolic terms against the returned Emperor, to the effect that "Napoleon had no right to see France again! So let us rally around our King, the father of his people ... the worthy descendant of Henry of Navarre!"[18] He also dealt vigorously and competently with the incipient mutiny in the north. His old friend, Mortier, was sent northward with orders to shoot the leaders of the revolt if necessary. Mortier succeeded in having the ringleaders arrested and the revolt collapsed.

However, despite all his energetic if last minute activities, Soult's days as Minister of War were numbered. The disastrous events in the south, with regiment after regiment going over to Napoleon, with Ney following suit and the royal princes fleeing in panic, were in no way Soult's fault but an immediate scapegoat was needed. Had the Minister sent an army to Lyons that would welcome the returning Emperor? Was his opposition to the summoning of the Chambers another example of his treachery? Had his 'agents' sabotaged the Chappe semaphore system? In fact there was no question of Soult betraying the King and each suggestion to this effect was more absurd than the last. The best evidence for Soult's loyalty was given by Napoleon himself. Long afterwards he talked frankly to Dr O'Meara in St Helena. "Appearances may have been against Soult but he did not betray the King. He was in no way privy to my return: indeed he thought I was quite mad when he first heard that I had landed."[19] Wellington, too, no doubt based on the knowledge he had acquired as British ambassador in Paris, strongly defended, in discussion later, Soult's decision to send troops to Lyons which were there as a potential threat to Murat and for no other reason.[20]

But most of the King's ministers, led by the Abbé Montesquieu, came to quite a different conclusion at the time and they demanded Soult's resignation. The King, while still maintaining confidence in him, felt that he would have to resign in order to appease the indignant and highly embarrassed royal advisers after almost the whole regular army had gone over to the Emperor. When Soult handed the King his sword, the King returned it saying he was sure it would only be drawn in his service – an ironic moment! At the end of his last ministerial meeting Soult was escorted out of the Tuileries by two of the men who had now become his admirers, Blacas and Vitrolles. At the gate outside, Soult raised his plumed hat in salute to the considerable crowd gathered on the pavement. He then made a dignified departure with his family to his country estate at Villeneuve L'Etang. His short but hectic three months as Minister of War was at an end. He was succeeded by his old enemy, Clarke, the crafty Duke of Feltre.

In the impossible circumstances which existed during this brief explosive period, Soult probably did as much as he could have done to sustain the royal government. In an absurdly short time he had tried to transform the old Imperial army into a new army to serve the restored royal rulers of France. As a result he incurred in almost equal measure the cordial dislike of both the Bonapartists and the Royalists and he was quite unjustly accused by either side of disloyalty and treachery. The fact that he was caught in the middle in this way meant that he had probably got things about right, doing with some considerable courage what he believed to be in the best interests of France. He was to face much the same political problems and with the same ill success in the next few months. But at least he played some part in preparing that splendid French army that was to meet its fate at Waterloo.

18

THE HUNDRED DAYS

LOUIS XVIII's dismissed Minister of War was living in retirement at his country house, Villeneuve L'Etang, when hardly a fortnight after his departure great events took place in Paris. The King and the royal government left precipitately for Ghent and Napoleon was installed once again in the Tuileries. Saint-Chamans, when he visited Soult, found him as busy as ever supervising the men working on his estate. He told his former a.d.c. that he had refused two invitations from the Emperor to come to the Tuileries. Finally he had been persuaded by Savary and his old divisional general, Clausel, to have a talk with Napoleon. They had evidently spoken together very frankly. Soult had made no secret of the fact that he had tried to have Napoleon arrested when he landed. Napoleon had certainly read Soult's very hostile proclamation in the *Moniteur*. But the Emperor was a realist. He recognized how men behaved in various political situations and knew Soult through and through. What matterd most was to have good soldiers around him. But for the present Soult had insisted that he wanted to live quietly at home as a private citizen.[1]

What made Soult change his mind and agree to become major general or chief of staff of the new Army of the North that Napoleon was creating? Undoubtedly Napoleon had great need of him. Not only was he one of the greatest marshals but after his recent service as Minister of War under the Bourbons he was also a great political prize – much more so than Suchet, who again was an alternative candidate and whom, on looking back, Napoleon may have preferred. But Napoleon had more serious reasons than mere political propaganda for wanting Soult. He admired his military and administrative capabilities, even if he was not to make proper use of them in the forthcoming campaign. He also recognized that he was probably the most hard working of all his marshals. It is sometimes said that Napoleon was defeated at Waterloo partly because Soult rather than Berthier was his chief of staff. Of course Soult was a far better commander of troops than Berthier, who had proved useless when for brief periods he had been left in command of the Grande Armée. Nor did Soult lack staff experience. The historian, Houssaye, often a stern critic of Soult, claims that Soult's only experience as chief of staff had been when he served Lefebvre during the Revolutionary Wars. But of course he was a highly successful major general and chief of staff to King Joseph at Ocaña and during the conquest of Andalusia. He had also briefly understudied the overworked and ailing Berthier at the beginning of the campaign in 1813 with the possibility of becoming his successor. But, as noted already, Soult was a chief of staff on the Prussian model – fighting the battle himself and simply keeping his commander-in-chief informed. This had worked well with the gallant old Lefebvre and with the militarily incapable Joseph, but it would be no good at all with a genius such as Napoleon. Berthier had the gift, which Napoleon had found invaluable, of interpreting orders with speed and lucidity, but he had his faults too, especially when, as with Soult, he was jealous of the man to whom he was transmitting those orders. A carelessly drafted message sent by the hand of a single staff officer who was murdered en route had caused Soult to be very roughly handled by the British cavalry at the beginning of the Peninsular War, and subsequently he had been sent off to invade Portugal with a timetable drafted by Berthier which was quite impossible to fulfil. Indeed, in a discussion much later, Wellington was to comment that, from what he had heard, Berthier scarcely deserved his high reputation.[2]

The Emperor was aware of Soult's inexperience of what might be described as the 'clerical' side of the chief of staff's duties. Realizing that he would anyway take a little time to play himself in, Napoleon intended to keep a close watch on him and indeed to act as his own chief of staff if necessary, although this was bound to lead to confusion and would add to his personal burdens. Soult was given some excellent assistants including Bailly de Mortholon, who had been Berthier's right-hand man. Unfortunately, the self-confident Napoleon did nothing to exploit Soult's other military advantages. From his service in the Revolutionary Wars he was familiar with the whole area where the critical battles were to be fought; Ligny and Waterloo were only a few kilometres from the battlefield of Fleurus where Soult had greatly distinguished himself in 1794. More importantly, no other marshal then available had anything like the same experience of fighting against the British and against Napoleon's principal opponent, Wellington. It was a tragedy for France that Napoleon paid so little heed to these facts.

In deciding to appoint Soult – and he made the appointment a week or two before Berthier's accidental death or suicide –[3] Napoleon was taking a risk. Soult had created many enemies among the Bonapartist officers because of the strong line he had adopted as Minister of War. But again the Emperor was a realist. When the campaign began he expected that personal animosities would subside especially if, as he confidently expected, he was victorious. He also recognized that it was partly due to Soult's hectic activities directed against himself when he was Louis XVIII's Minister of War that most of the half-pay officers and many of the old soldiers had returned to the colours, providing some of the components of the Army of the North. Also two of Napoleon's closest advisers agreed with the Emperor's decision; one was the ever loyal Davout who had taken over from the miserable Clarke as Minister of War and was in a good position to judge what his old comrade in arms, Soult, had accomplished at the Ministry; the other was Savary who, as is evident from his *Memoirs*, had been an admirer of Soult ever since they were both involved in security measures against Royalist and English spies along the Channel coast around Boulogne ten years before.

From all this it seems probable that it was largely at Napoleon's request that Soult returned to serve him. Houssaye argues that the initiative really came from Soult but Napoleon was not someone who could easily be persuaded to make an appointment against his will. However, it was certainly true that Soult could not bear to be unemployed when dramatic events were taking place so near him. In his *Justificatory Memoir*, which he prepared just before having to leave France after Waterloo, he said that, as a marshal of France, he could not "keep his sword in its sheath" when his country was threatened with invasion. "I fought the Prussians and the English at Fleurus and Waterloo. If that is a crime then I am guilty."[4] There was also the question of national unity. On his return Napoleon had begun to create the elements of a 'Liberal Empire', causing many of those who had been his strong opponents to rally around him – his quarrelsome brother, Lucien, Benjamin Constant, the political philosopher, and Carnot, the old 'organizer of victory'. Soult had little in common with any of them but, as his first biographer wrote, "He was one of the men like Carnot for whom patriotism meant unity."[5] There was naturally also a strong element of ambition in Soult's patriotism; he simply could not bear to be on the sidelines in a crisis.

On May 9, a month and a half after his first talk to Napoleon, he was appointed major general, i.e. chief of staff, of the Army of the North. Along with ten other marshals, including Davout, Ney, Masséna and Suchet, he became a peer of the French Empire and with Ney, Jourdan and a newly created marshal, the cavalry general Grouchy, he rode beside the Emperor's carriage at the great ceremony in the Champ de Mai which was to celebrate the 'Acte Additionel' inaugurating the Liberal Empire. Once again he had recourse to the *Moniteur* to justify his action. "The flight of the Bourbons," he proclaimed, "and their appeal to foreigners to help them to return to the throne has destroyed the engagements that have been made with them."[6] After his strident proclamation in the *Moniteur* against Napoleon only a few weeks previously, the Royalists naturally made the most of this new announcement. In the Royalist *Journal Universel*, published in Ghent, they referred to "the Marshal who celebrated the obsequies of Louis XVI and then the resurrection of Napoleon – who was Louis XVIII's minister while Bonaparte was plotting and Bonaparte's chief of staff when Louis XVIII was betrayed."[7] Of course Soult was very far from being alone in these changes of front. Like all the others who had done the same, he could firmly justify his actions as being caused by a higher loyalty to France itself. He tried unsuccessfully to get his two chief a.d.c.s, Brun de Villeret and Saint-Chamans, to join him again. When Saint-Chamans refused he got a very cold lunch indeed at Villeneuve L'Etang.[8]

Soult was not involved in the Emperor's various political activities – the new constitution ushered in by the 'Acte Additionel' and the totally unsuccessful attempts to negotiate with the Allied governments. When it was clear that the Allies intended to invade France once more, Napoleon took urgent steps to clear up pockets of Royalist resistance in the south (earning for Grouchy a very 'political' marshal's baton) as well as to check dissension in the Vendée. Then, with his newly organized Army of the North, he decided to seize the initiative and move at once against the strongest Allied concentration - the Anglo-Netherlands army led by Wellington and the Prussian army of Blücher – both of them in the neighbourhood of Brussels. Further south Rapp commanded a single corps called the Army of the Rhine, based on Strasbourg, while at Chambéry Suchet led the Army of the Alps. These were defensive forces designed to keep the Austrians at bay while Napoleon took the decisive action in Belgium.

It has been said by Houssaye that "only brilliant staff work" could have achieved the very rapid and secret concentration of large forces that took place in north-eastern France at the end of May. With Soult as major general there were five army corps commanded and positioned at first as follows. I Corps under Drouet d'Erlon was stationed at Lille; II Corps under Reille was at Valenciennes; III Corps under Vandamme was at Mezières; IV Corps under Gérard was at Thionville, and VI Corps under Lobau with the Imperial Guard was in reserve. The various formations came from places as far distant from one another as Paris, Lille and Metz and consisted of nearly 90,000 infantry, 22,000 cavalry and 11,000 artillery and engineers with some 300 guns.[9] The army could have been substantially larger but Napoleon was determined to move fast before the Allies were fully prepared. Moreover, if he had fought a purely defensive war it would have meant abandoning nearly a third of France to the enemy.

Undoubtedly it was the most extraordinary army that Napoleon had ever commanded. It has been well described as follows: "Impressionable, critical, without discipline and without confidence in its leaders except for Napoleon himself, it was haunted by the dread of treason and, on that account perhaps, liable to sudden fits of panic: it nevertheless loved war for its own sake, fired with a thirst for vengeance – more excited, more eager for the fray than any other Republican or Imperial army before it. Napoleon had never before handled an army that was so formidable and so fragile."[10] Much of this turbulence and many of these internal suspicions affected Soult personally. Since a large part of d'Erlon's corps was involved in an insurrection against the previous government, many senior officers including d'Erlon himself had been threatened by Soult with prison or with death; the fiery Vandamme, who had been one of Soult's generals of division in the Grande Armée, had written to Davout, when he was appointed major general, saying that he must treat the appointment as null and void unless it was confirmed by Davout himself. Vandamme also complained that his corps, with only 18,000 men, was smaller than most of the others while he objected strongly to serving under Grouchy who had been made a marshal so recently and was a mere cavalry general.[11] Before Rapp got an independent command there were complaints to Soult about his incompetence from several of his senior staff and there was almost universal antagonism to Bourmont's Royalist background. Bourmont had gone over to Napoleon at the same time as Ney and he had been kept in the army at the insistence of Gérard. Then he deserted to the Bourbons again before Waterloo. "Be careful of Soult – he will betray you!" said a private soldier to Napoleon at the beginning of the campaign. "Keep calm," the Emperor replied, "I will watch him carefully."[12] Jealousy and rivalries had always been intense in the Grande Armée. They were now much more bitter. Such dissent affected the outcome of the forthcoming battles but, despite their bitter feelings against some of the senior officers, the veterans still believed that Napoleon was invincible; he had only been conquered by the snow in 1812 and by treason in 1814. Wellington commented that the spirit of the French army was quite as high as during the Revolutionary Wars.

On June 5 Soult, on the Emperor's orders, moved the five corps of the army with the Imperial Guard nearer to the frontier. A very tight security blackout was still maintained and units of the National Guard replaced the regular troops as they advanced so that warnings of major troop replacements were not given to the enemy. "Never had Napoleon's intelligence been so lucid!"[13] wrote Houssaye. But, under the Emperor's direction, much of the credit for this very rapid and highly secret concentration of forces must surely go to Soult and his staff. However, Soult was criticized for not sending quicker instructions to Grouchy about his cavalry units which had not got moving until the Emperor, who had left Paris on June 11, had arrived at Laon. When the cavalry finally got movement orders their advance was so hasty that the horses were in danger of being exhausted before the campaign began. There were also delays in giving orders to Vandamme's and Gérard's corps now making up the right wing under Grouchy, and to Lobau's corps, forming the reserve. This was because Soult tended to send only single officers with his orders, instead of the half dozen that Berthier might have used and some of the officers lost their way. These were blunders due to Soult's inexperience of the details of staff work, but he really should have had proper advice from his assistants. He was also plagued with disciplinary problems. Villages which had welcomed the arrival of the Bourbons earlier were sacked and, no sooner had the army entered Belgium, than there was an orgy of pillaging with the Imperial Guard setting a specially bad example. Soult's gendarmerie general (provost marshal) came near to resigning.

Despite these various problems and confusions, the army had moved with lightning speed, still in conditions of great secrecy, and now occupied a strong position in a kind of hinge between the armies of Wellington and Blücher, with the bridges over the River Sambre firmly secured. Wellington's forces were concentrated to the south and west of Brussels and Napoleon's immediate instinct was to envelop Wellington from the west and then march straight on to Brussels while Blücher's army was held in check by Grouchy's two corps on the right. When he found that he was confronted by most of Blücher's army in full force, he changed his tactics completely. Ney, who had accompanied the army without any specific command, was put in charge of Reille's and d'Erlon's corps on the left with orders to attack the British vigorously at Quatre Bras while the Emperor launched his first main attack on the Prussians. Soult and his staff had coped with these rapid and complicated changes of tactics competently although Soult was opposed to giving Ney so important a command because of his past unreliability. In the end Soult was to be proved right.

Meanwhile Napoleon prepared to launch his attack on Blücher and, soon after 8 am on July 16, Soult sent out the appropriate orders to Ney and Grouchy. But Ney, who had not handled troops in action for over a year, was very dilatory. Reille, who had had plenty of experience of attacking the British in Spain and southern France, was likewise cautious while d'Erlon, similarly experienced, had not yet joined up with the rest of Ney's army. Grouchy was also having difficulties in getting his two corps ready to attack the Prussians. Both Vandamme and Gérard still resented the fact of being commanded by a recently promoted cavalryman. Soult sent message after message to Ney requesting him to move faster and he arranged for part of the main cavalry reserve under Kellerman to reinforce him, but he has been criticized for not making sure that Vandamme and Gérard fully accepted the command situation on the right flank. Vandamme was incorrigible and was ready to blame the late arrival of orders from Soult for his own slow movements. The Emperor's intention to attack the Prussians with the two halves of his army being mutually supportive was well reflected in his major general's clear dispatch sent to Ney at 2 pm. It ran as follows: "HM's intention is that you should attack whatever force is before you and, after vigorously driving it back, you are to turn in our direction so as to bring about the envelopment of the Prussian forces. If in fact they are overthrown sooner HM will manoueuvre in your direction so as to help you in the same way."[14]

As soon as Napoleon had launched his ferocious attack on the Prussians with Vandamme's and Gérard's corps, he realized that Blücher was determined to stand his ground. So here was a fine opportunity to annihilate him. Soult was instructed to send off another message to Ney ordering him to attack the Prussian right flank. Soult ended his dispatch with the words: "The fate of France is in your hands." Immediately after this message was drafted there was confusion, and there are a number of contradictory reports of what exactly happened. Because Napoleon appreciated by now that Ney was going to have his hands full with the British, a second message was composed, either handwritten or even to be delivered orally, telling Ney to get on with the job at Quatre Bras but to release d'Erlon's division forthwith to turn westward and attack the Prussian flank. Soult entrusted these various communications to a highly intelligent staff officer, Major Baudus. Unfortunately, Napoleon insisted on duplicates of the various messages being sent by another hand. The only other staff officer available for this second task was Colonel Forbin-Janson, a man in no way qualified for his post. He was a purely political appointee, having commanded a group of Bonapartist partisans in the

Nièvre in 1814; otherwise he had seen no active military service. He would have received short shrift if he had served under Soult much longer, and indeed came in for precisely that treatment from Ney when he reached him, unfortunately a little time before Baudus. The colonel was so alarmed by the irascible marshal that he only gave him the messages about fighting the British and apparently forgot altogether to hand over the vitally important message about d'Erlon. Nor does he seem to have made any personal contact with d'Erlon himself. In fact, before Baudus arrived with the right messages d'Erlon appears to have received Napoleon's instructions from yet another intermediary, Colonel de Laboydyère, one of the Emperor's own a.d.c.s. D'Erlon must have recalled those occasions in Spain in 1812 when he had been a kind of 'shuttlecock' batted to and fro between Soult and King Joseph. As his latest biographer, Pierre Germain, implies, he was not one of the most intelligent of Napoleon's generals and he found it hard to reach firm decisions. He had been uncertain about heading the revolt against the King when he was commanding in Lille a few months previously and he had nearly ended up in prison as a result. However, having now received a direct order from the Emperor, he sent off his chief of staff, Delacombe, to explain the situation to Ney and then marched westward to make the critical flank attack on the Prussians. The furious Ney, who had not been properly briefed about d'Erlon's westward march at least until the arrival of Baudus, was now facing an even larger Allied force at Quatre Bras. Accordingly, with characteristic insubordination, he defied the orders that Soult sent him and instructed d'Erlon to turn around once again so as to bring him some much needed reinforcement. The wretched d'Erlon had almost reached the Prussian right flank – indeed his sudden appearance alarmed Vandamme who thought at first it was another Allied army – when he received Ney's strongly worded message of recall. Since Ney was his immediate superior, he felt in a bizarre fashion that he must obey him. Despite the Emperor's direct order to the contrary, he thought that Ney must be in such desperate straits facing an Allied army of 20,000 men that he really had to march to his aid. In the event he was too late to help at Quatre Bras, while his failure to turn the Prussian flank at Ligny meant that, although Napoleon decisively defeated Blücher, with some 16,000 casualties and another 10,000 fugitives, he failed to win the overwhelming victory that he badly needed. However, the news of Ligny was good enough for Soult to send off a victory message to Prince Joseph in Paris – his last communication as an imperial marshal with his old enemy, the Emperor's elder brother. Meeting d'Erlon with Ney's forces around Quatre Bras later that evening, Napoleon is supposed to have said, hardly hiding his chagrin: "You have dealt a blow to the cause of France, general, but carry on at the head of your cavalry and pursue the English rearguard."[15]

Blame for this very muddled business must be shared by the Emperor himself, who had no Berthier at his elbow and who insisted on sending duplicate messages by the hand of a totally inexperienced staff officer; by Ney, who was at first dilatory and then grossly insubordinate in countermanding the Emperor's orders; by d'Erlon, who tried to serve two masters and ended up serving neither; and by Soult, who, despite the nine separate messages that he sent that day to Ney in the Emperor's name or his own, did not properly sort out the confusing messages transmitted by the incompetent Forbin-Janson which cut across the orders carried by his own trustworthy staff officer, Baudus. In the endless post-mortems that have since taken place on the whole affair, most of the principal participants have left full accounts covering their own points of view. Soult, although defended by the faithful Baudus, was too busy, as a minister under Louis Philippe, to write *Memoirs* covering this period of his career and to some extent his apologia has gone by default.[16]

It was apparent on the following day that Blücher's army, although badly mauled, was still in being. Napoleon had therefore three options. He could follow up his victory at Ligny by attacking Blücher again with the bulk of his army, leaving Ney to hold Wellington at bay; he could attack Wellington with his main army, leaving Grouchy with a small skeleton force to keep watch on Blücher; or he could virtually divide his army into two, attacking Wellington with the larger part comprising Reille's, d'Erlon's and Lobau's corps and the Imperial Guard, while leaving Grouchy with Vandamme's and Gérard's corps to pursue Blücher. This third course, which had dangerous possibilities and caused Soult particular concern, was the one which the Emperor followed.

In order to keep aligned with Blücher as he retreated, Wellington had retired to the strong position of Mont St-Jean south of Brussels and near to the village of Waterloo. It was here that on June 18 Napoleon proposed to attack him. A reassuring dispatch had been received from Grouchy the previous evening saying that, in accordance with orders sent to him by Soult in the Emperor's name, he was pursuing Blücher in the direction of Wavre – not as Napoleon had first hoped towards the much more distant Liège. However, Grouchy affirmed that he was following hard on Blücher's heels and would prevent him from joining up with Wellington in the Brussels area.

The Emperor did not read Grouchy's dispatch until the following morning. As it seemed to indicate that Grouchy was carefully obeying the orders given to him, it did not appear to need an urgent reply. Immediately after an early breakfast the Emperor called a staff conference at his headquarters at Le Caillou. It was here that Soult was decidedly critical of the Emperor's decision to divide his army before attacking the strongly entrenched Allied positions at Mont St-Jean. In view of his own unrivalled experience of fighting Wellington and his veterans, he said to one of his staff beforehand that it was "a great mistake to separate so large a force of some 30,000 men from the main army which is facing the English". He shared Napoleon's over-optimism about the state of Blücher's army and believed that a weak infantry corps with some cavalry was all that was needed to keep watch on the Prussians.[17] He repeated these views at the staff conference. If such a force had been properly led, perhaps by Soult himself, it might well have succeeded in keeping the Prussians away from Waterloo on that fatal day while Napoleon crushed

Wellington. With only three corps supported by the Imperial Guard, Soult considered that the Emperor faced a very difficult task. Over ten years ago, after the battle of Fleurus, he had stormed this very plateau, driving the retreating Austrians into the forest of Soignes beyond. This had involved some fierce fighting although the Austrians were already a defeated army and had suffered severe losses in the battle; nor was their fire-power anything like as accurate and effective as that of Wellington's army. Soult thought that to make a direct frontal attack on the Allied line facing devastating British rifle fire would be highly dangerous. He had already advised the Emperor the night before to recall Grouchy; now he was supported in his views about the danger of attacking the Allied line frontally by Reille, whose previous experience of fighting the English was equal to his own. Several times, particularly in Spain, Soult had done what he thought was right in defiance of the Emperor's views. However, to get one's own way in an independent command was quite different from overriding the Emperor when acting as his chief of staff. Indeed Napoleon resented even senior officers arguing against him in an open conference and he flatly rejected Soult's advice. He is reported to have said to Soult and Reille, "Because you have been beaten by Wellington you consider him to be a good general. I say that he is a bad general and that the English are bad troops. It will be a 'lunch time affair'!" To which Soult replied sardonically, "I hope so!"[18]

It is possible that Soult's warnings about the effectiveness of Wellington's forces when they were in a strong defence position contributed to the fateful delay in Napoleon launching his attack, until all his preparations were complete. But it had been raining heavily for the last 24 hours and the Emperor did not want to move until he could make effective use of his artillery. On his instructions Soult had ordered that all forces should be prepared for action by 9 am, but the onslaught was postponed until later in the morning. The strength of the army was just under 75,000 men including the Imperial Guard, numbering some 20,000, and the reserve cavalry, about 20,000 strong. Of the three infantry corps commanded by Reille, d'Erlon and Lobau, d'Erlon's corps was much the largest. Napoleon was determined that the main attack should be delivered by d'Erlon on the centre of the Allied line. But Ney did not keep a tight control over all his forces because, as the great onslaught began, one of the divisions on the left of Reille's corps turned what was intended to be a feint attack against the strongly fortified farm house of Hougoumont into a ferocious and bloody encounter. The Emperor's youngest brother, Prince Jérôme, made continuous and wholly unsuccessful attempts to capture this desperately defended strongpoint for most of the day.

As the battle got fully under way, with d'Erlon's corps furiously attacking the centre of the Allied line, it was obviously neccessary to send a further message to Grouchy. Supposedly Soult drafted this dispatch, but although it was not "the ambiguous document that was not worth the time it cost in writing it", as Thiers described it,[19] neither Napoleon nor Soult deserve much credit for it or for the delay in sending it. A Polish staff officer, Zenowicz, had been waiting for it for hours and both the Emperor and his major general should have realized that Grouchy, with his command problems, should not have been left without a reply for so long. The dispatch was prepared at about 1 pm. It certainly was not a dynamic document. Abbreviated, according to Houssaye, it read as follows: "Your movement on Wavre conforms to HM's dispositions. Meanwhile the Emperor orders me to inform you that you should always manoeuvre in our direction and bring your army closer so that you can join up with us before any force can impose itself between you and us. I do not instruct you on your line of march. It is for you to note our position and to dispose your forces accordingly so that you are always ready to crush any enemy that tries to threaten our right flank."[20]

Before the message was sent, Soult with his eagle eye appears to have been the first to discern the famous cloud of dust beyond the French right flank. The Emperor was sure it was Grouchy. But a captured officer made it clear that it was a Prussian force. At once Napoleon concluded that it was Bülow's corps, perhaps detached from Blücher's main army. Accordingly a postscript was added to Soult's dispatch urging Grouchy to move at once and encircle this corps. The Emperor was confident that the odds were still distinctly in his favour and if Grouchy could only crush Bülow's corps his victory could be even more decisive.

Alas for the French, there was no likelihood of this and indeed the dispatch reached Grouchy too late to affect his operations. Yet common sense should have told him what to do. A constant sound of gunfire had been coming from the Mont St-Jean area and Gérard had urged the Marshal to move at once in that direction. Gérard considered that he himself ought to have been made a marshal after Ligny and his relations with Grouchy were almost as bad as Vandamme's. He failed completely to make Grouchy change direction. Grouchy had been ordered by the Emperor to move on Wavre and he stuck rigidly to this line of march. Soult has been blamed for not sending him quicker and more precise instructions but, since the original orders came from Napoleon himself and no further speedy initiative had come from him, it is hard to imagine that Berthier would have acted any differently if he had been there. It was Grouchy's inexperience and obstinacy that was really to blame, coupled with the failure of both Napoleon and Soult to send him orders more rapidly.

Meanwhile, in the continuing frontal attack on the Allied defences which had caused Soult so much concern, Reille's divisions were still battling away unsuccessfully at Hougoumont. But the main French attack continued to be directed against the centre of the Allied line. Lobau's corps had been brought forward to defend the French flank against an increasingly strong Prussian build-up. D'Erlon's vigorous infantry attacks were followed by an overwhelming, but very premature, French cavalry attack, ordered by Ney himself, which caused the Emperor and Soult much anxiety. They agreed that he was being as unreliable as he had been at Jena and elsewhere. A violent assault by a combined force of all arms at last captured the crucial farm of La Haye Sainte but the Allied line was not broken and Prussian pressure on the French right was increasing alarmingly. In this narrow field of operations the Emperor was directly involved in all these desperate events and with the final dramatic crisis. At last the Imperial Guard, 'The Immortals' led by Ney, advanced majestically against the British line. In a short time there was disaster and the Imperial Guard were recoiling down the hill in the face of devastating rifle fire and the onslaught of the British Guards Brigade. Soult could do little to help during these disastrous events but in the final moments of defeat it was characteristically he who kept his head. When Napoleon wanted to lead a forlorn charge against the enemy and several of the a.d.c.s were rushing wildly around trying to get themselves killed, Soult laid hold of the bridle of the Emperor's horse and with General Gourgaud guided him firmly away from the battlefield.[21]

French losses in the battle were some 25,000 killed and wounded with about 16,000 prisoners or deserters. Soult, who had taken over command after Napoleon had hastened back to Paris, succeeded in stemming the rout, gathering together the shattered infantry and cavalry formations at Philippeville in southern Belgium and making contact with Grouchy whose two corps had seen practically no action since Ligny. Retreating back to Laon, Soult restored some semblance of order. On paper, taking into account the French forces under Rapp and Suchet, Napoleon would still have had some 115,000 men to stem the Allied advance from the north-east, but a series of messages from Soult to the Emperor and to Davout graphically described the state of the army. On June 22 he recorded that the greatest confusion reigned among the generals, many of whom supported the Duke of Orléans whom later, as Louis Philippe, Soult himself was to serve; others had deserted the army and had gone to Paris. There was disaffection everywhere, especially among the staff officers, and even the soldiers were selling their arms and equipment to the peasants. Events in Paris had moved to a crisis. When Davout sent Soult and Grouchy a copy of Napoleon's abdication announcement, Soult's first reaction was to try to minimize the effect this would have on the troops' morale and he discussed with Reille what precautions would be needed when the announcement was made public. From Paris Davout was still hopeful that the enemy advance could be stemmed in the forest of Compiègne or by holding the crossings of the Oise. Soult, that master of successful retreats, might have achieved this. However, he was in utter despair at the state of the army and, "being without an Emperor to serve," as he told Davout, insisted that he must resign the command "on health grounds". He handed over to Grouchy at Soissons. Grouchy, whose own conduct in the campaign was soon to be so severely criticized, recorded in his *Memoirs* later that Soult was obviously trying to mend his broken fences with the Bourbons. As usual Soult, the political realist, must have considered that his own personal position would certainly be precarious if and when the Bourbons did return.[22] There is no evidence that he gave any support to the alternative of the Emperor's baby son being proclaimed as Napoleon II and, back in Paris, he made a speech in the House of Peers saying that the best hope for the country was to bring back the King as soon as possible.[23]

After serving first as Louis XVIII's Minister of War and then as Napoleon's major general, Soult could expect some pretty rough treatment from the returning Bourbons and soon after his speech in the House of Peers he left Paris to return to his distant home of St-Amans in Languedoc. The rough treatment was indeed to begin during the weeks before he was forced to leave the country.

It is easy to criticize Soult's role in the Waterloo campaign – to suggest that he was a "fine fighting general, but quite unused to the detailed staff work that he was called upon to undertake",[24] or that he was "a great manoeuvrer of armies who was employed not to manoeuvre anything except the Emperor's thoughts".[25] Others have considered that Suchet would have made a better chief of staff or deplored the absence of Berthier who would have relieved the Emperor of some of the detailed work that fell upon him because of Soult's staff limitations.[26] On the other hand, Berthier made blunders too and had certainly already begun to feel the strain of overwork in both the 1813 and 1814 campaigns. Suchet would have been an unknown quantity but his selfish failure to cooperate with Soult in the Pyrenean campaign and in the defence of southern France, as well as the alacrity with which he joined the Bourbons after Napoleon's first abdication, have already been noted. Yet surely what really matters is Napoleon's own opinion. Apart from some barbed comments on Soult's failure to employ enough staff officers to carry messages, the Emperor, who was strongly critical of both Grouchy and Ney, did not blame Soult at all. Indeed at St Helena he told Dr O'Meara that Soult was in fact "an excellent major general".[27]

Napoleon made no use of Soult's expert knowledge of fighting the British and of opposing Wellington in particular; nor did he benefit from Soult's past experience of campaigning over the whole Waterloo area. Indeed it has been truly said that chief responsibility for the outcome of this short campaign can only be laid at the door of the Emperor himself. "A high degree of personal control was possible on so restricted a battlefield as Waterloo but there is scant evidence of Napoleon exercising more than a negative influence once the battle was joined. The Emperor may have been unfortunate in the weather but this factor does not remove one iota of responsibility for the lethargy, indolence and absent-mindedness that he displayed at different critical moments..."[28] Neither Berthier, nor Suchet, nor Soult could have saved him from all this.

19

EXILE AND RETURN

SOULT left for his home in the Midi on July 3, soon after his speech in the House of Peers. In the aftermath of Waterloo France was again in turmoil. The army, now commanded by Davout, had retired beyond the Loire while what was called grandiloquently the 'Revolution of June 30' brought back the Bourbons once more. The Midi was not a safe place for those who had been fighting alongside the Emperor. Bordeaux and Toulouse were Royalist strongholds and even in Castres, a few miles from Soult's home, a municipal officer had disposed of a prize mule given him by Soult lest he should be considered a friend of the Marshal's! The Midi, where the Duke of Angoulême was for a time almost an independent ruler, was the centre of the so-called' White Terror' in which Royalist gangs, sometimes calling themselves 'Vedettes' – the followers of Angoulême – captured and even put to death those suspected of Bonaparte sympathies. The most tragic victim was Marshal Brune who was torn to pieces by a Royalist mob and his body thrown into the Rhône near Avignon. All kinds of rumours were going around about Napoleon himself. He was actually on his way to surrender to the British navy at Rochefort, but some suggested that he was really going south with Soult and Davout so that he could use the army to crush the Royalists and continue the war.

Prudence dictated that Soult should make his way through the mountainous region of the Massif Central. When he reached St-Flour, two-thirds of the way along what his friend Brun called his 'bizarre journey home', he found Royalist sympathizers everywhere. Brun gave him shelter in his château of Malzieu but in the early hours of the morning a mob of Royalists appeared, intent on laying hands on him. He was reluctantly persuaded to take refuge in an attic over the bedroom occupied by the heavily pregnant Madame Brun, while his host told the excited Royalists that he had already departed. The following night, escorted by a group of Brun's family and friends, he did leave for Mende, the capital of the department of Lozère. On the way they were confronted by another mob of Royalists from a neighbouring commune which had suffered severely from the activities of a Bonapartist prefect. They included the servants of a prominent local family, the Lescures, National Guardsmen and priests. Soult's party had great difficulty in forcing their way through and at one time it looked as if they would have to take to the high mountains. Finally they reached Mende where Soult was imprisoned in the prefecture, having given his word not to leave until authorized to do so by the government. He then suffered the humiliation of being 'investigated' by the local council. He claimed that one reason for his journey was to offer his services to the Duke of Angoulême. Some of the council accepted this but the Vicomte de Lescure and his friends remained hostile; they were convinced that Soult was partly responsible for the return of Napoleon from Elba and they thought that his present purpose was to arouse Bonapartist sympathizers and soldiers in the south against the Royalist government. During his incarceration the Marshal was subjected to the jeers of his captors and was roughly handled on the staircase of the prefecture by several National Guardsmen. All the time Brun de Villeret was working tirelessly on his behalf. Brun was in touch with Angoulême who, at the instance of the Comte de Bruges, had made him the local military commander of the department with full powers to release Soult. The Marshal then went on his way with an escort of gendarmes. This move was only just in time as some units of the half disbanded Army of the Loire, many of them furious at the treatment Soult had received, began to arrive in Mende. He had been colonel of the *chasseurs* of the Imperial Guard, and a bitter attack by a *chasseur* regiment on the Mende Royalists for persecuting one of the marshals that they admired most could have resulted in a serious outbreak of violence. Still farther south, Soult was attacked by some more Royalists near the village of Lacaune in his own department of the Tarn. They accused him of causing thousands of unnecessary deaths by fighting the battle of Toulouse after Napoleon had abdicated. He had to take refuge from his assailants in gardens and hedges on the outskirts of the village. At last he and his escort managed to escape and to make their way in comparative safety to his home in St-Amans.[1]

After this hectic journey Soult must at first have been much relieved that he had left Louise and the children behind in Villeneuve l'Etang. There was no reason to expect that they were in danger but this country property was partly requisitioned by the Royalist government and then pillaged by Allied troops, forcing the family to take refuge in Paris. By now the White Terror was at its height; Brune and other generals had been murdered; Ney and some prominent Bonapartists were on trial for their lives, and Ney at his trial had repeated the assertion which he had made when he first rejoined Napoleon that Soult had been involved in a plot to bring the Emperor back from Elba. Soult's old antagonist, Sir Robert Wilson, found out from a clerk in the Ministry of War that Soult might well be put on the 'death list' too and he determined to warn him. This 'English eccentric' had also helped with the rescue of Napoleon's minister, Lavalette.

During his imprisonment at Mende, Soult had begun, with Brun's help, to prepare a *Justificatory Memoir* of his conduct and when he got back to St-Amans he completed it with some local legal help. It was a well-argued document describing in some detail his past career, beginning with his service as military commander in Brittany after the First Restoration. He was rather too effusive about the Quiberon monument but he was on firmer ground when he described his hard working life as Minister of War trying to draw together the returning *émigrés* and the veterans of

Napoleon's armies against the background of a nearly bankrupt economy. He emphasized that he was in no way involved in bringing Napoleon back from Elba and gave the familiar explanation that the troops that he had sent to south-eastern France were there in response to Talleyrand's plea to put pressure on Murat. He added that when he resigned he had received a warm letter of commendation from the King. During the Hundred Days his only 'crime' had been to fight for France against the invading armies of Prussia and England. Rather surprisingly, he referred to some edict of Henry VII of England for the classic argument that no subject should be punished for obeying his current ruler. In general he affirmed that he was no more a traitor than most other Frenchmen. It was the ultimate and reasonable defence of the 'Collège des Girouettes' – the 'weathercocks' – which included so many of his other comrades in arms.[2]

Soult sent his *Justificatory Memoir* to the president of the civil court in Castres who had been one of his political enemies. However, the president suggested some sensible amendments before sending the document on to Paris. From then on he and Soult became close friends. But, before the *Memoir* reached the capital, Soult's name had been placed at the head of a list of 38 people who were to be banished from their homes and placed under police supervision pending a decision by the two Chambers on their future. The order was made on July 24, but it did not appear in the official *Moniteur* until December. Those on the list were then given two months in which to leave France. The Marshal had no intention of remaining at home, especially after Sir Robert Wilson's warning. So with much help from various local friends he quickly left St-Amans, travelling by night in the local diligence driven by its owner, posing as a businessman from Limoges. He was stopped outside St-Amans by two villagers who insisted on giving him some money. Then, probably with the acquiescence of the government, who were no doubt glad to be rid of him, he made his way to the German border at Mauberge. His first objective was his wife's homeland, the Duchy of Berg, where Louise and the children joined him. The French government forbade him to return and he remained in exile for the next three years.

As already noted, Soult with his German wife had made himself well liked both as a young general of brigade in the Rhineland during the Revolutionary Wars and also as governor of Berlin during the critical months after Tilsit. Now he took refuge in the house of his formidable mother-in-law, Frau Berg, in Barmen. Then, with the ready approval of the Prussian government, he made his home at Schloss Hardenburg near Düsseldorf. Prussian police agents kept an eye on him but their reports were entirely favourable. It was not for nothing that he had once been called by the Rhinelanders their *Wundermann*, and he obviously intended to do nothing to prejudice his eventual return to France.

It was at this time that he began writing his *Memoirs* which were also intended to give a more general commentary on the history of his times. The *Memoirs* were to be divided into four periods. The first part was to cover his early military life and the

Revolutionary Wars; the second part the camp of Boulogne and the wars of the Third Coalition in Germany and Poland; the third part the war in Spain and Portugal and the fourth part the campaigns in Germany, France and Belgium from 1813 to 1815. But he made very slow progress, inhibited, to some extent, from making political judgements by the existing situation in France. Although he continued writing at intervals, even during his renewal of active political life under King Louis Philippe, he had only finished the first part covering his early life and the Revolutionary Wars by the time of his death. It was left to his son, the second Duke of Dalmatia, a distinguished diplomatist who unfortunately did not live long after his father, to publish this first section of the *Memoirs*.

Soult's writings are certainly not a literary masterpiece – not surprisingly considering his poor education. But they are more than mere campaign records and are probably as good as many of the voluminous military memoirs that were now pouring out from the pens of most of Napoleon's former military leaders. They were totally lacking in bombast and, considering the bitter jealousies and animosities that convulsed the French Republican armies, they are remarkably restrained in their comments on his comrades in arms. They also give a 'plain soldier's view' of such political issues as the venal incompetence of the Directory, the danger of alienating conquered people by the policy of 'living off the land', the political risks of the Brumaire *coup d'état* and the seizure of power by Napoleon Bonaparte. Considering that Soult had become very much more than just a 'plain soldier' (if indeed he had ever been one) it is a great pity that he had no time to complete any more of his *Memoirs*. He left copious memoranda and much correspondence in the possession of his descendants which have mostly ended up in the château of Epoisses in Burgundy, the home of the de Guitaut family. It was left to his great granddaughter and her husband, Antoinette and Louis de Saint-Pierre, to edit and publish some of these papers.

For a man of action such as the Marshal, his stay in the Rhineland must have seemed endless. It was also a sad time personally for Louise and himself. Hector and Hortense were completing their education but another daughter, Caroline, born in 1817 when Louise was in her 40s, died after a few weeks. In the intervals of writing, Soult had a good circle of friends, both German and French, and at first he used to say that Germany was much friendlier than France. Perhaps with an eye to becoming in due course a country landowner in St-Amans, he began to study rural agriculture. However, after three years, he was in despair about his future and on the anniversary of his father's death he wrote miserably to his mother saying that he did not know whether he would ever experience true happiness again. If time hung heavily on his hands in Germany, this same period in France was described with equal scorn by the son of another of Napoleon's generals. Victor Hugo called it "the period when David the painter was said to have no talent, Carnot no honesty, Soult had never won a battle and Napoleon was no longer a genius!"

Louise returned frequently to Paris and used all her considerable powers of persuasion and skill to secure her husband's return. She had always been on excellent terms with her husband's a.d.c.s and she enlisted the help of Saint-Chamans who once more re-entered his old chief's life. Saint-Chamans spoke to Angoulême on Soult's behalf and found that both he and the King were well disposed. A note of caution, however, was struck by the new Minister of War, Marshal Gouvion St Cyr, who thought that Soult had such a high reputation among the old veterans of Napoleon's army that it might be dangerous to recall him. The wheel had really come round full circle.

By 1819 the political climate in France had changed. For the time being the extreme Royalists, the Ultras, were no longer in power. Decazes, the King's favourite, was the most powerful individual in the government which was formally presided over by General Dessolles who had been with Joseph Bonaparte in Madrid and had been admired by Soult as a capable administrator in Andalusia. Dessolles has been well described as the first of those 'illustres épées', ('valuable swords'), as Soult was to become later, who were included in cabinets to provide cohesion to various French governments under both branches of the House of Bourbon.[3] It was Decazes's intention to work towards a political situation akin to the First Restoration in 1814 when there had been a real attempt to bring together both the Royalists and the ex-Imperialists. Soult had played an important part in this period of reconciliation and, in May 1819, he and his friend, Savary, as well as (ironically) his old bugbear, Exelmans, were allowed to return to France together. The incorrigible Duke of Berry said to him: "If I had been in charge you would have been shot!" Soult retorted that he "had never even been put on trial". After an audience with the King it was rumoured that Soult would soon be made Minister of War again,[4] but his 'misdemeanours', such as they were, were too recent and, in any event, the period of the Decazes/Dessolles ministry was to be short-lived. Soult went first to his property at Villeneuve l'Etang which had suffered so much at the hands of the Royalist government and also from the soldiers of the Allied armies.[5] Then he quickly made for his home in the village of St-Amans. St-Amans was to be his home base for the rest of his life. He told Saint-Chamans that he would "never again" become involved in French politics.[6]

For the next eleven years, when the senior branch of the Bourbons ruled France, Soult was out of the mainstream of political life. He was wealthy enough to retain his large house in the Rue de l'Université in Paris but at first he and Louise spent much of their time in St-Amans. His redoubtable old mother had looked after his household there and, when he returned, she continued to occupy the place of honour at his table; Soult usually talked to her in the patois of her native 'Black Mountains'. Another important member of the family was his strong-willed spinster sister, Sophie, who was a kind of village dictator and looked after his affairs with a rod of iron when he and Louise were away.

While he was at St-Amans he continued to write his *Memoirs* but, being far more a man of action than of letters, he became increasingly involved in business interests and in the economic development of this very backward area of France. As he said, "If our department were better known and better administered, we could really work miracles."[7]

A year after his return to France Soult's marshal's baton was restored to him, and apart from increasing business enterprises, he became more active socially both in St-Amans and in Paris. His younger brother, Pierre, with his wife, were frequent visitors. Pierre had been his devoted aide-de-camp before serving him as commander of his light cavalry in the Peninsula and then becoming a baron of the Empire. Like his elder brother, he was to lead something of a public life under the July Monarchy. His younger brother Francis, known as Chevalier Soult, who had been a prefect under the Empire and then French consul in Charleston, South Carolina, also visited his elder brother regularly, but sadly died in 1823. The youngest brother, Antoine, had long ago been killed in action.

Naturally Soult's relations with the faithful Brun de Villeret were as close as ever. Brun had advanced quickly in the political world. Not only was he the president of his local council but, under the moderate government of Decazes, he was elected a member of the Lower Chamber for the department of Lozère. As he was a frequent visitor to Paris he made full use of the Soults' town house. He also had a room in their home at St-Amans. The Soult family, in turn, visited him in Lozère. Their first visit was not a great success. Brun had gathered together all his family and the friends who had escorted Soult on his hectic journey south in 1815. On this occasion the Marshal's manner was distinctly cold, which upset Brun very much since most of his guests had risked their lives on his behalf five years before. No doubt Soult did not relish being reminded of these embarrassments nor did he greatly enjoy the idea that, for the time being at least, his former a.d.c. occupied a more prominent position than himself on the political stage.

Soon their relationship was as close as ever again. Brun introduced Hector Soult to the daughter of the Liberal banker and future cabinet minister, Lafitte. Although that introduction did not prosper, it was under Brun's auspices that the charming Hortense met and married the Marquis de Mornay, another Liberal Royalist like Brun himself and the nephew of Napoleon's close adviser, Caulaincourt. More importantly, Brun's family relationship with the ever active Comte de Bruges helped Soult to rebuild his links with the royal family.

The murder of Artois's son, the Duke of Berry, signalled the return to power of right-wing Royalists and, when Artois succeeded to the throne as Charles X on his brother's death, successive ministries continued to be from the right. Against this background Soult has been accused of an undue deference to right-wing Royalism partly because, as a very senior marshal, he bore one of the sceptres at Charles X's coronation, carried out with traditional splendour at Rheims. Also, perhaps rather foolishly, he took part in one of Charles X's religious ceremonies, bearing a lighted candle, thus causing some 'mauvaises plaisanteries' behind his back. Nevertheless, unlike many of the other marshals, he never re-established a close relationship either with Louis XVIII or Charles X. He played no part in the new French invasion of Spain in 1823 which was designed to restore King Ferdinand VII to his throne. The invasion was partly organized by Soult's old subordinate, Victor, as Minister of War, while two of his old comrades, Moncey and Oudinot, provided the professional knowledge that the army commander, Angoulême, badly needed. Nor had he worked his passage back as successfully as the wily Suchet who was a sorrowing figure at Louis XVIII's death bed. He was the only one of Napoleon's marshals not to be made a peer of France until he was included in the contemptuously named 'batch of 76' in 1827. In fact he maintained a consistent political posture as a Liberal Royalist and he took his stand as a Liberal when at last he became a member of the House of Peers. He also retained his close ties with the Duke of Orléans, the future Louis Philippe, but the likelihood of Orléans ever succeeding to the French throne seemed remote when the Duchess of Berry, a few weeks after her husband's assassination, gave birth to a baby, the future Comte de Chambord and eventually the legitimist pretender to the French throne. Soult also maintained Bonapartist ties. For example, he remained like many Napoleonic officers an enthusiastic freemason, receiving to his great delight from British hands the masonic regalia from a Scottish lodge to replace the regalia that he had lost in Spain. Through his son's marriage in 1825 he was also deeply enmeshed in the Napoleonic world. The mother of Moina Saligny, Hector's first wife, had been married to a Neapolitan duke created by King Joseph Bonaparte; she was also the niece of the two famous Clary sisters who became the Queens of Spain and Sweden respectively. The mother then married again Duke Décrès, who had been Napoleon's Minister of Marine. When Moina died at the early age of 24, Hector married as his second wife Marie Louise Desprez, the daughter of Joseph Bonaparte's a.d.c. who, as we have noted, had been such a burden to Soult in Spain and was now a distinguished general.

A visitor who went to see Soult's famous collection of pictures in Paris at this time described him as follows: "We were received by the Marshal, a middle sized though somewhat corpulent personage from 50 to 60 years of age, with dark curling hair rendered rather conspicuous by the bald patch in the middle of his head while his sunburnt complexion accorded well with his dark intelligent eye. His plain stock, plain dark coat and loose trousers which, capacious as they were, could not hide his bow legged form, suggested the soldier rather than the courtier – the marshal rather than the duke. If he had been encountered in London he might have been taken for an East or West Indian sea captain."[8]

At home in the country Soult worked as hard as ever on his various industrial and commercial enterprises. In fact very soon – and particularly as a minister under the July Monarchy – Soult became a good example of the closer links which were beginning to develop between businessmen and the official classes. The wealth that he had acquired during the Napoleonic wars could be put to excellent use in various industrial and commercial enterprises. Indeed he probably had a much keener business sense than any of the other marshals. Such activities developed not only in his native department of the Tarn but in the Midi generally. In 1827, with the support of the Parisian banker, Bérard, he established a company to produce coal in the valley of the River Alès as well as factories in Saint-Pons, Castres and Mazamet. A more ambitous project was the setting up in 1829 of a major industrial combine at Sault-de-Sabo near Albi. Here he went into partnership with the brothers Talabot, acquiring rights for a permanent monopoly of traffic on the neighbouring Beaucaire canal. This was to develop after 1830 into a vast expansion of the business activities of the Talabot brothers, much helped by Soult's membership of the Chamber. There was no suggestion of corruption but it was one of the first examples of close cooperation between businessmen and politicians which was such a feature – and not always an agreeable one – of nineteenth-century France.[9] Despite all his business acumen, Soult was unenthusiastic about railways and he refused to support a project to construct a railway from Bordeaux to Cette through Castres and Mazamet which would have brought much greater economic benefits to the department; doubtless he feared that it would spoil the beauty of the country home that he was planning to build near St-Amans. To this day Mazamet is the terminus of a small branch line.[10] After the Marshal's death his immediate descendants, who were to represent the department of the Tarn for the next 100 years, continued to interest themselves greatly in the affairs of the region.

Soult's other main preoccupation in the country was to build a house for himself and for Louise. He chose a beautiful site just outside the village of St-Amans with a magnificent panoramic view of the Black Mountains, the home of his mother's family, the de Greniers. In building the house he wanted to get away from those turreted 'châteaux' which in imitation of the country's ancestral past would soon spring up all over nineteenth-century France. Soult used to say that he was his own ancestor and he wanted to create a 'pleasure pavilion' in the middle of a park. The whole property amounted to several thousands of hectares – a fair proportion of which is still owned by his descendants. In the middle of his park Soult built 'Soultberg', a name which commemorated both his wife's name and his own. It took three years to build – from 1827 to 1830 – mostly with the help of army engineers and almost inevitably it became known as 'Château Soultberg'. It has some fair-sized reception rooms, a library and a small theatre but it is by no means on a grand scale. It commands magnificent views but is in fact a rather commonplace and uninteresting building.

During all these years Soult played little part in the internal politics of France. On the other hand, as he neared the age of 60, he was beginning to build up a firm reputation as a patriot soldier – the 'grand old man' of Napoleon's marshals. The two other 'greats' – Davout and Masséna – were both dead; Ney and Murat had been executed; Berthier had probably committed suicide, and none of the other marshals came near to equalling Soult's reputation. His portrait was painted for the Paris salon of 1824 and, despite some Royalist sneers, people who saw it commented that he certainly looked as if he was well qualified to command an army. His public pronouncements were also making news. When a neighbour introduced his son as "a comrade from Waterloo", Soult replied sharply, "I did not know that I had any comrade there except Marshal Ney!"

Soult's most famous public relations victory was over the reception at the Austrian embassy when he, Mortier and Marmont were introduced as Marshals Soult, Mortier and Marmont instead of as the Dukes of Dalmatia, Treviso and Ragusa – titles which were all taken from places that were now parts of the Austrian Empire. Characteristically it was Soult who took the lead in the violent public protest. Villèle, the President of the Council or head of the government, tried to effect a compromise by offering to get Soult made Duke of Soult-Austerlitz. Twenty years ago Soult would have gladly accepted such an offer from his Emperor. Now he rejected it with scorn. He refused to visit the Austrian embassy again at that time and, as many patriotic Frenchmen followed his example, Ambassador Apponyi's reception rooms became conspicuously empty.

If the follies of Charles X and of his new chief minister, the Prince de Polignac, had not led to the July Revolution of 1830 Soult might well have continued as an ageing military patriot increasingly well respected but with no part to play in the politics of his country. But the idiocy of the King and of his minister led to the dethronement of Charles X, to the July Revolution and to the succession of Soult's friend, the Duke of Orléans, as King Louis Philippe. So all was changed and once more Soult was brought back into the centre of the French political scene where he was to remain for most of the remainder of his life.

20

THE "ILLUSTRE ÉPÉE"

"FROM THIS MOMENT Soult draws his sword and throws away the scabbard!" This was the characteristically dramatic – or melodramatic – remark which Soult is supposed to have made when he heard the news of the July Revolution while visiting one of his factories at Sault-de-Sabo near Albi.[1] He wrote at once to the provisional government offering his services. After fifteen years of comparative inactivity he remained ambitious; his intelligence and ability for concentrated and hard work were as great as ever; and at 61 he longed to return to the centre of affairs.

The July Revolution was something of a political enigma. How far was it an echo of 1789? Some Republicans, who were to take the lead 18 years later, evidently thought that it was. Louis Blanc was an admirer of Robespierre; Lamartine admired the Girondins; Lafayette was once more commandant of the National Guard. For their part, Guizot and his friends saw it as a copy of England's Glorious Revolution of 1688 with King Louis Philippe as William III. Were the ministers now to be all powerful with a king, as Thiers proclaimed, "who reigned but did not rule"? Certainly there were strong left-wing political forces which had lain dormant during the reigns of Louis XVIII and Charles X not only in Paris but all over France. Against a background of much social and economic distress there were also similar political upheavals throughout Europe. In France Republican and more extreme groups were given greater rein. But there were other quite different strands – bourgeois supporters of the new regime, the Orléanists, the Bonapartists for whom nostalgic memories of the Empire were newly strengthened by the so-called 'legend of St Helena', and, especially in western France, the Legitimists, the supporters of the dethroned Charles X and his family.

To bring some order into the state of confusion, a strong central government and an efficient and vigorous army was badly needed. Louis Philippe as 'King of the French' had at first neither of these. His first ministry was an association of liberal and conservative Orléanists with the banker, Lafitte, as President of the Council and Marshal Gérard as Minister of War. Gérard was an intrepid soldier – he had to no avail urged Grouchy to march to the sound of the guns at Waterloo – but he was a timid minister unsuitable to deal with the riots and more serious civil disturbances which were soon to break out all over France.[2]

Abroad the new regime was looked upon with intense suspicion and alarm. The July Revolution seemed partly to have caused the other European uprisings. Would the other great powers try to take action against France? Moreover, the friendless government of Louis Philippe had taken over a new commitment in Algeria. How far could this be sustained against so many internal and external pressures? A strong minister was needed at the centre who could not only provide some stability but also turn the army into an efficient and homogeneous force which could deal with France's many foreign and Algerian problems as well as with domestic troubles. Marshal Soult seemed to meet this need. The King used to refer to him as his old comrade in arms from the Revolutionary Wars. As Duke of Orléans, Louis Philippe had fought briefly in the Republican army at Valmy before going over to the Allies. Soult was by far the most prestigious of Napoleon's surviving marshals. Later the King was to make some political use of the 'St Helena legend' and here was a Napoleonic marshal who had been strong enough from time to time to defy the Emperor; he had been a Liberal Royalist under Louis Philippe's predecessors but he had also been a robust patriot who had won much approval on such occasions as the affair of the Austrian embassy. The King guessed that he would be little interested or skilled in day-to-day politics but, as he was determined not to be relegated to a largely ceremonial role, it would be very helpful to have a ' strong man' at his side through whom he could himself try to govern. More important still, he needed a highly efficient professional soldier to reorganize the army in order to defend France in her present isolated state and to deal with the many internal problems.

Soult's papers and correspondence have made it clear that he quickly built up a close personal and political relationship with the King, with Queen Marie Amélie and, even more important, with their able son, now called the Duke of Orléans, who was so tragically killed in a carriage accident before he could succeed to the throne. Orléans was to marry a Mecklenburg princess with whom Louise Soult, herself a German, was soon on close terms. Soult was also on friendly personal terms with the King's other sons. He was careful to maintain these close ties. There are often slighting references to Louis Philippe's 'illustre épée' but the links between the King, his family and his famous subject was a unique feature of the July Monarchy.[3]

In November 1830 Soult succeeded Gérard as Minister of War. "I am going to Paris to make an army," he told a friend. "That was my first duty in France's present situation!"[4] When he began work in the ministry he resumed the formidable timetable that he had adopted sixteen years before, as Louis XVIII's Minister of War. He rose at 4 am and was at his office an hour later working through the day with only a brief midday meal. In the evening there were receptions and dinner parties which often turned into working dinners. At night the servants had strict orders to wake him if there was any hint of a 'happening'. As the work load increased he had an annex built on to his mansion in the Rue de l'Université in order to make offices for some of the staff of the ministry. This was 'taking work home' with a vengeance! Of course much of his time was spent out of the office, accompanying the King on tours of inspection, reviewing troops on his own or dealing personally with many of the civil disturbances that plagued the early years of the reign.[5]

Soult's first period as Minister of War lasted from 1830 to 1834. Following the death of Casimir Périer in 1832 he became President of the Council as well. During his initial period at the Ministry of War he had two main tasks. The first was to use the army, as he found it, to deal with France's many problems in a very unfriendly Europe and with some equally serious internal problems. His other more long-term task was the reorganization of the French army.

Of the foreign problems the most immediate related to Belgium. Leopold of Saxe Coburg, the widower of George IV's daughter, Charlotte, had accepted the throne of Belgium when the country broke away from the Netherlands. He was to marry Louis Philippe's daughter and, as King of the Belgians, he was firmly supported by both France and Britain. This was another serious disturbance to the concert of Europe, like the Revolutionary movements which were active elsewhere on the continent. The Belgian situation was handled through an ambassadors' conference in London at which Talleyrand represented France. Like Soult, Talleyrand had his own direct link with the King through Louis Philippe's sister, Princess Adelaide. By the time Soult became Minister of War there remained many outstanding Belgian problems. Marshal Gérard commanded the troops but serving with him was the Duke of Orléans so that, in addition to his formal communications with Gérard, Soult obtained much background information from Orléans with whom he corresponded regularly.[6] Soult had first to ensure that France could sustain any general European attack which might be launched in support of the government of the Hague. With the full agreement of Casimir Périer, the President of the Council, he adopted the old Napoleonic device of bringing forward the call-up date of the class of 1831 and also encouraged the enlistment of volunteers. Reinforcements were brought back from eastern France and a sizeable reserve army, partly composed of National Guardsmen, was based near Paris. The French army supporting the Belgians was stationed a few miles from Waterloo. It was now required, in accordance with the directions of the London Conference, to withdraw behind the French frontier. In a letter to Soult, Orléans strongly objected to this, partly because Antwerp was still held by the Dutch, while the Belgians were quite unreliable and constantly created difficult administrative problems. Soult told both Gérard and Orléans that they must accept the decisions of the ambassadors' conference "since the wind from London was blowing sharper than ever".[7] But he also insisted on sending a number of senior French officers to occupy key positions in the Belgian army. The most distinguished of these was his old 'bugbear' from the Peninsular War, François Desprez, King Joseph's old a.d.c. who had made the famous ride from Paris to Moscow carrying Joseph's violent complaints to his brother about Soult. Since then the wheel had turned. Desprez had created a staff college in France before serving with distinction in the French invasion of Spain in

1823 as well as in Algeria, while his daughter had married, as his second wife, Soult's son, Hector. Soult now sent him to organize a Staff College in Belgium; he bacame a Belgian national and he died in harness in Brussels. Soult sent other military specialists to Belgium, including an able artilleryman, General Evain, who also became a Belgian national. However, he was quick to recall other officers, including an infantry general, who were unsatisfactory.

When Soult succeeded Casimir Périer as head of the government he was still faced with the difficult problem of Antwerp, which the Dutch refused to give up in defiance of the London Conference. Moreover, some of the other European powers remained sympathetic to King William of Holland, whose family was closely related to the royal family of Prussia. There was therefore a serious risk of a direct attack on France herself. Writing to Soult at this time, Orléans asserted, "France must make its intentions clear: it is for you, Marshal, beyond anyone who can decide this!"[8]

Soult had in his cabinet the three political heavyweights, Guizot, Thiers and Broglie but, as President of the Council with the full support of the King, he played an important part in the exchanges that now took place. In his correspondence with Orléans he commented that the political initiatives of the European powers sounded suspiciously like the Brunswick Manifesto of 1792. This was the right patriotic note to strike. Sharp notes in this sense were sent to the various French diplomatic representatives in European capitals and Soult declared publicly that "war was possible – even likely".[9]

To Soult and the rest of the Cabinet the capture of Antwerp was the touchstone: it would show whether the other European powers were prepared to go to war on behalf of Holland. Antwerp must be captured since the Dutch were in flagrant violation of past decisions of the London Conference. Soult struck the right patriotic note by proclaiming publicly, "We have never asked permission to fire a gun in Europe. There is no need to ask permission to fire 40 guns now!"[10] When plans were made to capture Antwerp there were the usual problems of cooperation with the Belgians who were understandably averse to letting the French take the lead in the operation. But it was evident to Soult that the untrained Belgian troops, even with French officers advising them, would be quite unable to take the city. So, with the full agreement of the British, Antwerp was attacked by the French at the end of 1832. It took about a month to capture the city. The French *Official Gazette* was right when it stated plainly that "France had settled by force a question that had obstinately resisted a settlement for two years. At the same time an alliance had been built up with England which was to last a long time."[11]

Although France and England were frequently to be at odds with each other in the future, the London Conference laid a groundwork of cooperation which not only brought France out of her position of isolation but at least tipped the balance away from the fierce Anglo-French hostility of the last 100 years. Talleyrand in London played a large part in all this but Soult's intervention was also important. A few years later Soult was to make another major contribution to cementing ties between the two nations. In recognition of his services to Belgian independence as head of the French government King Leopold conferred on him the Grand Cordon of the new Order of Leopold, with the patent dated suitably from Antwerp.

As Minister of War, Soult had to provide an army for Casimir Périer's belligerent expedition against the Austrians at Ancona. Developments in Spain and Portugal necessitated keeping a French army of observation in the Pyrenees once more. The situation in the two countries was much the same with youthful and foolish queens – Isabella in Spain and Maria Gloria in Portugal – being threatened by uncles who disputed their rights to their thrones and advocated more extreme conservative policies. France and England maintained cautious if mutually suspicious support for the two young monarchs. Thiers and some other French ministers advocated armed intervention but Soult and Talleyrand favoured the more cautious policy of the King and, partly because Soult controlled the army, their views prevailed.

The extension of French interests in Algeria was also a constant strain on French military resources. Almost immediately after he had assumed office in 1830, Soult had to send substantial reinforcements to help his old divisional commander, Clausel, who was the first of many governors general appointed by Louis Philippe's government. This action much depleted the army that he was trying to build up to defend France in case of war with Europe. These governors general ruled over Algeria, with varying success, during the period of the July Monarchy. There were serious problems of morale and the Duke of Orléans emphasized to Soult that soldiers returning from North Africa often affected the discipline of the rest of the army. Soult has been criticized for not himself taking a more active part in the Algerian War. His experience of fighting guerrillas in Andalusia might have proved invaluable. But he was compelled to leave active operations to those on the spot. On one point, however, he was absolutely firm, in opposition to Guizot and other ministers. For the present Algeria must remain a military problem, both in day-to-day operations and in matters of colonization. He set his face determinedly against the appointment of a civilian governor general and it was on this issue that he was eventually to resign.

Soult also faced a whole range of law and order problems. His old opponent, Wellington, was concerned with potential Chartist riots in England. Soult had much more serious difficulties. Economic distress and Republican sentiment had led to outbreaks of violence in Lyons and elsewhere. In 1831 Soult acted as military adviser to the Duke of Orléans in suppressing serious riots in Lyons. Once again his old assistant, Brun de Villeret, who was the military commander in the neighbouring department, provided some additional troops and acted as Soult's chief of staff. Three years later Soult was called on to quell an even more violent insurrection in Lyons, and did so with great firmness. There were also a number of serious disturbances in Paris itself, provoked partly by Legitimist religious ceremonies on the anniversary of the murder of the Duke of Berry, and partly by the funeral of the left-wing General Lamarque. These riots had strong Republican support. Louis Blanc suggests that Soult himself showed some sympathy for some of the uprisings as if he wanted to gain supreme power for himself with the help of the army.[12] This suggestion seems rather absurd in view of the Marshal's very close relations with the King and with the royal family. There is no evidence to suggest that he wanted to become a kind of French Bernadotte or an earlier version of General Boulanger.

There were also Legitimist uprisings in the Vendée. These were rendered more dangerous at first by the presence of the widowed Duchess of Berry who landed in the south in the summer of 1834 and proclaimed her small son, the future Comte de Chambord, as King of France. In what turned out to be a ludicrous chain of events, she was captured and then wrote to Soult, as being the only member of the government grand enough to receive her letters, complaining of her conditions of imprisonment and reminding him of her husband's 'helpfulness' when Soult himself had returned from exile in 1819. As the Duke of Berry had cheerfully informed Soult at the time that he deserved to be shot, his wife's present letters were not very persuasive. But while the duchess was in prison it was discovered that she was heavily pregnant, either as a result of a liaison or a secret marriage with a Neapolitan courtier. Her father-in-law at once disowned her; the government felt they could safely release her and she returned to southern Italy, leaving the Legitimist cause in considerable disarray.

Throughout these different crises Soult pursued with single-minded devotion and intense hard work the effective rebuilding of the French army. During the period from 1815 to 1851 there were no less than 27 Ministers of War in France with an average length of service of only sixteen months. Moreover, the minister was almost invariably a senior army officer and, while exercising great authority within the army, was usually under the control of the civilian government. The House of Peers and the Chamber were full of active or retired soldiers but there was no real 'army lobby' which had any influence on the government of the day. The great exception to these short-term appointments was Soult, who as a result of his nine years overall service at the Ministry of War during the July Monarchy stood the best chance of achieving a continuity of policy. A recent military historian has described his work at the ministry as perhaps his greatest contribution to his country.[13]

Despite his length of service there and the support of the King and of the Duke of Orléans, Soult's army reforms faced strong opposition. This came from many of his civilian cabinet colleagues and also from the Chamber where, in addition to the army officers and ex-officers, there were numerous 'pacifist' elements among both the Orléanists and the Republicans.

A particular problem arose over the higher direction of the army. During the Restoration, infantry and cavalry committees had been established to give some unity to each of these arms of the service. The two committees had then been combined into a central committee. Soult, who had vigorously supported the creation of a staff college by General Desprez, gave his full support also to this central committee in the hope that it would become a kind of 'Conseil Supérieur de la Guerre'. But various ministers and members of the Chamber were hostile, fearing that it would give the Minister of War too much power. Conservative elements in the army also regarded the central committee as little more than a collection of interfering upstarts. When Soult left office in 1834 the central committee was abolished.

Soult faced many other problems. In 1818 Louis XVIII's reforming Minister of War, Marshal Gouvion St Cyr, had introduced into the army an element of conscription – the 'Appel' – to supplement the voluntary system originally guaranteed by the Restoration Charter. Conscripts were to serve for six years but there was a ballot system which enabled those better off to buy themselves out. This limited form of conscription was designed to add an annual contingent of 40,000 men which would provide for an army of some 240,000. In his *Journal*, de Castellane, eventually to become a marshal himself, strongly criticized many of St Cyr's reforms. He recognized that 'the Owl', as St Cyr was known to the soldiers because of his solitary personality, was highly intelligent – as well as being an excellent violinist. But he had limited regimental experience and was remote from normal service life – the exact opposite of Soult. He had also created a corps of inspectors general who were primarily responsible for army promotions. They were of lieutenant general rank and they made the army very top-heavy. Furthermore, with the laudable intention of preventing favouritism, he required all officers to serve at least four years in any grade before being promoted. This slow rate of advancement caused many of the more active and intelligent officers to leave the army in disgust. The invasion of Spain in 1823, although it was more or less a 'military promenade', was something of a shambles, exposing St Cyr's reforms as little more than skin-deep. The cavalry and artillery had been neglected at the expense of the infantry; staff at various levels were too numerous and too costly; transport was inadequate; there was a medley of uniforms but poor equipment. In criticizing these shortcomings both privately and publicly, Soult must have wondered whether he would ever have the chance of bringing in the reforms that were so badly needed.

After the Revolution of 1830 the army was still in poor shape and there were now many additional problems. A number of ex-Bonapartist officers who had refused to serve earlier now came forward, like Soult himself, to offer their services to Louis Philippe. There were also the so-called 'Heroes of the Revolution' – many with strong Republican sympathies, who joined the reconstituted National Guard. As Minister of the Interior, Guizot was at first responsible for this new National Guard. He divided it into two regiments, one static and one mobile, while National Guard units were attached to each regular army regiment.

One of Soult's first tasks at the Ministry of War was to make the regular army less top-heavy. He dealt drastically with some of the senior ex-Bonapartist officers as well as with St Cyr's inspectors general. In a purge of senior officers he got rid of

88 lieutenant generals and 136 'maréchaux de camp'. He was also very doubtful about the military capabilities and indeed political sympathies of the new National Guard. The commandant – the age-long Lafayette – was retired and the various elements of the National Guard were brought together to fulfil a purely defensive role that was quite distinct from the regular army.

Soult also made drastic reforms to the system of regular army promotion. Instead of officers having to remain at least four years in one rank he devised a more elastic procedure. Junior lieutenants had to have served two years as an NCO or to have been a cadet either at St Cyr or at the Ecole Polytechnique which, incidentally, Soult saved from virtual extinction. Afterwards about half the promotions to higher rank would still depend on seniority but the remainder would be 'at the King's discretion', thus providing for a fast promotion stream which could be speeded up still more in time of war. There were soon some quick promotions, especially in the technical and less glamorous branches of the service. Inevitably Soult was criticized for seeking to surround himself with a clique of youthful military supporters. But this was an exaggeration. General Bonnet, the personnel chief of the artillery department, was probably nearer the truth when he commented that Soult's relationship with the army was "like that of an old man with a young wife."[14] These promotion reforms lasted until modern times.

There remained the larger question of the length of military service. Soult had inherited an army that was quite insufficient for France's defence and for her overseas commitments. Only about a third of the army were regulars, so the conscript element was of great importance. Soult had to decide between a larger annual intake of conscripts with a shorter length of service or a smaller intake with a longer period of service. Remembering the severe losses suffered by the brave but ill-trained 'Marie Louises' during the last years of the Empire he had little doubt that quality was more important than quantity. As usual he wasted little time in theoretical discussions. His aim was to build up an army of half a million men with a trained reserve of 200,000. Under the Soult Law of 1832 the length of military conscription was fixed at seven years. By cutting down the number of exemptions he hoped for an annual intake of 120,000 men, with the ultimate aim of creating an army, part regular and part conscript, of half a million with a substantial reserve comprising those men who had obtained a temporary or provisional exemption from conscription. He also provided barracks and training cadres for the reserves. His plans were much curtailed by the 'pacific' elements in the government and the Chamber who regarded a half-trained reserve army as a threat to the state. The annual conscript intake was limited to 80,000 and a reserve army hardly came into being at all. In the end the number of army effectives never approached Soult's goal of half a million and, in any case, this would have been a smaller number than Bismarck was able to raise among the German states in 1870.

In addition to these organizational reforms, Soult concerned himself with every aspect of army life, seeking to put right the inadequacies of past years. In cooperation with the radically minded Duke of Orléans and, from time to time, with Thiers, he tackled the difficult problems of training, pay, service regulations, equipment and uniforms. He introduced improvements in military law and reformed army prisons. Naturally he made sure that his native Languedoc was included among the reforms. A big army remount depot was built in Castres and the old cavalry barracks was reconstructed as one of the most attractive military headquarters in the Midi. Nor did he forget his wife's home town, the sword-making centre of Solingen in the Rhineland, which began to supply swords for the French army. Naturally, such special attention to local interests aroused suspicions of corruption. There were critical articles in the press but these were not substantiated and Soult was awarded damages for an article in *The Tribune* alleging bribery. In fact Soult was wealthy enough to make accusations of this nature unlikely.

While he was carrying out his military reforms the army was actively engaged in Belgium or in operations against civil disturbances in France. After the Belgian campaign it was concentrated in big military establishments at St-Omer, at Wattignies and at Rocroy. His friend and collaborator, Orléans, commanded a mobile reserve at Versailles but both paid visits of inspection all over France. Orléans was in fact as well informed about military problems as Soult himself. Soult busied himself with strengthening France's various frontier fortresses ranging from Dunkirk in the north to Antibes, close to the existing frontier with Piedmont, in the south. He also inspected with the King the newly constructed port of Cherbourg and coastal fortifications on the coast of Brittany where he had been army commander in 1814.

The fortification of Paris itself was another important defence priority. Although he had been so busily engaged in defending southern France at the time, he was well aware of the ease with which the Allied armies had captured Paris after Napoleon's magnificent campaign in the north-east in 1814. Effective defence of the capital was urgently needed. To the governments's surprise, the issue raised much indignation both in the Chamber and outside. Some people feared that the fortifications might be used against Parisians themselves while others thought they would spoil the beauty of the city. Accordingly, preliminary work on the fortification was stopped. Most sensible politicians and soldiers hoped that it would soon be resumed and Orléans told his friend Soult, "I always find you accessible to truth at the most difficult moments."[15] However, Soult's civilian colleagues, especially Guizot and Thiers, had strong and often conflicting views on the subject which was not resolved finally until Soult's long period of office as head of government after 1839.

The Marshal's military reforms, now and later, were carried out with varying degrees of support or opposition from his civilian colleagues. What he achieved was partly due to his own determination and partly to the support of the King and of Orléans. In the end he did at least lay the foundations of an efficient and united army which made France a formidable military power for succeeding decades – even able to recover from the disasters of 1870. Despite such crises as Louis Napoleon's military coup in 1851, General Boulanger or the Dreyfus affair, there is some truth in the comment by Marshal Franchet d'Esperey that "as a result of Soult's revolution the army got away from party conflicts and became completely 'national'. Whatever were the political regimes it was France that the army served."[16]

Of course Soult's reputation has suffered from the much greater reputations of Guizot and Thiers, both of whom were also prolific writers. Indeed it is often hard to realize that Soult was an important minister under Louis Philippe at all. He was quite different from anyone else in the Cabinet. He did not write elegantly nor did he speak clearly in the Chamber; indeed his increasing years combined with his strong Languedoc accent made him hard to understand when he was speaking in public. However, at Cabinet meetings, in his own office in the Ministry of War or when talking to the King he had a strong and decisive personality. With Casimir Périer, President of the Council in 1831-2, he reached a fair *modus vivendi*. This was important because Casimir Périer was an able man who often presided over meetings of ministers instead of the King. Having once threatened to replace Soult by his old antagonist, Jourdan, he decided, according to Guizot, that the government could not do without "this valuable sword".[17] Casimir Périer did not hamper any of Soult's army reforms and all the ministers agreed broadly on the policy towards Belgium. There are indeed some indications that Soult was regarded abroad as being more influential than in fact he was. Lord Aberdeen commented in the British House of Commons in September 1831 that he did not trust Marshal Soult "since he seemed to be getting all that he wanted in Algiers, Italy and Portugal".

Soult was very valuable to Louis Philippe and to the government in another way. At a time when the 'legend of St Helena' was beginning to take hold of people's imagination it was useful to have at hand a very distinguished Napoleonic marshal. The government wanted to get some benefit from imperial nostalgia; the Arc de Triomphe was nearly finished; the Emperor's statue was restored to its place on the monument in the Place Vendôme. But what made Soult even more valuable was that his relationship with his old master had been, to say the least, 'at arm's length'. So he was just the man to deal with some of the surviving members of the Bonaparte family. Queen Hortense, Napoleon's stepdaughter, had provoked much Bonapartist enthusiasm when she visited Paris and, a few years later, her son, Louis Napoleon, was to make two rather futile attempts to seize power. Napoleon's surviving brothers, Joseph and Lucien, were firmly kept out of France and Joseph was quite sure that this was due to "the malign influence" of his former chief of staff, Soult.

During the period 1832-4, when Soult succeeded Casimir Périer as President of the Council, Soult's relations with his two leading civilian colleagues, Guizot and Thiers, became seriously strained. They were strongly contrasting characters: Guizot, the dry Protestant, an ex-history professor with an admiration for English institutions that bored most Frenchmen; and Thiers, a fat, vivacious, bespectacled little man with an ardent admiration for Napoleon whose history he was soon to write. In their different ways they both scorned and disliked Soult, partly for his obstinacy in Cabinet and partly for his poor performance in the Chamber. They were also jealous and suspicious of his close relations with the King, recognizing Louis Philippe's apparent intention of trying to rule with Soult acting as his agent.

Guizot, however, was a reasonable man and in his *Memoirs* he provided what must be a fair assessment of Soult at this time. "He had no established ideas or political objectives, no decided party and no permanent supporters. His profession and his fame enabled him to dispense with them. He conducted policy as he had commanded in war 'for the good of the state' and he was always ready to change courses or his allies as occasion demanded. Using a kind of 'political polygamy' he was not deficient in the spirit of government, in resolution or in perseverance. It would be equally dangerous to rely on his discretion or to mistrust his fidelity. He required security and also his own personal advantage. He had no fear of responsibility and he covered the King with his name. The King found him in no way over-pretentious except for occasional bouts of short-lived jealousy. His mind was rude and somewhat incoherent. But he was fertile in resource, of indefatigable energy and very strong physically. He had great natural authority even with his equals and enough artifice to evade embarrassing discussion."[18]

At first Soult himself was particularly contemptuous of Guizot and of his ally, the Duke of Broglie. "As an old soldier their arrogance and their ability aroused his antipathy".[19] His relations with Guizot were to improve, however, over the years. On the other hand Soult could not stand the sight of Thiers, once hurling at him in a moment of fury the untranslatable obscenity "foutriquet".[20] Soult's differences with both Guizot and Thiers were personal but they were also political. The Lyons riots of 1834, which Soult firmly suppressed, caused strains in the Cabinet as to the fate of the ringleaders. The crisis in Spain, when Don Carlos tried to seize power from the young Queen and her mother, the Regent, provoked disagreement among ministers as well; the bellicose Thiers still favoured armed intervention but the King and Soult remained firmly opposed to it. However, the occasion of Soult's resignation in 1834 was over Algeria. There had been continual problems with a series of different governors general. As has been noted, Soult was determined that the conquest and eventual settlement of Algeria must, for the present, remain a military problem; a civilian governor general would only be appointed, as it were, 'over his dead body'. In the event this issue was used as an excuse for Guizot and Thiers to combine in getting rid of Soult. In July 1834 the Marshal resigned in high dudgeon, departing immediately for his distant home in St-Amans.

His resignation was highly embarrassing both to the King and to the royal family on personal and on political grounds, as testified by their agitated letters to him on his departure. As the King commented mournfully to a foreign diplomat, "I am aware of Soult's faults but he had very many excellent qualities. Among other things he never courted popularity."[21] In his *Memoirs* Guizot was to write very apologetically about Soult's departure. "He always supported govenment policy," he declared, "and his defection split the Cabinet. His departure was indeed a double fault because we were really quite wrong to press for a civilian government in Algiers."[22] Talleyrand also criticized Soult's enforced departure. He and Soult had never been close during the Empire but they had appreciated each other's activities over the Belgian problem, while Soult had learnt something about the importance of close Franco-British relations from Talleyrand's highly successful diplomatic mission in London.

Soult was now 65. His first three and a half years as one of Louis Philippe's chief ministers had been both eventful and important. He still retained in full measure the admiration and affection of the King, the Duke of Orléans and the rest of the royal family. This was his strength. When he went home the King left him in no doubt about his own feelings. "I ceaselessly regret that you are so far away," he wrote. "I have so much appreciated your good, loyal and great services to France and to me all the time you have been my minister."[23]

21

AMBASSADOR EXTRAORDINARY

OVER THE NEXT few years the King made repeated efforts to persuade Soult to return to office. As Orléans wrote to him: "My father longs for your return to head the government which is far too much dominated by 'the coterie' and the doctrinaires." By this of course he meant Guizot and his friends. He added that there was "torpor and stagnation" in the army after Soult's departure.[1]

Meanwhile the government, which had been on such close terms with the Whigs in England since the settlement of the Belgian problem, must have viewed with some concern the possible return to power of the Tories led by Sir Robert Peel and the Duke of Wellington. This was not to occur for a year or two but the duke was one of the most famous figures in England and his friendship was important to France. Soult had become acquainted with his old antagonist when he was Louis XVIII's Minister of War in 1814 while Wellington was the British ambassador in Paris. This was one of the reasons why Louis Philippe and his ministers decided to send Soult to London as his special representative at Queen Victoria's coronation in 1838. The visit turned out to be a spectacular success and Soult himself regarded it as one of the greatest episodes of his career.

A young official in the tax office who was in the crowd watching the coronation procession passing through the streets of London wrote in his diary that Marshal Soult undoubtedly stole the show. "His stern features, his snow white hair and his solemn red face ... did he use rouge ... made an unforgettable impression on all the bystanders."[2] Here was the last and by now much the most famous of the great soldiers who had fought alongside Napoleon in what was then called the Great War. Moreover, so much of his fighting had been against the British. He had been one of the great organizers of the formidable invasion army based on Boulogne, 34 years before, and he might well have led the advance guard of that army; he had pursued Sir John Moore all across northern Spain in 1808-9 and, having failed to defeat him, had put up a memorial in his honour; he had been driven out of northern Portugal by Wellington but, due to the follies of King Joseph and Marshal Victor, he had narrowly failed to surround Wellington's army after Talavera; he had fought a bloody battle against the British at Albuera; he had been close to trapping Wellington again at the Tormes in 1813; he had with difficulty held the British in check for months in southern France when Napoleon's Empire was tottering and, as a man of action rather than a military clerk, he had watched ineffectively while his imperial master was defeated at Waterloo. This great Frenchman, who had only glimpsed England before through the eye of a telescope across the Channel coast, now rode triumphantly along the streets of London. It has been said that arrivals at the Abbey at the end of the procession were greeted with loud applause ... "the loudest being for the Duke of Wellington until Marshal Soult appeared".[3]

The Marshal's coronation coach must have caused quite a sensation. It was shaped like a gondola, coloured blue with the upper parts painted in silver. Soult's armorial bearings covered the side panels of the coach and the ducal coronets which surmounted the lamps appeared to be encrusted with jewels. The whole equipment cost what was at that time the considerable sum of 42,000 francs.[4]

The official welcome accorded to Soult was very warm. The bitter and often obscene cartoons of Napoleon by Gilray and Crookshank were still on sale in London and the young Queen had recorded that the French Emperor was "our bitterest foe", but she received Marshal Soult graciously and made him feel very much a friend. However, the main responsibility for looking after the veteran fell upon the Duke of Wellington. Characteristically, the Duke confided to George Seymour beforehand that he hoped that Soult's arrival would not coincide with the anniversary of one of his defeats. "Indeed he would be puzzled to find a day in the present season when he would not have a disagreeable recollection!" However, when the two old soldiers met in Lady Salisbury's drawing room, Wellington stole up behind the Marshal, saying, "I've got you at last!" and very soon they were recalling former battles and campaigns with great animation and delight. Lady Salisbury described Marshal Soult as a "gentlemanlike old man – rather as I would have expected William Penn or George Washington to be like". However, as a British patriot, she could not help remarking that, although he and Wellington were exactly the same age, Wellington's eyes shone more brightly than Soult's![5]

The 69-year-old Marshal was accompanied on his visit by his son the Marquis of Dalmatia, the future ambassador, by his son in law, the Marquis de Mornay, and by members of two famous Bonapartist families, the Duke of Vicenza (Caulaincourt) and the Duke of Bassano (Maret). With great tact the British also attached to his suite for the visit two members of the Napier family who, since Peninsular days, had been his warm admirers, Colonel Napier and his cousin, Admiral Napier.

Marshal Soult was invited to take part in most of the festivities which followed the coronation. On July 9 he was an honoured guest at the great review in Hyde Park in the presence of the Queen. In command of the parade was the Marquess of Anglesey who had lost a leg at Waterloo, and among the troops who marched past the review stand were Soult's old opponents, the Rifle Brigade, the regiment which, with others in the Light Division, formed the rearguard during Moore's retreat to Corunna. Two days later Soult accompanied the Duke of Wellington when, as colonel in chief, he inspected the regiment in the Tower of London. Soult subsequently paid another three-hour visit to the Tower, when he was received with full military honours. Later he was present with the Duke of Wellington at a dinner given in his honour by the Royal Artillery at Woolwich. Probably no foreign soldier, as distinct from a sovereign, had been given so many military honours during these hectic post-coronation weeks. The Marshal was also an enthusiastic sightseer and delighted his hosts by paying long visits to Windsor Castle, to the British Museum, to the National Gallery, to London Docks and even to a house of correction. In return for all this hospitality he gave, in conjunction with the French ambassador, two magnificent dinners and balls at which members of the royal family and most of the leading political and social figures in London were present.[6]

Soult's visit to England was nevertheless rather more than just a splendid military, social and sightseeing affair. After spending about a fortnight in London he and his party set off on a rapid but comprehensive visit to Manchester, Liverpool, the Black Country and Birmingham. Visits to the industrial North and Midlands were at that time comparatively rare even for the royal family and absolutely unprecedented for a distinguished foreigner. But Soult, the French patriot, anglophile and shrewd businessman, was determined to see for himself something of industrial England.

Accompanied by his family and the other distingished Frenchmen, with the two members of the Napier family still in attendance, he travelled to Manchester where he visited various factories and public institutions, including a large industrial warehouse in the centre of the town which had been brilliantly illuminated for the occasion. Speeches were exchanged at an elaborate banquet when Soult declared that he would never forget the welcome the town had given him. True to his early rising habits, he then left at 6 am for Liverpool by the newly extended Liverpool and Manchester Railway and, when his train was delayed outside Liverpool by some derailed goods trucks, he seems to have finished most of the rest of the journey to the Adelphi Hotel on foot. Here he waived aside the offer of breakfast so as to lose no time in visiting the St John's Market and other industrial establishments. A launch had been put at his disposal so that he could get the best possible view of the dockyards, the shipping and the factories that lined the wharves. With his usual tireless energy, he embarked so early on the launch that several of the English guests were left behind. After a two-hour cruise, the Marshal disembarked and visited the Exchange, the Town Hall, the Custom House and some ships in the harbour. Another meal had been prepared for him in one of the ships, but in his eagerness to see as much as possible in the short time at his disposal, he gracefully refused to call a halt to his hectic progress. This continued until his exhausted hosts were finally able to lead the elderly Marshal and his weary party to a magnificent dinner at the Town Hall followed by a reception attended by a thousand guests. The guest of honour mingled freely with them, using as interpreters his son, his son-in-law and the Napier family. This rapid and detailed visit by a man of 69 has surely some parallel in modern times.

On the following day the tireless Soult and his party visited the Menai Bridge by sea and immediately afterwards left for Wolverhampton and Dudley, having a good look en route at the famous Iron Bridge over the River Severn. Once again he moved so fast that he had finished the lunch provided for him before his principal host had appeared. The party then left for Birmingham.

The visit to Birmingham was the highlight of the whole tour. After inspecting a great number of industrial establishments, including an armaments factory, the Marshal and his party were entertained to a lavish party at the Town Hall. In his first speech at dinner Soult paid a warm tribute to the city and hoped there would be a great increase in the links between Birmingham and France. Then in answer to another toast he made a second, more important speech. After praising the skill and magnanimity of the English, and of the Duke of Wellington against whom he had fought so often, he went on to express the firm hope that there should be peace between France and England for ever. "From henceforth there should be no possibility of war between the two countries. A perpetual alliance had been established so that there should be no rivalry between them save in the arts of peace. As neighbours France and England had too many interests in common to disturb that peace!" These high-flown sentiments were received with great applause.

Next day, still unwearied, the Marshal left Birmingham, visited Kenilworth, had breakfast at Warwick Castle and returned that evening to London. There, after delaying his departure from England to attend another royal reception, he finally embarked from Sheerness to return to France on July 29. The Channel was rough and at first he thought he would have to land at Boulogne. In the event he sailed on to Le Havre but there was a muddle over the reception arrangements. A guard of honour was hastily assembled but the civic authorities had not been informed and Soult was merely greeted by the prefect in his private capacity. So, instead of carrying out a full day's inspection of Le Havre as he had intended, he and his party drove straight on to Paris. The *Times* of August 3 1838 could not resist pointing out the confusion awaiting him on his return to France after the enthusiasm of his reception in England. It suggested that suitable punishments might well be meted out to those responsible![7]

No doubt Louis Blanc much exaggerated when he described Soult's visit as the most significant event of the Queen's coronation.[8] But the visit had undoubtedly been a great success. The July Monarchy badly needed to retain her ties with England as her principal European ally. Talleyrand had laid the foundation in the London Conference on Belgium: Guizot was an anglophile to the limit: royal visits were soon to be exchanged between Louis Philippe and Queen Victoria. But this tour by the famous Marshal Soult, Britain's friendly foe, was an important element in the whole process. As for his forthright speech on Anglo-French relations in

Birmingham, due allowance must be made for his natural euphoria towards the end of a unique and exciting journey. There were of course to be many serious difficulties between France and England in the future ... the problem of Mehemet Ali almost at once ... sharp colonial rivalry ... Fashoda ... and other problems. But it may not be too much of an exaggeration to say that Soult's whole visit including his Birmingham speech was a faint and distant pointer to the 'Entente Cordiale'.

22

ONE OF THE LONGEST TERMS AS HEAD OF GOVERNMENT IN FRENCH HISTORY

SOULT HELD THE TITLE OF President of the Council from 1839 to 1847 – with one short break in 1840 – one of the longest terms as head of government in French history. Naturally the significance of the post varied greatly according to the holder. It was not necessarily a sinecure. Early in Louis Philippe's reign Casimir Périer certainly gave it reality, and so too, on occasion, did Soult, notably in presiding over a left and right of centre coalition without any of the leading politicians such as Thiers, Guizot or Broglie. He was then very much in control under the general direction of his great admirer, the King. During his second period as President of the Council from 1840 to 1847 he remained a powerful figure during the early years and, as Minister of War until 1845, he retained a firm grip on the army. Even when increasing age and infirmity caused him to spend more and more time in his country home, Soultberg in the Tarn, his control over the army continued, and of course in the Midi he was much nearer the centre of military operations in Algeria than in Paris. By the end of 1844, when he was 75, he was begging the King to relieve him of the office of Minister of War and for the last two years of his official life he was President of the Council more or less in name only. Guizot, for whom he gradually acquired a growing respect, was chief minister for most of this time, but Soult's correspondence with the King and the royal family on a wide range of subjects continued unabated, although the death in a carriage accident of his close friend, the Duke of Orléans, heir to the throne, was a great blow to the old soldier. The widowed duchess remained an intimate friend of Soult's German wife, Louise, and she continued to pay regular visits to Soultberg.

When Soult became President of the Council and Minister of Foreign Affairs in 1839 there had been renewed civil disturbances in Paris. Europe was now on the eve of the 'hungry Forties' which were to cause unrest and turmoil in most European countries including England and, within ten years, would sweep away the July Monarchy itself. But, for the moment, Soult's government brought tranquillity to France. As his son Hector commented: "In the midst of all this my father put an end to the confusion by forming a ministry with the King's consent."[1] Guizot said that it was a ministry without a concerted policy but it ended the longest constitutional crisis of the reign and it was in a real sense 'the King's government'. Also, perhaps for the first time, it reflected the majority view of the Chamber despite the absence of the great orators like Guizot and Thiers.

Having achieved calm at home, Soult, as Minister of Foreign Affairs, was faced almost at once with the horrible complexities of the Eastern question. No doubt some of the decisions taken during the next few months were those of the King, acting through Soult, who despite his intelligence and his political subtlety was inexperienced in everyday diplomacy. Moreover in Britain he was confronted by a colleague – or sometimes an antagonist – who was every bit as wily and fast-moving as any of the generals against whom he had fought in the Peninsula – Lord Palmerston. Fortunately Soult was well served by his officials in the department, especially by Dessages, the secretary general of the ministry.

The crux of the problem in May 1839, as it continued to be, was the future of the ramshackle Ottoman Empire. Turkey was threatened on two sides – by Russia, which under the Treaty of Unkiar Skelessi, was empowered in certain circumstances to intervene in the country 'to preserve its independence', and by the Sultan's overweening subject, the ruler of Egypt, Mehemet Ali.

Neither France nor Britain wanted to encourage Russian aggression against the government of Turkey and, in his various dispatches to Bourgency, the French chargé d'affaires in London, Soult affirmed that it was France's wish "to act reciprocally with England in the most perfect accord".[2] Fresh from his own recent visit to England, where he had publicly proclaimed the merits of a permanent alliance between the two countries, this was not surprising. He had always been specially fearful of Russia's aggressive intentions. As far back as 1800, when he helped to drive Suvorov out of Switzerland, he had affirmed in his *Memoirs* that "one day it might be necessary for all Europe to combine against Russian aggression".[3] The predominant part that Russia had played in the wars against Napoleon merely confirmed his fears.

According to Bourgency's reports to Soult, Palmerston did not treat the Russian danger so seriously nor did he seem to act with sufficient firmness against the intransigence of the Sultan; indeed Soult and the French government found it increasingly difficult to follow the twists and turns of Palmerston's policy. There was much discussion through diplomatic channels about Anglo-French naval intervention if there was a serious attack by Russia on the Sultan and Soult succeeded in obtaining sufficient financial credits for this from the Chamber. The French government was also in favour of bringing Austria into the discussions and of setting up an ambassador's conference in Vienna. After some hesitation Palmerston agreed. His suspicious attitude towards France was partly caused by the French relationship with Mehemet Ali. Louis Philippe and his chief minister, Soult, made no secret of the fact they considered that France had a special and continuing interest in Egypt. Little more than a generation ago Napoleon had conquered the country, taking with him not only soldiers but scientists and technicians. Soult had not served in the Army of Egypt but his letters to the King showed that he fully supported French interest in the eastern Mediterranean. Neither France nor Britain could possibly accept Russian wishes for what amounted to the virtual dismemberment of the Ottoman Empire but, when the Sultan rashly broke his agreement with Mehemet Ali and attacked him, the policies of France and Britain began to diverge. Soult himself was dissatisfied with French diplomatic representation in Constantinope and with Mehemet Ali in Alexandria, so he took the unusual step of sending two of his senior military advisers to urge restraint on both contestants. It was in fact from Colonel Callier, the military officer sent to Alexandria, that France and Britain learned that Mehemet Ali had totally defeated the Sultan's army at the battle of Nezib; the Turkish fleet had surrendered and the Sultan himself had abdicated in favour of a child successor.

French and British policies now became sharply divided. A major point of disagreement was whether, after his victory, Mehemet Ali should be allowed to extend his territories and to occupy Syria. Palmerston, fearing that this might weaken the Turkish government still more, told the French chargé d'affaires, "I look for no prejudice in this issue on the part of Marshal Soult."[4] It was, in fact, strange that so far during the crisis, France had only been represented in London by a chargé d'affaires. However, when Sebastiani, the ambassador, returned from leave, he fared no better. He was summoned by Palmerston to his country house at Broadlands to be told that Mehemet Ali could be confirmed as hereditary ruler in Egypt but that any substantial increase in his territories would fatally weaken the position of Turkey. The Russians appeared now to accept British views because, as Palmerston asserted, "Russia hated France".[5] The Russian attitude was partly caused by Tsar Nicholas's continuing dislike of Louis Philippe as a usurper. A compromise under which Mehemet Ali would be allowed to retain Acre was finally dismissed by Palmerston who declared firmly that there could be no unity between Britain and France if the French government did not take a strong line with the ruler of Egypt. At first Louis Philippe and Soult asserted that it was unacceptable to limit Mehemet Ali's power even if this caused a rupture of the alliance with Britain, to which they attached so much importance. Sebastiani was recalled from London on the grounds that he was too pro-Turkish and was replaced by Guizot. Soult might well have continued to take a tough line if he had remained Minister of Foreign Affairs and he expressed amazement at the possibility of a Russian army crossing Asia Minor in order to do battle with the forces of Mehemet Ali. However, after the fall of Soult's government in 1840, France was left in an isolated position. In London Guizot got an agreement with Palmerston to confirm Mehemet Ali as hereditary ruler in Egypt provided that he surrendered any other territory that he had acquired. This was confirmed in the treaty of July 15 1840. As the anglophile Guizot commented, the Mehemet Ali affair had revived some of the old hostility between France and England, but he added with characteristic sententiousness, "There was no doubt that the two countries must march along side by side on the great path of liberal and pacific progress."[6] Louis Philippe and Soult had been worsted in a battle of wits against the formidable Palmerston but at least the independence of Turkey had been preserved against the Russians. A more serious test would come fourteen years later in the Crimean War.

While he had been busy negotiating and disputing with Palmerston over one part of North Africa, Soult had been much occupied with another African territory which was even more important to France – Algeria. France's conquest of Algeria presented many very difficult problems. Earlier in his career Soult would undoubtedly have gone out there to take command himself, putting his guerrilla experience in Andalusia to good effect. But he was now too old to do so; he simply had to leave the war to be waged by a series of governors general of varying ability. For example, Drouet d'Erlon, of Peninsular and Waterloo fame, was a complete failure. Soult received from his close friend, the Duke of Orléans, the most sensible reports on the Algerian problem. Orléans had gone to Algeria at the end of 1839 after a tour of the Midi in which he had been conducted over the battlefield of Toulouse by Soult's old divisional general, Clausel. From Algeria he wrote a series of letters to Soult which showed that he had quickly grasped many elements of the Algerian problem. He pointed out that there were already some parts of the province of Constantine which were suitable for French civilian settlement. On the other hand, a firm military regime was needed elsewhere, with Moslem tribal rule preserved as far as possible. In his view the French troops were like the Romans of old, doing all the initial hard work, but there would also be a need for some form of civilian colonial settlement to prevent the return of the fanatical Moslem leader Abd-el-Kadir and his friends. Soult fully agreed with Orléans's conclusion that "the strong influence of France in North Africa would be a great thing for the world".[7] In his advice to Soult, which certainly impressed the old Marshal, Orléans was facing up to some of the dilemmas which were to plague France in North Africa for the next century. In the short term, some of the problems might well have been avoided if Orléans, himself, could have been appointed governor general. There is no evidence that Soult ever advocated this but Orléans's advice influenced him and his colleagues very considerably.

In fact Soult's government, formed in 1839, fell in February 1840 on a technical vote in the Chamber over the size of the allowance to be given on his marriage to another of the King's sons, the Duke of Nemours. While this illustrated the influence which the Chamber now exerted on French governments, a period of more political confusion followed with Thiers succeeding Soult as head of the government.

As a dedicated admirer and historian of Napoleon, Thiers decided to advise the King to make an imaginative move which would attract to the July Monarchy some of the historical aura of the First Empire. The rather ridiculous attempts by the Emperor's nephew, Louis Napoleon, to seize power had ended in a long period of imprisonment in the fortress of Hamm, while the Emperor's surviving brothers were still forbidden to return to France. But the 'legend of St Helena' showed no signs of abatement and some of the glowing memories of the glorious past could surely be used to support the present regime. Under an agreement with the British government in 1840, the mortal remains of the great Emperor were to be brought back from St Helena by another of the King's sons, the Prince de Joinville, and buried in the Invalides. As by far the most famous of Napoleon's surviving marshals, it was obvious that Soult had a leading part to play in this, especially as he had once more become President of the Council in succession to Thiers while also becoming Minister of War again. This was in a Cabinet which included Guizot and many of the other leading politicians. As the King's closest supporter Soult had always been rather careful of his 'Bonapartism'. Although Minister of War at the time, he had not been present 'for political reasons' when the famous column of the Grande Armée at Boulogne, for which he had been so largely responsible at first, was at last completed and dedicated with the Emperor's statue surmounting it. He had shown no sympathy for Prince Louis Napoleon's 'junketings' and he was regarded with continuing dislike by his old chief, Joseph Bonaparte, still living in exile.

But the return of the Emperor's body from St Helena was a very different matter and he took charge, under the King, of all the final arrangements. The Emperor's body was transferred at Cherbourg from the Prince de Joinville's frigate, *La Belle Poule*, to a smaller craft to make a slow and stately journey up the Seine from Le Havre to the outskirts of Paris. The coffin was wrapped in a French flag embroidered by ladies living in St Helena. The cortege was met outside Paris by a party led by Marshal Soult who went on board the funeral vessel and prayed solemnly over the coffin. There then followed the last solemnities at the Invalides. Soult handed Napoleon's sword to the King, who in his turn gave it to the faithful Bertrand, one of the Emperor's companions at St Helena, for him to place on the coffin. It was a poignant moment in the old Marshal's life. He had been born in the same year as his imperial master: now he was in his 70s. After the ceremony was over it fell to him to entertain all those who had been involved in the Emperor's last sad exile.[8]

As Minister of War the Marshal was soon fully occupied again with army administration and with continuing military reforms. In his second group of reforms, begun in 1839, he had regulated the organization of the general staff which had tended in the past to be altered at the whim of successive Ministers of War. Now it was to be divided into active and reserve sections. He laid down that the army should have six marshals in peace time but that this number could rise to twelve in time of war. To become a marshal one had to have commanded an army or specialist services like the artillery or the engineers in the face of the enemy. He prescribed the number of lieutenant generals and 'maréchaux de camp'. Of course, general officers on retirement could always be called forward again for active service.[9]

The most serious defence problem which he and other ministers had to face remained the fortification of the city of Paris. This difficult issue had been left over from Soult's previous tenure of office from 1830-4. It was as important as ever and continued to generate excited feelings in the Chamber, particularly from those who still believed that fortifications would be used against the people of Paris rather than against the enemy; others continued to be vociferous about the aesthetic harm which forts might cause to the capital's beauties and, of course, there were budgetary problems too. A secondary question was whether the defences should be a series of isolated bastions which, as a professional soldier, Soult preferred, or whether there should be a continuous ring of fortifications. The debates in the Chamber were long and confused; Soult had originally introduced a bill for detached forts but then under pressure he was compelled to change to a continuous fortified ring. He did not show up well in the fierce debates that ensued, and perhaps Guizot was being charitable in commenting mildly that he had not displayed his customary tactical skill.[10] In the eyes of the King he could still do no wrong and Louis Philippe was to call the ring of fortifications that were eventually built as "contributing to the safety and glory of my reign".[11] During the King's visit to Queen Victoria, Wellington told Guizot that the fortifications would now prevent a rapid march of the enemy on Paris, "doing for your capital what the ocean does for us".[12] Paris remained ringed by these fortifications until the end of the First World War.

Military problems kept Soult busy enough for Guizot to comment that he was now content with his position and "no longer made importunate pretensions".[13] He was not directly involved, for example, in the fresh difficulties which arose over the Spanish Marriages question. A fair picture of him at this time is provided by a Royalist writer, the Marquis de la Rochefoucauld, no great admirer of the July Monarchy, who wrote: "He was without doubt one of the first generals of our age and one of the best organizers even if he paid too much attention to minute details." After commenting on his zealous service to all the changing rulers of France, he described his calmness and decisiveness in the face of danger. "He was not a political tactician but a fighter...war was more important to him than diplomacy. He was ambitious and never made any concession in maintaining power. Everyone knew that he kept his promises. Firm with his equals, even arrogant with his inferiors, he was subtle and persuasive with his superiors but he was so grand that the King was his only superior. He held the army in the palm of his hand. He did not care whether he was popular and he maintained absolute control. He was invariably polite but he could flatten you with a word. Those who dared to tell him the truth annoyed him but he had a regard for them. He loved money but primarily to maintain his position. He was often lavish but also miserly. He had an unconventional mind with much originality. His solemn face broke into a charming smile when he wanted to please somebody. As he grew older he became more melancholy. He was a great Frenchman."[14]

Soult became more and more concerned with the army and of course with the war in Algeria. His links with the King remained as close as ever despite the fact that he spent more time at Soultberg. From here he could still maintain a firm grip on army administration both directly and through his admirable secretary general in the

Defence Ministry, Martineau. Marshal de Castellane was a frequent visitor to Soultberg at this time and describes Soult's working day as still beginning at 5 am and continuing with short breaks for meals until midnight. There was a continuous flow of visitors, although by 1844 the number was diminishing. Soult's increasing infirmity prevented him, to the King's sorrow, from being present at Eu for the visit of Queen Victoria and the Prince Consort, although from afar he supervised meticulously all the military arrangements for the visit. Nor was he well enough to accompany the King and Queen on their return visit to Windsor. He was very sad about this, commenting to the King that "the union of the two crowns will cement the peace of the world".[15] He came to Paris at this time, as it were, 'to mind the shop' while the King and Guizot were away.

Much of his active work now consisted of supervising army operations in Algeria. These were now in the hands of Marshal Bugeaud who was highly dictatorial and a real thorn in the flesh of Guizot and the rest of the Cabinet. He would take orders only from Soult, who had to spend much time in composing quarrels between him and some of his subordinate generals. He compelled him to give up his plea of making a direct attack on Morocco as being too elaborate and perhaps provocative towards Britain. Instead there was a small sea-based expedition against Mogador on the Moroccan coast while Bugeaud defeated Abd-el-Kadir's forces at Isly near the Moroccan border. Bugeaud was made Duke of Isly but continued his intransigence, and only Soult's influence prevented him from adopting a wholesale military colonization of Algeria by soldiers and their families only.[16] Orléans's earlier advice had borne fruit with Soult and the rest of the Cabinet in opposing this purely military solution.

It says much for the King's admiration for the old Marshal and for Guizot's forbearance that Soult could go on controlling the army from his remote home in the Tarn. He was furious when his authority was assumed for a very necessary and urgent reform of the Ecole Polytechnique where some serious disturbances had taken place. He wrote indignant, even bad tempered, letters to the King and returned quickly to Paris to supervise the necessary reforms himself. When he was in the capital harmony was restored and the Marshal accompanied the King on a tour of the new fortifications. Then, on his return to St-Amans – he was now 75 – he asked at last to be relieved of his portfolio of Minister of War. There was much discussion about a successor but finally a stop-gap minister was appointed while Soult continued more or less in name only as President of the Council until his complete retirement in 1847. He came to Paris several times during this period, visiting with the King the rooms in the Palace of Versailles which Louis Philippe had arranged to commemorate his various military and administrative exploits. When he returned again to St-Amans, the King kept in close touch with him through his senior aide-de-camp, General Dumas.

These last two years were bad for the government. Two of Soult's former ministers were tried by the House of Peers for corruption while a scandal in high life shook the July Monarchy when the Duke of Praslin murdered his wife, who was Marshal Sebastiani's daughter, and then poisoned himself in prison. After Soult had retired the situation got worse. Serious budget deficiencies and bad harvests led to much popular discontent in Paris and all over France. There were the famous 'political banquets' in which, inspired by Lamartine and Louis Blanc, strong Republican feelings were expressed. According to the official *Journal des Débats*, the Chamber became quite uncontrollable. The King no longer had his 'illustre épée' at his side to quell the disturbances. Soult did not even feel strong enough to accept the honorary post of governor of the Invalides on the retirement of Oudinot.

There was one great honour, however, that he did not refuse. A few weeks after his retirement Louis Philippe took the exceptional step of creating him a marshal general. Thus he joined the select group of Turenne, Villars and Saxe in becoming only the fourth marshal general in the whole history of France. This high honour naturally delighted him and he was accorded a number of exceptional privileges, including the provision of a squadron of light cavalry to act as a kind of permanent guard of honour at Soultberg.

While the King and Guizot faced an increasingly disturbed political situation in Paris, Soult in his old age was involved only in local affairs. He was a quarrelsome grandee in the Tarn, engaging in vigorous disputes with local farmers and agricultural leaders. But it was perhaps characteristic of this strong-willed old man that the secretary of the hostile chamber of agriculture in Castres, Anarchasis Combes, became his great admirer and first biographer. At this time his authoritative spinster sister, Sophie, tried hard to make him become a sincere Catholic but, like Napoleon, he retained a cynical attitude towards the church. Priests to him were little more than 'religious officials' who had their uses from time to time but that was all.

When the July Monarchy was toppling in February 1848, Soult was in Paris. He visited the Tuileries but was not physically able to give his beleaguered sovereign any help. His son, Hector, was far away in Berlin as French ambassador, but his son-in-law, Mornay, provided some valuable assistance to the widowed Duchess of Orléans and to her little son, the Comte de Paris, obtaining through Louise's family and other sources passports for them to go to Germany. Sadly Soult himself returned to St-Amans. Here in the political turmoil that followed it is significant that his sympathies were for the strong-willed Cavaignac as President of the Second Republic rather than for Louis Napoleon Bonaparte.

How would Soult, the 'pragmatic Bonapartist' have fared under the Second Empire? Napoleon III, himself a great pragmatist, would surely have loaded him with additional honours. But he died on December 12 1851, only a few days after the *coup d'état* in which the Prince President made himself President for life as a preliminary to becoming Emperor.

At Soult's funeral there was, of course, a full gathering of the family and many of the famous in the snow-covered village of St-Amans, soon to be renamed St-

Amans-Soult. But the political crisis in Paris had prevented some of Soult's senior military and civilian colleagues from being present. The service was conducted by the Archbishop of Albi and Soult's marshal's baton with his sword broken after his death lay amongst the glittering array of his decorations which included the Golden Fleece awarded to him by King Joseph of Spain. A huge marble mausoleum outside the church at St-Amans commemorates him and his innumerable victories. His military spirit and his political skills lived on among his family. The tomb itself is surrounded by many memorial tablets recording those of his descendants who have represented the Tarn in the Chamber of Deputies as well as three Reille-Soult brothers, two of whom, in their 20s, were killed in action in the First World War while the third one disappeared on active service in the Second World War.

Louise did not long survive her husband. She died the following year, having been received formally into the Catholic church shortly before her death. Sophie Soult, the Marshal's dominant sister, who had tried so hard to convert them both to Catholicism, is buried in a simple mausoleum in the cemetery near the church.

The character of this great, complex man is hard to summarize. He was a brilliant soldier, one of the chief architects of the Grande Armée and one of the creators of the modern French army. He was a subtle politician (if somewhat rough and lacking in finesse), a fine civilian administrator, an art admirer and an art plunderer. Aloof by temperament, he was immensely determined and physically very strong. Above all he was a French patriot, serving, like so many of his contemporaries, each government of France as it existed and as it changed. Perhaps the fairest summary of his last years came from André Berton, writing in the *Journal des Debáts* not long after his death: "Marshal Soult must be subjected to the judgement of posterity not only as one of the great men of war (one only excepted) but indeed as a great man in all the events of contemporary history. Finally at an age when most men seek for rest he took a full part in the government of his country. In a field that was new to him he could use those qualities which he had used in war and peace for 25 years. The lieutenants of the Emperor were poorly prepared by the rough but noble art of war for the business of representative government but the old Marshal after a lifetime of war and of administration exercised in the government of France the greatest patience, firmness and vigour." Guizot would probably not have accepted all this. Certainly King Louis Philippe and his brilliant son, the Duke of Orléans, would have done so. It is perhaps a fitting last epitaph for Marshal Jean de Dieu Soult.

Appendix: Marshal Soult's Art Collection and Library

Soult had a magnificent collection of Spanish paintings, many of them acquired directly from monasteries in Seville, and elsewhere in Andalusia and in Granada. Some came from King Joseph when he and Soult still remained friendly and after the King had suppressed the Spanish monasteries. Commissioner Frédéric Quillet acted as Soult's principal agent.

There are plenty of stories of Soult's plundering activities, many of them much exaggerated. The best known story relates to his acquisition of Murillo's *Immaculate Conception,* which 'saved a man's life'. Soult is supposed to have told the prior of a Spanish monastery that if the picture, which had been hidden away, were not produced, he would be hanged. The picture was produced and the prior's life was saved. The picture was Soult's favourite. It was hung in the salon at Soultberg. Later it was acquired by the Louvre.

At the Treaty of Paris in 1814 King Louis XVIII and the French government refused to return the pictures acquired in Spain. They were not made to do so by the Treaty. After Waterloo Soult had more difficulty in retaining his collection but, surprisingly, his personal possessions, including the pictures, were respected, despite his exile in Germany. On his return from exile most of the pictures were displayed in his mansion in the Rue de l'Université in Paris. They filled the walls of the salons, the bedrooms and the stairs. When he became a Minister under Louis Philippe he refused to offer the pictures for sale to the state. In later years, when he no longer lived much in Paris, some of the pictures were transferred to Soultberg.

After Soult's death the sale of this huge picture collection was arranged by his son and daughter. The sale took place in Paris in three sessions on May 13, May 20 and May 22 1852. The sale realized the sum of 1,467,351.50 francs – a huge price in the middle of the nineteenth century. A list of the pictures, the prices paid for them and some of the buyers are set out in the manuscript copies below from *Le Moniteur Universel* for May 20, May 21/22 and May 23 1852.

The pictures have found their way to galleries and to private collections all over Europe and America. Some of them are on public display, notably in the Louvre, the National Gallery in London, the Wallace Collection, the Walker Art Gallery in Liverpool, the Hermitage in Leningrad, art galleries in Genoa and Budapest, the National Gallery in Washington and the National Gallery in Ottawa.

A more detailed list of the pictures with an indication of their ultimate destination appeared in *Beaux Arts,* No. 47 of June 1987.

Soult's magnificent library was auctioned in Paris on February 20 1978. It contained not only military memoirs but books on history, travel, exploration, science, nature study and medicine. Old enmities seem to have been buried in fine editions of Marshal Ney's *Memoirs,* autographed by Ney's son, and of Marshal Suchet's *Memoirs,* autographed by Suchet's widow. Surprisingly, the central feature of the library was not military but travel and scientific discovery. As the sale catalogue commented: "No auction in the last decades has provided such a collection covering the great scientific discoveries of the beginning of the nineteenth century."

It had certainly been a long and splendid intellectual journey for the uneducated notary's clerk from St-Amans-Labastide.

Le Moniteur Universel des 20, 21/22 et 23 Mai 1852

La vente eut lieu en trois vacations dirigées par MM. Bonnefonds de Laviale et Georges, en présence de M. le comte de Nieuwerkerke, directeur gal des Musées.
Le montant des vacations s'éleva à 1467351, 50 francs. Les comptes rendus sont signés Hercule Robert.

Vacation du 19 Mai:

– un tableau (?) de Fyt
– "la vision de St Jean" de Alonzo Cano – adjugé à 12100,..
– "la vision de l'Agneau" d° – d° 2550,..
– "la vision de Dieu" d° – d° 3700,..
– "la Vierge" Jean Bellin
– "la Conception" Murillo – d° 586 000,.. (préemption des Musées Nationaux)
– "St Pierre aux liens" d° – d° 151 000,..
– "Jésus et St Jean enfants" d° – d° 63 000,..
– "le Christ portant sa croix" Sebastien Del Piombo d° 41 000,..
– "les enfants du peuple" Murillo – d° 9000,..
– — tableau (?) de Fernandez Navarette d° 25 000,..

Vacation du 20 Mai.

– "L'Hotellerie italienne" Philippe Napolitain d° 355,..
– un portrait d'homme Sebastien Gomez d° 300,..
– "La conversion de St Mathieu" Jean Pareja d° 385,..
– "l'enlèvement des Sabines" Henri Van Balen d° 1505,.. à M. Ferdinand de la Neuville (tableau sur cuivre).
– "le combat des Romains et des Sabins" d° 1920,..
– "L'ange Gabriel" Zurbaran – d° 2555,.. (considéré comme le chef d'oeuvre de Zurbaran)
– Portrait d'un militaire espagnol d° – d° 705,..
– "la délivrance de St Pierre" Ribeira d° 1500,..
– "les noces de Cana" François Herrera le jeune d° 2450,.. à M. Roux (gde toile en frise).
– "Ste Lucie" Zurbaran – d° 485,..
– "Ste Agathe" d° – d° 1540,..
– "la vierge, l'enfant Jésus et Ste Rose" Geminiani d° 1600,..
– "La vierge au rosaire" Juan de Las Roelas d° 5800,.. à M. Georges.
– "Un évêque donnant la communion à une jeune fille" Alonzo Cano – d° 7000,.. à M. Roux.
– "Ste Agnès" d° – d° 4000,.. à M. Mundler.
– "les funérailles d'un évêque" Zurbaran – d° 5000,.. à M. Georges.
– "St Laurent" d° – d° 3000,.. à M. de Bruni.
– "la scène d'épidémie" Murillo – d° 20 000,.. à M. F. de la Neuville.
– "Jésus portant sa croix" attribué à Ribera d° 2050,..
– "Mater Dolorosa" Murillo – d° 10 600,.. à M. Townend, de Manchester (ce tableau est considéré comme "un des diamants de la collection").
– "Miracle de San-Diego" d° – d° 85000,.. à M. Georges.
– "la fuite en Egypte" d° – d° 51 500,.. à M. Roux.
– "la voie de douleurs" Morales d° 24000,.. à M. Townend, de Manchester.

Vacation du 22 Mai

– 6 petits tableaux de Zurbaran – adjugé 11 500,.. l'ensemble.
– "St Antoine" d° – d° – (la mise à prix 1000,.. n'a pas été couverte).
– "St Antoine de Padoue et l'enfant Jésus" Murillo – d° 10 200,..
– "le repentir de St Pierre" d° – d° 5500,..
– "Christ en croix" d° – d° 3100,..
– "St Paul" de frère François Morelli d° – (la mise à prix 300,.. n'a pas été couverte).
– "St Pierre repentant" Ribera d° 350,..
– "St André" Guerdia d° 380,..
– "Intérieur d'Estaminet" David Teniers d° 1210,..
– "le choc de cavalerie" Pierre Sesagoas d° 1660,..
– "la marche d'un détachement" d° d° 1400,..
– "St Jean" Alonzo Cano – d° 4800,.. } "deux charmants petits tableaux".
– "St Jacques" d° – d° 4900,.. }
– "Naissance de la Vierge" Murillo – d° 90 000,.. à M. Georges.
– "la glorification de la Vierge" d° – d° 5000,.. à M. Georges.
– "le denier de César" Titien d° 62 000,.. à M. Woodburn, de Londres ("oeuvre de vieillesse du Titien, inférieure pour la composition et la touche à l'exemplaire de Dresde").
– "la Ste Famille" Ribera d° 9150,.. à M. Mundler.

Bibliography

Original Sources

Archives in the Château of Epoisses, examined for me by Comte Hervé de Guitaut.

Archives de la Guerres, Vincennes.

Archives Départmentales de l'Haute Garonne. Information about the battle of Toulouse by J-P Escalettes, C. Cau and J. Sicart.

Archives Départmentales de Morbihan. Information about Quiberon.

Correspondance de Napoléon I. 1858–1869.

Napoleon's Confidential Correspondence with King Joseph. English translation. 1855.

Stadtarchiv of Solingen in the German Federal Republic. Information about Soult in the Rhineland, his marriage and his German wife.

Unpublished letters from Napoleon to Soult covering the period of the camp of Boulogne and the early stages of the War of the Third Coalition which were in the family's possession – made available to me by the Commune of St-Amans-Soult.

Secondary Sources

John Aitchison. *Ensign in the Peninsular War.* Letters edited by W. F. K. Thompson. 1981.

Brito Aranha. *Invazoes Fransezas em Portugal.* 1909.

Jacques Bainville. *Napoléon.* 1932. English translation by Hamish Miles. 1938.

D. Plunket Barton. *Bernadotte. The First Phase 1763–1799.* 1914.

La Bastide. *Général Comte Heudelet.* 1938.

Dr Fernand Emile Beaucour. *Lettres, Décisions et Actes de Napoléon à Pont-de-Briques.* 1979.

A. F. Becke. *Napoleon and Waterloo.* 1939.

Général Bigarré, Aide de camp du roi. *Mémoires.* 1893.

Sebastian Blaize. *Mémoires d'un aide-major sous le premier empire, – guerre d'Espagne.*

Louis Blanc. *Histoire de Dix Ans 1830–1840.* 1844.

Georges Blond. *Le Grande Armée.* 1979.

Commandant P. Boppe. *Les Espagnols à la Grande Armée.* 1986.

F. de Bourrienne. *Memoirs of Napoleon Bonaparte,* translated and edited by Edgar Sanderson. 1908.

Captain William Bragge. *Peninsular Portrait.* Letters of Captain William Bragge, edited by A. C. Cassells. 1963.

Denis Brogan. *The French Nation from Napoleon to Pétain 1814–1940.* 1959.

Général Brun, Baron de Villeret. *Cahiers,* published by Louis de Saint-Pierre. 1953.

Arthur Bryant. *Jackets of Green.* 1932.

Arthur Bryant. *Years of Victory.* 1944.

Baron du Casse. *Mémoires et correspondance politiques et militaires du Roi Joseph.* 1855–8.

Maréchal de Castellane. *Mémoires.* 1896.

Général de Caulaincourt, Duc de Vicence, Grand Ecuyer. *Mémoires.* 1933.

Manual Pinheiro Chagas. *Historia de Portugal.* 1903.

Muriel Chamberlain. *Life of Lord Aberdeen.* 1983.

David Chandler. *The Campaigns of Napoleon.* 1966.

David Chandler. *Napoleon's Marshals.* Article on 'King Nicolas-Soult' by Dr Paddy Griffith. 1982.

Comtesse Chastenay de Lanty, *Mémoires.* 1896.

Commandant le Clerc. *Campagnes de Maréchal Soult dans les Pyrenées Occidentales. 1813–1814.* 1894.

Edward Charles Cocks. *Intelligence Officer in the Peninsula. Letters and diaries of Major the Honourable Edward Charles Cocks,* edited by Julia Page. 1986.

Capitaine Coignet. *Cahiers.* 1909.

Anarchasis Combes. *Histoire Anecdotique de Jean de Dieu Soult.* 1870.

Owen Connelly. *Napoleon's Satellite Kingdoms.* 1965.

Louis Constant. *Mémoires Intimes de Napoléon I*, published by Maurice Demelle. 1862.
Baron de Corneau. *Souvenir des guerres d'Allemagne.* 1906.
R. F. Delderfield. *The March of the Twenty Six.* 1962.
Edouard Détaille et Jules Richard. *L'armée française.* 1885–1889.
Christopher Duffy. *Austerlitz.* 1977.
Général Mathieu Dumas. *Souvenirs, publiés par son fils.* 1839. Soult provided the author with important documents from the Spanish War.
R. P. Dunn-Pattison. *Napoleon's Marshals.* 1909.
Charles J. Esdaile. *The Spanish Army in the Peninsular War.* 1988.
Comte d'Espinchal. *Souvenirs Militaires.* 1901.
Général Fantin des Odoards. *Journal.* 1895.
Général Apollinaire Fée. *Mémoires.*
Comte de la Forêt. *Correspondance 1808–1813*, edited by G. de Grandmaison, 1905.
Général Maximilien Sebastien Foy. *Histoire de la guerre de la Peninsula sous Napoléon*, published by Comtesse Foy. 1828.
Pierre Germain. *Drouet d'Erlon. Maréchal de France.* 1985.
Pieter Geyl. *Napoleon. For and Against.* 1949.
Gabriel Girod de l'Ain. *Joseph Bonaparte, le roi malgré lui.* 1970.
Michael Glover. *Legacy of Glory, the Bonaparte Kingdom of Spain 1808–1813.* 1931.
Richard Glover. *Britain at Bay.* 1873.
Guy Godlewski. *Souvenirs de Napoléon.* 1983.
Captain Alexander Gordon. *Journal of a Cavalry Officer in the Corunna Campaign*, edited by H. C. Wylly. 1913.
Vice-Amiral Grivel. *Mémoires.* 1914.
G. Guénin et J. Nouillac. *La Consulat, L'Empire et la Restauration. Lectures Historiques.* 1923.
E. Guillon. *Les guerres d'Espagne sous Napoléon.* 1902.
François Guizot. *Mémoires pour servir l'histoire de mon temps.* 1856–1860. English translation by J. W. Cole. 1858–1861.
François Guizot. *Memoirs of a Minister of State.* English translation. 1864.
George Healy. *Reminiscences of a Portrait Painter.* 1894.
Christopher Hibbert. *The Recollections of Rifleman Harris.* 1970.
Lieutenant James Hope, 92nd Highlanders. *Letters from a British Officer during the Recent Memorable Campaign.* 1819.
Alastair Horne. *Napoleon, Master of Europe 1805–1807.* 1979.
Dr François Guy Hourtoulle. *Ney, le brave des braves.* 1981.
Henry Houssaye. *1814.* 1888.
Henry Houssaye. *1815.* 1893–1905.
Henry Houssaye. *The Return of Napoleon.* English translation by T. C. Macaulay. 1934.
Henry Houssaye. *1815, Waterloo.* English translation by A. E. Mann. 1900.
Maréchal Jourdan. *Mémoires Militaires.* 1898.
Jacques Jourquin. *Dictionnaire des Maréchaux du Premier Empire.* 1986.
F. M. Kircheisen. *Napoleon*, English translation by Henry Lawrence. 1931.
Général Lejeune. *Mémoires.* 1897.
Countess of Longford. *Wellington – The Years of the Sword.* 1969.
Countess of Longford. *Wellington – Pillar of the State.* 1972.
A. G. Macdonnell. *'Napoleon and his Marshals'* 1934.
Louis Madelin. *Conférences prononcées à la Société des Conférences.* 1926.
Louis Madelin. *Histoire du Consulat et de l'Empire.* 1940–1943.
Philip Mansel. *Louis XVIII.* 1981.
Baron de Marbot. *Mémoires*, English translation by A. J. Butler. 1892.
Gilbert Martineau. *Napoleon's Last Journey.* 1926.
Frédéric Masson. *Napoléon et sa famille.* 1897–1900.
Dimitri Merezkovsky. *The Life of Napoleon*, English translation by Catherine Zvegintzov. 1929.
A. F. Miot, Comte de Melito. *Mémoires*, edited by A. von Fleischmann. 1893.
Sir Charles Napier. *Passages of Early Military Life*, edited by his son, General W. C. E. Napier. 1884.
Priscilla Napier. *The Sword Dance.* 1971.
Sir William Napier. *History of the War in the Peninsula and in the South of France.* 1851.
Jacques de Norvins. *Mémorial.* 1896.
Sir Charles Oman. *The Peninsular War.* 1907.
Dr Barry O'Meara. *Napoleon in Exile.* 1827.
Didier Pacaud. *Jean de Dieu Soult.* 1986.
Alan Palmer. *Alexander I, Tsar of War and Peace.* 1974.
Roger Parkinson. *Moore of Corunna.* 1976.
Baron Percy. *Journal des Campagnes.*
Régine Pernoud. *Histoire de la bourgeoisie en France.*
Colonel R. W. Phipps. *The Armies of the First Republic and the Rise of the Marshals of Napoleon I.* 1926–1939.
Colonel Pion des Roches. *Mes Campagnes.* 1889.

William Plomer. *Ali the Lion.* 1936.

Duc de la Rochefoucauld. *Esquisses et portraits.* 1844.

Comte Roederer. *Journal.* 1909

Michael Ross. *The Reluctant King.* 1976.

Duc de Rovigo (Savary). *Mémoires.* 1828.

Comte Alfred de Saint-Chamans. *Mémoires.* 1896.

Sarazin, Maréchal du camp. *Notice Biographique sur le Maréchal Soult* from *L'histoire de la guerre d'Espagne et de Portugal. 1789–1812.* 1814.

Charles Sellers. *Oporto Old and New.* A Historical Record of the Port Wine Trade. 1899.

Georges Six. *Dictionnaire biographique des généraux et amiraux français de la révolution et de l'empire.* 1934.

Lieutenant General Sir Harry Smith. *Autobiography,* edited by G. C. Moore Smith. 1902.

Maréchal Soult. *Mémoires.* Preface by his son, le Duc de Dalmatie. 1856.

Maréchal Soult. *Mémoires. Espagne et Portugal,* presented by Louis and Antoinette de Saint-Pierre. 1955.

Maréchal Soult. *Correspondance politique et familière avec Louis Philippe et la famille royale,* presented by Louis and Antoinette de Saint-Pierre. 1957.

Maréchal Soult. *Mémoire Justificatif.* 1815.

David Stacton. *The Bonapartes.* 1966.

Philip Henry, 5th Earl of Stanhope. *Conversations with the Duke of Wellington 1831–1851.* 1880.

Gilbert Stenger. *The Return of Louis XVIII,* English translation by Mrs Stawell. 1966.

Général Baron Thiébault. *Mémoires,* edited by Fernand Calmette. 1896. English translation by A. J. Butler. 1894.

M. A. Thiers. *History of the Consulate and the Empire under Napoleon I.* English translation, edited by D. Forbes Campbell. 1845–1890.

Jean Tulard. *Napoleon, The Myth of the Saviour.* English translation by Lady Teresa Waugh. 1984.

Vidal de la Blanche. *L'Evacuation de l'Espagne et l'invasion dans le Midi.* 1894.

Duke of Wellington. *Dispatches.* 1844–1847.

Friederich Wencker-Wilberg. *Bernadotte.* 1936.

Brigadier Peter Young. *Napoleon's Marshals.* 1973.

Newspapers and Periodicals

Beaux Arts, No. 47. Information on Soult's magnificent collection of pictures. June 1987.

Bergische Zeitung. Article on Soult. March 6 1935.

Birmingham Gazette. Soult's visit in 1838 to the industrial North and Birmingham. July 30 1838.

Bononia, 'Le Télégraphe Chappe' by P-A. Wimet. 1988.

Boulogne-Sur-Mer, 'Regards sur le passé'; 'Boulogne ville impériale' by P-A. Wimet, 1983.

Bulletin de la Commission Départmentale du Pas de Calais. 'Napoléon et Bruix à Boulogne' by D. Durand. 1978.

Bulletin de la Société Belge d'Etudes Napoléoniennes', No. 53, 1989. Article on Soult's pictures. 1987.

Cahiers de Vieux Boulogne, No. 3. 'Le Camp de Boulogne, bluff, erreur ou grande espérance' by Jacques Cassar; 'Le Palais Impérial' by P-A. Wimet; 'L'Espionnage les Anglais savaient tout' by Guy Bataille.

Délégation à l'action artistique de la ville de Paris. Article on Soult's house in Paris. 1987.

Deutsche Zeitung. Article on Soult, February 16 1949.

Die Heimat, Articles on Soult, 1931 and 1967.

Journal des Débats. 1851.

Meine Heimat. Article on Soult. 1939.

Monatschrift of the Berg Historical Society. Article on Soult, 1898.

Revue de Boulogne et de la Région, No. 281. 'Le Maréchal Soult' by Mabille de Poncherille; 'La Baraque de l'Empereur' by P-A. Wimet, 1962.

Revue de Boulogne et de la Région, No. 292. 'Monsieur de Chanlaire et le cheval Napoléon' by P-A. Wimet. 1964.

Revue de Boulogne et de la Région. Nos 323 and 327. 'Correspondances inédites du Général Marchand' by P-A. Wimet. 1970.

Revue de l'Institut Napoléon. 'Daru et la campagne de 1805' by P-A. Wimet.

Solingen Zeitung. Article on Soult, August 23 1908.

Sud. Monthly Review No. 12 published in Mazamet, Tarn. 1981.

The Times. Article on the French occupation of Switzerland, April 10 1798.

The Times. Coverage of Soult's visit to London as King Louis Philippe's representative at Queen Victoria's coronation and his subsequent visits to the industrial North, the Black Country and Birmingham. July 6, 9, 14, 17, 19, 20, 21, 27 and August 3 1838.

Westdeutsche Zeitung. Article on Soult in the Rhineland by Dr R. Geocke. 1883.

NOTES

Main sources abbreviated

M.S.	*Mémoires, Maréchal Soult.* Preface by his son Hector, Duc de Dalmatie.
M.S-S and P.	*Mémoires, Espagne et Portugal.* Presented by Louis and Antoinette de Saint-Pierre.
M.S-LP.	*Maréchal Soult. Correspondance politique et familière avec Louis Philippe et la famille royale.* Presented by Louis and Antoinette de Saint-Pierre.
M.J.	*Mémoire Justicatif.* Maréchal Soult.
Beaucour	*Lettres, Décisions et Actes de Napoléon à Pont-de-Briques 1798–1804.* Dr Fernand Emile Beaucour.
B de V.	*Cahiers de Général Brun, Baron de Villeret.* Published by Louis de Saint-Pierre.
Du Casse	*Mémoires et correspondance politiques et militaires du Roi Joseph.* Baron du Casse.
Chandler, *Campaigns*	*The Campaigns of Napoleon.* Professor David Chandler.
Chandler, *Marshals*	*Napoleon's Marshals.* Professor David Chandler. Article on 'King Nicholas Soult' by Dr Paddy Griffith.
Le Clerc	*Campagnes du Maréchal Soult dans les Pyrenées occidentales 1813–1814.* Commandant le Clerc.
Combes	*Histoire Anecdotique du Jean de Dieu Soult.* Anarcharsis Combes.
Corr: N.	Correspondance de Napoléon I.
Corr: N-S.	Unpublished letters from Napoleon to Soult which were in the possession of the family.
Corr: N-J.	Napoleon's Confidential Correspondence with King Joseph. English translation.
Esdaile	*The Spanish Army in the Peninsular War.* Charles J. Esdaile.
Glover M.	*Legacy of Glory. The Bonaparte Kingdom of Spain 1808–1813.* Michael Glover.
Glover R.	*Britain at Bay.* Richard Glover.
G. and N.	*Le Consulat, L'Empire et la Restauration. Lectures Historiques.* G. Guénin et J. Nouillac.
Guizot M.M.T.	*Mémoires pour servir l'histoire de mon temps. (Memoirs of My Time).* English translation.
Guizot M.M.S.	*Memoirs of a Minister of State.* English translation.
H.H. *1814*	*1814.* Henry Houssaye.
H.H. *1815*	*1815.* Henry Houssaye.
H.H. *1815 Waterloo*	*1815 Waterloo.* Henry Houssaye. English translation.
Jourdan.	*Mémoires Militaires.* Maréchal Jourdan.
Longford *Y. of S.*	*Wellington. The Years of the Sword.* Countess of Longford.
Longford *P. of S.*	*Wellington. Pillar of the State.* Countess of Longford.
Madelin	*Histoire du Consulate et de l'Empire.* Louis Madelin.
Mansel	*Louis XVIII.* Philip Mansel.
Marbot	*Mémoires.* Général Marbot. English translation by A. J. Butler.
Masson	*Napoléon et sa famille.* Frédéric Masson.
Napier	*History of the War in the Peninsula and in the South of France.* General Sir William Napier.
Oman	*The Peninsular War.* Sir Charles Oman.
Pacaud	*Jean de Dieu Soult.* Didier Pacaud.
Ross	*The Reluctant King.* Michael Ross.
Rovigo.	*Mémoires.* Duc de Rovigo (Savary).
Saint-C.	*Mémoires.* Comte Alfred de Saint-Chamans.
Thiébault	*Mémoires.* Général Baron Thiébault, edited by Fernand Calmette. English translation by A. J. Butler.
Thiers	*History of the Consulate and the Empire.* English translation edited by D. Forbes Campbell.
Tulard	*Napoleon, The Myth of the Saviour.* Professor Jean Tulard. English translation by Lady Teresa Waugh.
Wellington	Dispatches of Field Marshal the Duke of Wellington.

1. The Making of a Marshal: The Revolutionary War in Germany

1. J-C Averous of St-Amans-Soult has provided me with much information about the *gentilhommes verriers* of the Black Mountains. From Eric Hemming of Bushey Heath I have learned much about the English branch of the de Grenier family.
2. The house has now been turned into a number of separate apartments.
3. 'Les Révolutions Industrielles à Mazamet 1750–1900' by Remy Casals points out that no more than 1 per cent of Mazamet's total production of cloth was used by the army.
4. My information about Soult's early life comes partly from his descendants, partly from *Jean de Dieu Soult* by Didier Pacaud, Président de la Société de Sciences et Belles Lettres du Tarn, partly from the commune of St-Amans-Soult and partly from a commemorative article in the monthly review *Sud*, published in Mazamet.
5. Some evidence for this comes from *Letters of a British Officer during the Recent Memorable Campaign* by Lieutenant James Hope of the 92nd Highlanders. Hope met a French officer who had been Soult's captain in the Royal army.
6. Edward Détaille et Jules Richard, *L'Armée Française.* See also the very full information in Chandler, *Campaigns.*
7. Rovigo, vol. 1, pt. 1, p. 3.
8. M.S., chaps 3, 4 and 5 *passim.* Soult strongly criticized Jourdan's failure to coordinate.
9. Dunn-Pattison, *Napoleon's Marshals,* p. 94. This highly coloured story finds no place in Soult's own precise *Memoirs.* It was described long afterwards in *The Times* of July 11 1838 when Soult was in London representing Louis Philippe at Queen Victoria's coronation.
10. M.S., chap. 6, p. 165.
11. H.H., *1815 Waterloo,* chap. 1, p. 318.
12. There is a colourful picture of the activities of the 'Sambre et Meuse' in *Bernadotte. The First Phase 1765–1799* by D. Plunket Barton.
13. But the old saying that all Napoleon's soldiers carried a marshal's baton in their knapsacks is nonsense. In 1804 he had created fourteen active and four honorary marshals: some of these were mainly for political reasons. After 1804 seven generals and a Polish prince were made marshals. Further down the ladder promotion could be at a snail's pace. Coignet, the intelligent memoir writer, enlisted in 1799, became a corporal in 1807, a sergeant in 1809 and finally an officer in 1812.
14. Tulard, p. 151.
15. The Comte de Guibert, the military writer under the French monarchy, strongly advocated it. See Chandler, *Campaigns.*
16. Soult's conduct in Bonn is fully described by Dr R. Goeche in an article in the *Westdeutsche Zeitung,* 1883. The article is based on local archives. However, against the background of German fears of a resurgent France at that time, he may have painted a rather grim picture of French activities in the Rhineland.
17. M.S., chap. 8, p. 372. But Didier Pacaud, the author of *Jean de Dieu Soult,* has provided me with much fuller information.
18. Corr: N. no. 7998.
19. Soult's marriage to Louise Berg and his future relationship with the town of Solingen have been described in information supplied by the Stadtarchiv of Solingen. There are also interesting articles in *Monatschrift* of the Berg Historical Society 1898; in the *Solingen Zeitung* of August 23 1908; *Die Heimat* of 1931 and 1967; *Meine Heimat* of 1937; the *Bergische Zeitung* of March 6 1935 and the *Westdeutsche Zeitung* of February 16 1949.
20. M.S., chap. 10, p. 355.
21. Ibid., chap. 10, p. 357.
22. M.S-S and P., p. 12.

2. The Making of a Marshal: Switzerland and Italy

1. M.S., chap. 12, p. 69.
2. Ibid., chap. 14, p. 218.
3. Ibid., chap. 15, p. 305. Combes, p. 36.
4. Ibid., chap. 15, p. 538.
5. Ibid., chap. 15, p. 298.
6. Ibid., chap. 15, p. 303.
7. Ibid., chap. 15, p. 339.
8. Combes, p. 31.
9. Thiers, vol. 1, book 3, p. 137.
10. M.S., chap. 17, p. 4.
11. Ibid., chap. 17, p. 117.
12. Thiébault, vol. 3, p. 15 and pp. 522–5, also *passim* in the *Journal of the Siege of Genoa.*
13. M.S., chap. 24, p. 347.
14. Ibid., chap. 24, p. 376.
15. Chandler, *Marshals.* Griffith, *King Nicolas-Soult,* p. 465.
16. For French relations with Ali Pasha see, *inter alia,* William Plomer, *Ali the Lion.*
17. M.S., chap. 24, p. 385.

3. The Invasion that Never Took Place

1. Tulard, p. 193.
2. Beaucour, *Introduction.*
3. Much of the information about Boulogne has been supplied by Pierre-André Wimet of the Commission Départmentale d'Histoire et d'Archaeologie du Pas de Calais.
4. Bourrienne, *Memoirs,* English translation, p. 239. Professor Tulard comments that these *Memoirs* are full of inaccuracies.
5. Priscilla Napier, *The Sword Dance,* p. 159.
6. Glover R. Some of his material is taken from Edouard Desbrières, *Projets et Tentatives de Débarquement aux Isles Britanniques.*
7. Beaucour, p. 85.
8. Ibid., Introduction. Dr Beaucour and Pierre-André Wimet were largely responsible for the preservation of Pont-de-Briques. Soult visited Napoleon there constantly.
9. Ibid., p. 189.
10. Rovigo, vol. 1, pt. 2, p. 5. The Duc de Rovigo (General Savary), who got to know Soult well at this time, gives a graphic description of all these works.
11. Corr: N. No. 7020.
12. Beaucour, p. 509.
13. *Bononia,* The Bulletin of the Friends of Boulogne Museums. *La Télégraphe Chappe* by Pierre-André Wimet.

14. Norvins, *Mémorial sur Boulogne,* vol. 3, p. 104.
15. Information on these inter-service operations has been supplied by Pierre-André Wimet. See also Georges Blond, *La Grande Armée* and Glover R.
16. Philippe de Ségur, *Histoire et Mémoires,* vol. 2, p. 332.
17. See for instance Corr: N. nos. 7186, 7244 and 7272; also Corr: N-S which have been in the possession of the Soult family.
18. Saint-C., pp. 87–8.
19. B de V., pp. 33–4.
20. Saint-C., pp. 10–11.
21. Vice-Amiral Grivel, *Mémoires.*
22. Dellard, *Mémoires Militaires,* p. 194.
23. *Revue de Boulogne et de la Région,* nos. 323 and 327. 'Correspondance inédites du Général Marchand'.
24. Corr: N-S., 19th Prairial, Year XIII. For Joseph's appointment of colonel of the 4th Regiment see Corr: N 7683.
25. This entertaining anecdote is based on information contained in Girod de l'Ain's *Joseph Bonaparte – le roi malgré lui.* See also Ross, *The Reluctant King.*
26. Kircheisen, *Napoleon.* English translation by Henry St Lawrence, pp. 288–9.
27. For the background to Napoleon's invasion plans see for example Corr: N 7133, 7144, 7159, 7332, 7494, 8369, 8429, 8473 and 8566 – far more than letters addressed to any of the other Marshals. See also Glover R., Georges Blond, *La Grande Armée* and O'Meara, *Napoleon in Exile.* Soult's possible role in the invasion is a matter of speculation.
28. Corr: N. no. 7383.
29. Corr: N. no. 7998.
30. Corr: N-S. 24th Germinal, Year XI.
31. Pacaud, pp. 50–1.
32. Information about these various activities comes from many Boulonnais publications, especially *Cahiers de Vieux Boulogne,* no. 3 and *L'Espionnage: les anglais savaient tout* by Guy Bataille.
33. A full history of the column from the time when it was first planned until its formal rededication after being damaged in the Second World War appears in various numbers of the *Revue de Boulogne et de la Région.*
34. Dunn-Pattison, *Napoleon's Marshals,* p. 97.

4. "The First Tactician in Europe"

1. Christopher Duffy. *Austerlitz,* p. 41.
2. See for instance the article by Pierre-André Wimet in the *Revue de l'Institut Napoléon,* no. 121 of Oct. 1971.
3. Chandler, *Campaigns,* Appendix D, p. 1103.
4. Général Bigarré, *Mémoires,* quoted by Christopher Duffy in *Austerlitz,* p. 14.
5. Baron de Corneau, *Souvenirs des guerres d'allemagne,* p. 207.
6. Kircheisen, *Napoleon.* English translation, pp. 323–5.
7. Christopher Duffy, *Austerlitz,* p. 14.
8. Corr: N., no. 9340.
9. Corr: N-S passim.
10. Thiébault, vol. 3, pp. 423–5.
11. Corr: N., no. 9397.
12. Thiébault, vol. 3, p. 412.
13. Dr Guy Godlewski, *Souvenirs de Napoléon,* p. 327.
14. Général Lejeune, *Mémoires,* vol. 1, p. 36. A characteristically colourful description.
15. Capitaine Coignet, *Cahiers,* p. 112.
16. Christopher Duffy, *Austerlitz,* p. 114.
17. Thiébault, vol 3, pp. 508–10.
18. Brigadier Peter Young, *Napoleon's Marshals.*
19. Much of my account of Austerlitz is based on Christopher Duffy's marvellously detailed study, Thiers, on Lejeune's *Mémoires* and on Coignet's *Cahiers.*

5. From Vienna to Königsberg

1. B de V., p. 37.
2. Ibid., p. 38.
3. Saint-C., p. 35. An objective assessment of Soult.
4. Chandler, *Campaigns,* pp. 467–8.
5. A full description of Soult's advance is in Chandler, *Campaigns,* and in Corr: N-S. of Sept. 29 and Oct. 7, 8 and 12 of 1806.
6. Corr: N, nos. 10977 and 10980.
7. B de V., pp. 40–1.
8. Ibid., p. 46.
9. Marbot. English translation, vol.1, pp. 238–9.
10. B de V., p. 47.
11. Baron Percy, *Journal des Campagnes,* vol. 1, p. 133.
12. Capitaine Coignet, *Cahiers,* p. 136.
13. Saint-C., p. 55.
14. Corr: N., no. 11780 – the 5th Bulletin of the Grande Armée.
15. Marbot. English translation, vol. 1, pp. 255-6.
16. Saint-C., pp. 56–60.
17. The volumes of Larrey's *Memoirs* and his medical studies personally inscribed to Soult in the Marshal's library testify to their close friendship.
18. Tulard, p. 151.
19. In his *Histoire du Consulat et de l'Empire,* Louis Madelin compares Ney's dilatoriness in allowing Lestocq's Prussians to reach the battlefield before his own corps with Grouchy's conduct at Waterloo. Vol. 6, p. 270.
20. Brun de Villeret gives a graphic description of living conditions in IV Corps at this time.
21. Général Mathieu Dumas, *Souvenirs.*
22. Corr: N., no. 12953.
23. Saint-C., p. 89. The letter has been among the family papers.
24. Thiébault, vol. 3, p. 87. As Duke of Dalmatia Soult's coat of arms comprised a red shield with three leopards' heads in gold surmounting the escutcheon of a duke of the empire. Jacques Jourquin, *Dictionnaire des Maréchaux du Premier Empire,* p. 89.
25. Thiers, vol. 8, book 28, p. 75. Soult's official endowment amounted to 305,777 francs drawn from a variety of sources including the Grand Duchy of Warsaw, Westphalia, Hanover and Swedish Pomerania as well as from the French government. This compared with Berthier's endowment of over a million francs and the endowments of Masséna and Davout with over 800,000 francs. See Jacques Jourquin, *Dictionnaire des Maréchaux du Premier Empire,* pp. 97 and 102.
26. B de V., pp. 59–60.
27. Ibid., p. 58.
28. M.S-S and P., p. 12.

6. "The Duke of Damnation"

1. Napier. Volume 1, Preface, page XVI.
2. Esdaile, passim.
3. M.S-S and P. p. 11. 'The three "greats".'
4. Ibid., p. 30, footnote 2.
5. Napier, vol. 1, book 4, p. 254.
6. Corr: N-J., no. 451.
7. M.S-S and P., p. 32, footnote 1.
8. Ibid., p. 46, footnote 1.
9. Esdaile, pp. 89 and 134.
10. Dr O'Meara, *Napoleon in Exile*, vol. 1, p. 232.
11. M.S-S and P., p. 44, and Napier, vol. 1, book 4, p. 301.
12. Du Casse, vol. 5, p. 243.
13. Captain Alexander Gordon, *Journal of a Cavalry Officer in the Corunna Campaign.*
14. Soult's *Journal of Operations*, quoted in Napier, vol. 1, book 4, p. 305.
15. Rovigo, vol. 2, pt. 2, pp. 18–19.
16. Corr: N-J., no. 465.
17. Corr: N-J., no. 14731.
18. Roger Parkinson, *Moore of Corunna*, p. 172.
19. Muriel Chamberlain, *Life of Lord Aberdeen.*
20. M.S-S and P, p. 45. According to an account of the Royal Green Jackets 'Corunna Walk' in 1984 which followed the route of the great retreat 175 years later, one of Romana's descendants told the party that the British had plundered and burnt down the family castle. Nevertheless, since the British had really saved Spain, she entertained them all generously!
21. Napier, vol. 1, book 4, p. 313.
22. A. G. Macdonell, *Napoleon and His Marshals*, p. 175.
23. Corr: N-J., no. 482.
24. Oman, vol. 1, p. 574.
25. M.S-S and P., p. 49.
26. Christopher Hibbert, *The Recollections of Rifleman Harris.*
27. Priscilla Napier, *The Sword Dance*, p. 205.
28. Général Lejeune, *Mémoires*, p. 116.
29. B de V., p. 68.
30. Napier, vol. 1, book 4, pp. 329–30 footnote.
31. Rovigo, vol. 2, pt. 2, p. 20.
32. Corr: N-J., no. 465.
33. Napier, vol. 1, book 4, p. 357.
34. In the presence of Spanish officials and British embassy representatives Captain/now Major/ Blackmore, the leader of the expedition, was invited by the mayor of Corunna to unveil the memorial plaque to Sir John Moore on the wall of a new building which had replaced the original house.

7. "King Nicholas" – Fact or Fantasy?

1. M.S-S and P., p. 63. Du Casse, pp. 305–7.
2. Ibid. Saint-Pierre, the publisher of the *Memoirs*, makes his own views quite plain on pp. 64–5.
3. Jourdan, p. 171.
4. M.S-S and P., p. 68.
5. E. Guillon, *Les guerres d'Espagne sous Napoléon.*
6. Rovigo, vol. 1, pt. 2, p. 275 footnote.
7. John Aitchison, *Ensign in the Peninsular War*, p. 40.
8. M.S-S and P., p. 78.
9. Ibid., p. 31.
10. Thiébault. English translation, vol. 2, p. 256.
11. Pinheiro Chagas, *Historia de Portugal*, vol. 8, p. 8.
12. Ibid., p. 12.
13. Saint-C., pp. 131–2.
14. M.S-S and P., p. 90.
15. Charles Sellers, *Oporto Old and New. A Historical Record of the Port Wine Trade.* For this and general information about the French occupation of Oporto I am indebted to several correspondents both Portuguese and British.
16. B de V., p. 74.
17. Pinheiro Chagos, *Historia de Portugal*, vol. 8, pp. 13 and 26.
18. M.S-S and P., pp. 92–3.
19. Napier, vol. 2, Appendices.
20. Pinheiro Chagas, *Historia de Portugal*, vol. 8, p. 15.
21. B de V., p. 74.
22. M.S-S and P., p. 93.
23. Saint-C., pp. 138–9.
24. M.S-S and P., pp. 93–4. These contain the text of Soult's circular letter.
25. Marbot, vol. 2, p. 365.
26. Jourdan, p. 191.
27. Saint-C., pp. 138–9.
28. Pinheiro Chagas, *Historia de Portugal*, vol. 8, p. 20.
29. Thiébault. English translation, vol. 2, p. 259.
30. Wellington Dispatches to Castlereagh, April 24 1809, vol. 4, p. 270.
31. Ibid. to Frere, April 24 1809, vol. 4, p. 267.
32. Ibid. to Castlereagh, April 27 and May 7 1809, vol. 4, pp. 273 and 310.
33. Longford, *Y. of S.*, p. 179.
34. G. La Bastide, *Général Comte Heudelet.*
35. Napier, vol. 2, book 7, p. 109.
36. Saint-C., p. 149.
37. Ibid., p. 150.
38. Wellington Dispatches to Villiers, May 5 1809, vol. 4, p. 345.
39. Ibid. to Richmond, May 22 1809, vol. 4, p. 565.
40. John Aitchison, *Ensign in the Peninsular War*, pp. 43–4.
41. B & V., pp. 93–108. A memorable account of a memorable series of interviews.
42. M.S-S and P., pp. 111–12.
43. Ibid., p. 113
44. Ibid., p. 114.
45. The original letter is in the family archives.
46. M.S-S and P., p. 116.
47. Tulard, p. 271.
48. Saint-C., p. 140.
49. Pinheiro Chagas, *Historia de Portugal*, vol. 8, p. 27.

8. Supremo in Western Spain

1. Thiébault, vol. 4, p. 344.
2. Saint-C., pp. 157–8.
3. Dr François Guy Hourtoulle, *Ney, le brave des braves.*
4. B de V., Appendix 3. Recriminations continued even after Soult's death forty years later. There is a letter dated February 19 1852 from Jomini to the Marshal's son in the family archives in Epoisses. Jomini refers to the 'cruel misunderstanding' when in his *History* Thiers attributed to Soult all the blame for the abandonment of Galicia "without thinking of consulting me on the subject". When Jomini found out the terms of the Convention he declared that Soult had acted quite correctly in first

clearing Romana's forces out of Orense and then marching to Zamora "to resume co-operation with King Joseph's army".
5. Saint-C., p. 149.
6. M.S-S and P., p. 127.
7. Esdaile, p. 137.
8. Jourdan, p. 229.
9. Stanhope, *Conversations with the Duke of Wellington,* p. 11.
10. Esdaile, p. 133.
11. M.S-S and P., p. 126.
12. Du Casse, vol. 6, p. 266 and *passim.*
13. Ibid., vol. 6, p. 278.
14. Corr: N-J no. 546.
15. Oman, vol. 2, p. 562.
16. Napier, vol. 2, book 8, p. 163.
17. Saint-C., p. 159.
18. Corr: N-J., no. 547.
19. Jourdan, p. 273.
20. Napier, vol. 2, book 8, p. 185.
21. Wellington Dispatches to Richmond, August 8 1809, vol. 4, p. 567.
22. Ibid. to Richmond, September 13 1809, vol. 4, pp. 567–8.
23. Longford, *Y. of S.*, p. 208.
24. On the subject of Spanish military operations I have received much helpful advice from Charles Esdaile, author of *The Spanish Army in the Peninsular War.*
25. Napier, vol. 2, book 8, p. 212.
26. Wellington Dispatches to Castlereagh, August 8 1809. WP 1 274/21.
27. Corr: N. 15848 containing a political assessment based on an aide memoire by General Clarke, the Minister of War.

9. King Joseph's 'Commander-in-Chief'

1. M.S-S and P., p. 148.
2. Masson, vol. 6, p. 76.
3. Jourdan, pp. 272–3.
4. Jacques Jourquin, *Dictionaire des Maréchaux du Premier Empire,* p. 17.
5. Glover M., pp. 145–6.
6. Masson, vol. 6, p. 84.
7. Glover M., p. 148.
8. Chandler, *Campaigns,* pp. 145–6.
9. Corr: N-J., no. 554.
10. B de V., pp. 107–8.
11. M S-S and P., p. 153.
12. Wellington Dispatches to Marquess Wellesley, May 22 1811, WP 3132/2.
13. Esdaile, pp. 121–3.
14. Corr: N-J., no. 566.
15. See for example Corr: N, no. 15986 and many subsequent letters.
16. M.S-S and P., p. 159.
17. Thiers, vol. 12, book 38, p. 123.
18. Esdaile, pp. 115 and 143.
19. Glover M., chapter heading.
20. Jourdan, p. 294.
21. Oman, vol. 6, pp. 169–70.
22. B de V., pp. 107–8.
23. Esdaile, p. 144.
24. M.S-S and P., p. 163.
25. Napier, vol. 2, book 10, pp. 298–9. Napier is also quoted in M.S-S and P., p. 165.
26. Général Bigarré, *Mémoires,* p. 270, quoted by Ross in *The Reluctant King.*
27. Ross, pp. 192–3.
28. Wellington Dispatches to Marquess Wellesley, June 11 1809, WP 1 259/1.
29. Vice-Amiral Grivel, *Mémoires.*
30. Masson, vol. 6, p. 97.
31. Corr: N-J., no. 586.
32. Ibid., no. 596.
33. M.S-S and P., p. 176.
34. Ibid., pp. 177–8.
35. Esdaile, p. 115.

10. 'Viceroy in the South' – The French Power Base in Spain

1. Wellington Dispatches from Roche to Wellington, March 6 1810, WD 1/243, quoted by Esdaile, p. 155.
2. Owen Connelly, *Napoleon's Satellite Kingdoms.*
3. Corr: N-J., no. 629.
4. Ibid., no. 630.
5. Napier, vol. 2, Appendix 17, p. 478.
6. M.S-S and P., p. 181.
7. Corr: N-J., no. 632.
8. Ibid., no. 608.
9. Du Casse, pp. 319–21.
10. This matter is examined in detail by Charles Esdaile in his book, *The Spanish Army in the Peninsular War.*
11. M.S-S and P., p. 260.
12. Julia Page, *Charles Cocks, Intelligence Officer in the Peninsula,* p. 135.
13. P. Boppe, *Les Espagnols à la Grande Armée.*
14. M.S-S and P., p. 184.
15. Ibid., p. 185.
16. Esdaile, pp. 141, 161–3, 176.
17. Ibid., p. 163.
18. Ross, p. 270.
19. Général Lejeune, *Mémoires,* vol. 2, pp. 38–72.
20. Saint-C., p. 179.
21. Esdaile, pp. 165–6.
22. M.S-S and P., p. 259.
23. Ibid., p. 259.
24. Ibid., p. 262.
25. Ibid., p. 264.
26. Ibid., p. 262.
27. Ibid., p. 263.
28. Général Apollinaire Fée, *Mémoires,* p. 135.
29. Julia Page, *Charles Cocks. Intelligence Officer in the Peninsula,* p. 135.
30. Ross, p. 176.
31. Corr: N-J., no. 639.
32. M.S-S and P., p. 267.
33. Ibid., p. 232 footnote.
34. Ibid., p. 263.
35. B de V., pp. 127–8.
36. M.S-S and P., p. 264.
37. Ibid., pp. 128–32.
38. Thiébault. English translation, vol. 5, p. 380.
39. Saint-C., p. 205.
40. A. G. Macdonnell, *Napoleon and His Marshals,* p. 258.
41. Comte d'Espinchal, *Souvenirs Militaires,* vol. 12, p. 67.
42. Ross, p. 162.
43. Napier, vol. 1, book 4, p. 339.

44. Comte d'Espinchal, *Souvenirs Militaires,* vol. 2, pp. 46–7.
45. Combes, pp. 78–9.

11. Defending the French Power Base in the West

1. Esdaile, p. 159.
2. M.S-S and P., pp. 191–2.
3. Corr: N., nos. 17131 and 17145.
4. Chandler, *Marshals,* Griffith 'King Nicolas-Soult', p. 468.
5. Thiébault. English translation, vol. 4, pp. 412–15.
6. M.S-S and P., p. 13.
7. Corr: N-J., no. 694.
8. Oman, vol. 4, section 23, p. 68.
9. M.S-S and P., p. 224.
10. Dr O'Meara, *Napoleon in Exile,* vol. 2, p. 194.
11. Jean Maximilien Lamarque, *Organisation Militaire,* quoted by Oman, vol. 6, p. 591. On the other hand Soult seems to have been fully conscious of the need to change plans. In his own *Memoirs* he writes: "When orders are given away from the theatre of operations they may have to be changed completely." M.S., vol. 2, p. 145. In general my account of Albuera is based on the study by Dr Paddy Griffith in his article on 'King Nicolas-Soult' in Chandler's *Marshals.* Errors are my own.
12. Rovigo, vol. 3, pp. 52–3.
13. Chandler, *Marshals,* Griffith, 'King Nicolas-Soult', p. 468.
14. Saint-C., p. 145.
15. Arthur Bryant, *Years of Victory,* p. 508.

12. Operations in the South and South-East of Spain

1. Esdaile, p. 175.
2. Corr: N., no. 17131.
3. Jourdan, p. 317.
4. M.S-S and P., pp. 191–2.
5. Esdaile, p. 181.
6. Wellington Dispatches to Marquess Wellesley, August 29 1811, WP 12/1/4.
7. B de V., pp. 122–4.
8. Napier, vol. 4, book 15, p. 43.

13. The Abandonment of Andalusia and War in Central Spain

1. Masson, vol. 4, p. 467.
2. Jourdan, p. 403.
3. Pierre Germain, *Drouet d'Erlon. Maréchal de France.*
4. Masson, vol. 4, p. 468.
5. Ibid., vol. 4, p. 470.
6. Esdaile, p. 159 quoting *El Redactor General* for March 1 1813.
7. Masson, vol. 4, p. 476.
8. Jourdan, p. 401.
9. Comte de la Forêt, *Correspondance 1808–1813.*
10. Napier, vol. 4, Appendix 10, contains the full text of the letter to King Joseph.
11. Ibid., vol. 4, Appendix 11, contains the text of the letter to Clarke for the Emperor's eyes.
12. Pacaud, p. 111.
13. Sebastien Blaize. *Mémoires d'un aide major sous le premier empire,* p. 212.
14. Masson, vol. 7, p. 483.
15. M.S-S and P., p. 334
16. Esdaile, p. 169.
17. John Aitchison, *Ensign in the Peninsular War,* p. 218.
18. Jourdan, p. 442.
19. Oman, vol. 6, section 34, pp. 150–1.
20. Masson, vol. 8, p. 17.
21. Julia Page, *Charles Cocks. Intelligence Officer in the Peninsula,* p. 130.
22. Oman, vol. 6, section 4, p. 175, quoting a dispatch by Wellington.
23. Ibid., vol. 6, pp. 167–8.

14. Interlude in Saxony

1. B de V., Appendix 1(6).
2. There had been rumours earlier, according to one of Wellington's senior officers, that Soult might take over from the ill and overworked Berthier as Napoleon's chief of staff, being succeeded as overall commander in Spain by Suchet (A. F. Becke, *Napoleon and Waterloo*). His appointment to this post later, during the Hundred Days, was, therefore, not surprising.
3. Chandler, *Campaigns,* pp. 882–7.
4. Ibid., pp. 889–98.
5. Général de Caulaincourt, Duc de Vicenze, *Mémoires,* vol. 3, pp. 353–4, 456.

15. The Last Offensive in Spain

1. Corr: N., nos. 19930 and 20299.
2. Napier, vol. 5, book 21, p. 198.
3. Rovigo, vol. 3, pt. 2, p. 97.
4. Masson, vol. 8, p. 141.
5. Ibid., vol. 8, p. 142.
6. Comte Roederer, *Journal,* pp. 310–14.
7. Ross, p. 218.
8. Napier, vol. 6, Appendix 3, The Muster Rolls.
9. Esdaile, p. 174.
10. Wellington Dispatches to Bathurst, July 12 1813, p. 524.
11. Wellington sent a copy of Soult's proclamation to Bathurst. Dispatches, p. 586.
12. Oman, vol. 5, section 38, p. 591.
13. William Bragge, quoted by Lady Longford in *Y. of S.,* p. 324.
14. Napier, vol. 5, book 21, p. 226.
15. Oman, vol. 6, section 38, pp. 736–7.
16. Le Clerc, p. 67.
17. Ibid., p. 77.

16. The Defence of Southern France

1. William Bragge, quoted by Lady Longford in *Y. of S.,* p. 334.
2. Oman, vol. 7, section 41, p. 135.
3. Wellington Dispatches to Bathurst, October 9 1813, p. 177.
4. Oman, vol. 7, section 40, pp. 90–2.
5. Napier, vol. 5, book 22, p. 198.
6. Wellington Dispatches to Bathurst, November 21 1813. WD 1/381, quoted by Esdaile, p. 175.
7. Wellington Dispatches to Beresford, March 7 1814, p. 557.
8. Masson, vol. 3, p. 245.
9. Ross, p. 221. An earlier choice had been Lucien's daughter, Lolotte, but Lucien's defection from his brother ruled out this possibility.
10. General Sir Harry Smith, *Autobiography,* vol. 1, pp. 145–6.

11. Vidal de la Blanche, *L'Evacuation de l'Espagne et l'Invasion dans le Midi.*
12. Le Clerc, p. 287.
13. Ibid., p. 322.
14. Corr: N., nos. 21, 365.
15. Major John Blakiston, *Twelve Years of Military Adventures.*
16. Most of my information on the battle of Toulouse has been provided by Jean-Paul Escalettes, who in collaboration with the archives section of the Department of Haute Garonne has become a real expert on the battle.
17. M.J., p. 3.
18. Oman, vol. 6, Section 38, p. 589.

17. Louis XVIII's Minister of War

1. Baron de Vitrolles, *Mémoires,* vol. 2, p. 34.
2. M.S-S and P., p. 13.
3. Comtesse Chastenay de Lanty, *Mémoires,* p. 563.
4. Jean Gourhaud of the Archives Section of the department of Morbihan has supplied me with some of the background to this affair. Even Soult's laudatory biographer, Anarchasis Combes, admits that it was an embarrassing matter for the Marshal.
5. Philip Mansel, *Louis XVIII,* p. 194.
6. B de V., p. 190.
7. Comtesse Chastenay de Lanty, *Mémoires,* p. 565.
8. Cussy, *Souvenirs,* quoted by Guénin and Nouillac, p. 296.
9. Puymaigre, *Mémoires,* quoted by Guénin and Nouillac, p. 245.
10. M.J., p. 9.
11. B de V., p. 190.
12. Lord Oxford was a descendant of Queen's minister, Harley, who had been so much involved with France during Louis XIV's reign, 100 years before!
13. Philip Mansel, *Louis XVIII,* p. 207.
14. Gilbert Stenger, *The Return of Louis XVIII,* English translation, p. 294.
15. H.H., *1815,* P.R., pp. 104–6.
16. Thiers, vol. 8, book 28, p. 75. See also Jean Gabriel Eynard, *Journal,* quoted by Guénin and Nouillac.
17. Descriptions of the house in *Délégation à l'action artistique de la ville de Paris,* 1987 and in 'Bulletin de la Société Belge, Etudes Napoléonienne', 1987.
18. Gilbert Stenger, *The Return of Louis XVIII,* English translation, p. 308.
19. Dr O'Meara, *Napoleon in Exile,* vol. 1, p. 386.
20. Stanhope, *Conversations with the Duke of Wellington,* p. 65.

18. The Hundred Days

1. For Soult's initial refusal to serve Napoleon see Saint-C., pp. 297–9, and Combes, p. 107.
2. Stanhope, *Conversations with the Duke of Wellington,* p. 248.
3. Berthier had fallen from a window at Bamberg Castle in Germany while he was watching Allied troops marching past on their way to invade France.
4. M.J., p. 28.
5. Combes, p. 108.
6. H.H., *1815 Waterloo.*
7. Gilbert Stenger, *The Return of Louis XVIII,* English translation, p. 355.
8. Saint-C., p. 299.
9. Chandler, *Campaigns,* p. 1020.
10. H.H., *1815 Waterloo,* quoted in Chandler, *Campaigns,* p. 1023.
11. Archives de la Guerre, Vincennes.
12. Thiers, vol. 20, book 60, p. 45.
13. Archives de la Guerre, Vincennes.
14. Chandler, *Campaigns,* p. 1040.
15. Pierre Germain, *Drouet d'Erlon,* pp. 175–6.
16. These confusions have been exhaustively described by memoir writers and later historians including the notes of Colonel Baudus; H.H., *1815 Waterloo*; Thiers; A. F. Becke, *Napoleon and Waterloo*; *Waterloo,* by Book Club Associates, edited by Lord Chalfont, and Pierre Germain's new Life of *Drouet d'Erlon.* An authoritative account is in Chandler, *Campaigns.*
17. H.H., *1815 Waterloo,* pp. 244, 254, 256, 416–17.
18. H.H., *1815 Waterloo,* English translation, book 3, p. 178.
19. Thiers, vol. 20, book 60, p. 109.
20. H.H., *1815 Waterloo,* English translation, book 3, pp. 191–2.
21. Dr O'Meara, *Napoleon in Exile,* vol. 2, pp. 161–2. These contain General Gourgaud's account of the last dramatic moments.
22. H.H., *1815 Waterloo,* English translation, book 3, pp. 191–2.
23. M.J., p. 22.
24. Lord Chalfont, Prologue to *Waterloo,* by Book Club Associates.
25. Longford, *Y. of S.,* p. 487.
26. This is certainly the view of Jacques Champagne in his major contribution to *Waterloo,* by Book Club Associates.
27. Dr O'Meara, *Napoleon in Exile,* vol. 1, p. 105.
28. Chandler, *Campaigns,* p. 1092.

19. Exile and Return

1. B de V., pp. 199–222; also discussions with Bertrand de Viviés of Viviers les Montagnes, Tarn, a descendant of the Vicomte de Lescures and articles by him in local historical reviews.
2. M.J., *passim.*
3. Philip Mansel. *Louis XVIII,* p. 361.
4. Ibid., p. 310.
5. Villeneuve L'Etang, which the Soults had taken much trouble to develop with artificial streams and lakes, was sold to the Duchess of Angoulême in 1823. She in turn sold it to Louis XVIII's minister, Decazes. Finally it was sold to Napoleon III who pulled down the house and built a new château. Information on this was supplied to me by Comte Antoine de Guitaut, Soult's great-great-great-grandson.
6. Saint-C., p. 64.
7. Combes, p. 131.
8. Dunn-Pattison, *Napoleon's Marshals,* p. 112.
9. Some of Soult's numerous business activities are described in vol. 2 of the *Histoire de la Bourgeoisie en France,* by Régine Pernoud.
10. Considering Soult's cordial dislike of railways, it is ironic that the two main lines now used by the 'Trains à Grande Vitesse' to Dijon and to Lyons pass within a respectful, if not a great, distance from the splendid château of Epoisses, the home of

Soult's descendants.

20. The "Illustre Epée"

1. Combes, p. 146.
2. I have heard him likened in his youth to Conan Doyle's mythical Napoleonic hero who claimed him as a cousin!
3. Some of the letters in the family archives exchanged between Soult, Louis Philippe and members of the royal family were published in 1959 by Soult's great-granddaughter, Antoinette de Saint-Pierre, and her husband, Louis.
4. Combes, p. 147.
5. Much evidence of Soult's hard work appears in the papers in the Archives de la Guerre at Vincennes.
6. M.S-L P. More letters were exchanged between Soult and the Duke of Orléans during these years than with the King himself.
7. Ibid., p. 13.
8. Ibid., p. 53.
9. Ibid., p. 56.
10. Combes, p. 157.
11. Ibid., p. 157.
12. Louis Blanc, *Histoire de Dix Ans,* vol. 3, p. 89.
13. Chandler, *Marshals,* Dr Griffith's article on 'King Nicolas-Soult', p. 471. I am indebted to Dr Griffith for much information on this subject. Where I have erred the mistakes are of course mine.
14. Combes, p. 155.
15. M.S-LP., p. 81.
16. M.S-LP., p. XLII.
17. Guizot M.M.T., English translation, vol. 2, p. 168.
18. Guizot M.M.T., original. A less objective estimate appears in the English translation.
19. Louis Blanc, *Histoire de Dix Ans,* vol. 3, p. 328.
20. It was said that, when his mother-in-law, Madame Dorsne, asked Thiers how he had replied to this obscenity, he pretended that he had not heard it. Madame Dorsne then suggested that, to pay Soult out, Thiers should write a history of the war in Algeria without mentioning Soult's name. Thiers never wrote about the Algerian War but, in his treatment of Soult in the *History of the Consulate and the Empire,* he may well have been taking his mother-in-law's advice!
21. M.S-LP., p. 94. According to the reminiscences of George Healy, the young American artist who painted Soult's portrait at that time, Thiers and Guizot fidgeted in the anteroom while the King broke the news of his enforced departure to Soult. Finally, the door opened to allow the King's pear-shaped head to appear as he whispered, "Patience, gentlemen – just a little patience – we are weeping together!"
22. Guizot M.M.T., English translation, vol. 2, p. 250.
23. M.S-LP., p. 102.

21. Ambassador Extraordinary

1. M.S-LP., p. 117.
2. The tax officer was my great-great-great-uncle. His diary is in my possession.
3. Cecil Woodham Smith, *Queen Victoria.* However, according to Longford *P. of S.*, "As the procession preceded Her Majesty out of the Abbey, Wellington's were the loudest cheers." Bernard Levin comments on the competitive conclusions of these two distinguished writers in *The Times* of January 23 1973. Chateaubriand was more cynical. He wrote: "The English love a show. Soult was not treated by the English ladies like Marshal Blücher whose moustaches they kissed!" *Memoirs from the Tomb,* vol. 7.
4. Combes, p. 105. Much to the annoyance of Louis Napoleon when he was Prince President, the coach was eventually sold to a scrap merchant for 2,000 francs!
5. Longford *P. of S.,* pp. 324–5. Dunn-Pattison, *Napoleon's Marshals,* pp. 113–14.
6. A full description of Soult's many activities in London is contained in relevant copies of *The Times,* kindly sent to me by Mr Ibbott of *News International.* Additional information has been supplied by Colonel Elliot and Colonel Baker of the Royal Green Jackets Headquarters in Winchester.
7. Descriptions of Soult's visit to the industrial North, to the Black Country and to Birmingham appear in relevant copies of *The Times* and in the *Birmingham Gazette* of July 30 1838, sent to me by Mr Patrick Baird of the Public Libraries Department of the City of Birmingham.
8. Louis Blanc, *Histoire de Dix Ans,* vol. 3.

22. One of The Longest Terms as Head of Government in French History

1. M.S, Introduction.
2. Guizot M.M.T., English translation, vol. 4, p. 333.
3. M.S., chap. 15, p. 305.
4. Guizot M.M.T., English translation, vol. 4, p. 349.
5. Ibid., vol. 4, p. 359.
6. Guizot M.M.S., English translation, p. 128.
7. M.S-LP., pp. 185–93.
8. Gilbert Martineau, *Napoleon's Last Journey.*
9. M.S-LP., p. 43.
10. Guizot M.M.S., English translation, p. 32.
11. M.S-LP., p. 230.
12. Guizot M.M.S., English translation, p. 36.
13. Ibid., p. 13.
14. La Rochefoucauld, *Esquisses et portraits,* p. 326.
15. M.S-LP., p. 222.
16. Ibid., p. 282.

INDEX